Praise for William Kennedy's

Riding the Yellow Trolley Car

"There is a spirit of grace and generosity here as Kennedy delights in each of his subjects. He continues to ride his yellow trolley with wonder and delight, and the reader is just as delighted to take the journey with him."
                                    —*San Francisco Chronicle*

"The writer who emerges here sounds not merely interesting but delightfully genuine. . . . This eclectic collection both entertains and enriches . . . [showing] Mr. Kennedy's accelerating maturity, [and] his acquisition of a sinuous, powerful prose style."
                                    —*The Dallas Morning News*

"Funny, charming, and certainly indicative of the subterranean personal and literary roots that bore glorious fruit in his novels."
                                    —*Kirkus Reviews*

"It is a grand souvenir of a long career."   —*Los Angeles Daily News*

"Whether he's discussing his taste for oysters or the plight of the homeless, there's a touch of the poet about Kennedy, making his writing a great pleasure to read no matter what the subject."
                                    —*Library Journal*

"It is Kennedy's voice that makes this collection sparkle; he is a personable, unique writer, one who studies his craft as well as plies it."
                                    —*Booklist*

PENGUIN BOOKS

RIDING THE YELLOW TROLLEY CAR

William Kennedy is a novelist who began his writing career as a journalist. His previous work of nonfiction, *O Albany!*, was published in 1983. In 1993, he was elected to membership in The American Academy of Arts and Letters.

The author at work on the sports desk of the Glens Falls *Post-Star* when he was twenty-two, had hair, and smoked Camels, none of which he is, has, or does anymore.

William Kennedy

Riding the Yellow Trolley Car

SELECTED NONFICTION

PENGUIN BOOKS

PENGUIN BOOKS
Published by the Penguin Group
Penguin Books USA Inc., 375 Hudson Street, New York, New York 10014, U.S.A.
Penguin Books Ltd, 27 Wrights Lane, London W8 5TZ, England
Penguin Books Australia Ltd, Ringwood, Victoria, Australia
Penguin Books Canada Ltd, 10 Alcorn Avenue, Toronto, Ontario, Canada M4V 3B2
Penguin Books (N.Z.) Ltd, 182–190 Wairau Road, Auckland 10, New Zealand

Penguin Books Ltd, Registered Offices: Harmondsworth, Middlesex, England

Published in the United States of America by Viking Penguin,
a division of Penguin Books USA Inc., 1993
Published in Penguin Books 1994

10 9 8 7 6 5 4 3 2 1

A leatherbound signed first edition of this book has been published by
The Easton Press.

Photographs are from the author's collection.

Page 496 constitutes an extension of this copyright page.

THE LIBRARY OF CONGRESS HAS CATALOGUED THE HARDCOVER AS FOLLOWS:
Kennedy, William.
Riding the yellow trolley car/William Kennedy.
p. cm.
ISBN 0-670-84211-7 (hc.)
ISBN 0 14 01.5992 4 (pbk.)
I. Title.
PS3561.E428R54   1993
814′54—dc20   92–50398

Printed in the United States of America
Set in Bodoni Book
Designed by Francesca Belanger

This book is dedicated to all journalists with a novel in the desk drawer.

ACKNOWLEDGMENT

The author herewith extends his gratitude to the editors of the publications in which the articles in this book originally appeared, first for the work they originally gave him, and second for the chance to see the work in print a second time.

AUTHOR'S NOTE

The idea of publishing a collection of my interviews, book reviews and other nonfiction writing is more than twenty years old, but other work always took precedence over it. The problem lay in the beginning: how to find the time to wade through a lifetime of writing and come up with what had survived, what had died on the shelf. Last year an erstwhile newsman, constant reader and good pal of mine offered to do the wading; choices were then made, and so the book began to take shape. For that reason I am most grateful to that early editor, Joseph F. Gagen.

I must also tip my hat to Al Silverman, venerated bookman and my splendid editor at Viking.

CONTENTS

I. The Writer on the Examining Table

The Beginning of the Book:
Riding the Yellow Trolley Car   3

The Beginning of the Writer: Eggs   9

A Memoir: Hearst Is Where You Find Him
(And I Found Him in Albany)   12

Early Assignments:
Langford, Prominent Cat, Dies   16
Albert the Swimmer   17
Tracking the Missing Leopard   19

A Speech: Be Reasonable, Unless You're a Writer   21

The Hopwood Lecture: Writers and Their Songs   26

An Interview: Tap Dancing into Reality   39

Fragments of a Talk with *The Paris Review:*
Ironweed and Style   59

An Argument: Rejection and Henry James
(Ironweed award speech to National Book Critics Circle)   66

Winning the Pulitzer:
Who Are You Now That You're Not Nobody?   69

II. Examining Writers: Some Interviews and Essays

A Week with the Verbivorous Joyceans:
    The Quest for Heliotrope   77

Bernard Malamud:
    On the Short Story   93
    On *The Fixer*   95
    Pictures of Fidelman: A Review   98

Ernest Hemingway:
    His Clear-Hearted Journalism   102
    His Dangerous Summer   105

J. P. Donleavy: Captivated by Ginger:
    A Non-Interview   114

James Baldwin: The Distractions of Fame   120

The Beat Generation:
    Ginsberg's Albany Pain   125
    Where Did They Go? Everywhere.   129

Jerzy Kosinski: On Still Being There   133

Walker Percy: Grim News from the Moviegoer   137

Saul Bellow:
    Intellectual Activity: A Form of Resistance   141
    If He Doesn't Have a True Word to Say,
        He Keeps His Mouth Shut   144

E. L. Doctorow:
    A Strong Voice in the Universe   155
    Shimmering *Loon Lake*   158

Norman Mailer: An Eavesdropper at the Lotos Club   161

Robert Penn Warren: Willie Stark,
    Politics, and the Novel   165

Damon Runyon: Six-to-Five: A Nice Price   174

III. Thirteen Reviews, One Review Rebutted

Samuel Beckett: The Artful Dodger Revealed   183

The Lime Works: Thomas Bernhard's Citadel   188

Players: DeLillo's Poisoned Flowers   192

Something Happened: Joseph Heller's
    Great Monologue   195

Ionesco's Remarkable Irreducibility   200

Far Tortuga: Peter Matthiessen's Misteriosa   204

O'Hara's Letters: A Quest for Celebrity   209

The Grapes of Wrath at Fifty: Steinbeck's Journals   212

Malcolm Muggeridge's Wasted Life   219

Frank Sullivan: Serious Only About Humor   222

The Fan Man: Kotzwinkle's Buddha as a Saint
    of Dreck   226

Nathanael West: The Stink of Life and Art   230

Nothing Happens in Carmincross: Benedict Kiely's
    Deathly Variety Show   233

Freedom of the City: Clive Barnes Is Wrong About
    Brian Friel   237

IV. Ten Latin Writers, Plus Translator

Gabriel García Márquez:
    One Hundred Years of Solitude   243
    The Yellow Trolley Car
      in Barcelona: An Interview   246

Gregory Rabassa: Keeper of the Golden Key:
    An Interview   268

Carlos Fuentes: *Distant Relations*   274

Osman Lins: *Avalovara*   279

Lygia Fagundes Telles: *The Girl in the Photograph*   285

Jorge Amado: *Tereza Batista:*
    Home from the Wars   289

Carlos Castaneda: *Tales of Power*   292

Ernesto Sábato: *On Heroes and Tombs*   297

Julio Cortázar: *A Manual for Manuel*   307

Pedro Juan Soto:
    Spiks   310
    To What Extent Was Enrique Soto
        the Creation of Pedro Juan Soto?:
        An Interview   314

Mario Vargas Llosa:
    Aunt Julia and the Scriptwriter   326

V. Exotic Life Forms Beyond Fiction

Frank Sinatra: Pluperfect Music   333

Pablo Casals: Master Class at Marlboro   339

Satchmo: "All My Days Are the Same"   344

Paul McCartney: The Major Possum Game   351

Jiggs: "What's the Matter with Father?
    I Saw Him Drink Water."   357

The Photography of Stillness:
    Muckraking the Spirit   360

Marshall McLuhan's Message Is . . . ?   364

Diane Sawyer: The Subject Is Beauty   369

"Tropicality" Defined   371

Rudolph Valentino: He's No Bogart   375

Cassius Clay Arrives   379

Ballet: Everybody Loves a Fat Girl, Right?   382

Roberta Sue Ficker Is Going to Become
    Suzanne Farrell   385

The Cotton Club Stomp   390

The Making of *Ironweed*   403

The Homeless: Do They Have Souls?   414

VI. Albany Resurgent: More Reports from the Native

O Albany!: Remarks to the Publication Party   421

Jack and the Oyster   423

The Capitol: A Quest for Grace and Glory   432

Talking to the High Court   440

Jody Bolden or Bobby Henderson:
    Either Way the Music Was Great   444

The Charcoal Man: Warming Up to the Press   449

Barney Fowler: The Quest for Curmudgeonous Joy   454

Radicalism and Dwight MacDonald:
    Not What They Used to Be   459

Requiem for a Lady at the Bottom of the World   464

Baseball at Hawkins Stadium:
    "Here's Your Son, Mister."   469

Family:
    My Life in the Fast Lane   478
    Dana's Ironic Hiccups   483
    Snapshots: Two Grandfathers   489

PART ONE

The Writer on the Examining Table

THE BEGINNING OF THE BOOK:

Riding the Yellow
Trolley Car

The Yellow Trolley Car is a realistic, or perhaps surrealistic, vision I may, or may not, have had in Barcelona in 1972 when I was there to interview Gabriel García Márquez. When my wife, Dana, and I crossed into Spain at Port Bou, we asked at the tourist window for some literature on Barcelona and were given a brochure that detailed the trolley lines in the city, by number and destination. At Columbus Plaza we tried to find the trolley that would take us to Antonio Gaudi's Sagrada Familia church, one of Barcelona's wonders. A vendor of fresh coconut at the plaza explained that there hadn't been any trolley cars in Barcelona for fourteen or fifteen years.

Why, then, were they still mentioning them by name in the tourist literature? The coconut vendor had no answer and so we boarded a bus instead of a trolley and rode toward Gaudi's monumental work. We stood at the back of the bus and watched the mansions and apartment buildings make splendid canyons out of the street, which at times looked as I imagined Fifth Avenue must have looked in its most elegant nineteenth-century moments. And then I said to Dana, "Look, there's a trolley."

She missed it, understandably. Its movement was perpendicular to our own. It crossed an intersection about three blocks back, right to left, visible only for a second or so, then disappeared behind the canyon wall.

When we reached García Márquez's house we talked for some hours and eventually I asked him, "What trolleys still run in Barcelona?" He and his wife, Mercedes, both said there were no trolleys in Barcelona. Mercedes remembered a funicular that went somewhere.

3

"This one was yellow," I said, "and old-fashioned in design."

"No," she said. "The funicular is blue."

García called his agent, Carmen Balcells, on the phone. "Is there a yellow trolley car in Barcelona?" he asked. "I'm here having an interview with Kennedy and he saw a yellow trolley." He listened, then turned to us and said, "All the trolleys were yellow in the old days."

He asked about the blue trolley, but Carmen said it was outside of town, nowhere near where we had been. In a few minutes she called back to say that about two years ago there was a public ceremony in which the last trolley car in Barcelona had been formally buried.

What had I seen? I have no idea.

"To me," García said, "this is completely natural."

He had already told us a story of how a repairman woke them and said, "I came to fix the ironing cord."

"My wife," García said, "from the bed says, 'We don't have anything wrong with the iron here.' The man asks, 'Is this apartment two?' 'No,' I say, 'upstairs.' Later, my wife went to the iron and plugged it in and it burned up. This was a reversal. The man came before we knew it had to be fixed. This type of thing happens all the time. My wife has already forgotten it."

In a later year a friend pointed out that I had included trolley cars in all my books except *Legs*, and in that I included a train. I grew up riding trolleys to school, hated to see them displaced by the mundane bus, and obviously gave them a significant place in my imagination.

When I wrote about my Barcelona vision, I equated riding the trolley with writing fiction, but in trying to find a title for this collection of essays, journalism, reviews, interviews, and other pieces that seem to create their own categories, it became clear I should also equate the trolley with writing nonfiction.

That said, I must also say that I am torn. García Márquez, in an interview in *The Paris Review*, said he didn't think there was any difference between fiction and nonfiction. "The sources are the same," he said, "the material is the same, the resources and the language are the same. *A Journal of the Plague Year* by Daniel Defoe is a great novel and *Hiroshima* is a great work of journalism."

And in a panel discussion in Albany that opposed fiction to nonfiction,

Mary Gordon raised a comparable argument: "Do we have to say that *War and Peace* is more important than *The Confessions of St. Augustine?* . . . I think that's an unnecessary and a false choice and I think it's a very human thing. People like to feel that they know where they stand, that there is a truth, there is a superior genre."

I find validity in both arguments; and genius is genius in whatever form. But I also believe that fiction, at its most achieved, comes from a source—a profound wellspring in the unconscious—that is not accessible to nonfiction, unless the form is stretched to the point where it overlaps with, or is indistinguishable from, fiction.

It is axiomatic that nonfiction is the collection and interpretation of information; and that fiction is information *invented* and interpreted. If done well, fiction reads the soul of a nonexistent being, dramatizes it, and creates an effect on the reader that is beyond the reach of reporting, or analytical or theoretical writing.

That said, nonfiction is the genre at hand, and I love it extremely well. I have worked in it all my writing life, and have enormous respect for its pitfalls and its exalted reaches.

I began my writing career as a newspaperman, and fragments from those early days are here, along with the story of my first effort at fiction. My original career plan was to live the life of the reporter who could go anywhere and write about anything, and, on the side, toss off an occasional short story to satisfy the craving for art; also to help pay the rent, newspaper salaries being scandalously low.

This is not how it worked out. I quit newspapering in 1957 to write a novel, but was back in the city room two years later. I quit again two years after that to finish a novel, yet continue to work part-time as a journalist even to this rainy July day in the early summer of 1992. I have covered sports, crime, trials, slums, city hall, politics, race, movies, books, and theater. I've done investigative work, raked muck, written columns and editorials, been an editor, and I've loved it all. But along the way something happened to my head and I turned into a novelist.

Yet I valued the nonfiction experience and always dreamed of making a book out of it: this book. The earliest story in the collection, the demise of Langford the cat, dates to 1954, and the most recent, a story about Damon Runyon, a hero of mine, I wrote a month ago. I have included, in large measure, pieces about literature, other art forms, pop culture and Albany. I left out my writings on politics, crime and other hard news; though they may turn up another day.

The problem from the beginning was in deciding what work survived, what had gone rancid. One piece that survived was a review of Hemingway's journalism, and I quoted him saying this:

The "newspaper stuff I have written . . . has nothing to do with the other writing which is entirely apart. . . . The first right that a man writing has is the choice of what he will publish. If you have made your living as a newspaperman, learning your trade, writing against deadlines, writing to make stuff timely rather than permanent, no one has any right to dig this stuff up and use it against the stuff you have written to write the best you can."

Of course you have the right to do this yourself, if you can live with it, and I decided I could. This book, in a way, is a writer's oblique autobiography (of his taste, if nothing else). It is the tracking of a writing style as it develops. It is about reading, and it can stand as a chorale of contemporary voices, also a chorale of my own assumed voices. It is a historical chronicle of what some of the world's best writers were writing in the decades the book spans, and it is an analysis of how fiction is written: writers talking of their craft, their ideas.

The latter element is the result of my own need to know. I was still an apprentice in fiction when I moved back home to Albany from Puerto Rico in 1963, starving for conversation about writing and literature. I'd worked for the *Albany Times-Union* from 1952 to the spring of 1956 and now I was back, writing anything that appealed to me, working half-time. I also became a stringer for a new national newspaper, Dow Jones's staid *National Observer*; and I self-propelled myself into covering, among other things, the literary life upstate for these two papers.

I sought out James Baldwin, Norman Mailer, Bernard Malamud, Saul Bellow, and others, and when writers like Allen Ginsberg and Robert Penn Warren came to town I was there, cajoling them into telling me how they created literature, how they imagined it, lived it. Of these literary encounters, I've included only those that still seem worth reading twenty or more years after the fact.

After I did these interviews, my editors decided I was such an aficionado of writing that I should become a book reviewer. Also, because

I had lived in Puerto Rico, I was considered expert in Latin American literature, and so I was thrust into assuming a point of view on the works of others: a critic, can you believe it? This was not what I was supposed to do in life. I was a newsman, a writer. I well knew where, in descending order, Beckett had ranked the critic: moron, vermin, abortion, morpion, sewer-rat, curate, cretin, and finally, "crritic!"

But there I was, working in the eighth circle of judgmental hell, and somehow glad to be there. I relished being force-fed good books, even less-than-good books, for it is also important to know how a book is badly written. The reviewing paid next to nothing, but I took what came. I remember the late David Boroff, also working for the *Observer* and one or two journals of opinion, calling what we were doing "dirty-shirt journalism," for at these wages you couldn't afford to send out your laundry.

It was painful to read a bad book and then have to write a negative review. I did a few, but even when I was right I regretted it. In time I sent back books I knew I'd have to knock. I found no pleasure, as some critics do, in denigrating the work of others; my ego was never so needy, nor was rejection my way to define a critical canon. I remember an academic friend, who liked almost nothing, telling me I shouldn't be so ready to praise, but should look for the flaws in any work. I decided this was literary sadism in the service of highmindedness. Not my way. I mentioned flaws when I thought I'd found them, but I was far more interested in discovering what I felt was valuable in a work, and illuminating that.

Eventually I resented reviewing, and writing essays, and even doing journalistic work, for it took time from fiction writing; and yet there was always the pleasure of completing any piece of writing, serious or frivolous, to my own satisfaction. And although I've gone for long periods of time without writing nonfiction, I always come back to it—to challenge the imagination in a new way, or to take on an assignment too good to reject, or to extend my knowledge of a subject, or to redefine my memory. What's more, *any* work that lets me run loose with the language needs no other justification.

One of the high points of my reporting came in 1973 when I was in Dublin to cover a week-long symposium of James Joyce scholars. By what I presumed to be happenstance, but which I would like to think was something mystically richer than that, I was driving along and

stopped at a street corner, looked up, and saw the sign ECCLES STREET.
I quickly found number 7, where Leopold and Molly Bloom lived.

It was one of four row houses, gone now but part of their façades still
erect, including, at number 7, two boarded-up windows, the doorway
nailed over with corrugated aluminum, a black iron picket fence in front,
and the chalky discoloration where the 7 used to be. The bedroom door
from number 7 had been installed at The Bailey, a Dublin pub. Grass
and weeds grew just beyond the doorstep in the now vacant lot that was
once the house. What remained had been marked long ago by a reverent
Joycean or two: over the absent door, erratically printed in faded black
paint, and also carved on a horizontal board, was the name "Molly
Bloom." There was also the mark of, perhaps, an anti-Joycean: the word
"shit," the only legible item among the faded bits of graffiti.

It is probably psychically confusing to visit a house in memory of
people who lived there but never actually existed. And yet in *Ulysses*
such is the detail available about the Blooms and how and where they
lived that they have a bygone reality equivalent to our dead relatives'.
Through the use of the real in service of the fictional, said one scholar,
Joyce "canonized the obsession with being Irish—the whole love of
place, of knowing a particular street in Dublin and talking all night
about it."

As to myself, there on Eccles Street, what I was doing was journalism.
But I was also, as I now know, riding the yellow trolley car.

1992

THE BEGINNING OF THE WRITER:

Eggs

My first short story I wrote for *Collier's* magazine. *Collier's* didn't know this when I wrote it. It was called "Eggs" and concerned a man who goes into a diner and orders scrambled eggs. The counterman doesn't want to serve him eggs and suggests goulash. The man insists on his eggs, the counterman reluctantly serves them, the man eats them and leaves. End of story. I was eighteen, my first year of college. After I wrote "Eggs" I showed it to my mother and as with everything else I had done in life she thought it was very good. I also showed it to my banjo teacher, Mike Pantone. Very good, he also said. He did not say it was very *very* good, which is what he said when I played well during my banjo lesson.

I showed the story to my father and he read it at the breakfast table while eating eggs of his own. He liked soft-boiled eggs with a teaspoon of sugar on them, and tea with three teaspoons of sugar. I never saw him eat scrambled eggs. What could he know of my story? He read it and said, "What the hell is this?"

"It's a story, a short story," I said.

"It's about a guy who goes in and eats eggs," he said.

"That's right," I said.

"What the hell kind of a story is that?" he said.

"It's a realistic story," I said. "I'm sending it off to *Collier's*."

"They publish stuff like this?"

"Every week," I said.

"Who the hell wants to read about a guy who goes in and eats eggs?"

"The whole world reads *Collier's*," I said. "The whole world eats eggs."

"Is this what you learned in school?" My schooling had cost serious money.

"I don't want to argue about it," I said. "You either like it or you don't."

"Take a guess," my father said.

Well I'd show him. I sent it off to *Collier's* that afternoon and I've still got the rejection slip to prove it. I never showed any more stories to my father. This is known as writer's block. However, I reread the story last week for the first time in forty-five years and my father emerges from that day as a masterful literary critic. A retarded orangutan could write a better story than "Eggs."

Be that as it may, writing the story was valuable for an assortment of reasons. It was the first step of a career. It proved I'd get better because I couldn't get worse. It acquainted me with rejection and I didn't die from it. It taught me that whether they're right or wrong, don't trust your parents with literature. It was about a particular place, the diner down the block, that I went to five nights a week, and about a counterman named Herbie who had been a batboy for the Yankees and was a pal of mine who died of cigarettes and who was such a singular man that I wrote "Eggs" two more times in later years. I called it "Counterman on Duty" and then just "Eat," and the story got better without getting good. Finally I abandoned it and put Herbie in a novel under another name and there he is at last, even though he missed out on *Collier's*.

Eudora Welty once wrote that a writer should write not about what he knows, but what he doesn't know about what he knows. I translate this to mean that the writer should understand and value mystery. But the only mystery about "Eggs" is why I didn't know it was awful. In time I did put some of my own mystery into the places I wrote about, and my fiction improved.

I'm sorry my parents didn't get to appreciate what happened to me as a writer. My mother died while I was still trying to get my short stories published, and my father was at the cusp of senility when I published my first novel. But he bragged about the book down at the State Supreme Court, where he worked. He said it was about how two thousand cows get swept out to sea in Puerto Rico. Actually the book is set in Albany and doesn't have any cows. But you can see how with that kind of imagination and critical apparatus in my genes it was inevitable that I'd become a writer.

1989

Hearst Is Where You Find Him (And I Found Him in Albany)

Charlie Davis was an old and amiably cynical newspaperman who had the falsest set of false teeth I ever saw, who had genius when he played high-low seven-card stud, who owned a bad stomach (every night he drank a cup of soup, every night he threw it up), a backwardly sloping bald pate with straight white threads hanging off it like icicles, a belly like a bowling pin, a talent for making up a front page so that you wanted to read every story, a reverence for authority that came from a lifetime of working for William Randolph Hearst and a penchant for uttering zingers.

It was 1952, the Korean War period, and I was a brand-new cityside reporter on the *Albany Times-Union*, a Hearst paper in a town run by a wondrously powerful and epically corrupt Irish Democratic boss machine that hadn't lost an election in thirty years. I'd done a year in the sports department of the *Glens Falls* (N.Y.) *Post-Star*, two years on Army newspapers in Georgia and Germany, and now I was getting a fair share of bylines on hot Albany stories and cool features. Charlie Davis eventually took notice of my potential for rising in the ranks.

"Hey, kid," he said to me, "what are you aimin' at?"

"I dunno, Charlie," I said with a young man's candor. "I suppose I'm just out to tell the truth as I see it and write it in the best way I can."

Charlie leaned back in his swivel chair in the slot of the copy desk and laughed with professional glee. "Son," he said, "you're in the wrong business, the wrong town, and on the wrong newspaper."

But it was Charlie who was wrong. The *Times-Union* was exactly the right place for me. The job let me live in and learn about my own city.

The editors, before long, let me write the way I wanted. And so between 1952 and 1956 I covered everything worth covering, except heavy politics. Also the *Times-Union* was the paper where I'd first come across Damon Runyon, my earliest writing hero, and there was something mythic in that.

There was also Hearst himself, The Chief.

From 1952 until I left town in 1956, I slept with a crucifix of you-know-who, plus a pair of photographs, hanging over my bed. One photo was an artsy shot of the Eiffel Tower I'd taken on a weekend pass to Paris, and the other was a framed head-and-shoulders portrait of Hearst that I'd liberated from a dusty file drawer of the *Times-Union*'s morgue. The Chief's portraits no longer hung in the newsroom, or anywhere else in the building, this perhaps because he was now dead.

Nevertheless, I was conscious of the power he, along with Jesus and the city of Paris—Hearst, God and mammon—exercised over my life. And so I stole and hung The Chief on my bedroom wall.

Hearst, and the *Times-Union* (a morning and Sunday paper), were emblematic of an age that had ripened before I was fully awake to the life around me. Popeye, Maggie and Jiggs, the Katzenjammer Kids, Ripley's Believe It or Not, the *American Weekly* with its exotic artwork and its stories of mummies, murder and the evils of vivisection (nowhere else in the world, before or since, have I read so much about the evils of vivisection), the brilliant Westbrook Pegler before and after he turned into a journalistic fascist, and the great Runyon, all arrived with notable fanfare, surrounded by large and compellingly black headlines and the magnetism of spankingly fresh news. Buying tomorrow's morning newspaper from an aging paper boy in an all-night coffee joint at 2:00 A.M. is a mystical experience to which no television news addict can ever attain.

I tried to get a copy-boy job at the *Times-Union* when I was in my last year of college but I didn't make it. Three years later I was sitting in the office of the paper's managing editor, George Williams, and he was reading my Army newspaper columns and telling me, "I like your leads," and all of a sudden I was a general assignment reporter.

George was a great character, irascible, slightly daft as all editors out of the *Front Page* era were supposed to be. I put him in my novel *Billy Phelan's Greatest Game*, called him Emory Jones, and elaborated on a true story Bill Lowenberg, a pal of mine who went to work for Hearst in the early 1930s, told me. It had to do with a night editor failing to take note of a major change in one of The Chief's editorials concerning President Roosevelt, and of all Hearst papers, the *Times-Union* was alone the next morning in failing to carry the new and critical view of FDR. Emory, on a later occasion, met The Chief when his train pulled into the Albany station:

"The Chief received Emory Jones, who presented him with the day's final edition, an especially handsome, newsy product by local standards. The Chief looked at the paper, then without a word let it fall to the floor of his private compartment, and jumped up and down on it with both feet until Emory fled in terror."

Thus did authority from on high arrive at Albany.

But that authority related principally to national and international matters. Local editorials were homegrown, as were local political allegiances. Hearst may have been antipathetic to New Deal Democrats, but in Albany the local Democrats and the *Times-Union*'s editors and publisher were as close as Siamese twins. If a reporter put a hostile question to the mayor, by the time he got back to the city room the mayor would have called George Williams to complain. George would thereupon ream the offender sideways for insubordination to an elected Democrat, take the city hall story away from him and send him out to cover a manure auction.

That's how it was until 1960 when Gene Robb, the *Times-Union*'s publisher, led the consolidation of the *T-U* and the *Knickerbocker News*, a Gannett daily. The machine always threatened both newspapers with withdrawal of city and county legal advertising (as much as $300,000 a year) if they became critical of city hall. In light of this, the two papers' traditional economic competitiveness argued for discretion. But after Robb controlled both papers, he kicked discretion out the door and began a new era in Albany journalism.

I left the paper in 1956 because I was bored and repeating myself, covering yet another St. Patrick's parade, another ax murder. The final straw was the story I wrote after a two-hour interview with Louis Armstrong at the Kenmore Hotel. The news editor (not Charlie Davis) looked at it and tossed it in the wastebasket. "Just another bandleader," he said. I retrieved the story, complained to the boss and the story ran. But by then I was suffocating.

A month later I was working on a new daily in San Juan and I stayed away from Albany for seven years, most of that time in Puerto Rico, less than a year in Miami. I also turned myself into a half-time newsman and full-time novelist (aspiring), and came back to Albany in 1963 to discover Hearst and the political machine at war. The newspaper business, the town and the paper were no longer recognizable.

I hired on again as a part-timer and wrote features for a while, then turned into a muckraker. Nobody censored me, and my stories about political corruption, civil rights and black radicalism ran around the block. Our executive editor, Dan Button, quit to run for Congress against the machine, and he won. This wasn't the Hearst paper anybody in Albany over the age of six was used to reading, but on we went and I became one of the machine's public enemies.

It was sporty stuff but you can't do that forever either, and so I turned into a movie critic to change my mood. Then Gene Robb died and the paper's radicalism died with him. In a matter of months the new editors were running a condensation of a vanity press book attacking the welfare system and its recipients ("Lawrence Lazy," "Sally Stupid," "Sonya Sleepy"). Also the new managing editor refused to consider even the idea of a story of my experience during the 1970 peace march on Washington, or one on student riots at a local college. "Irresponsible people," he said, were getting too much publicity. He preferred the story of hardhat construction workers in Manhattan attacking student protesters. I slowly tuned out and left the paper finally in 1970 during this man's tenure.

Well, he passed out of the picture too, as did the fellow who dumped Satch in the wastebasket. The legacy of Gene Robb survives in the present-day *Times-Union*, which is cozy with no politicians and has an edge to its coverage.

We all evolved over the years, and in 1983 I published my notes on this evolution—thirty years of Albany-watching—in a book called *O Albany!* I neglected therein to thank properly The Chief and all his subalterns, cosmic and regional, for my roller-coaster ride through the hills and dales of their dynamic inconsistency. But here and now I have rectified that.

I am still taking notes, however.

1987

Langford, Prominent Cat, Dies
Albert the Swimmer
Tracking the Missing Leopard

Langford, Prominent Cat, Dies

Langford, widely known North Albany cat, died Friday night at the Albany Animal Hospital. He had undergone surgery earlier in the week for the removal of a tumor and was on the way to recovery.

Then on Saturday his owner, Jerome Kiley of 1232 Broadway, announced to a gathering at Jack's Lunch, at 1247 Broadway:

"Langford took a turn for the worse and they had to gas him."

The animal's fame was so widespread throughout the North End that a wave of sentiment inundated Jack's customers and almost spontaneously a collection was made to buy Langford some flowers.

Jack Thorpe and John Itzo, owners of Jack's Lunch, Gratton Finn, George Brown, Joseph Sheehan and several others contributed to the fund for the floral wreath.

"We got about six dollars altogether," Thorpe said.

Langford, who was three years old at the time of his death, was described by acquaintances as being "tan, gentle, something like an Angora, and fat—almost as big as a dog."

He was said to have been a fussy eater and to have subsisted solely on a diet of chicken livers. He also slept on a bed, constructed especially for him.

His treatment at home was so preferential, in fact, that Jerome Kiley often confided to intimates:

"That cat lives better than me."

16

Kiley, who weighs about 250 pounds and stands six feet, three inches, is self-employed. He repairs and cleans beer coils for tavern owners.

The floral piece was put together by another acquaintance of Langford's, John M. Tracey of the Danker Flower Shop. It contained, among other things, a few strands of pussy willows. And perched atop the flowers was the figure of a bird, bearing a card addressed to Langford. The message on the card read:

"I don't have to worry about you anymore."

In addition to his parents, who are unknown, Langford is survived by an estimated forty-six children, plus innumerable brothers, sisters, cousins, uncles, etc.

Funeral services and burial were private.

1954

Albert the Swimmer

The oil slick on the Hudson River drifted lazily out to sea on the ebb tide and on the dock of the Albany Yacht Club Albert Black, twenty, slobbered himself with all-purpose grease.

The bright sunlight warmed the skin but a chill wind reminded bystanders that this was not ideal swimming weather. Black dipped a hand in the river and sloshed it about.

"It's cold," he said.

The 187-pound young man from West Atlantic City, New Jersey, was preparing for a 156-mile swim from the Albany Yacht Club (now at Rensselaer) to the Statue of Liberty (still in the same old place).

SWIMMER'S AIMS

Three associates and two newsmen were at the dock to watch the start of what Black hopes will be a record-breaking swim. He figures to shatter the speed record set by Marilyn Bell of Canada for thirty-two miles. He also claims that if he makes New York Harbor (present estimate: sixty-one hours), he will have made the first nonstop swim of the Hudson.

A swimmer since he was two, Black has trained for this event for three years. Last January, his plans went awry when a chlorinator in a hotel swimming pool exploded. He inhaled the gas it exuded and was hospitalized ten days. He was told he would never swim again, but last week, upon discharge from doctors' care, he decided to swim the Hudson lengthwise.

Robert George of Somers Point, New York, and Jack Cantrell of Philadelphia will precede him by ten feet in a rowboat. Bill Jones of Pleasantville, New Jersey, will follow down Route 9-W by automobile.

WELL SUPPLIED

Cantrell sat alone yesterday in the boat which was stocked with soup, chocolate bars and other goodies, while Black greased himself.

"Bring the boat around, Jack," someone said.

Jack pulled on the oars and the boat banged into the dock. He smiled thinly and pulled on the oars again. The boat started downriver.

"No, Jack," he was told. "Back this way."

"I'll get the hang of it," he said.

Jack is going to row halfway on the trip.

EXPLAINS GOALS

Swimmer Black is making this swim, he says, to "prove to people and myself that when you're hurt you can overcome it if you work." Also because "if you want to do a sport, don't do it halfway." Also because "I'd like to have Atlantic City and New Jersey and the United States known as the home of someone who set an important record."

Also because his sponsor is an Atlantic City restaurant owner who stands to gain substantial local publicity.

He donned a rubber cap and slipped on a nose clip and goggles. He looked very strange. The nose clip caused him to talk like a man with a head cold. He walked to the dock's edge leaving a trail of greasy footprints.

"DURE HE'D WARB"

"Are you nervous?" he was asked.

"Yedd. You always are before yo duo subthig."

"It's a little chilly. Aren't you cold?"

"No. I'be nide and warb." He patted the grease on his chest.

It was 1:31 P.M. then and with a wave to observers he leaped into the water, flailing the air with legs and arms like a mixed-up frog. He swam out a ways while George stepped into the boat and Cantrell guided it cautiously away from the dock.

He paddled patiently for two or three minutes, beginning to feel the penetrating chill of the water. Then he had a sudden thought.

"Brig more grease," he yelled half-frantically to Jones. "I'be going to need more grease."

Jones nodded and waved. The boat and swimmer Black moved out into the river. Next stop, Miss Liberty?

1955

Tracking the Missing Leopard

It was beastly hot when we started out on the safari. The afternoon sun was blistering the paint on our Buick.

We were after leopard: Great White Hunter Bill Kuenzel and I. Kuenzel carried the cameras. I was armed with an Ebony Jet Black, Extra Smooth, No. 6325 pencil.

The leopard had been ranging in rural Ojus in North Dade since it broke away from its owner, Mrs. Bonnie Tindall of 2330 NE 197th Street, Thursday morning.

It was three feet long, a foot and a half high, brown, black and white. It had been known to eat dish towels, furniture and sweaters. We could take no chances.

Jaba Gatito was the leopard's name and it had been sighted twice Friday near the Maule Industries rockpit.

It had also attacked a tomato in the Tindall back yard during the night. Large toothmarks were found in the tomato's carcass.

We approached the Tindall house cautiously. No sign of life anywhere. I got out of the car and rang the doorbell. It went "ding dong"—the only sound for miles around.

I wondered what to do if I spotted it. I had no gun. No knife. Only an Ebony Jet Black, Extra Smooth, No. 6325 pencil. But you don't think of yourself. You think only . . . the leopard must be caught. Or do you?

I got back in the car.

The Humane Society of Greater Miami had its hunters out searching all day. They hadn't found anything either.

We drove along a road next to a rockpit, looking for tracks. All we could see were tire marks. The sun was scorching. We were thankful for the breeze.

We saw a herd of animals grazing on a grassy plain.

"Look there!" I told Kuenzel.

He turned his trained hunter's eye on the herd.

"They're Shetland ponies," he said.

There were two other ferocious-looking animals in an adjacent field. Kuenzel identified them right away as cows. They had a mean look.

We drove along the wilds of NE 22nd Avenue. The undergrowth was dense. Our right front wheel snapped a twig.

We stopped at the Greynold Park Stables. L. O. Grassman said a party of twenty had canceled its riding date because of the leopard.

While we were at the stables a saddleless horse broke out of the stable and ran off. It seemed the whole animal world had gone on an emancipation kick.

We went back to the Tindall home and I pushed the doorbell again. It repeated that same ominous "ding dong."

Mrs. Bonnie Tindall, a fifteen-year-old bride of twelve days, came to the door. No, she said, the leopard hadn't returned. They just moved into the house and they had no place to keep the leopard except outside.

She kept it on a chain, with a garbage can nearby so it could crawl inside during a storm.

Mrs. Tindall had been looking all day for her leopard, she said. She said she has a girl friend who owns a lion.

It was getting late. Kuenzel snapped his first picture of the day—of Mrs. Tindall. We drove back the same way we came. The sun wasn't nearly so beastly any more.

We saw a goat on the way home.

1957

Be Reasonable, Unless You're a Writer

Shelley believed that poets—and by that he meant all imaginative writers—are good people. He writes in his essay "A Defence of Poetry" that "cruelty, envy, revenge, avarice, and the passions purely evil, have never formed any portion of the popular imputations on the lives of the poets." Thank you, Mr. Shelley. However, he also thought that writers don't necessarily know what they're doing.

He attributes to them great power to change opinion or institutions beneficially. And this power, he writes, is "seated on the throne of their own soul." And further, "electric life . . . burns within their words." But he concludes—with some chagrin, I suspect—that the writers themselves are the ones most sincerely astonished at the manifestation of their own power, for he sees this power derived less from *their* spirit than from the spirit of the age working through them.

This spirit of the age, this sensitivity to what is temporal, is what American writers are sometimes thought to be lacking. That is a confusion, and a serious one. Such criticism was very much in evidence last year during the International PEN Congress in New York, when a parade of foreign writers castigated their American counterparts for being too removed or aloof from, or indifferent to, the pressing needs of society. I found myself under siege in 1985 in Germany in a similar conversation with several writers. One German novelist concluded that there was no such thing as political writing among modern American novelists.

This is, to say the least, very silly; especially when you consider the work of Ralph Ellison and Toni Morrison and Norman Mailer and Grace Paley and E. L. Doctorow and Richard Ellman and Robert Stone and

Saul Bellow and William Styron and Alice Walker and William Herrick and Tim O'Brien and Don DeLillo and so on and so on. Make your own list.

Not all these writers I've named would agree on what is proper to the temporal element of writing, the political temporality if you will. But I know that as writers of serious intent they understand the self-destructive element in the temporal—that being the appeal of propaganda, or partisan writing. Hemingway's famous line on this subject is, "All you can be sure about in a political-minded writer is that if his work should last you will have to skip the politics when you read it." Yet politics abounds in his own writing, the politics of war, for instance, in the retreat from Caporetto during the Italian campaign in *A Farewell to Arms*; or the stories of the Spanish Civil War, in which political attitudes among the combatants are central to the meaning. These works have not gone dead in fifty or sixty years, and you do not have to skip them when you read Hemingway's books; and so it is not the matter, and it is not the subject, that goes dead. Survival depends on the way the work is written, the way the writer does it.

How does the writer do it? How does he write about the temporal without falling fatally into the pit of propaganda? Consider Franz Kafka's novel *The Trial*. Was there ever a more telling blow struck against totalitarianism? Here, without doubt, was a stunningly original attack on the state and on its courts—was it not? But then, again, wasn't it really the analysis of a neurosis? Or take Kafka's shorter work "In the Penal Colony"—clearly an attack on the church, and on every dogmatic form of theology or ideology, wasn't that what it was? Or was it, too, like *The Trial*, a case of the writer looking into the center of his own deceitful mind and finding something other than a one-for-one metaphor reflecting this morning's political logic?

Propaganda is *logical*. It takes sides, foursquare. It argues, it finds enemies and targets, it promotes or opposes love and allegiance toward the object being propagandized, whether it be the flag, the revolution, the mother church or the genocidal death machine. Love me or leave me, it argues. If you're not with the revolution or the death machine, you are against it. Such directness is the function of reason, and synthesis, and unity. But writers are made of another fabric; and their fabric is the imagination.

"Reason is to the imagination," says Shelley, "as the body to the spirit, as the shadow to the substance." He defines poetry, or writing, as the expression of that imagination, and he likens the imagination to the wind—an ever-changing wind—blowing over a mythic aeolian lyre, and by this motion creating an ever-changing melody. This is *unarguably* what the literary imagination does. It does not reach for, nor does it arrive at, simple conclusions. It is more concerned with centering on the action of things, the fluid condition of things, the whatness of things, the open-endedness of things, than it is with formulating prescriptions for proper revolutionary or reactionary behavior.

Albert Camus is one of the most political of writers, but consider his line, "I like men who take sides more than literatures that do." He points out that if the merit of a piece of writing is imposed either by law, or by professional obligation, or by terror, then where is the merit? Camus writes in his diary: "It would appear that to write a poem about spring would nowadays be serving capitalism. I am not a poet, but I should have no second thoughts about being delighted by such a poem if it were beautiful. One either serves the whole of man or one does not serve him at all."

The work by Camus that seems to be universally valued is *The Stranger*. It is a most political piece of work and, as with the work of Kafka, you search it in vain for conventional logic, or an appeal to reason. An appeal to unreason is closer to what it is: mirror images of certain dark unknowns of our deepest selves, a revelation of relationships that exist not on a basis of one-to-one, but of one-to-ten, or one-to-forty. The reward in reading it is similar to that provided by betting long shots at the track.

My uncle Peter, who was a horseplayer, once pointed out to me a forlorn citizen of the world, a man in tatters who was picking a cigarette butt out of the gutter. "There's a guy," he said, "who used to play the favorites." You can't win much of anything playing the favorites. It's too logical. Too much reason, too much method, goes into it. It is important to remember Gallant Fox, the world's best horse in 1930, going off at

1-to-2 in the Travers Stakes at Saratoga. But in the stretch here came Jim Dandy, a 100-to-1 shot, and Jim wins it going away. Wrote Damon Runyon: "You only dream the thing that happened here this afternoon."

The tale goes to the core of the kind of writing I've come to value: first dreaming, and then executing, the improbable, and on good days, the impossible. This involves a serious reliance on intuition, and an enduring reverence for the irrational. It has very little to do with reason. Let me quote from the diary of Lionel Trilling, the literary critic and teacher, and a man of reason if there ever was one. Trilling saw a letter that Ernest Hemingway had written to Clifton Fadiman, the critic, and Trilling thought the letter crazy, arrogant, scared, trivial, absurd and written when Hemingway was obviously drunk.

And Trilling could write this: "Yet [I] felt from reading it how right such a man is compared to the 'good minds' of my university life—how he will produce and mean something to the world . . . how his life which he could expose without dignity and which is anarchic and 'childish' is a better life than anyone I know could live, and right for his job. And how far-far-far- I am going from being a writer—how less and less I have the material and the mind and the will."

This is sad about Trilling, and, to me, no news at all about Hemingway. Even Hemingway's unfinished fragments now turn up on the best-seller list, twenty-six years after his death, and I'm glad to have them.

Trilling saw in Hemingway the same qualities Shelley valued in poets: the electricity of their words, the power of their imagination and the anarchy of their melodious minds. And then Trilling posed these questions to himself: how can Hemingway do it so well with such a disordered mind, and why can't I and my orderly colleagues do the same? Well, as we used to say so frequently in my religion class, that's a mystery.

And mystery is not only great sport, it's also, as Luis Buñuel cleverly pointed out, the basic element in all works of art. But even if writers know all that, and even if they grudgingly admit that Shelley might have a point about their not always knowing what they're doing, they also perceive that this isn't a flaw in their makeup, but a happy gift of a particular kind, like being born double-jointed or with hair that falls out and reveals a noble brow; and these writers continue to write with enormous pleasure, and with reverence for the art. For with whatever marginal gift of *reason* that may have been doled out to them, they concluded long ago that not only was writing truly worth pursuing, it was the most important thing they could do with their lives.

1987

THE HOPWOOD LECTURE:

Writers and
Their Songs

I was working as a newspaperman when I was drafted into the army during the Korean War, and I decided to write a continuing column about it called "This New Army," which was what everybody was calling that same old army in those days. I wrote about how unbelievably stupid sergeants and corporals were, how unspeakably dreadful army food was, and how very peculiarly the general behaved when he noticed I was marching out of step.

When these columns were published back in Glens Falls, New York, enlistments in this new army dropped to zero, the first time I changed the world with my writing. This change was testified to by the local doomsday recruiting sergeant, who packaged off my clippings, along with a formal complaint, to Fort Benning, Georgia, where I was taking basic training in a heavy-weapons company of the Fourth Infantry Division. Because I could type, somebody had made me the company clerk, and so I also got to answer the phone. A call came in one day and guess who it was for? Me. The major who ran the division's public information office was calling.

"Kennedy," he said to me, "that was a funny column you wrote the other day about the general."

"Thank you, Major," I said. "I'm glad you liked it."

"I didn't say I liked it and don't write any more." And then he added, after a pause, "Come up and see me and maybe I'll give you a job."

Well I did, and he did, and for the next two years I spent my days writing for army newspapers in the United States and Germany—Germany because our Fourth Division became the first American troop unit to go back to Europe after World War II. I was also thrown in with the literate and subliterate malcontents who populated the public information section, most of them also draftees and ex-newsmen, and four, including me, aspirants to writing of a different order—short stories, novels, films, plays; we weren't particular.

These years were seminal for me, the period in which I dove head first into literature. One of my great pals was Frank Trippett, a brilliant newsman from Mississippi who had not only seen and talked to Satchmo, he had actually attended a lecture by William Faulkner. Closer than that to the Empyrean no man I knew had ever ventured. Four or five nights a week we would gather in our enlisted men's club in Frankfurt, arguing, over heilbock and doppelbock, the relative merits of Sherwood Anderson, Hemingway, Dos Passos, Steinbeck, Caldwell, Fitzgerald, Mailer, Algren, Katherine Anne Porter, Flannery O'Connor, James Jones, Irwin Shaw, Thomas Wolfe. "Wolfe said it all but Faulkner said it better," was the youthful anthem from Mississippi.

I tried then and since to read everything that all these writers ever wrote and I have succeeded, perhaps by half, though I'm still working on Faulkner. I also began writing what I thought of as serious short fiction. I had written stories in college, all derivative and blithering, but now I was beginning to match myself against these maestros I'd been reading. At first I was such an amateur I couldn't even imitate them, but in the year or two after I left the army I managed to write dialogue that sounded very like Hemingway and John O'Hara, I could describe the contents of a kitchen refrigerator just like Thomas Wolfe, I could use intelligent obscenity just like Mailer, I could keep a sentence running around the block, just like Faulkner. But where was Kennedy?

I came to loathe the stories, as did my family, my friends, and fiction editors from coast to coast. Nevertheless, by diving into literature I had baptized myself as a writer. I have since come to look upon this as a religious experience; not because of its holiness, for as a profession it is more profane than sacred, but because of its enmeshment with the Catholic Church's supernatural virtues of faith, hope, and charity—as I had learned them.

Charity, of course, is what the writer supports himself with while he is finishing his novel.

Hope is the virtue by which he firmly trusts that someday, somewhere, somebody will publish his novel.

But it is in the virtue of faith that the writer grounds himself (or herself) in the true religious experience of literature; and faith was defined early on for me as a firm belief in the revealed *truths*—truths of God as religion would have it; truths of the writing life, as I would have it.

"How may we sin against faith?" the catechism used to ask itself, and then it provided four answers:

Sin number 1: "By rashly accepting as truths of faith what are not really such." I take this to mean that the writer should learn how to tell the difference between literary gold and dross. Michelangelo said a work of sculpture is created by cutting away the unnecessary part of a block of marble. Georges Simenon removed all words from his work that were there just to make an effect. "You know," he said, "you have a beautiful sentence—cut it." But it was Hemingway who forever codified this issue when he said: "The most essential gift for a good writer is a built-in, shock-proof shit detector. This is the writer's radar and all great writers have had it."

Sin number 2: "By neglecting to learn the truths which we are bound to know." This is a large order. It means you should read the entire canon of literature that precedes you, back to the Greeks, up to the current issue of *The Paris Review*; and if you have any time left over, you should go out and accumulate an intimate knowledge of politics, history, language, love, philosophy, psychology, sex, madness, the underworld, soap opera, your cholesterol level, and whether the Beatles will ever have a reunion.

Sin number 3: "By not performing those acts of faith, which we are commanded to perform." This means you should write even on Christmas and your birthday, and forswear forever the excuse that you never have enough time.

Sin number 4: "By heresy and apostasy." This means writing for the movies.

You see here before you a heretic and an apostate. My life after the army was a tissue of muddle, a pilgrimage through ignorance, anxiety, and innocence, but a pilgrimage with some discernible milestones. Five

years after leaving the army I would get married, write my first play and
my twenty-fifth short story, then quit journalism to write a novel. I would
write the novel and it would be awful. Seven years after the army I
would become managing editor of a daily newspaper. After nine years
I would quit journalism again to finish another novel. I would be showing
improvement in novel writing, but not much. After fifteen years of work
as a half-time journalist, half-time fictionist, I would become a movie
critic. After seventeen years I would publish my first novel. After nineteen years I would become a book critic. After twenty-two years I would
become a teacher. And then, after thirty-one years, I would write my
first movie script, may God have mercy on his soul.

I was not always a heretic. For a time I was a true believer in journalism, lived it passionately, gained entry to worlds I had no right to
enter, learned how to write reasonably well and rapidly, was never bored
by what I was doing, found it an enduring source of stimulation, met
thousands of the crazy people who inhabit it and learned madness from
most of them. I loved the tension, the unexpected element of the news,
the illusion of being at the center of things when you were really at what
approximated the inner lining of the orange peel.

Also I learned who I was, in certain small but significant ways. I
became, as I mentioned, a managing editor, a position to which I had
been obliquely gravitating since the beginning; for in wanting to learn
all there was to learn about writing, I also wanted to learn all there was
about what you did with writing after you wrote it. I became an escalating
figure in the editorial room: from lowly slug in the sports department,
to army columnist, to inquiring reporter and rewrite man. I harangued
myself onto the police beat, became Saturday city editor, feature writer,
substitute night city editor, general reporter; city editor when the reigning
figure went to lunch and never came back; acting managing editor when
the boss infarcted myocardially. And then, at long last, managing editor.

When this happened to me—over the objection of my second self,
which had always wanted to be a daily columnist until the seductive
muse of fiction deflowered my pencil—I contemplated the new condition
and wrote to a contemporary of mine who had also become a managing
editor. He'd been a youth-page writer for a local daily when I was still
in college, and I always envied him that head start. Now here we were

in perfect equanimity, managing editors both, he in Albany, I in Puerto Rico, and I apprised him of this, also reminding him of what Mencken had once written: "All managing editors are vermin."

I remained verminous for two years, for we had started this newspaper from scratch and it was a challenge unlike any other I'd known. I never worked harder, never found more pleasure in the work, yet always longed to be out of it, for the job had interrupted my novel in progress, and I yearned to return and see how it would turn out. It took me those two years to accumulate the courage and wisdom to quit a lucrative, fascinating job, live off my savings and a weekend editing job, and work five full days on fiction. What I had finally come to realize was that I'd learned all I wanted to learn about newspapering, and that I could never learn enough about how to write fiction; for the more I learned, the more difficult writing became; and that is still so today. I don't mean to be simplistic about journalism, which is mired in the complexity of randomness. It was a great training ground for a writer; but I'd reached my limit with it and knew in my soul that I was a committed novelist, whose work is grounded in the complexity of unconscious logic.

The problem then became the quest for the elusive Kennedy voice. I had ceased to be consciously emulative of anyone in my work, but what I was left with was what I now think of as the voice of literary objectivity, a journalistic virus, an odious microbe that paralyzes the imagination and cripples the language. "Cut, cut, cut," counsels Simenon; but what is left after all the cuts? Is there something new on the page? Something original? Is there energy in the sentence, power in the scene? In the interest of curbing excess, has the heart been cut out of the story? In the relentless quest for realistic action and surface, has the intellectual dimension been excised, or avoided?

In recent years a number of very good young writers have been, and are still being, castigated, even vilified, because of the brevity of their styles and content. This is the critical assault on so-called minimalism, that word a critic's invention that is not a new subject for assaulting purposes. Forty years ago the critic Philip Rahv looked around and found the novelists of that day excluding the intellect in favor of depicting life on its physical levels (which is the journalistic way, of course). Rahv accused the American writer of "a disinclination to thought and . . . an intense predilection for the real," and found also that less gifted writers following Hemingway's method were producing "work so limited to the recording of the unmistakably real that it could be said of them that their art ended exactly where it should properly begin."

The transition from journalism to fiction is always a precarious trip, for journalism foists dangerous illusions on the incipient fiction writer. The daily journalist is trained, for instance, to forget about yesterday and focus on today. There is also a car parked downstairs, ready to carry him off into tomorrow, and so every new day becomes, for him, a tabula rasa. This is deadly. The fiction writer who puts little or no value on yesterday, or the even more distant past, might just as well have Alzheimer's disease; for serious fiction, especially novelistic work, has time as its essence and memory as its principal tool.

The journalist is also under pressure to believe that merely his presence at the great moments—whether he be first on the scene after a murder of passion, or witness to the fall of an empire—gives him the stuff of fiction. This is true to a point, but the stuff in question is merely raw material. The writer who believes he has a ready-made work of fiction spread out before him in his notes, needful only of a bit of sprucing and spicing, is deluded. He is a victim of the cult of experience, the impulse that sends writers, who can find no value in the quotidian, off to wars and revolutions to find something to write about. More than experience is called for.

In recent months in this country we have witnessed a rather tub-thumping, hog-stomping, name-calling literary argument on this subject, begun by our contemporary Tom Wolfe, a notable tub-thumper and baroque hog-stomper of high journalistic achievement and repute, who moved into the realm of fiction with an extraordinarily successful first novel, *Bonfire of the Vanities*. Having succeeded, he now would like others to succeed also by writing novels like his. The debate over this has flourished in the pages of *Harper's* magazine and the *New York Times Book Review*, among other places, and Mr. Wolfe has had his say twice on the subject. Also, his argument has been deconstructed by some notable figures in contemporary literature, Philip Roth, Mary Gordon, John Hawkes, and Robert Towers among others, and its parts have been handed back to Mr. Wolfe, somewhat the worse for wear. Even so, there is merit in his point of view. I mentioned to him last month that I'd followed the exchange with great interest and had heard several arguments on both sides of the issue. That surprised him. "If there's anybody on my side," he said, "I haven't heard from them."

The essence of Mr. Wolfe's side of the argument is that American literature in the last half of this century has gone down the tube of privacy, inversion, neo-fabulism, magical realism, absurdism, and so on, and that the only way to rescue it is through a return to realism of a nineteenth-century order, writing akin to that of Dickens, Trollope, Thackeray, Zola, and Balzac. The means of achieving this movement back to the future of the novel, says Mr. Wolfe, is reporting.

He writes: "I doubt there is a writer over forty who does not realize in his heart of hearts that literary genius, in prose, consists of proportions more on the order of 65 percent material, and 35 percent talent in the sacred crucible."

Mr. Wolfe also believes that, because of the way fiction has been written in the past twenty-five years, "Any literary person . . . will admit that in at least four years out of five the best nonfiction books have been better literature than the most highly praised books of fiction."

This latter notion has at least two memorable antecedents, one an essay by Norman Podhoretz, the editor of *Commentary* magazine, written some thirty-odd years ago. As Mr. Wolfe does today, Mr. Podhoretz back then found fiction wanting in imagination, in disciplined intelligence, and also lacking a "restless interest in the life of the times."

Discursive writing, argued Mr. Podhoretz, had taken over the province that the novel had voluntarily surrendered—that province being the criticism of morals and manners. In short, the novel had no contemporary social relevance, he said, and the real art form of the age was the magazine article.

Similarly, the critic Leslie Fiedler, the great doomsayer of our era, all but exulted back in the early 1960s that the novel as a form was just about dead, that the public for novels had become subliterate, that the artistic faith that had sustained writers was dead, and, what's more, America never had an unequivocal avant-gardist among novelists of the first rank anyway.

In a subliterate era, he wrote, who needs fiction? For, what *documentary realism* once promised to give people in *novel* form, nonfiction was providing more efficiently, more painlessly. As to the myths the subliterates always look for—boy gets girl, good guy kills bad guy, etc.—television and film were providing them more vividly than the novel, and at less intellectual cost.

Some truth there, alas, in Mr. Fiedler's argument. Even so, it's very troublesome being a novelist when critics with a license to kill keep saying you're dead. Such complaints also cheer up *serious* people who do not find their own predilections and prejudices reflected in the novels they read. They see instead a hostile fiction that supports dangerous ideas and does not strike sufficiently critical attitudes toward the social forces and institutions that oppress certain multitudes, or certain elites. They see the literature of the age being written by the disengaged, the alienated, the untalented, the Philistines, the dropouts, the solipsists, the anarchists; and who will save us from drowning in all this irrelevance? these serious people wonder.

I could join Tom Wolfe's argument happily and point out my own black beasts of contemporary literature; but I am more inclined to defend this literature and its creators for several reasons.

What is fundamental to the counterargument is the number of great books that have been written that did not directly concern their own time, but have prevailed as classic works nevertheless.

Consider only three of these books written out of their own age: *Benito Cereno* by Melville, written in 1856 of an event from 1797, but emblematic of the racial conflict that prevailed throughout the long era of slavery, and relevant even today; *The Red Badge of Courage* by Stephen Crane, written thirty years after the Civil War had ended, but a masterpiece of that war that speaks to all soldiers of any war; Hawthorne's first novel, *The Scarlet Letter*, written in 1850, probing the conflict between the Puritan culture of the seventeenth century and the privacy of love, but a cautionary tale of secrecy and shame whose meaning has endured, will endure.

Should we have told these writers that their choice of time was out of joint? Clearly their books are relevant not only to their own time, they are relevant to all time. I don't believe it matters whether a writer crisscrosses continents in search of today's material. I believe that what Alfred Kazin wrote is the truth: ". . . every writer criticizes life and society with every word he writes. The better the writer, the more this criticism and his imagination will fuse as one."

Or consider Tolstoy on the same subject:

An artist's mission must not be to produce an irrefutable solution to a problem, but to compel us to love life in all its countless and inexhaustible manifestations. If I were told I might write a book in which I should demonstrate beyond any doubt the correctness of my opinions on every social problem, I should not waste two hours at it; but if I were told that what I wrote would be read twenty years from now by people who are children today, and that they would weep and laugh over my book and love life more because of it, then I should devote all my life and strength to such a work.

How can anyone have the audacity to tell a writer what and how to write? The writer, of necessity, is the sole judge of that, for the making of these decisions is evolutionary, a process of trial and rejection, of finally choosing among infinite possibilities the method, and story, and characters that allow the work to be written at all. I could never fault any writer for not writing about the age, for in my own experience it has been extremely difficult; and I offer only one example.

My time in the army represented two years of my life, and not merely life lived, but life reported on through a newsman's eye—reporting on the army, on Germany, on the cold war getting hot, on an innocent abroad, on fraternization with frauleins, on the black market, on army skulduggery, on leftover Nazism, and much more. I had, and still have, some of that world at my fingertips; and also I've gone back twice to Germany to rekindle my memory.

Why? Well I wanted to write about it all, and did write about it—in short stories over a decade; and all those stories died. I also wrote about two hundred pages of a novel about it, and that too died. Why do my stories die when clearly I have at least 65 percent of them living right there in the file cabinet? Obviously, in my case, because it is not the *material* that makes a work of fiction come to life. It is, in fact, almost impossible to say what it is that does that. Material can begin a piece of work, emotion and ideas can keep it going, but in order for the work not to self-destruct along the way, something else must happen. The writer must find himself in a strange place full of unknowns, populated by characters who are not quite strangers but about whom little is certain, everything is to be discovered. There must be a transformation of the material, of the characters, of the age, into something that is intriguingly new to the writer. "Art," wrote Boris Pasternak, "is interested in life at the moment when the ray of power is passing through it."

The writer, when he is functioning as an artist, understands when this power is at hand, and he knows that it does not rise up from his notepad but up from the deepest part of his unconscious, which knows everything everywhere and always: that secret archive stored in the soul at birth, enhanced by every waking moment of life, and which is the source of the power and the vision that allow the writer to create something never before heard or seen on earth.

This creation of the new is what a good reader seeks and will recognize. Listen to Seamus Heaney, for instance, on what he expects from good poetry: "You want it to touch you at the melting point below the breastbone and the beginning of the solar plexus. You want something sweetening and at the same time something unexpected, something that has come through constraint into felicity."

Or E. M. Forster trying to define *Moby Dick*. He calls the book a yarn about whaling interspersed with snatches of poetry, also a battle against evil conducted too long or in the wrong way, also a contest between two unreconciled evils; and then he throws up his hands: "These are words," says Forster, "a symbol for the book if we want one, but . . . the essential in *Moby Dick* is prophetic song, which flows athwart the action and the surface morality like an undercurrent. It lies outside words."

Prophetic song. Nice work if you can get it.

Almost, but not quite, just by the nature of Melville's effort, one might conclude he was striving for that song from the outset. But to think that is to believe in creation as nothing more than conception; that the song, the achievement, was already present in the embryo. If this were true, what then can we say of Melville's years of gestation among whales, his months of research ("I have swam through libraries," his narrator writes in *Moby Dick*, and the same was true of Melville), and his year and a half of writing and rewriting the text? One of his biographers pointed out that although seventeen months seems a short time for the composition of such a book, it would have been an unusually *long* period given the manic pace at which Melville was writing.

An ancillary note: Nathaniel Hawthorne, to whom Melville became a soul mate during the writing of *Moby Dick*, had taken ten years for his own literary embryo to mature into the form and substance that became *The Scarlet Letter*.

Writers (and their songs) grow like plants, like trees, like children, like disease, like love. They go through stages of fragility, woodenness, pubescence, death, and passion. You'll note that I have put death before passion. This corresponds to the crucifixion, burial, descent into hell, and resurrection that befalls all literary careerists who keep the faith. Fitzgerald's noted line, "There are no second acts in American lives," was cockeyed and trivializing. He was talking about stardom. Resurrection has come to many American writers—Melville, the most egregiously belated case, and Faulkner, and Henry James, and Kate Chopin and Willa Cather, and Edith Wharton, and Fitzgerald himself (though he was dead at the time); and it is now happening with Hemingway. It even happened to Faulkner when he was still alive, the problem being that no one knew he was alive, his books all out of print. Then suddenly they were *in* print and still are, along with those of the other writers in this group, who have all been elevated to a cosmic status that will long outlast the stars as Fitzgerald perceived them.

Not all of these writers wrote of their own age, though most did; and most of them were realists; but not Melville, and not always James, who wrote romances and took excursions into the world of ghosts. In the words of Maupassant, they each made themselves "an illusion of a world," each according to his or her sex, knowledge, style, talent, joyful or melancholy disposition, mythic or mordant mind.

So whose realism is this anyway?

And what of dreams? Are they part of realism?

And what of the surrealistic episodes that all of us have gone through but try not to accept as real? Kafka and Borges and García Márquez have made them real, without doubt, just as they were supposed to; because they found it necessary. "The great artists," said Maupassant, "are those who impose their particular illusion on humanity."

I am delighted to report to you that pursuing my own particular illusion I have just finished a section of a new novel in which I use—at long last—that experience I had in Germany so many years ago. I am also pleased to report that I have transformed it to such a degree that it no longer resembles anything I lived through. The character who inhabits this transformed experience is forever doing things that are wild and illegal and outrageous; not at all like me, which may be the reason I could never before write about the place. Yes. Absolutely. That last possibility is so clearly accurate that I hereby aver its truth: that I couldn't write it *because* I had lived it; because I knew it *too well*; because I knew *how it would come out:* boringly, as it always had.

The writer usually feels that any successful transformation of the work is a form of personal growth; but also that he's transformed his chosen art form, the novel, a micromillimeter or two, as well. Mr. Fiedler, and other undertakers who have come after him, tend to think otherwise. As the novel replaced narrative poetry as the reigning form, so the movies and television will replace the novel, is their view. Since the form of the novel no longer progresses, they argue, since it doesn't redefine itself beyond what the modernists—Joyce, Proust, Mann, etc.—were able to do, then it is doomed to repeat itself, grow moldy, and become an esoteric genre only antiquarians will pursue henceforth.

Maybe it is all too true that the attention span of the reading audience is now at the level of a manic Siamese cat, and that the future of the word lies with magazine journalists and screenwriters; but I don't buy it. I've worked in those usurping forms and will work in them again. I love them both. But I live for the novel and will never believe it is less than what Henry James called it—the great form, in which *anything* is possible.

Back in the late 1950s, when I was trying to read the complete shelf of William Faulkner, I kept coming across speeches or interviews in which he talked of uplifting man's heart. In his Nobel speech he said it was the writer's "privilege to help man endure by lifting his heart." In a literature class at the University of Virginia he said: ". . . the artist believes what he's doing is valid in that it may do something to uplift man's heart, not to make man any more successful, but to temporarily make him feel better than he felt before, to uplift his heart for a moment."

This uplift business baffled me. I was reading and rereading *The Sound and the Fury* and *Sanctuary* and *Light in August* and *The Wild Palms* and *Absalom, Absalom!*—tales of incest and whoring and rape and dying love and madness and murder and racial hate and miscegenational tragedy and idiocy—and saying to myself, "This is uplift?"

But I kept reading and found I couldn't get enough; had to reread to satisfy the craving, and came to answer the question in a word: yes. I felt exalted by the man's work, not by reveling in all the disasters, but learning from his language and his insights, and his storytelling genius, how certain other people lived and thought. I was privileged to enter into the most private domains of their lives and they became my friends, or people I'd keep at least at arm's length, or people I pitied, or feared, or loved. This was truly an uplifting experience, something akin to real friendship, and I began to understand the process by which writing reaches into another person's heart.

Now let me mention two letters I received from a man who had read my novel *Ironweed*. About four years ago he wrote the first letter. He was moved by the book and had to write and tell me. Two years later came the second letter, in which he hinted he might have known the street life, the drinking life of a bum, just as *Ironweed*'s hero, Francis Phelan, knew it. The letter writer was now living with his sister, doing handyman's work for her, and staying out of trouble. His sister didn't like drunks, and would even cross the street to get away from a wino. Then her brother pressed *Ironweed* on her, got her to watch a home video of the film of it, and got her to read the book. At the end she found herself crying, and she said to her brother, about Francis, "You know, he wasn't such a bad guy."

That would be quite enough for me, but the story has a coda. The sister no longer fears winos, no longer crosses the street to get away from them. She now gives them her loose change. And at Christmas she passes out to them, one and all, half-pints of muscatel.

This is a true story. It is a realistic story of our age. It has been transformed somewhat by the writer, who is very glad to have written it.

1990

AN INTERVIEW:

Tap Dancing into Reality

*I*t's the writer's dream: the National Book Critics Circle Award for fiction; a MacArthur Foundation "genius" award of a quarter of a million dollars; the Pulitzer Prize for fiction; movie deals, fame, acclaim, wealth, a success story so improbable that even Frank Capra might have turned it down.

But it's true. It's as real as this man sitting on the porch of his house outside Albany, a novelist whose life reads like a novel, who spent years of struggle and anonymity, writing books that, despite praise and plaudits, never seemed to sell.

"I was broke," Kennedy says. "I didn't have any future. I didn't have anything." Nothing, that is, but the writer's craft, nothing but the redemptive satisfaction of his own creativity as he came "to understand that the writing itself was the most important element in my life."

Kennedy's literary odyssey began in good Irish fashion when he turned his back on the parochial world of pols and prelates and left Albany for Puerto Rico. But, also in good Irish fashion, he remained a prisoner to the place, with a knowledge of himself now as "a person whose imagination has become fused with a single place. And in that place finds all that a man needs for the life of the soul . . ."

Bill Kennedy has it all now. But sitting with him on a soft summer afternoon, warmed by the sun and the smooth assurance of a glass of Irish whiskey, you realize that the work goes on, that while the fame and good fortune are welcomed and even relished, they are still beside the point. For Bill Kennedy the point is what it has always been: the sentence: words strung together into complexity, words transubstantiated into life, words that jump off the page.

39

What follows are some of Bill Kennedy's reflections on life, art and the Irish-American experience, a self-portrait of an artist in progress.

—Peter Quinn

QUINN: John Updike in a recent piece in the *New York Review of Books* mentions a story that he wrote called "The Happiest I've Ever Been." He says that "while composing a single paragraph I had the sensation of breaking through a thin sheet of restraining glass to material previously locked up." Did you ever have a similar kind of experience, a moment—an epiphany—when you knew you were going beyond the material?

KENNEDY: Yes, I wrote something once and I showed it to a friend of mine. He asked, "*Who* wrote this?" and I knew I was on to something. But it happened to me seriously when I was in Puerto Rico. I was working on a first novel that has never been published and when I read back the next morning what I'd written the day before I knew I had done *something*, probably just as Updike knew what he had done. It's when you discover that there's something else going on in your head, when you find the right metaphor, or symbol, or whatever it is you're groping for—and suddenly the work begins to blossom in directions that you couldn't possibly conceive of before then. That's precisely the way I felt with *Ironweed* which is the most recent example that comes to mind. You create the structure, you create the character and a number of events, and then you find out that what you've done is beyond what you intended to do. Of course, you understand the new developments as soon as you touch them, and in my reading of that paragraph back in Puerto Rico, I realized I knew more than I had given myself credit for knowing. It comes out of your fingertips as you write, the unconscious becoming conscious at the instant that you need it. It first seems a very happy, wonderful accident, but it's not so accidental—it's really everything that you always were and hoped to do that is emerging.

QUINN: What about the "muse," the sense of something speaking through you? Some writers seem to experience its presence. Have you?

KENNEDY: Never had that. I never understood the muse. I used to wait for it when I was a kid. I'd stay home on Thursday afternoons and expect it to arrive. That was my day off, and also the muse's day off. It never did show up, but I'd like the stuff anyway. Nobody ever bought any of it, so I felt there was some other element in writing that I didn't understand. That was a question I asked in *The Ink Truck*. "What is it that I don't understand? What is it that I can't figure out?"

With *Legs*, I began to understand writing a little more clearly. I would work for hours sometimes and nothing would happen, but then after ten or maybe eleven hours, suddenly, something *would* happen. I used to go to a friend's lake house and put in time. I knew I wanted to say something, thought I knew what I wanted to say—I had all the material, but nothing would come together. I couldn't figure out what to do or how to do it. But after those long hours, I would begin to write, and feel very good about what I'd achieved by the end of the day. I came to understand in those days that writing itself was what was important. It was enough. I mean I was broke, didn't have any future, didn't have even a prospect. But I would come away from those sessions at the lake house feeling quite happy. It was amazing. I went over to Cape Cod. I went up to the Adirondacks, all by myself, and just hung out and wrote. At the end of the day, I would be ecstatic about the fact that I had produced whatever number of pages it was. I was somehow making something worthwhile out of nothing at all.

QUINN: There's a scene in *Legs* that strikes me as being one of those moments when you felt both a sense of "breaking through" and a sense of achievement. It's the scene where Legs's girlfriend, Kiki, is hiding in a closet. It's a tautly woven, exciting example of what—for lack of a better phrase—is called "stream of consciousness."

KENNEDY: That's a true fact of her life. Kiki was actually arrested in a closet in her friend's house. She was hiding when the police came and got her. I guess I got to know Kiki. I felt it one afternoon when I was writing about her. That piece didn't get into the book, but it was a most ecstatic afternoon, another one of those moments when I felt I had done something that I hadn't expected to do. It was a leap beyond the surface of Kiki. I had gotten beyond the journalistic sense of who she was and into what she truly was, the kind of kookiness of her life, the voluptuousness of her life, and it was all in this page and a half that never got into the book. It was giving definition to something that had not been very clear before, and that is what I really loved. It was a new sense of writing, a breakthrough in saying things obliquely.

QUINN: John Gardner has described the writing process as getting to the point where you just look at your characters and let them act, let them live their lives. They're so real that you're writing down what people are doing, rather than attempting to invent. Have you ever had that experience?

KENNEDY: That's the idea of the characters running away with the writer. I've never really felt it. I must say that's probably true for some people. Maybe it was true for Gardner, but it's not been entirely true for me. My way is to impose myself, my new information, my new interest, my new attitudes on anything in the book. Whatever I read tends to turn up in the next chapter. You may not know that I read it yesterday afternoon, it may be something that happened back in 1846, but quite possibly it can turn up in the writing as a brand-new perception.

QUINN: You spent several years writing *Legs*. How well did you get to know him? Was he a real person for you?

KENNEDY: I believed I knew Jack Diamond, but it took me a long time. I started to write him in the first person, and I couldn't, because I didn't know him. I started to write his life as a movie script which would become a novel, a form that now is a cliché, and I could see it was a cliché even then. I only got about two chapters done, and then I was asking myself, "Where am I going to put the camera now? Where is the cameraman going to stand?" All those artificial aspects of the constructed world, the stylistic world, were intrusive and ridiculous, so what I did was spend about two and a half years trying to figure out how to tell that story. I wrote it eight different times. I finally arrived at a narrator who could see Diamond in the round, and when I did that, I began to see Diamond myself. And then I began to wait for him on the road. I figured he'd be a nervous hitchhiker and I'd pick him up. Dana, my wife, had a dream about him being on the front lawn after the book was finished. She went out on the porch and there was Diamond. He rolled around in the grass and kicked his legs up in the air, and Dana asked, "What's going on?" Legs said to her, "Bill got it just right." That's Dana's dream, not mine.

QUINN: *The Ink Truck* was your first novel. It's said that there's a special relationship between authors and their first novels, a parent's pride in their firstborn. Do you feel that way about *The Ink Truck*?

KENNEDY: Yes. I love it. Some people badmouthed it after the fact, and before the fact for that matter. Actually, it sold as soon as I had finished it. It sold the first time out. I had a little problem trying to sell it before it was finished, but when it was done, my agent sent it over to Dial Press, where Ed Doctorow was the managing editor, and he bought it. Thereafter, it went out of print fairly quickly, but that's the nature of first novels. Writers who are serious about themselves don't worry about that. If you're going to cut your wrists after your first novel, you're not a writer. After the twenty-eighth novel, and nobody will buy it, well . . . But you think of Farrell. He never quit. It's an admirable thing, because he was getting pleasure out of what he was doing. If there are enough people who understand that, if there are other writers getting some pleasure out of reading your twenty-eighth novel, then maybe that's enough.

QUINN: What about the influence of other writers on you? James Joyce must certainly be one of them?

KENNEDY: Yes, absolutely. I've been reading him just lately. I've read books about him, by him. There's no end to that man. He's the greatest man of letters in the twentieth century. I don't think there's a close second. If there is, it's Faulkner.

But Joyce has transcendence. Leopold Bloom is someone who is never going to die in the history of literature. Faulkner did great things. He did wonderful, wonderful things. But there's nothing like Leopold and Molly, the Blooms, in all of twentieth-century literature. I don't know where the hell you go to find their equal.

QUINN: What about the similarities between you and Joyce?

KENNEDY: Similarities? I don't aspire to similarities.

QUINN: People have compared the opening of *Ironweed* to "The Dead" and to the "Circe" chapter in *Ulysses*. Is there any validity to that?

KENNEDY: I wish I had heard somebody say that, but I never heard that before. Joyce is Joyce. He's by himself, and I wouldn't make any comparisons. No, it's not an attempt at conscious imitation, if that's the question.

QUINN: Your careful reconstruction of Albany, your fascination with place, certainly evokes Joyce's obsession with Dublin.

KENNEDY: That's true enough. Joyce made things easier for all of us. He prompted us to become aware of our entire heritage, including dish-pans and the jakes in the back yard.

QUINN: You both are absorbed with the place where you grew up.

And you both left it. Did you choose, as Joyce did, "silence, exile and cunning," and set out to chronicle Albany at a distance? Or did you pack up all your cares and woes and only gradually come to understand your relationship to Albany?

KENNEDY: Silence was imposed on me by all my editors. My might-have-been editors. Exile came because I couldn't stay in Albany any longer and still function effectively. I had to go elsewhere. I went to Puerto Rico, which is exile under the American flag. It's as far away as you could get, and still be in the U.S.A. But cunning was not in my kit bag. I never felt that that was necessary. I was always aboveboard. I always put out my work for stomping, whatever I did. And I usually got stomped. But I never felt that it was necessary to retreat and stay home and nurse my wounds and never try again until I had a masterpiece. That was never my understanding of how to write, or how to live as a writer. Somewhere along the line I came across a phrase about "renewing your vulnerability." And that seemed to me a most important thing for a writer. You renew your vulnerability. Constantly. You start out feeling so vulnerable that you're afraid the criticism will kill you. But if you're not afraid of being vulnerable, if you say, "Go ahead, hit me again, I can take it," you get a thick skin.

You get that as a journalist. Letters to the editor demanding "Throw this guy in the river." Or "Why did you hire him to begin with? This man should be destroyed." Or "This is a radical," or "This is a liberal"—or some other dirty word. You get to live with that. I remember I wrote a series of articles on the slums of Albany back in the sixties. The mail attacking me came in like you couldn't believe. I got hate calls and hate mail from grand bigots, wonderful bigots, really *creative* bigots. It didn't faze me, because I realized early on that when you get into the business of putting yourself out on the public chopping block, you have to figure you're going to get chopped at.

QUINN: With *Legs* did you set out to write an Albany cycle?

KENNEDY: No, I chose the word "cycle" because it connotes an open-ended and related series of novels.

QUINN: Your first three novels are set in Albany in the Depression, which really seems to have captured your imagination. Why?

KENNEDY: *Legs* was 1931, and that was researched to discover that era. And once I discovered the twenties and Prohibition and the gangland world, I began to see that it had tentacles that went forward, that people I was writing about in *Legs* were going to be significant in future books I wanted to write. When I got around to writing *Billy Phelan*, which was the next one, it should have taken place in 1933, which was only two years after Diamond died, but I felt what I needed to do then was to move deeper into the Depression, into the grit of it, into the end of it, the feeling of coming out of it. I set *Billy Phelan* in 1938, which was just before the war begins and was also a political year. I manipulated history to suit myself. I made the real-life kidnapping of Dan O'Connell's nephew take place five years later than it actually had, and I used the "blackout," for instance, in *Billy Phelan*, but placed it in 1938. Dan O'Connell [Albany's political boss] "blacked out" Governor Dewey in '42 or '43. He had the civil defense behind him when he turned off the electricity so nobody in Albany could hear Dewey's radio speech attacking the Albany politicians.

QUINN: *Ironweed* is the latest completed part of the cycle. You said in a recent interview that it came "like a bullet." Is that because you had lived in that world for so long, were so familiar with it from all the research you'd done, that you already knew the characters?

KENNEDY: No. *Ironweed* was something else, and had a preexistence in both journalism and early fiction. In that unpublished novel I wrote in Puerto Rico I created Francis Phelan, just one of several characters in a family chronicle. Then, in 1963, I wrote a series of articles on a wino couple for the *Albany Times-Union*, and I fused the fiction and nonfiction when I started to create Francis Phelan again for *Billy Phelan*. The early work was all dead at this point, which is what usually happens when you leave it in the drawer, so I began from scratch, and Francis emerged as a new and more complex character in *Billy*, so much so that I knew he should have his own book. So by the time I got to him in *Ironweed* I knew far more about the history of the city, and I was reflecting a complexity of life that I had not been able to get to in the first novels. I felt I was into higher mathematics, and that I really knew this man. And the book was written in just about seven months.

QUINN: You mentioned Farrell before. Are there any other Irish-American writers who've had an impact on your writing?

KENNEDY: Fitzgerald, if you call him an Irish-American. Actually, he was the original Yuppie. The Yuppie Irishman.

QUINN: There are similarities between *Legs* and *Gatsby*. Several critics
have mentioned them.

KENNEDY: Deliberately so. *Gatsby*'s a great book, I think. And I
make that comparison in homage as much as anything else. I wouldn't
want anybody to think I was cavalierly using the narration of Marcus
Gorman about a gangster without understanding the precedent. But I
also feel that the narrator in *Gatsby* was boring as a character, and I
don't think Marcus is. Fitzgerald's narrator came to life only when Fitzgerald let him stop talking about himself and allowed us to see him in
action. That, very clearly, was when he leaped off the page for me.

QUINN: *Legs* and *The Great Gatsby* are both about outsiders trying to
force their way into America. Is that right?

KENNEDY: Right. But you never see Gatsby doing it seriously. There
are some people who have made the analogy that Diamond *is* Gatsby,
but I don't think Gatsby was like Diamond. I don't think Gatsby was a
gangster. I think he was just a thief. I don't think he was a killer. People
said he killed a man *once*, but they said that about everybody in the
twenties.

QUINN: That's the American story. The immigrant or the immigrant's
son forcing his way in.

KENNEDY: The ambition was always to reach fame and fortune. Some
people tried to shoot their way into it. Some survived, were acquitted,
or just got rich and went straight. Big Bill Dwyer did that. He was one
of the great rumrunners, and he wound up in Café Society, Palm Beach,
racetracks, hobnobbing with the rich, hanging out in tuxedos. A number
of Irish-Americans chose that route.

QUINN: Any other Irish-American writers besides Fitzgerald whom
you value?

KENNEDY: O'Hara, even though he tried to bury his Irishness and
come on as a WASP clubman. But his stories still have great vigor and
wit. I got lost in his novels, that deluge of information that now seems
the trademark of the pulp writers. Eugene O'Neill was a great favorite
of mine, especially his *Iceman* and *Long Day's Journey*. Wonderful Celtic
gloom and irony in those works. I liked Farrell's *Studs Lonigan* but I
never wanted to write like that—the naturalism of the city. I was too
interested in the dream element in life, the surreal. Flannery O'Connor
is terrific, now and always. I always thought Edwin O'Connor's *The Last*

Hurrah was a marvelous book. I fell off the chair reading those great lines about the Curley days and I could see he understood the tension between the church and politics extremely well. But I also felt he was leaving out things either to be polite to the church or to Irish society, or perhaps out of squeamishness. I felt at times that he didn't reflect Irish-American life as I knew it. I felt I had to bring in the cathouses and the gambling and the violence, for if you left those out you had only a part of Albany. The idealized Irish life of the country club and the Catholic colleges was true enough, but that didn't have anything to do with what was going on down on Broadway among all those raffish Irishmen. They were tough sons-of-bitches, dirty-minded and foul-mouthed gamblers and bigots, and also wonderful, generous, funny, curiously honest and very complex people. I felt that way of life had to be penetrated at the level of harsh reality—its wit, anger, sexuality, deviousness. It also needed to have the surreal dimension that goes with any society in which religion plays such a dominant role. Those lives are worth recording, and I'm not done with them by any means.

QUINN: Do you think, in fact, there is such a thing as an "Irish-American literary tradition"?

KENNEDY: When we talk about Irish-American writers—or Irish-American anything—we're talking about an evolution. You can't really be negative about Finley Peter Dunne, or Farrell, or Fitzgerald, or O'Hara, or O'Connor. They all lived in a certain time and reflected that time. And for some of them, maybe, there was a sense of marginality about their background. There was an uncertainty. Certainly, in the days of Fitzgerald and O'Hara there was. The Irish were aspiring to rise in the world. You had Finley Peter Dunne satirizing those "donkey" Irishmen in order to make them become something beyond what they could become. Everybody is a climber. Everybody is trying to come up from below. That's the first law of motion in America. Nobody wants to live in the Five Points in New York City forever. Nobody wants to live with the stereotypes that were associated with Irish thugs—the derbys and the cockeyed look, the readiness to break your ankle for a nickel or your wrist for a dime.

God knows where I am in all of this, in this evolution, but I *know* all that has come before. I know that those who came before helped to show me how to try to turn experience into literature. I know all that came before in the same way I know that the Irish ascended politically to become Jack Kennedy. After Jack Kennedy, anything was possible. Goddammit, *we've* been President, and you can't hold us back anymore.

QUINN: Is there a certain defensiveness about the Irish? We know all about the lecherousness and the sinfulness but we prefer to present outsiders with the other face, the saintly side.

KENNEDY: I just got a letter from the son of the owner of a bar in Albany. You know what he told me? He said, "Dan O'Connell told my father that he closed all the poolrooms in Albany, so how come you've got a poolroom in *Billy Phelan*?" O'Connell didn't want any poolrooms in Albany, he said, because they were corrupting influences on kids.

QUINN: As opposed to cockfights?

KENNEDY: Or as opposed to saloons? And whorehouses? Dan took tribute from them all. I don't see how you can leave all that out if you're going to talk about life in the twentieth century. Irish-American life or any kind of life.

QUINN: But haven't the Irish been blessed by a wonderful sense of guilt? Isn't that part of their Catholicism?

KENNEDY: I don't think Catholics feel that much guilt anymore. They're more and more like other Americans.

QUINN: Isn't the loss of guilt the loss of a wonderful strength? Isn't it one of the essential ingredients in the Irish-American mind, as it is in the Jewish-American mind? It's the one thing you can be sure of never losing.

KENNEDY: Well, there's always a sense of sin. I don't think we're ever going to lose that. Norman Mailer was unnecessarily worried about the loss of sin, in terms of sex, back in the sixties. He was suggesting that the only thing that makes sense is to have sex when you're sinning. Otherwise, it's no fun.

QUINN: But isn't Catholicism one of the things that makes those earthy Irishmen you write about unique? The tension created in their lives by the church?

KENNEDY: That's only part of it. You only go to church on Sundays, and maybe you talk about it the rest of the week. But politics is far more important than church, because politics is survival. You could postpone your concern about the salvation of your soul. You could always say, "I'll get to that when I get old," and if you got a heart attack, God forbid, and died in the blossom of your youth, the chances are you would go to Purgatory.

QUINN: What about the Catholic element in your novels? One reviewer has seen in *Ironweed* a parallel between the liturgy of the Catholic church and the events of the three days the book encompasses. Is he right?

KENNEDY: Absolutely, but not for reasons of celebration and liturgy. In *Ironweed*, it was all accidental because I had already created the time frame in *Billy Phelan*.

I created it because I had to have it all happen during the pre-election period. That was the whole purpose in *Billy Phelan*. So I made the kidnapping take place in an election year. Then it moves forward into the campaign. Once I had that, I went back, and if you notice, *Billy Phelan* and *Ironweed* end on the same day. And they do that only because having created the dynamics of Billy meeting his father, the logical thing when I dealt with Francis was to see him in those postconfrontational days with Billy—to discover what it was that made him go home.

Francis Phelan wouldn't go home until he knew that Annie had never condemned or blamed him. So first come these two things: the invitation from Billy and the knowledge about Annie. They stay in his mind. He dries up. And he wants to go home. All of *Ironweed* is this tap dancing into reality, trying to figure out, "How am I going to do it?" Talking to Helen, getting rid of Helen, walking back, putting her in the car with Finny, walking up to where he used to live, confronting that reality, going back and making some money so he could buy a turkey, and so on.

QUINN: Editors kept turning down *Ironweed* because they said it was too depressing. Nobody would want to read a novel about bums. But it's actually a very hopeful novel, isn't it? A novel about redemption? And forgiveness?

KENNEDY: "Redemption" is the key word. That's what it's all about. It parallels the *Purgatorio*. When you talk about the liturgy or Catholic thought, you think of Dante, and eventually you think of the *Inferno*, and the *Purgatorio*, and the *Paradiso*. From the epigraph, you enter my book with Dante, and it's a journey through planes of escalation into a moment of redemption out of sin. Francis cleanses himself. It reflects something I think is profound about human behavior. I don't look at it in the way that I used to when I was a kid, when I believed in everything, believed it was the only way to look at the world. Today I believe Catholic theology has great humanistic dimensions, great wisdom about how to achieve peace of mind in relationship to the unknown, the infinite. Maybe it's a palliative. Maybe it's one of the great lollipops of history. At the same time, it's beautiful. It's as good as I could see on the horizon. I don't need Buddhism, or Zoroastrianism—I've got Sacred Heart Church in North Albany.

QUINN: All Saints Day is taken from Irish mythology. It's based on the Celtic feast of Samhain, when the barriers between the living and the dead disappeared. Was Irish mythology a conscious part of *Ironweed*?

KENNEDY: No, it was not. I didn't know that about All Saints Day. I just grew up with it as a holy day. But I'm finding out all kinds of things about myself, things that are pushing me, nudging me into places I'm not yet fully aware of.

Much of it seems parallel to what I know about contemporary Irish life. Maybe, if there's such a thing as collective unconsciousness, then this was part of it: a kind of grip that still holds. It's really remarkable that the Irish, like the Jews, have held on so to their identity, that there was this triumphant resistance to death and genocide and their obliteration as a people. But in this case, the Irish link wasn't conscious. My consciousness as a Catholic was sufficient.

QUINN: The Irish poet Patrick Kavanagh has written that he lived in a place where literature wasn't supposed to happen. It was too conventional, supposedly. Did you ever face that stumbling block? The thought that literature happened in places grander or more exotic than Albany?

KENNEDY: Oh yes, from the very outset. I understood that Melville went to school here. I understood that Henry James touched down here, in one of his less cosmic moments. Bret Harte was born here, and left immediately. Those kind of moments, that's about as much as you used to expect out of Albany. But then I began to figure that it couldn't be all that bad, I found out that Albany was, and is, a great place. There are not all that many people who lived and died in Albany creating literature that would endure through the ages. But there was a sense of the place being valuable, and this was *tremendously* important. As soon as I began to understand this, I realized that the town was unexplored.

QUINN: Was it out of the newspaper articles you wrote about Albany that you began to sink yourself into its history? To sense its depths?

KENNEDY: No, I was writing in Puerto Rico about myself and my wife and my ancestors trying to understand it all, and then I realized I didn't understand, and that was it. That ignorance was the main drive: to come back at some point in my life, settle in and do some research in the library, and try to understand. I never expected that I would stay forever.

How can you write about a place if you don't understand what the street names mean, or who the mayor is, or what the machine was all about? I was writing from Puerto Rico at a point when I didn't really understand the political bossism in Albany. I hadn't paid sufficient attention when I was working at an Albany newspaper. I just said, "I'm *mildly* opposed to it." I was very self-righteous.

QUINN: One of the main components of Albany is its powerful, Democratic machine, an Irish-American machine. For the Albany Irish, you've written, "politics was justice itself; politics was sufficient unto itself." What did you mean by that?

KENNEDY: When I grew up, there was no sense of morality in regard to politics. If you were Irish, you were obviously a Democrat. If you were a Democrat, you were probably a Catholic. If you were a Catholic, you obviously gave allegiance to the church on the corner, and to Dan O'Connell who was a pillar of the church, inseparable from the bishop and the priests, and who was revered and prayed for. But Dan was also profiting from the whorehouses, the gambling joints, the all-night saloons and the blackout card games. He was in collusion with the grafters and the bankers, getting rich with the paving contractors.

No matter what it was in town, wherever you could make an illegal dollar, that's where the Irish were, that's where the politics were, that's where the church was, that's where the morality was. And it was all fused. You couldn't separate it because the families were so interlocked, and the goodness walked hand-in-hand with the evil. But it wasn't *viewed* as evil. It was viewed as a way to get on in the world. Objective morality didn't interest Albany. The Irish didn't care about it. They understood that *they* had been deprived and now they were not. Now they were able to get jobs. In the previous era, when the Irish were not in power, they had *not* been able to get jobs. Their families were starving, and starvation for them was immorality. So once they took power, O'Connell became kind of a saint. He became the man who would save your soul by putting you to work.

QUINN: Was he a Robin Hood?

KENNEDY: Of course he was a Robin Hood. Of course he was also a rascal. I don't know what the original Robin Hood was like. Maybe he has been romanticized out of existence, but there's no question that Dan O'Connell as we knew him was a Robin Hood. He certainly gave away a lot of money.

Nobody really knows how much he died with. What came out in the papers was ridiculous. A quarter of a million or so. But they would spend $200,000 in five-dollar bills every election day. He was raking it in from all quarters. All the beer drinkers in the county were adding to the party's profits, and Dan O'Connell controlled the beer. Thousands and thousands of fortunes were made in this town through politics.

QUINN: Politics was the Irish stock market?

KENNEDY: Yes, the Irish stock market. I never thought of that. That's a great phrase. You've invented something.

QUINN: Politics, then, is one of the common threads among the American-Irish? If anything united them, it was that. In Kansas City, Boston, Albany, New York, always the same story.

KENNEDY: What else could they do? They could have done other things if they had the education, but they didn't. They were the people of numbers. That was the important thing about them. They were not the people of knowledge, the people with connections to power, the people of Harvard and Wall Street. What they knew was politics. What they knew was the church. What they knew was their Irishness. What they knew was clannishness. The network was a great strength. It let Dan O'Connell hold on to the allegiance of the masses. In the face of the most vile declarations by enemies, in the face of the obvious stealing that was going on, and despite the slimy meat and the whorehouses, Dan went on and on and on.

QUINN: Albany is more than a setting for your novels. It becomes kind of a character. But do you think of yourself as a *regional* writer in the way that Flannery O'Connor thought of herself as a Southern writer?

KENNEDY: Yes and no. All regional writers are trying to capture the uniqueness of their region, obviously. And most writers who use regions are trying for universality, to speak to life outside the region. It depends, I suspect, on how well you are able to make your cosmos, however small—Milledgeville, Georgia, or Albany, New York, or Dublin, or the *Pequod*—become a center of vitality, a center of ubiquity, a center of spiritual life that will transcend any kind of limitation that geography imposes. If you never find that center, all you're doing is floating free. Until you have a Milledgeville, or unless you're a genius like Beckett, you can't coalesce your meaning. Creating life in an abstract place— that's very hard to do, you have to really have genius.

QUINN: Do you think you could move to a place, let's say to Scarsdale, stay there for two years, study the place, become familiar with its characters, and then create the same sort of magic that you've done with Albany?

KENNEDY: I don't think so. I would probably begin to impose my knowledge of Albany on Scarsdale. I tried to do that in Puerto Rico, and I couldn't do it. I didn't understand Puerto Rico that well. In those days, I could write about Puerto Rico as a reporter, but I didn't really understand the dynamics of the place, what was going on in the *soul* of Puerto Rico, in the *soul* of San Juan. When you don't have that, you don't have anything, as far as I'm concerned. You can do all the navel-gazing you want and until it's centered on a place, it seems to me that it's a vagrant pursuit, a Sunday afternoon in the park, or with the soap operas. It's an absence of significance. If you don't have the place, you don't have the dynamics of the society that exists in that place, and they're very different in Scarsdale from Albany, or San Juan, or Dublin. Georgia is not in any way equivalent to North Albany, where I grew up. No matter how Catholic Flannery O'Connor was, she's writing about a society where you have peacocks on the front porch, you have blacks and whites with active hostility toward one another, and that's not where I grew up.

QUINN: What about Ireland? Does it ever tug on your imagination? Any of the Albany cycle spinning its way back there?

KENNEDY: I've been to Ireland several times. I'll go again in quest of my ancestors, like so many other Irishmen in this country, to comprehend origin and consequences. But it's very unlikely that I will ever set a novel in Ireland because I don't know enough about the places. It's a foreign country to me. I've thought about writing about Ireland,

I've been to the North, I've lived in Dublin, but I feel I don't know enough about any particular place to give me what I'd need for a novel. I'm thinking seriously about the Irish-American experience, which is not the *Irish* experience. I feel that I'd be a fraud if I went to Ireland and tried to write significantly about somebody there, when I'm not from there. I'm from Albany.

I believe that I can't be anything other than Irish-American. I know there's a division here, and a good many Irish-Americans believe they are merely American. They've lost touch with anything that smacks of Irishness as we used to know it. That's all right.

But I think if they set out to discover themselves, to wonder about why they are what they are, then they'll run into a psychological inheritance that's even more than psychological, that may also be genetic, or biopsychogenetic, who the hell knows what you call it? But there's something in us that survives and that's the result of being Irish, whether from North or South, whether Catholic or Protestant, some element of life, of consciousness, that is different from being Hispanic, or Oriental, or WASP. These traits endure. I'm just exploring what's survived in my time and place.

I don't presume that I could go back in time and find out what was going on in Belfast or Dublin before my own day, to go back as a fiction writer and reconstitute it. For me, it's a question of imagination. I don't feel I own those Irish places, but I do own Albany. It's mine. Nineteenth-century Albany is mine as well. It's a different time and in many ways a different place from what it is now, but I feel confident I can reach it.

QUINN: Do you think your fascination with place is particularly Irish?

KENNEDY: The natural world is always very important to writers. You use it wherever necessary. But it's not peculiarly Irish to have a sense of a place. For me, fiction exists, finally, in order to describe neither social conditions nor landscapes but human consciousness. Essays, documentary films, editorials in newspapers can persuade you to a political position. But nothing except great fiction can tell you what it means to be alive. Great fiction, great films, great plays, they all center in on consciousness, which always has a uniqueness about it, and that uniqueness is what a writer can give you that nobody else in the world can give you: a sense of having lived in a certain world and understood a

certain place, a certain consciousness, a certain destiny, a grand unknown, all the squalor and all the glory of being alive.

And if you reduce fiction to political or social argument, or to a kind
of sociological construct, you lose its real strength. When you think of
Chaucer or Boccaccio, you remember the individualistic elements of
their characters in the same way you remember the people in, for example, Sherwood Anderson's *Winesburg, Ohio*. They don't go bad. Great
fiction doesn't go bad.

QUINN: Do you write with a certain audience in mind? Do you have
an ideal reader?

KENNEDY: You know who I write for? I write for people like me who
used to appreciate Damon Runyon sentences. I write for people who
appreciate writing first, who understand the difference between an ordinary sentence and a real sentence that jumps off the page at you when
you read it.

I'm working on a preface for a new book about the state capitol. As
always when I do research, I read an incredible amount of horseshit
that's been published on the subject. Tons of it. The same old stuff
rewritten and rehashed every which way. But every once in a while a
historian gets hold of something and creates a real sentence, maybe one
in a whole book of essays, but it stops you. You look at it and say,
"Terrific sentence." That's the reaction I'm looking for.

QUINN: Does writing—the creation of a "terrific sentence"—ever get
easier?

KENNEDY: Some things get easier. Journalism gets easier. I'm not
sure it gets better. Fiction, at least for me, seems to get more complicated.
Not that it's hard to write a sentence or a paragraph, but it's hard to
believe that the current sentence or paragraph is new and that I'm not
just saying something that's been said a hundred times before. Making
it new, that's what's hard. I don't expect it will ever get any easier. I'm
not counting on it.

QUINN: Do you ever look back at what you've written, and say, "I've
learned so much since then. I know so much more now"?

KENNEDY: Yes, absolutely. But it doesn't mean the writing gets easier
just because you know more now. . . . Because what you have to do
now is not repeat yourself, at least try not to repeat yourself. You feel
that maybe you're in better command of the language, of your ability to

write a sentence, of your ability to conceptualize, of your ability to create a new character. But the process is problematical. It's still a great game. That's what the whole thing is still all about, as far as I'm concerned, what it's always about: the invention of something out of nothing. That's the classic definition of what writing is. And I believe this is the whole satisfaction that comes from writing: That you're able to create something, out of nothing, that seems new to you.

Maybe you don't have the same response to it that you had as a kid, when you were discovering these wondrous elements of your unconscious, or your talent, or even the nature of your existence. But at the same time, what I feel about my life is that there are still so many unknowns. When I begin to write, I begin to confront things that I never confronted before. I begin to invent things, willfully going into the unknown. As I face the challenge of an empty page tomorrow morning—and that's what I live for—what I need to do is discover something that will surprise me, something that I've never done before, written before, seen before, heard before.

It's not as if you want to write science fiction, or go to another genre or invent another bizarre character. But you must penetrate into something beyond an ordinary story. You start with an ordinary story. You have a man or a woman moving quietly through life. A man and woman in trouble, both of them. And there's a classical way to create the clichéd situations about how they meet and get back together, or how they stay together for forty years. But you can't do any of those things. You must do something that *you* have never done before. And how do we do that? Mostly, it seems to me, through language. It can happen through dialogue—sometimes through language alone. When your language is leading you in, it's like watching the sea, and the sea is never the same. And it's never the same sentence. And as long as it isn't, you're in good shape. As soon as it becomes the same sentence again, you're all washed up.

QUINN: Your next project, besides the new novel, is to write screenplays for *Legs*, *Billy Phelan* and *Ironweed*. Any trepidations? Any fear that Hollywood might hurt your writing?

KENNEDY: No, I don't have that kind of conflict. I believe it's a very rare writer in the twentieth century who can separate himself from films. They're such an enormous and important part of our imaginative lives.

Only hermits haven't been influenced by them. And I love the movies. I'm glad to be a part of the movies. I don't confuse them with novels. I don't see them as competition. I think the novel is far superior to the film because of its complexity. But I think the film can also do many things that engage you in ways that no novel can. You can't get quite such an exciting vision of womanhood from a book as you can with Garbo or Monroe or Ava Gardner on the screen. When you see these people idealized up there, there's nothing quite equivalent to it in literature. Literature is an extension of your imagination, but here's an incomparable illusion of visual reality.

QUINN: How different is screenwriting from writing a novel?

KENNEDY: Very different. I'm glad to write the screenplays for the films that are going to be made out of my books since I've got *some* control on each of them. I respect films very much. I think film can be a tremendously exciting medium. It's been that for me all my life, from the time I was a kid on up to the time I began discovering Ingmar Bergman. The whole idea of the translation of any kind of life into cinema is important, because it's a medium that reaches so many people. And if you can reach those people with something that's valuable to you, it's the same as reaching them with your novel in a certain way.

QUINN: What do you most want to preserve from your novels when they're made into films?

KENNEDY: I'd like to preserve the whole novel, but you can't. You can't preserve the language. You can't preserve the unconscious center of Francis Phelan's soul as it's articulated in *Ironweed*. You're not going to be able to depict it, except maybe in a fleeting scene or phrase. You're not going to be able to put that into the movie. One medium is language, the other is the visual. Movies can only do so much. The novel is the supreme form of explaining how it is that any human being exists on this planet, complexly, with a history, with a soul, with a future, with a present, in an environment. You can get some of the environment, you can get a bit of the language, you can get the look of things in the movies. But you only get a small bit of the soul. You can't get the density of the unconscious, you can't get the ineffably complex element of what it means to be alive. It's all but *impossible* in the movies.

At their best, movies can only suggest great complexity. John Huston, Orson Welles, Bergman, they've done it. They've required us to be alert to complexity. But maybe only two percent of the movies ever made have required this of the audience.

QUINN: A final question. We've talked about the "Irish-American experience," literary and otherwise. I don't know if we've come to any conclusions but, in your opinion, what is it that unites us?

KENNEDY: What unites us? It's song, drink, wit, and guilt.

QUINN: No politics?

KENNEDY: That's included in all four.

1985

FRAGMENTS OF A TALK
WITH THE PARIS REVIEW:

Ironweed and Style

INTERVIEWER: Success came to you very late. *Ironweed* was turned down by thirteen publishing houses. How could a book which won the Pulitzer Prize be turned down by so many publishers?

KENNEDY: Yes. Thirteen rejections. Remember that character in "Li'l Abner," Joe Btfsplk, who went around with a cloud over his head? Well, I was the Joe Btfsplk of modern literature for about two years. What happened was that I sold this book, then my editor left publishing; so that threw the ball game into extra innings. They gave me an editor in Georgia and I said, "I don't want an editor in Georgia; I want an editor in New York." They didn't like that. She was a very good editor, but she only came to New York every two months. Georgia is even more remote from the center of literary activity than Albany. She was living on a pecan farm, as I recall. So that got the publisher's nose out of joint. My agent was not very polite with them and finally we separated. In the meantime, my first editor came back to publishing and, finding that Joe Btfsplk cloud hanging over my head, was not terribly enthusiastic about taking me back. So I went over to Henry Robbins whom I had met at a cocktail party. Henry at that point was a very hot New York editor. He had just gone over to Dutton. Everybody was flocking to him. He was John Irving's editor. Joyce Carol Oates moved over there. Doris Grumbach moved in; so did John Gregory Dunne. It looked like Dutton was about to become the Scribners of the new age. So anyway, at the cocktail party he said, "Can I see your book?" And I said, "Of course." I sent it to him and he wrote me back this wonderful letter saying that he loved the idea of adding me to their list. I picked up the paper a week later and he had just dropped dead in the subway on his way to work. So I then went over to another publisher where a former editor of mine had been; she was somewhat enthusiastic, thought we might be able to make it if there were some changes in the book. And then she was let go. I bounced about nine more times. Then fate intervened in the form of an assignment from *Esquire* to do an interview with Saul Bellow, who had been a teacher of mine for a semester, in San Juan. He had really encouraged me at a very early age to become a writer. So he took it upon himself—I didn't urge him, and I was very grateful to him for doing it—to write my former editor at Viking, saying that he didn't think it was proper for his former publisher to let a writer like Kennedy go begging. Two days later I got a call from Viking saying that they wanted to publish *Ironweed* and what did I think of the possibility of publishing *Legs* and *Billy Phelan* again at the same time.

INTERVIEWER: How would you assess your development as a stylist?

KENNEDY: Somewhere back in the late sixties a friend of mine named Gene McGarr—we were sitting in the Lion's Head in Greenwich Village one afternoon—said to me, "You know, Irishmen are people who sit around trying to say things good." That is the purest expression of style I've ever come across. I remember being enormously impressed by Damon Runyon's style when I was a kid because it was so unique. It just leaped out at you and said, "Look at me! I'm a style!" And Hemingway had a style. These people were egregiously stylish. Then I read Graham Greene and I couldn't find a style. I thought, why doesn't this man have a style? I liked his stories enormously, and his novels, but what was his style? Of course he has an extraordinary style in telling a story, great economy and intelligence. Obviously these were adolescent attitudes toward style, valuing ways of being singular. I admired journalists who had style, Red Smith and Mencken. You wouldn't mistake their writing, you'd know it right away. What I set out to do very early on, in college, was to mold a style; and then I realized it was an artificial effort. I was either imitating Red Smith or Hemingway, or Runyon, or whomever, and I gave up on it. I realized that was death. Every time I'd reread it, I'd say that's not you, that's somebody else. As I went on in journalism I was always trying to say something in a way that was neither clichéd nor banal, that was funny if possible, or dramatic if possible. I began to expand my language: sentences grew more complicated, the words became more arcane. I used the word "eclectic" once in a news story and it came out "electric." It was a willful strain at being artsy, so I gave that up too. And as soon as I gave up, I wrote the only thing that I could write, which was whatever came to my head in the most natural possible way. And I evolved into whatever it is I've become. If I have a style, I don't know how to evaluate it. I wouldn't know what to say about my style. I think *The Ink Truck* is an ambitious book in language. I think certain parts of *Legs* are also; but Marcus is still telling that story in a fairly offhanded way, using the vernacular in large measure. *Billy Phelan* goes from being inside Martin Daugherty's mind, which is an educated mind, to Billy Phelan's, which is only street smart, and the narration is really only in service of representing those two minds. This was very different from what I came to in *Ironweed*, where I set out at the beginning to use the best language at my disposal. I thought my third-person voice was me at first, but the more I wrote, the more I realized that the third-person voice was this ineffable level of Francis Phelan's life, a level he would never get to consciously, but which was there somehow. And that became the style of the telling of the story; and the language became as good as I could make it whenever I felt it was time for those flights of rhetoric up from the sidewalk, out of the gutter. Francis moves in and out of those flights sometimes in the same sentence. A word will change the whole attitude toward what he's thinking, or talking about, or just intuiting silently. I think that as soon as you abandon your overt efforts at style, that's where you begin to find your own voice. Then it becomes a matter of editing out what doesn't belong—a subordinate clause that says, "That's Kafka," or "That's Melville," whoever it might be. If you don't get rid of that, every time you reread that sentence you think: petty larceny.

INTERVIEWER: The first chapter of *Ironweed* sets the tone for the rest of the book by showing us Francis Phelan through the eyes of the dead, and through his own encounters in memory with the ghosts from his past, with many shifts back and forth in time. The first chapter has a literary magic about it that persists throughout the book and makes the book work in a unique way—but I wonder if you encountered any editorial resistance to the narrative technique when you took *Ironweed* to publishers.

KENNEDY: Considerable. There was one editor who said it was not credible to write this kind of a story and put those kinds of thoughts into Francis Phelan's mind, because no bum thinks that way. That's so abjectly ignorant of human behavior that it really needs no comment except that Congress should enact a law prohibiting that man from being an editor. I also sent the first few chapters to *The New Yorker* and an editor over there said it was a conventional story about an Irish drunk and they'd had enough of that sort of thing in the past, and they wished me well and thought it was quite well done, and so on. That seemed very wrongheaded. It's hardly a conventional story about an Irish drunk when he's talking to the dead, when he's on an odyssey of such dimensions as Francis is on. I'd never read a book like it, and it seems to me that that's a comment I hear again and again. But again, you have to put up with editors who don't know what they're reading. One editor said there were too many bums in the book and I should get rid of some. And a friend of mine said, "I understand, I love this chapter, but there's an awful lot of negative things in it, there's vomit and a lot of death and violence and there's a lot of sadness, you know, and it's such a downbeat chapter that editors won't want to buy it. Maybe you should alter it to get the editors past the first chapter." Well, there was no way I could take his advice; I had written the book, and it was either going to stand or fall on what it was. I also felt that there was no real merit in the advice, although it was an astute observation about the way some editors are incapable of judging serious literature seriously. There were also people who just said, "I don't like it." Somebody said, "I could never sell it." Somebody else said, "It's a wonderful book, nobody's ever written anything better about this subject than you have, but I can't add another book to my list that won't make any money." These were more mundane, these were money considerations, but I think those other, more pretentious rejections had the same basis; they just didn't believe a book about bums was ever going to make it in the marketplace, but they didn't dare say so out loud. It's not simply a book about bums, you know, but that's the way it was perceived. I got a letter from Pat Moynihan after I won the Pulitzer and a story had come out on the AP wire, describing *Ironweed* as a book about a baseball player who turns out to be a murderer. Moynihan quoted that back to me in the letter, and he said, "Perhaps you will have a better understanding of what we poor politicians are up against."

INTERVIEWER: The most prominent characters in your novels are seekers after a truth or meaning or experience beyond the repetitive patterns of daily life. Do you find that your own worldview changes as a result of creating these characters and moving them through a series of life experiences?

KENNEDY: I think that my worldview changes as I write the book. It's a discovery. The only thing that's really interesting to me is when I surprise myself. It's boring to write things when you know exactly what's going to happen. That's why language was so important to me in journalism. It was the only way you could heighten the drama, or make it funny, or surprising. In *Legs* I was endlessly fascinated to learn how we look at gangsters. I discovered what I thought about mysticism and coincidence when I wrote *Billy*. I feel that *Ironweed* gave me a chance to think about a world most people find worthless. Actually, anybody who doesn't have an idea about what it is to be homeless, or on the road, or lost and without a family, really hasn't thought very much at all. Even though I'd written about this, the small details of that life weren't instantly available to my imagination until I began to think seriously about what it means to sleep in the weeds on a winter night, then wake up frozen to the sidewalk. Such an education becomes part of your ongoing frame of reference in the universe. And if you don't develop Alzheimer's disease or a wet brain, you might go on to write better books. I think that some writers, after an early peaking, go into decline. Fitzgerald seems to me a good example of that. He was writing an interesting book at the end of his life, *The Last Tycoon*, but I don't think it would have been up to his achievement in *Gatsby* or *Tender Is the Night*. But if you don't die, and you're able to sustain your seriousness, I don't think there's any rule that you can't supersede your own early work. I remember an essay by Thomas Mann about Theodor Fontane, the prolific German novelist who believed he was all done somewhere around the age of thirty-nine. But he lived to be a very old man, and published his masterpiece, *Effi Briest*, at age seventy-six. I believe in the capacity of the imagination to mature and I am fond of insisting that I'm not in decline, that the next book is going to be better than the last. It may or may not be, but I have no doubt I know more about how to write a novel, more about what it means to be alive, than I ever have. Whether another dimension of my being has faded, and will refuse to fire my brain into some galvanic achievement, I can't say. We may know more about this when the next book is published.

INTERVIEWER: You said before that you don't write novels to make money. Why do you write novels?

KENNEDY: I remember in 1957 I was reading in *Time* magazine about Jack Kerouac's success with *On the Road*. I felt I wasn't saying what I wanted to say in journalism, wasn't saying it in the short stories I'd been writing either. I had no compelling vision of anything, yet I knew the only way I would ever get it would be to give my imagination the time and space to spread out, to look at things in the round. I also felt that not only did I want to write one novel, I wanted to write a series of novels that would interrelate. I didn't know how, but this is a very old feeling with me. I came across a note the other day that I wrote to myself about "the big Albany novel." This was way back, I can't even remember when—long before I wrote *Legs*, even before *The Ink Truck*. It had to be in the middle sixties. It was a consequence of my early confrontation with the history of Albany when I did a series of articles on the city's neighborhoods in 1963 and 1964. I began to see how long and significant a history we had had, and as I moved along as a part-timer at the *Times-Union*, writing about blacks and civil rights and radicals, I began to see the broad dimension of the city, the interrelation of the ethnic groups. The politics were just incredible—boss machine politics, the most successful in the history of the country in terms of longevity. And I realized I could never tell it all in one book.

INTERVIEWER: Is this enormous sort of Yoknapatawpha County in your mind? Do the characters emerge as you think about them? You give the picture of being able to dip into this extraordinary civilization.

KENNEDY: Every time out it's different, but one of the staples is the sense that I have a column of time to work with; for example a political novel that could move from about 1918 to maybe 1930; and in there is a focal point on a character, probably the political boss. But that's not always enough, having a character. I once wrote a novel's worth of notes about three characters and I couldn't write the first sentence of the book. It was all dead in the water. There has to be a coalescence of influences that ignite and become viable as a story.

INTERVIEWER: What do you think the ignition thing is? It's rather frightening that you work on these things and do not know whether it's going to come together. How do you know?

KENNEDY: You don't. It's an act of faith.

INTERVIEWER: What is the feeling when you're done with a book?

KENNEDY: I remember the day I finished *Ironweed*. I came down and I said, "I'm finished." My wife was there and so was Ruth Tarson, one of my good friends; they had read most of the book along the way and they sat down and read the ending. Somehow they didn't respond the way I wanted them to respond. I was thinking of an abstract reader who would say what every writer wants you to say to him: "This is the best thing I ever read in my life." I knew something was wrong, though I didn't know what; I knew the elements of the ending should be very powerful. I thought about it and their lack of proper response. After dinner I went back upstairs and rewrote the ending, adding a page and a half. I brought that down and then they said, "This is the best thing I've ever read in my life."

—*Douglas R. Allen*
Mona Simpson

1989

AN ARGUMENT:

Rejection and Henry James

(*Ironweed* award speech to
National Book Critics Circle)

I am now as much awash in critical magnanimity as I was bathed two years ago in insolvent obscurity. The nature of this new status is extreme pleasure, but also part of it is residual bewilderment at the causes of the previous condition. I was once deeply resentful at the rejection of *Ironweed*—it was rejected thirteen times—but of course I am slowly coming out of that. As *Ironweed*'s hero, Francis Phelan, says to the ghost of the man who had tried to cut off his feet with a meat cleaver, "I don't hold no grudges more'n five years."

It is the substance of the rejections that is disconcerting; and that substance is twofold. First: My immediately previous novel, *Billy Phelan's Greatest Game*, was not only not a best-seller, it was a worst-seller. Was the book's lack of sales the author's fault? Well, I must have had something to do with it, but I won't take full blame. Yet its failure to galvanize the American imagination in 1978 dogged my future. The line I heard most frequently was that publishers would rather take the risk on a first novelist than on a fourth novelist with a bleak track record. I hardly think this the received wisdom of the ages—to reward the apprentice at the expense of the journeyman. Literature, I suggest, deserves a different ordering of values. Scott Fitzgerald's line that there are no second acts in American lives was the sad, solipsistic truth about that wonderful writer's self-destructive career; but for those who take this as wisdom it can be a pernicious fallacy.

Innumerable case histories illuminate my point, but I will focus only on Henry James, an optimist. After early success his popularity plummeted, but not his self-esteem. "I am in full possession of accumulated resources," he wrote in 1891. "I have only to use them, to insist, to persist, to do something more—to do much more—than I have done . . ."

He went on to seek fame in another direction, the theater, and poured his soul into the creation of a play, which proved to be an abysmal failure. He had already published forty books. And then, in the depths of his failure as a playwright, and at the age of fifty-one, he wrote: "I take up my own old pen again—the pen of all my unforgettable efforts and sacred struggles. . . . Large and full and high the future still opens. It is now indeed that I may do the work of my life." He went on to publish thirty-five more volumes, including his masterworks.

The second element of *Ironweed* rejections concerned subject matter more than economics. "Too many bums in this book," I was told. "Who wants to read about bums, and especially bums in Albany?" I again invoke Henry James, who wrote: ". . . we of course never play the fair critical game with an author, never get into relation with him at all, unless we grant him his postulates. His subject is what is given him— given him by influences, by a process, with which we have nothing to do. . . ." James argues that only the author's treatment of those postulates should be the subject of critical concern.

James (and if I may impose a parenthesis, he emerged into the light from an old Albany family), writing also of Ivan Turgenev's concern with the poor and the grotesque, said that the Russian viewed fictional character "through a broken windowpane." He added that one might collect from Turgenev's tales a "perfect regiment of incapables, of the stragglers on life's march," and spoke of such writers as explorers of "the great grimy condition."

My story of the straggler Francis Phelan was an effort to bring news of that condition, on down to the ninth circle of Francis's grimy soul.

These two rejective arguments against my novel have their own modern logic. I rebut them tonight, not on my own behalf—my life at this moment has transcended complaint—but on behalf of the numerous novelists whose work has been relegated to limbo, or worse, by prevailing editorial judgment. And the happy fate of *Ironweed* suggests that this judgment may, at times, be flawed. I proselytize, therefore, not only for a more open-minded attitude toward seasoned writers of talent, goodwill, and rotten luck, but also for a more recalcitrant attitude by those writers in the face of what people say is the inevitable.

I was enormously saddened recently to see the death of the word predicted by one of my heroes, Joseph Campbell. Literature is folding, is what he said—moving over into the visual field. I hope he will forgive my reluctance to accept his prediction. I am simply not ready to believe that we are done with storytelling and that all we will get hereafter are dancing images. In the beginning, another writer once said, the word was God. I think this is the motto writers ought to live by.

Invocation of the divine word also brings with it the notion of immutability; and perhaps it is true that there does come a time when acceptance has to set in; when we *must* bow before the inevitable. I recall an instance of this which is worthy of reflection. It took place in Albany during a conversation between the mayor and a party official who was trying to get a job for a fellow in his ward. The mayor was the late Erastus Corning, Albany's mayor for forty-two consecutive years, and also, at this point, the town's supreme Democratic party boss.

At any rate, the mayor listened and finally said, "No, no job. That fellow used to be a Republican."

"Yes," said his booster, "that's true enough. But he quit the Republicans and became a good Democrat. Just think of Mary Magdalene, Mr. Mayor. She was once a great sinner, but the church made her a saint."

"Yes," said the mayor, "but not in her lifetime."

1984

Postscript: I gave this speech in New York to a gathering of editors, critics, and writers, after being introduced at the event by Doris Grumbach, a novelist, biographer, teacher, editor, critic, and person of great substance. For two decades, as literary editor of *The New Republic*, and as a critic for major literary publications throughout the U.S. thereafter, she was, among other achievements, a champion of young and unheralded fiction writers. She has been a friend of mine for almost three decades, and was my benefactor in too many ways to count here. But this does seem the logical place, this time in print, to express gratitude for what she has done, and love for who she is.

WINNING THE PULITZER:

Who Are You Now That You're Not Nobody?

I was in Parsons bookstore in Dublin with David Hanly, the Irish novelist and journalist, and an old friend, buying some books by John Banville, another Irish novelist about whom I'd heard good things. One of the proprietors asked would I sign their writers' book, as Frank O'Connor, John Montague, Paddy Kavanagh and many others had done. I was glad to join such illustrious company and began to write something on a blank page. A young man entered, saw my pile of Banville books, saw me signing and inquired: was I John Banville? I said no, that I was someone else entirely. The young man excused himself but came over to me later and apologized for not knowing me. He had discovered that even though I wasn't Banville, I was somebody, and therefore: could he have my autograph?

The end of anonymity, even in Ireland, is pleasant enough, but it raises the new issue that the anecdote illustrates: who are you, now that you're not nobody? Prizes have come to me and to my work during the past two years, my books have been received with inordinate goodwill in this country and abroad, and even strangers seem to know me. In Central Park I was sitting for a photographer when a jogger passed by, called me by name and gave me a thumbs-up gesture. Very sweet. Very different from a few years back when only my children recognized me (and sometimes even they weren't sure who I had become) and the bank knew me only because of the absence of my mortgage payment.

There is money on the table now and so the mortgage department recognizes me from the photo on my book jacket. People want to give me loans and bond deals and credit cards, I am a friend of lawyers and brokers, and to certain charitable and cultural organizations I look like an annuity.

As a teacher it was beyond expectation that I would ever do much more than survive at subsistence level. I own only a bachelor's degree (at twenty-one I couldn't abide another lecture). Now invitations come in, five a day, to write, speak, teach or, when May comes, just to stand still and shimmer in the baccalaureated afternoon. I remember when all I wanted to do was make a few dollars to live on and talk literature to bright students. Now movies are there to write if I want that. People want me to write a play, a musical, a documentary film, a TV series, a history of their family, the story of their lives. Magazines want me to write about movies, books, the blues, baseball or myself.

It took me two weeks to work up this piece simply because I resisted yet another session of self-analysis. I succeeded finally because a friend raised a question worth pondering: "You seem to be becoming all the things you fantasized about in the lean years. So, what now? What do you do when you can do anything at all?"

We were in a taxi in Barcelona, near La Rambla. My wife, Dana, and I were in search of what in 1972 Gabriel García Márquez had called "the best secret restaurant in Barcelona." The month was October and we were at the end of a tour of six countries where my novel *Ironweed* was being published. Again García Márquez was in town, but not with us at this moment, which was why we were lost. We resorted to a map and saw the restaurant was near. I paid the driver, and we set off on foot to have dinner, perhaps another spectacular *perdiz*—partridge—as we'd had twelve years ago.

But our restaurant was elusive. The light worsened, the mood altered. I stopped a young couple and was asking directions when I heard Dana yell and I turned to see a youth in a white windbreaker yanking down on her shoulder bag. With one long double-handed stroke he broke the strap, tucked the purse under his arm and ran. I gave chase, yelling clichés in two languages: stop thief, *policia*, etc., seeing the distance between us widen as we ran uphill on the crooked street. I thought of Dana behind me, alone, and I slowed as the thief turned a corner. Would I tackle him? Wrestle the purse from him? Would he have a knife?

Suddenly I was at an intersection of three streets, hearing no footfalls, only silence, and the darkness deeper than ever. I went back to Dana, who had been reliving Nicolas Roeg's film *Don't Look Now*, in which a bereaved father believes he sees his drowned daughter running in the street, chases her, catches up and discovers the figure is a dwarf, who stabs and kills him. When I told our story, my Spanish publicist observed that if I'd been stabbed it would have been very good for the sales of my book.

The neighborhood of the theft had changed since 1972, when I'd relished its vitality at all hours, its exuberance with crowds and flowers and bookstalls on Barcelona's annual Day of the Book. This time we were warned against going there at night, but we didn't pay attention. After the theft I saw La Rambla for what it had become: an arena of drugs and raffish lowlife where even taxi drivers fear the violence. Franco is gone and the repression has lifted. Barcelona now spawns the free enterprise of the underworld. "A problem of the democracies," García Márquez explained to us.

We never got to his secret restaurant. The thief stole not only Dana's history—address book, notes, receipts—but also our airline tickets home. At the police station, a dismal, decaying building whose walls reeked of fascist memory, a genial policeman told us that thoughtful thieves sometimes took only the money and dropped the purse into a mailbox.

And the purse *was* returned the next day, all money, traveler's checks, papers and passport gone, but the tickets intact, that much of the future restored. We ate a late supper at our hotel after the theft. I had a *hamburguesa* instead of *perdiz*, the price of being willfully ignorant of the dangerous unknown.

The first stop on our tour had been Stockholm. My Swedish publisher, Lars Grahn, had come to Albany earlier in the year and marched in the North Albany Saint Patrick's Day parade with me, and later that evening we formally made him an honorary Albany Irishman. I talked to Lars about Ingmar Bergman and how he had transformed my vision of life and film after I saw a double bill of *Wild Strawberries* and *The Magician* in the 1950s. I've seen almost all of Bergman's films since then, some

of them six and seven times, and for me he is the grand maestro. Lars
said he would try to arrange a meeting with Bergman for me, an event
about which I used to fantasize.

Now here we were, Lars and Dana and I, at the Royal Dramatic
Theater, where Bergman was to have an open rehearsal of his production
of *King Lear*, a day away from opening night of the play's second season.
Bergman had sent word he would meet us, and we were escorted into
the actors' lounge. In he came in corduroy pants, green shirt, V-neck
sweater, tan windbreaker, his glasses on a string around his neck, his
gray hair sticking out over his ears, his smile broad and welcoming. He
kissed Dana's hand.

My first question to him was, would he make another film? Please,
would he make another film? I will save his answer for the moment, but
let me say we went on to talk for an hour about film and theater and
how he is terrified by the light and noise of New York City and how he
is "interested only in the faces" in his films now. He spoke of the muscles
around the mouth and how important they are in the filming of speech.
Dubbed films are unwatchable to him because of the way the dubbing
distorts faces.

He was interested in my involvement with Francis Coppola's *Cotton
Club*. He said he did not know Coppola personally but loved his cinematography. "Send him my admiration and love," Bergman said. "I love
what he does with film."

He was also interested in my own love of film. I told him that, like
him, I owned a projector when I was a child, a 16mm Excel that still
lights up but will not run. He wanted to know how success had affected
me. I don't remember what I said in reply. Probably I said what I usually
say: that I am trying to avoid substantial change, that the past was
valuable and I want to perpetuate some of it, that I will continue to write
novels, and an occasional film, perhaps; that I am too old to be undone
by sudden attention, that I love the recognition of the work. But even
as I was speaking I was struck that this supreme icon of the modern
cinema saw no need to keep the focus on himself, an unlikely development in the ego city most icons inhabit.

What I took away from the conversation was not only a personal
exhilaration, as well as his invitation to attend one of the great theatrical
experiences of my life, his *Lear*, but also the sadness of confronting the

mortality of art. For what he said was that he will not make another film; that *Fanny and Alexander* was, truly, his last; for he is weary. "You must be at your peak, always," he said, "in order to make only three minutes of film a day. You must do this no matter what happens, even if you have the flu."

Now he wants to direct works of theater and make an occasional chamber film, such as *After the Rehearsal*, his most recent, made for TV. "That is somebody else's production problem," he said. "If it isn't ready this week, you can rehearse another week and open when it's better." He said he wants his work to disappear. He knows the plays he directs will disappear and he wishes it could be that way with film. "But unfortunately the film remains.

"You do theater," he said, "and then it's gone, and only the memory remains with you." He gestured to an image on an imagined stage, then to the internalizing of that image, striking his stomach.

Bergman's vision seems to conflict with that of Faulkner, who said the writer wants to scrawl his name on the cave wall, "Kilroy was here." I think Faulkner was accurate about the writer at a certain stage of life, but as the writer matures, grows impatient with any buffoonery having to do with immortality, he passes into a Bergmanesque realism, which is a profound sadness.

I'm sometimes asked whether the good fortune that has come to me will be reflected in my work. Will I, in short, now write stories that end happily? The question is apparently fatuous but has some import. For there is a danger in being seduced by opportunity after long isolation; a hedonistic response to psychic hunger is as perilous as giving knee-jerk chase to a thief down a blind alley. Some writers go silent after success, or they explode with pomposity, or they squander their spiritual capital and shrivel. Success was such a diabolical burden to Thomas Heggen and Ross Lockridge that they took their own lives.

Fantasies are realizable. My visit with Bergman, indeed my whole present condition, corroborates this. But there are also fantasies, born of anxiety, that become visible in nightmares; and these, too, are out there waiting to become flesh.

Bergman stood and we shook hands in farewell. He said he had to tend to a crying actress. "I must hold her hand," he said. We left the theater and walked in the sweet Swedish rain, and I entered then a still point that even now endures—a moment in which the restless spirit, the consciousness glutted with actualized dream, and the sagely aggressive oversoul are all harmonious in the advice they offer up: Don't make a move. Tread softly. The next life you save may be your own.

1985

PART TWO

Examining Writers: Some Interviews and Essays

A WEEK WITH THE
VERBIVOROUS JOYCEANS:

The Quest
for Heliotrope

The airline clerk refused to cash my check for the price of a round-trip ticket, so I flashed assorted documents confirming I was en route to Dublin in search of James Joyce and literary truth and zap went the money problems. I wondered what the Franciscan who taught me religion and who liked to refer to Joyce as "that pig" would say, now that the drop of his name opened transatlantic corridors to truth-seekers. Here I was, about to join 176 literary scholars, two-thirds of them Americans, at the Fourth International James Joyce Symposium, a week-long revel in Joyce's real and imaginary worlds.

Americans have a mystical affinity for Joyce. The headquarters for Joyce scholarship in the world is the *James Joyce Quarterly*, published at the University of Tulsa, and the *Quarterly*'s advisory editors and consultants also interlock with the directorate of the more international James Joyce Foundation, which runs the biennial symposium.

The *Quarterly* recently printed a checklist of work about Joyce that had been published during 1970. This included 155 books, articles, or complete issues of magazines, with American scholarship dominating numerically.

An often-heard view is that the Irish have a greater awareness of Joyce today, principally because of the first two Joyce symposia, held in Dublin in 1967 and 1969. (The third was in Trieste in 1971; Joyce lived there for a time.) Irish newspapers covered those first symposia's lectures and discussions at unusual length and to the astonishment of many Dubliners.

How, they wondered, could this long-dead renegade author of foul-mouthed gibberish dragoon so many otherwise bright Americans into swarming all over the city and all over those filthy books in search of God knows what? The sin of the foreigners, to the Irish, was not only presumption but the reverence with which they treated Joyce. The Irish view their writers more with hostility than solemnity, and Joyceans were as solemn as bloody owls, so went the rumble. The gentlest comment I heard about them from an Irishman was that they were "an affectionate joke" to the Irish.

I had forgotten it, but it was swiftly pointed out to me as the Joyceans gathered at the National Library, that the Gresham Hotel, where I was staying, was where Gabriel and Gretta Conroy stayed on that immortal evening in "The Dead," when snow was general all over Ireland. "His own identity," Joyce wrote of Gabriel in that story, "was fading out into a grey impalpable world: the solid world itself, which these dead had one time reared and lived in, was dissolving and dwindling."

That world had indeed dissolved, but some of it was coming back to visual life in the library, where an exhibit of photos of Joycean time past was interwoven with some of his manuscripts and memorabilia. Kieran Hickey, who lent the photos and also directed a film, *Faithful Departed,* which used them and which was about to be shown, wrote in a flyer: "The Dublin through which the young James Joyce walked, that Dublin which he carried with him in his heart, in his mind and in his memory during his long years of exile, no longer exists. The destruction during the past decade of so much of the Victorian city removed most of what remained of the atmosphere of Joyce's world."

Hickey's film was lovely, a montage of photos of the time between 1880 and 1917, taken by Robert French, a once anonymous, now revered documentarist: O'Connell, and other streets of old, with their horsecars and wagons, men in derbies and boaters, women in shawls and straws, taking their pleasure, going to work, caught and stilled for our eyes.

"It is difficult now," Hickey wrote, "to see these fadographs of a yestern scene in anything but Joycean terms." Jack McGowran, the late actor who popularized Samuel Beckett's work for Dubliners with his television adaptation of Beckett fragments, narrated and closed Hickey's film with a line of Leopold Bloom's at Paddy Dignam's funeral in *Ulysses:* "All these here once walked round Dublin. Faithful departed. As you are now so once were we."

And so Joyce and Dublin were mutually evoked on a note of sacred humanism. Terence de Vere White, literary editor of *The Irish Times*, spoke briefly in the library, which was almost unchanged from the days Joyce read here, and he added a sour note to this Irish love song. Joyce, he said, neglected the library, giving it few of his manuscripts. And after he died, his wife, Nora, said he hated this country and she wouldn't give the library anything either.

Out on the sidewalk I met two delegates to the symposium, one named Knight, another named Day. Someone immediately wondered if Father Noon was attending this year and we were off on the punnyride. Even the Irish newspapers reflected the need to pun when Joyce's name was raised. A review of Anthony Burgess's new book on the hero, *Joysprick*, carried the equivalently organic headline: *Joystalk*.

We adjourned for a welcoming wine party at 86 St. Stephen's Green, part of University College, where the symposium would be held, and whose worn floors and stairs were still weighted with Joyce's spiritual tread from student days. In the men's room (sometimes called the Jacks), I turned up two bits of graffiti which kept the punning on course: "I know they have no 'arm in 'em, but I just can't find Jacks writers humerus." And one which would surely put the visiting pundits at ease: "Wholly, Holy, Holey, A Sponge Saint."

Yes, Mr. Joyce, it was apt. The gang was here to bathe in every drop of blessedness they could squeeze from you.

At the first *Ulysses* seminar two dozen people, a third of them women, sat in an old high-windowed classroom overlooking the splendid, sprawling Green, while a man on a panel discoursed funereally on "the comic in *Ulysses*." Joyceans seem to be willing to tolerate anybody at least once in their continuing quest for a new nugget of insight into the master. Of course, the symposium functions on attendance (twenty dollars a head) and the organizers strike a democratic attitude toward neophytes, nebbishes, and bores to avoid giving the gathering a more elitist image than it already has. The school back home usually kicks in at least part of the carfare for a professor invited to give a paper or speak on a panel, and the symposium's urge for self-perpetuation through such support counterbalances worry over the dud factor.

Academic obeisance to status is also part of the game. If a professor wrote a great paper on Joyce twenty years ago, it follows he will always write great papers, and so he is up there still as we doze, floating toward oblivion on the nuances of old nuances, the discovery of yet another Homeric allusion.

The young man at the front of the room was telling us that to Joyce, Bloom was not comic. Did he really say that or was he blaming somebody else for it? Must pay attention. The dynamics of the novel . . . the complex choreography of characters . . . the Catechistic style of Ithaca . . . the collision . . . the agon . . . the seguri . . . the seven samurai . . . the twee-twee-twee-qua-qua . . . zzzzzzz.

Movies. Joyce and movies. Somebody else talking. My head snapped to. Wandering Rocks chapter is a virtual blueprint for a script. . . . Yes, even camera angles dictated . . . It would be interesting to see . . . Yes, Joyce anticipated movie technique. . . . He opened the first cinema in Dublin. . . . He met Eisenstein.

Did he go to the movies in Paris? Someone who knew him there said, oh yes, indeed yes, even after his eyesight was so poor. His friends sat with him and filled in the gaps he missed, such as the famous topless film of the thirties, Hedy Lamarr in *Extase*, and there went Hedy in the buff, bouncing through the woods; and Joyce nudging his companion to ask, "What are they doing now?"

"Just so stylled with the nattes are their flowerheads now and each of all has a lovestalk onto herself and the tot of all the tits of their under-stamens is as open as he can posably she and is tournesoled straightcut or sidewaist, accourdant to the coursets of things feminite, towooerds him in heliolatry, so they may catchcup in their calyzettes, alls they go troping, those parryshoots from his muscalone pistil . . ."

This is a fragment of *Finnegans Wake*, a book which intimidates everybody. Unlike the committed Joyceans, I doffed my hat to its corpus long ago and moved on, planning to make other visits when I grew up or old or wise or crazier. At times, sections of it resurrected my spirit without rational explanation. The strange words alone, plus perhaps my reverence for them, reverence built on faith rather than reason, touched some inner region Joyce meant to touch in his readers and I responded emotionally to things I understood only in fragments.

Wake scholarship, then, was a source of awe, for these scholars had not only read all those incredible words; they went ahead and snippeted them up for digestion by others. They were connoisseurs of the arcane and esoteric, privy to the answers to the riddles of the sphinxes and the jokes of the cavemen.

And so with trepidation I entered the workroom of the Wakers, a classroom packed with fifty people, mostly middle-aged or middle-aging, only one recognizable as a student. There was a Jesuit in mufti with a black Smith Brothers beard, an old man with a white Hemingway beard, an effectual blonde, a dozen longhairs, a dozen straights in ties and coats, a pair of elderly women, one with a floppy hat, both of whom turned out to be old friends of the hero's. Many of the scholars knew one another and a few were renowned as Joyceans—Vivian Mercier, Father Robert Boyle, Nathan Halper, Bernard Benstock, and, chairing the action, Fritz Senn of Zurich, editor of *A Wake Newslitter*, a periodical devoted totally to Joyce's masterful puzzle.

I entered on a discussion of the *Wake*'s puns. Did they come clear when you read them aloud? someone asked. Yes, said one man. No, said another. Only sometimes, said a third, for there are puns which are purely visual and not pronounceable. The use of doodles was discussed, and our ignorance of the semantics of dead languages. Making up glossaries of *Wake* words, someone suggested, is a sterile exercise unless we simultaneously derive human value from the work. Ah ha, said a lady, this is an either/or attitude, and why do we have to have one? We work with induction and deduction in every other field. Someone cited Hart's Law, a creation of *Wake* scholar Clive Hart, that when you're reading the *Wake* and suddenly something hits you, you should go with it. Yes indeed, said a lady. I trained as a cryptanalyst and a basic rule was don't sit there and fiddle. Make a wild guess. The intelligent guess is so important. What you should do, someone else said, is to let it all flow past you, like Bach, and just feel it.

It is about a dream, someone said. But even if it's not about a dream, it works as if it were a dream. Making an inspired leap opens doors into other situations. It isn't a lock where you have a key and therefore have total comprehension. Wait, said another man, I know somebody who thinks it is a lock and if you have the key it will all open up. Personally, said another man, I think it's more like a key and you have to find the lock.

The words, a woman suggested, are complex, and if we get through them to the ideas behind them, perhaps we will find that those ideas are equally complex. I read it twice without help, said a man, and couldn't understand it and I was furious. A book should communicate. But then I began to read the commentators. Yes, said another man, we go to doctors and each one of them has a different diagnosis, but most ailments are self-curing. The point is that everybody who reads it says something different. Yes, but they also say that about *Hamlet*. The discovery of the Joyce notebooks in Buffalo was thought to be a breakthrough, said a man, but they turned out to be no help at all. You have to be Irish to understand it? Wrong. You have to know Shakespeare? Equally wrong. You just have to be a reasonable man. Listen, said one man, *Finnegans Wake* is a conscious work of art. It's less of a dream than the Buffalo notebooks. We've forgotten that one of the main points is the polarity of Shem and Shaun, two ways of approaching everything. We've always talked about the identities of contraries. One of the things it's giving us is multiple points of view at once. That's right, we lack a theory about *Finnegans Wake* but we all laugh at it. Yes, and we read it and sometimes it is all clear and sometimes it's nothing to us, but if you can get his association of ideas, his symbolic code, then you receive it. Wait a minute, a woman said, a graduate student told me every time her baby cried she read him a page of the *Wake* and he stopped crying. He was absolutely satisfied with the surface alone.

The two-hour session had no long or boring papers. It was a lively interchange among people who respected one another because of friendship or literary reputation or knowledge of Joyce. Wakers had more fun than Ulysseseans, playing games, whistling up meanings, cracking jokes, needling each other. No solemnity here. The impenetrability of the *Wake* was reinforced, and yet anyone's burden of ignorance would have been lightened a few straws by the session. For vast though the scholarship may be on the book, here were the specialists, people who've given great portions of their careers to the study of it, talking about how to read it, as if it were published last year instead of in 1939.

I sat through two other *Wake* sessions, all lively and full of wit, centering largely on the difficult Chapter Nine, but rambling everywhere, like the book itself: how Joyce used *Macbeth*, Wilde, Blake, Freud.

What did heliotrope mean in Chapter Nine? The speculation was vast, ingenious. One questioner suggested considering the heliotrope as an eagle, the only bird that can look at the sun and is therefore a symbol of Saint John and therefore the visionary and author of the Apocalypse.

Said Fritz Senn: "We have erred. We have not dealt with subjects of equal importance. It's possible we've overlooked an entire dimension. I would like to suggest that when we get together again groups split off and devote all their time to something like heliotrope."

Like so many, Senn looks for the big key to the book's riddle and is impatient with scholarship that is clearly ingenious in decoding sections of the *Wake* but that doesn't get nearer any larger meaning. He was equally impatient with Nathan Halper, whose plea to the group was to treat the *Wake* as a "humanistic document," and not an endless puzzle.

"I quite agree with him," Senn said when we talked after the last session, "but hasn't that been present here in our meetings somehow? To babble about humanity doesn't help me."

How would he assess the status of *Wake* scholarship?

"I've been discouraged. I'm waiting for more enlightenment. Halper says we have enough but it doesn't satisfy me. There's no way of measuring how far we've gone in linear terms. We've been moving on a plane and it should be a cube."

A quarter century ago an Irish critic wrote that any book in plain English that attempted to deal comprehensively with the *Wake* would have to be far longer than the *Wake* itself, for its author would have to "decant a quart of old wine from each of Joyce's pint bottles."

Did Senn see such a book coming to pass? Probably. "But there will always be a new theory that says the old theory is going in the wrong direction. It's the game we play. It makes us go on."

What Joyce knew intimately was Dublin. And no true Joycean goes there without exploring some segment of it relevant to Joyce's work. A map of the city, marked out with all the principal points Joyce described in *Ulysses*, is part of the kit bag symposiasts are given for their twenty dollars. For those more concerned with the man, the covers of the symposium's program were given over to photos of the façades and address plates of sixteen houses where Joyce lived, fourteen of them still standing and visitable.

By what I presumed to be an accident, but which I would like to think was something mystically richer than that, I stopped at a street corner, looked up, and saw the sign ECCLES STREET. I quickly found number 7, where the Blooms lived. It was one of four row houses, gone now but part of their façades still erect, including, at number 7, two boarded-up windows, the doorway nailed over with corrugated aluminum, a black iron picket fence in front, and the chalky discoloration where the 7 used to be. The bedroom door from number 7 is now installed at The Bailey, the Dublin pub. Grass and weeds grow just beyond the doorstep in the now vacant lot that was once the house. What remains was marked long ago by a reverent Joycean or two: over the absent door, erratically printed in now faded black paint, and also carved on a horizontal board, is the name "Molly Bloom." There is also the mark of, perhaps, an anti-Joycean: the word "shit," the only legible item among the faded bits of graffiti.

It is probably psychically confusing to visit a house in memory of people who lived there but never actually existed. And yet such is the detail available about the Blooms and how and where they lived that they have a bygone reality equivalent to our dead relatives'. Through this use of the real in service of the fictional, said one symposiast, Joyce "canonized the obsession with being Irish—the whole love of place, of knowing a particular street in Dublin and talking all night about it."

Darcy O'Brien, a Joycean from Pomona College, recently wrote in the *Joyce Quarterly* of his meeting with a Dubliner who'd been twenty years in the British navy and who was reading *Ulysses* for the twenty-fifth time: "He would become terribly homesick and he found that reading *Ulysses* was as close to being home as he could get. . . . The thing that brought him back to the book again and again was the authenticity of its Dublin speech and atmosphere."

Dubliners have a special sense of place that seems to relegate the rest of Ireland to the back porch, like Bugs Baer's line that after you leave New York everyplace else is Bridgeport. A woman in Galway told me she felt Dubliners were snobs: "They think the sun, moon, and stars shine on the durrrty, contammynated Liffey," she said with considerable vehemence.

I felt the Dublin sense of place one night when, flushed with Joycean detail, I toured an area in the center of Dublin that led into what was the old Kips, the vast brothel area, no longer functioning and some of it long gone, that Joyce used for his Nighttown episode in *Ulysses*.

It was after the 11:00 P.M. closing hour but a friend and I found an oasis and after a few discreet knocks we entered a room where two dozen people were drinking and the talk was still of place—a noted pub where Brendan Behan, Patrick Kavanagh, and other writers drank under a stained-glass window in what was known as the pub's Intensive Care Unit.

We were drinking in the place where a noted poet had sat upstairs by a window to observe the passing of John F. Kennedy's motorcade in 1963, his purpose to write of it. But the poet went on the nod and when the pub owner saw him dozing she shook him and said if he didn't stay awake he'd lose his place, for others wanted it. Then someone told her he was a poet and she went back and apologized and said it was all right if he slept as long as he was by the window when the motorcade went by. For as everybody knows in Ireland, poets can feel things without actually seeing them.

The evening was literary enough to satisfy any visitor with expectation of the Dublin pub tradition, and it was redolent of Joyce without being scholarly. Then the conversation veered back to the late Paddy Kavanagh and how he came into a pub one morning and asked the question:

"Were you here last night?"

"I was," said the bartender.

"Was I?" asked Paddy.

I bought Kavanagh's collected poems the next day, found the one about Joyce, his response to all that the symposium stood for in the mind of Irish literary chauvinists. He called it "Who Killed James Joyce?" Some excerpts:

> Who killed James Joyce?
> I, said the commentator,
> I killed James Joyce
> For my graduation.
>
> What weapon was used
> To slay mighty Ulysses?
> The weapon that was used
> Was a Harvard thesis.

How did you bury Joyce?
In a broadcast symposium.
That's how we buried Joyce
To a tuneful encomium. . . .

Who killed Finnegan?
I, said a Yale-man,
I was the man who made
The corpse for the wake man.

And did you get high marks,
The Ph.D.?
I got the B. Litt.
And my master's degree.

Did you get money
For your Joycean knowledge?
I got a scholarship
To Trinity College. . . .

Leslie Fiedler, in his Bloomsday address (June 16, the day on which the events in *Ulysses* occur) to the Joyceans in 1969, cited an incident which parallels the poem. It happened at The Bailey, where a group of Joyceans were gathered for drink and talk and a young Irishman suddenly rose up and told them: "I am an illegitimate grandson of James Joyce, and I want to tell you that he would spit on every one of you."

Said Fiedler: "Ah, the young man was wrong, alas, since I fear that Joyce would have approved rather than spit upon even what is worst about us and our deliberations. . . . He would have relished the endless *pilpul*, the Talmudic exegesis, in which the sacred is profaned without any feelings of guilt. He would have rejoiced, after all, at the soulless industry which has grown up around his tortured and obsessive works."

Fiedler then was knocking what he described as the scholarly Stephen Dedalus element in Joyce and Joyceans, and not the Bloom element— comic father, harassed Jew, self-appointed prophet—which he exalted.

His 1973 speech at mid-symposium Fiedler called "Joyce Against Literature," the title suggesting we could expect new shafts at the Stephenesque scholar, which Fiedler clearly was trying to unbecome. His subject was, again, *Ulysses*, which, he said, "straddles and crosses a border which maybe never existed at all . . . the line between belles lettres and schlock."

He spoke of *Ulysses* as a dirty book with ambivalent cultural pretensions. "It's easy to grant that it was an attack on Caesar and Christ," he said, "but we find it difficult to conceive that it was also an ambivalent attack on Flaubert and Henry James"—that is, on the notion of high culture. He cited Molly Bloom's soliloquy, her celebration of the flesh interwoven with an anti-literature stance: she dismisses Rabelais and Defoe, Joyce's favorites.

"Is Joyce using Molly to make fun of literature or is he making fun of Molly?" Fiedler wondered. "Joyce gives you the choice, always." But Joyce ended the book with her, and he ended on the note of her "yes" to fleshly impulses, and this contributed to Fiedler's conclusion on Joyce that "clearly as he would like to sustain the elitism—the artist as secular priest, and have his work pored over by exegetes for centuries," what Joyce really was was a "crap lover."

"He was a coprophile . . . a peeper at ladies pissing in the bushes," and also the purveyor of his own most obscene fantasies, "in short, a pornographer." He ticked off the porn that Bloom peruses, *Fair Tyrants*, by James Lovebirch, *The Awful Disclosures of Maria Monk*, *Tales of the Ghetto* by Sacher-Masoch, *Sweets of Sin*, books by a writer named Paul de Kock. None of it was hard-core porn, Fiedler said, but softer stuff. "I like to think Joyce would have liked Russ Meyer's films."

Fiedler talked of *Ulysses* as "metaporn"—Joyce imagining Bloom imagining Molly reading the porn—porn at a second remove. He talked also of Joyce's use of old soap-opera fiction, *The Lamplighter* and *Mabel Vaughan*, and added that he'd read all those nineteenth-century books which Bloom and Gerty McDowell knew and Joyce parodied, and gave this too as part of his justification for calling Joyce a coprophile.

"What I felt I had to do [in this speech] is throw the counterweight. If you don't know those books of the 1870s, then you don't know what he's doing." Fiedler's arguments were dense with substantiation of his viewpoint, his speech electric, his delivery manic, his appearance— rotund, gray-bearded, red-faced—somewhere between a sated satyr and a Jewish Santa Claus. The speech and rebuttal lasted two and a half hours, a high point in the symposium and the only time anyone seemed genuinely angry. Rebuttal was hostile. One man found the speech "pernicious." Many felt Fiedler was belaboring, grossly, what they already knew. His antiliterature thunder, his remark that he would rather be a Philistine than Matthew Arnold, made high art seem ridiculous, someone said.

He answered such attacks with his ambivalence. He hadn't argued that Joyce was either/or, but rather that he was both: an elitist as well as a pornographer, an Arnoldian as well as a crap lover. Fiedler himself wanted to close the gap between high and popular art.

Harry Staley, a Joycean from State University at Albany, New York, observed on the way out: "I don't take the aristocracy seriously, and I told Her Majesty that just the other day."

The Joyce legend attenuates. It grows closer to the day when there will be nobody alive who will remember the real man except through the haze of childhood. No literary legend has been better documented in this century, most notably in the great biography by Richard Ellmann. Yet the desire to know everything about his life, even after you feel you've already heard it all, persists. This was the case with the reminiscence of Mme. Maria Jolas, who, with her husband Eugene, founded *transition*, the Paris-based magazine in which the *Wake* appeared first as *Work in Progress*. The Jolases were close to Joyce and much of what she had to say had been reported in Ellmann's book. But her presence gave the recollections a force no biography could match and so her words became a high point of the symposium.

Madame Jolas was an honorary participant at the symposium, along with Dr. Carola Giedion-Welcker, an art critic who knew Joyce in Switzerland near the end of his life. Frau G-W too reminisced, briefly, about the man.

I also talked privately with Joyce's niece, Mrs. Bozena Delimata (daughter of Joyce's sister Eileen), who was close to Joyce's daughter, Lucia. What the three women revealed were random footnotes to the Joyce legend, footnotes to remind us (and the tendency was to forget) that Joyce was not a disembodied mind but a frail, drinking, singing, anguished, vulnerable, isolated, and introverted family man awash in heavy trouble as well as indomitable genius.

Here is some of what the women remembered:

Madame Jolas: She met him in 1927 and found him an "extraordinarily dignified man," even when drunk. Only Nora called him Jim; others called him Mr. Joyce. He was an "immense gentleman and comprehending friend" who didn't make friends easily, for that entailed the responsibility of empathy. He loved parties with intimates and they always ended in singing, often in a duet with Madame Jolas, and sometimes the party ended in dancing. He wouldn't drink until 7:00 P.M. or let anyone else in the house drink either. He was told by doctors to stop drinking white Swiss wine, that it would advance his blindness; but he kept on drinking.

He was "both father and mother," especially to Lucia, who did not get along with her mother and once threw a chair at her. Socially, Joyce "wouldn't move without his wife"—Nora was "absolutely essential" to him, although she wore down emotionally after Lucia's illness—schizophrenia. Joyce, when talking of the illness, once remarked: "And I'm supposed to be writing a funny book," meaning the *Wake*. Lucia is now sixty-five, in an English sanitarium, and "rather touchingly attached to this period of her life." Samuel Beckett took care of Lucia in France after Joyce was forced to leave her behind when he fled to Zurich, the Nazis having withdrawn permission for him to take her at the last minute. Beckett was, and remains now, "absolutely, inevitably loyal."

Madame Jolas went with Joyce's son Giorgio to make arrangements for the burial of Nora. The Swiss priest asked, without commenting, for birth dates of Giorgio and Lucia, both born out of wedlock; for Joyce had resisted formalizing his marriage religiously. Madame Jolas recalled that the priest behaved sympathetically. But at the graveside, after leaping off a trolley and donning his clerical garb as he walked toward Nora's open grave, he delivered the funeral prayers with the gratuitous remark that this was "a great sinner who is being buried."

And so in Joyce's long feud with the church, the church had the last, bitter word.

Dr. Giedion-Welcker: She said that at one stage in the writing of the *Wake*, Nora complained she couldn't sleep. Why not? "That man," she said, "he sits in there at his desk, writing and laughing out loud." Joyce, she said, had plans to write another book after the *Wake*, one on the order of a Greek tragedy or comedy, based on the Greek resistance to the Nazis.

Mrs. Delimata: She was close to Lucia and still communicates with her. "She writes to me every fortnight, always one letter: 'Please come and fetch me. I want to go to Ireland with you. My father and mother are in heaven and I'm all alone.' But there is no chance of letting her out; I asked about it and they won't."

A few years ago Lucia came to herself and said to Mrs. Delimata: "Was I much trouble? I'm sorry I was so much trouble to my father."

"Uncle Jim was so happy Lucia was getting better when she stayed with us in Ireland. But then she'd get spasms of wanting to commit suicide. Everybody wanted to keep her free as much and as long as possible but twenty doctors examined her. She used to go around half-dressed and went into the sea naked. People here would say, 'Of course it would be James Joyce's daughter that would do this.' Jim never stopped writing to Lucia to read this book and that book and go to this play and that.

"When my mother died in 1963 I started a guesthouse in Bray and called it *Ulysses*, but my heart didn't behave and I had to give it up. . . . I want to start a Joyce house in Bray, the one where he set the Christmas-dinner scene. The house is just the same as when he lived in it but I haven't been able to raise the money.

"The family? Some said Uncle Jim only wrote when he was drunk and they said he was half crazy. He loved my mother but years ago some of his other sisters would pretend he wasn't their brother at all. Aunty May came around and eventually kept a correspondence with Jim. Aunty Florry [who was eighty-one and dying in a nursing home] had nothing to do with Jim and blamed him for their mother's death. . . . Giorgio is in Germany and I understand he's very ill. . . . Jim was such a madcap. He'd get money from somebody and he'd go and buy a scarf, or some flaming thing. He wasn't very good with money. . . . But in 1938 he said to my mother he would get a beauty salon in Paris if I would study beauty culture in Ireland. I was starting in it when the war came. . . . He never forgot my birthday and he called himself my godfather, but by proxy he was, really. . . . He called me Baby. Lucia still calls me Baby. Lucia got a dressing gown from Beckett last Christmas."

A letter from Lucia: "Dear Baby, I hope you are all well. I wrote to Mr.——— my solicitor to send you 25 pounds. Did you get it I wonder? Mrs.——— says it is a lot of money so I don't know if he will let you have it. . . . I hope he will send you the money so that you can come to see me. I have a small room and there is a big tree just outside my window with lots of birds flying about all day. With lots of love, from Lucia."

The symposium ended on Bloomsday, with an early evening visit to the Martello Tower and then a dinner at the Royal Marine Hotel in Dun Laoghaire. The Joyceans descended from chartered buses and came up the walkway toward the tower, some in their new tweed caps and knitted sweaters bought the day before yesterday on Grafton Street. They stood hip to hip in the small museum, which was busy with photos, letters, Joyce's death mask by sculptor Paul Speck (that detail arranged immediately after his death by Frau Giedion-Welcker).

There in showcases, like rare Etruscan pottery, lay Joyce's last walking stick, his brocaded vest donated by Beckett, the guitar his friend Ottocaro Weiss photographed him playing, his books in so many languages.

Ulick O'Connor, the biographer of Oliver St. John Gogarty (the Buck Mulligan of *Ulysses*), recollected in a monologue for the tower visitors the days when Gogarty and Joyce had lived in this room. O'Connor had planned to bring back both their voices via recordings, to be heard here together for the first time since 1904, but Gogarty's son invoked a copyright and so Joyce alone, in his squeaky, simulated brogue, welcomed these benevolent invaders of his soul.

At the dinner which followed, two stunningly talented Irish singers, Anne Makower and Bill Golding, evoked for an hour the long-gone Joycean time with superbly rendered songs and patter, songs that were in the air in Joyce's day and which he used in his books—"I Dreamt I Dwelt in Marble Halls," "Love's Old Sweet Song," part of *Don Giovanni*, and, of course, "Finnegan's Wake," before which the singers gave the audience the compulsory Irish jab: "Let us remind these scholars who take him too seriously that concert Joyceans are aware that Joyce was a great *comic* novelist."

Madame Jolas said it was the kind of evening she'd often spent with Joyce, this music their common ground, and, "What a good account of this evening he could have given!" Paris was announced as the site of the 1975 symposium, two short Joyce films were shown, the symposium's organizers cracked in-group jokes, and since everybody was surfeited with song, literature, food, fellowship, and also deep into the French wine, the mood was as mellow and lyrical as a Tom Moore melody; and, some would say, just about as relevant to the contemporary world.

The most vituperative argument I heard against the Joyceans is not that they are solemn, which they generally are not as often as they are, but that as a group they are like Joyce: cultural imperialists and moral neuters; elitists turning up pointless esoterica·and framing it in prose that is often brilliant, often redolent of rancid socks. I heard an Irish Marxist denigrate Joyce as irrelevant today to the Irish masses who are still trying to overturn British colonialism in Northern Ireland and British economic imperialism in the Irish Republic. Marxists similarly attacked Joyce in his lifetime.

Benedict Kiely, the Irish short-story writer, told a story at lunch one day during the symposium about an Irish master of ceremonies at a Belfast musicale who came on stage and announced that "Mary Ann McGattigan will now sing 'The Londonderry Air.' " Someone from the balcony shouted down: "Mary Ann McGattigan is a whore!" The emcee, taken aback, stepped away, composed himself, and then returned to the microphone.

"Nevertheless," he said, "Mary Ann McGattigan will now sing 'The Londonderry Air.' "

The stalwart Joyceans, like that emcee, know that neither the artist nor his partisans ever bow to vituperation. The quest for heliotrope will continue.

1974

Bernard Malamud:

On the Short Story

On *The Fixer*

Pictures of Fidelman:
A Review

On the Short Story

"**I**t has many enticements. . . .

"Like a poem, it contains multitudes. . . .

"Its brief quality relates it more fittingly to our short lives. . . .

"Time flies because so much happens so quickly. . . .

"With a dozen or few more pages whole lives are implied and even understood. . . .

"When you put a dozen good ones together, you have a good book."

This is Bernard Malamud talking about the short story, a literary form he has worked in with more originality than almost any contemporary American writer. His newest book, *Idiots First*, is a collection of a dozen short stories. His first such collection, *The Magic Barrel*, won the National Book Award in 1959. The new work includes two fantasies, a section of a play, four stories with an Italian setting, "and the rest done in a realistic, expressionistic mode."

"I say expressionistic for I never really write a fully realistic tale," Mr. Malamud said in an interview at his office last week on the Bennington College campus, where he teaches literature.

"Fiction does not deal with pure, dead, documentary realism. As a fiction writer you take a realistic fact and abstract it and distort it and perhaps even fantasy it, and it comes out realism if it tells the truth about life."

Mr. Malamud puts his characters in a grocery store with no customers, in a railroad station where death is an employee, in a rooming house with a despondent writer, in Harlem searching for a Negro angel named Alexander Levine.

In these situations, in the words of the National Book Award jury, he "captures the poetry of human relationships at the point where reality and imagination meet."

Generally his characters are long-suffering, almost defeated, incredibly sad, pitiable. But he warns against misinterpreting his aims:

"Many people are victimized but some are gifted enough to pluck victory out of defeat, or even partial victory. A bad reading of my work would indicate that I'm writing about losers. That would be a very bad reading. One of my most important themes is a man's hidden strength. I am very much interested in the resources of the spirit, the strength people don't know they even have until they are confronted with a crisis."

This hidden strength, he explains, "is stored up through experience, you might say. A man lives through something and he learns. A man reads something and he learns. And some people use what they learn."

In *The Assistant*, Mr. Malamud's second novel (the first was *The Natural*, about a baseball player; the third was a story of a college professor, *A New Life*), he etched in stark events the life of a vagrant Italian, Frank Alpine, who becomes a clerk in a Jewish grocery store and encounters enough obstacles to give even a God-like hero the blind staggers. Circumstances and his own weaknesses send Alpine to his knees. But he always rallies, and in the long run achieves victory of a kind.

Mr. Malamud feels that "a man is always changing. And the changed part of him is all-important. I refer to the psyche, to the spirit, the mind, the emotions. I feel that a man's way out is his imagination and his will. He frequently does the impossible.

"In these times there is so much of a belief in unconscious determinism that people feel there is nothing they can do with their lives simply because they've had a past. I don't believe this. I believe that in a sense we are imprisoned, but that the chains have locks and the locks are openable."

Mr. Malamud at the moment is between works, a time when he generally produces short stories while a new novel is germinating. When you finish a short story, he says, "you breathe," whereas with a novel "there is a long time under water."

Mr. Malamud, now forty-nine, began writing as a child, but dates his "intensive, purposive apprenticeship" from 1940 to 1949, when he lived in a Brooklyn rooming house and later in Greenwich Village. In this period he wrote "dozens" of short stories and a novel, the latter eventually destroyed intentionally. He sold his first story in 1950 to *Harper's Bazaar*. Called "The Cost of Living," it is included in the new collection and was one of the bases for *The Assistant*.

"The artist's strongest protest against injustice," he says, "his best defense of the underprivileged of the world, is to tell their stories as works of art."

1963

On *The Fixer*

Bernard Malamud has written with his new novel, *The Fixer*, what he considers the best book of his life. It is an imaginative tour de force that shows the great power of his creative talents.

But he finds himself, through a publishing quirk, linked with the historical situation on which his plot is very loosely based. And the result is painful for this eminent literary man.

He talked of this during an interview in his office in a converted barn that is now a main building on the Bennington College campus.

Malamud's book is just published by Farrar, Straus and Giroux, and it is no secret that it is the author's version of the imprisonment (from 1911 to 1913) of Mendel Beiliss, a Jewish laborer in Kiev, Russia, who was accused of "ritual murder." Anti-Semitic conspirators used Beiliss, an innocent man, as scapegoat in their plan to fan anti-Semitic Russians to the frenzy of a pogrom. The murderers were known, and the crime had nothing to do with Jews. But Beiliss was nevertheless accused of stabbing a young boy forty-seven times to drain his blood for use in the making of matzos for Passover.

The story of the conspiracy against Beiliss, and his absurd trial, is told in scholarly detail by Maurice Samuel in *Blood Accusation*, a book just published by Knopf. Samuel, however, tells little of Beiliss's personal life or attitudes. That is Malamud's province.

But Malamud, who stands in the first rank of American novelists and short-story writers, has not merely transcribed Beiliss's circumstances into fictional form. He has created a new character, a product of history, myth, and the fertile Malamud mind.

Yet the linking of the novel with the Samuel book tends "to cut down the imaginative invention" in the minds of others, Malamud believes.

"I don't want my novel treated as a case history," he said.

Anyone who knows anything about literature will know from a reading of the novel that it is not a case history. It is an exploration of a man's mind as he suffers excruciating tortures of brutality, deprivation, and humiliation. Yakov Bok's jailers trick him, intimidate him, even try to kill him in ways that would not appear to be murder. But he survives through what Malamud terms "resistance of the mind."

A reading of the story, the author said, should make you "feel that you're in the presence of a man, and that he's using his resources as a man to stay alive."

Some readers, he says, have found the story "too depressing," but he terms these people "inadequate readers" who do not see "these elements of the story which are the sources of power."

Neither, apparently, do they see the Malamud humor, which is one of the author's great strengths. Yakov Bok is tragic, but Malamud makes him a ragtail, a gagster, has him walk into a closet by mistake, like Stan Laurel. As he contemplates the idea of a month in jail Bok thinks: "A month in jail is not a year and three weeks are less; besides if you wanted to look at it that way, rent was free."

Also, after excruciating months of prison and torture Yakov sees his attorney and finds out many in Russia are sympathetic to his plight.

"Should I hope?" he asks the attorney.

"If it doesn't hurt, hope," the attorney retorts.

The capacity to ask such a question, and the witty language of its answer, are part of the means by which Mr. Malamud feels that he "protects the reader from sheer laceration and gloom." The story is unquestionably painful to read. Malamud allows Yakov, nevertheless, to be almost comical in the midst of torture, a means, he says of being "objective and protective at the same time." This allows Bok, says the author, "to turn what is unpleasant into what a person can tolerate."

Bernard Malamud first heard of Mendel Beiliss from his father. The story of the man's suffering remained intriguing to him, but when he began to research it Beiliss proved to be fictionally inadequate. "He didn't fit the message I wanted to get across," the author recalled. "His suffering came to less than it should have come to. I had to invent a character—a folk hero, so that much that didn't happen to Beiliss could happen to him."

Beiliss's story was the outline. But Malamud also drew on the Dreyfus and Sacco-Vanzetti cases. Beiliss was never put in chains, but Yakov Bok is chained for months, as was Dreyfus. Bok's hallucinations were suggested by a line in an article about Vanzetti's hallucinations in prison. Many characters are total inventions by Malamud, others are composites; but the finished product is a panorama of fictional people who come to life through the author's talent. "They are more than the sum of their parts," he feels, and adds: "You cannot put anything together that you don't invent."

The story of Yakov Bok reaches back half a century for its plot, but its meaning is richly contemporary, most specifically in that the hero is the victim of a political situation involving civil rights. Bok is also an existential Jew, a confessed atheist who wrestles with the power and mythology of religion in his prison cell, trying to discover a meaning for what is happening to him, nurtured only by his own inner strength that refuses to yield to meaninglessness.

Malamud sees it further as "dealing with unprotected man—the way we feel unprotected before the A-bomb," and being modern in that. "But it's timeless too, I would hope," he added.

The Jewish aspect of the book is a deeply enriching factor, but the book is not merely a study of Jewishness. The Jew is Malamud's metaphor for any man who suffers. Totally alone with his suffering, the Malamud hero somehow manages to outwit fatalism and avoid despair. How does this happen to the unprotected, existential, persecuted man of this modern era? Other authors find modern man adrift in absurdity, bereft of meaning, hopeless of salvation. But Malamud's men are redeemed, always by themselves.

"It's an idea of yourself," Malamud said, "an ideal that makes human beings die for certain purposes. You find it in the philosophy of Spinoza [which Yakov Bok occasionally reads] who paid a serious price to promulgate his ideas of life and the universe as he saw it."

It's evident, he adds, in many acts of heroism. People who suffer dangers do so because they have "an attitude that it's worth it." Perhaps the suffering is to renew your own life, or for a woman, or an ideal, but "it does depend on an idea that you have."

"It's the same reason we live," he said. "I think most people do think they are living for something—some because their lives are comfortable with beer and TV, some because life is a challenge, a mystery, and some because they have nothing else to do. It varies. But it is the old eternal man that you admire most in literature—the man who must know where he is and who manages to oppose the gods and go on living."

What the Malamud hero represents is that "life is worth living, no matter what the odds." Says the author: "It's an affirmation of life we're dealing with here—people who find life too holy to waste." Of himself he says: "I'm a strong believer in possibility. I believe the surprises of life are extraordinary. I take pleasure that I have a family and that my position as a teacher and writer are not difficult for me."

He quoted the view of Thomas Hobbes, who said that life was "nasty, brutish and short," and Malamud adds: "As long as we have life we may outwit that view."

1966

Pictures of Fidelman: **A Review**

Innocence, guilt, stupidity, fateful Jewishness, and other abstractions have consistently ganged up on the heroes of Bernard Malamud's novels and stories, beating them bloody, driving them to madness, cajoling them into profound commitment, profound silliness.

Now comes art, aggravating Arthur Fidelman, a poor soul.

Fidelman has been on the scene for some time, in three short stories: "The Last Mohican," which appeared in Mr. Malamud's first story collection, *The Magic Barrel*, and also in "Naked Nude" and "Still Life," out of his second collection, *Idiots First*. But the Fidelman stories have seemed like a bunion on the body of Mr. Malamud's major literary concern. Fidelman was wandering around Italy when the major Malamudian personages were struggling for bread in urban ghettos. Fidelman was chasing art, a hoity-toity pastime, when Jewish shoemakers and grocers scrimped pennies.

Later Mr. Malamud moved his attention away from the ghetto, into the northwest with a Jewish professor of literature in *A New Life*, then to Kiev with Yakov Bok, *The Fixer*. He grew and changed as an artist. Now Fidelman represents another renewal—of subject matter, of literary style, of Malamud.

Mr. Malamud seems hardly to need a renewal, fresh from picking up both the Pulitzer Prize and National Book Award with his last work, *The Fixer*. But then the writer who doesn't perpetually renew himself, who is content to imitate his last success, is a writer who dooms himself to extinction. And Mr. Malamud is having none of that.

He has taken those three early stories, touched them up for verve and speed, added three new Fidelman tales, and packaged all six as a picaresque novel called *Pictures of Fidelman*. The achievement seems like ordinary high-level Malamud until the fifth story—or fifth chapter, if you will—called "Pictures of the Artist." In this episode, Mr. Malamud soars out of sight of all his previous stylistic achievements. He has made a collage out of artistic lore, artistic parody, quotations, parables, surrealistic story. The result is one of the most original short stories to come along in years, the high point of the book, a delight, a gem.

It also tells more about Fidelman, the sorry man who is trying to paint a masterwork, but at the same time trying to get in on life's action: "Unable to work, he wandered in the streets in a desolate mood, his spirit dusty in a city of fountains and leaky water taps. Water, water everywhere, spouting, flowing, dripping, whispering secrets, love love love, but not for him. If Rome's so sexy, where's mine?"

From time to time Fidelman finds love of a kind—with Annamaria, the painter, whose guilty secret he unlocks by accident; with Teresa, the chambermaid in the Milan brothel where Fidelman is held prisoner by a whoremaster; with Margherita, a forlorn Venetian wife; and with Beppo, her husband. But all love fails for Fidelman, just as all art fails. Some of his friends see him as a perfectionist, but Fidelman is what the sociologists call other-directed, both in his work and his subsequent judgment of it. He begins writing about Giotto, perceives with outside help that his writing lacks passion, and turns to the real thing, painting. He fails continually to paint a satisfactory portrait of Madonna and Child, though he persists through all of his days. He copies Titian, he sculpts in marble, he sculpts geometric space by digging holes in the ground: "Just as Giotto is said to have been able to draw a perfect free-hand circle, so could Fidelman dig a perfect square hole without measurement."

Hangers-on who talk knowledgeably of art are able to undermine Fidelman's confidence in his work. Outsiders are forever burning his writing, carving up his canvases. All art comes to nothing in Fidelman's grip, and he concludes, "If you're dead how do you go on living?"

The problem, as Mr. Malamud indicates with two quotations in his opening epigraph—one from Rilke, one from Yeats—is that you either perfect the life or the art. Fidelman's aim? "Both." And so he ultimately gets neither. He may have made the masterwork he wanted to make on half a dozen occasions, but he never had enough trust to let it stand by itself. He destroyed the work, or let it be destroyed, and yet nothing ever defeated his zest to make a masterpiece. In Venice, in the final story, he becomes a glass blower, working frantically to learn yet another phase of art.

"Why are you so fanatic about this accursed glass?" a friend asks. "After all, it's only glass."

"Life is short if you don't hurry."

"A fanatic never knows when to stop. It's obvious you want to repeat your fate."

"What fate do you have in mind?"

"Yours."

Fidelman's fate culminates when life, not art, forces him to leave Venice and return to America. He becomes a craftsman in glass back home, art behind him. Gray-haired, he thinks back over his life with melancholy: "I kept my finger in art. Fidelman wept when he was alone."

Pictures of Fidelman is yet another phase of Mr. Malamud's marathon study of failure and defeat, and though there is more mirth in it than in, say, *The Assistant* or *The Fixer*, there is ultimately less optimism. Frank Alpine and Yakov Bok, the heroes of those books, triumph over their fates in the long run, but Fidelman loses his battle to make a masterpiece. Finding anything less than that worthless, he settles for making love to men and women. Life, in a half-baked way, wins, art loses, and though we are all conditioned to revere life above art, Mr. Malamud makes the loss seem sad. Not quite a tragedy, but a painful waste: of Fidelman's time, of Fidelman.

1969

Ernest Hemingway:

His Clear-Hearted Journalism

His Dangerous Summer

His Clear-Hearted Journalism

"**N**ewspaper work," Ernest Hemingway once told an interviewer, "will not harm a young writer and could help him if he gets out of it in time. . . . Journalism, after a point has been reached, can be a daily self-destruction for a serious creative writer."

The attack on journalism by novelists is an old one, often valid. Each morning the reporter empties his head of yesterday's work; each story has its own set of ethics, often different from the reporter's, and he must reflect them honestly. Also, and probably most important, the relentless, horizontal newness of everything becomes a force field against the ruminative, vertical thought essential to fiction.

Yet Hemingway wrote journalism for forty years. Was he pulling our leg about its self-destructive qualities? Not at all, for he was never the conventional journalist, and in all but his early years he practiced the trade irregularly, mainly as a means to an interesting life or extra income. For example, in 1944 he was European bureau chief for *Collier's* magazine, but wrote "only enough to keep from being sent home."

What he wrote was always very special, as is clear from the collection of his articles and dispatches called *By-Line: Ernest Hemingway*, covering the period from his time as a *Toronto Star* reporter in the early 1920s to 1956, when he summed up his attitudes in "A Situation Report" for *Look* magazine. Interspersed are samples of his political reporting, his comments on the European social scene in the twenties, his superb reporting from the Spanish Civil War and World War II, an analytical series on the Far East in mid-1941 (then full of prophecy, now only dull), plus pieces on the Hemingway staples: bullfighting, fishing, hunting.

But it was not the range of his subject matter that made Hemingway unconventional. Many journalists make mush out of equally good material. Rather it was that even as a journalist Hemingway had what someone once called "a clear heart," which made for an almost instant point of view, and he put his personality, his tastes, even his prejudices into his articles. In the early years the story was refracted through Hemingway; in later years the story became a means of listening to the Hemingway mind.

And so most of his dispatches are still lively and readable twenty, thirty, even forty years later. They often take fictional form in terms of description, dialogue and narrative thread. They are vignettes, not news stories, though they tell the news.

Though a reporter named Ernest Hemingway perhaps figures a bit inordinately in the action, his account of the D-Day landing at Normandy may convey what that day was like better than any straight news report could ever do. He rode in a landing craft with the first wave, and his piece begins indirectly.

No one remembers the date of the Battle of Shiloh. But the day we took Fox Green beach was the sixth of June, and the wind was blowing hard out of the northwest. As we moved in toward land in the gray early light, the 36-foot coffin-shaped steel boats took solid green sheets of water that fell on the helmeted heads of the troops packed shoulder to shoulder in the stiff, awkward, uncomfortable, lonely companionship of men going to a battle.

The action, the scene, the detail of Hemingway's best fiction is present in his best journalism. When he tries to check in at a German inn in Bavaria in 1922 he pictures the German hostility to foreigners with a memorable five-page vignette that reads like fiction. He is conveying the thing that made the German arrogance important to him; he is illustrating it, not talking about it:

While we were eating they kept up a fire of comment in German on us *auslanders*. Then they got up to go. They started to come past our end of the table and I stood up and moved my chair forward to let them by. The space was too narrow. There was a perfectly clear way for them to get around the other end of the table. Instead, they grabbed my chair and pushed it. I stood up and let them through, and have regretted it ever since.

This dispatch could stand as a short story. It has the cast of characters, the setting, the conflicts, the secondary plot that lurked in so many of his stories, the good language. To be sure, there is some strained humor, some excess—bald statement, for example—that Hemingway the fictionist would not allow. He chose some of his dispatches to stand as fiction, but not this one. Critics can find fault with it, post facto, and figure out why. Probably because, for him, it didn't serve the deeper purpose that other stories did.

In 1931 he wrote that the

newspaper stuff I have written . . . has nothing to do with the other writing which is entirely apart. . . . The first right that a man writing has is the choice of what he will publish. If you have made your living as a newspaperman, learning your trade, writing against deadlines, writing to make stuff timely rather than permanent, no one has any right to dig this stuff up and use it against the stuff you have written to write the best you can.

But this has been done and the legions of Hemingway fans will be grateful. True, this journalism is not top-drawer Hemingway. But it is fascinating, for here in raw form are the bulls running in Pamplona's streets, the pseudo-artists in Paris, the cowardly lion-hunters, the old fisherman who loses his great catch to sharks, and much more that Hemingway transformed so magically into stories and novels.

"Prose is architecture, not interior decoration," he once said. As a journalist, he was just decorating the room. Later on he built his castles.

1967

His Dangerous Summer

Here we have a great writer who set out to write an epilogue that turned into a book-length manuscript that died of unwieldiness but was years later edited to its literary essence and became a book, truly, and is here with us now, and is good.

The epilogue was conceived by Ernest Hemingway in 1959 to conclude a new edition of his 1932 treatise on bullfighting as life and art, *Death in the Afternoon. Life* magazine editors heard of his plan and asked him to expand the piece into an article of a few thousand words, which they hoped to publish as successfully as they had published his novella, *The Old Man and the Sea.*

Hemingway's subject for the epilogue was the *mano a mano* (or hand-to-hand, a duel) between Spain's two leading matadors, Luis Miguel Domínguín and his brother-in-law, Antonio Ordóñez. Hemingway wrote to his close friend A. E. Hotchner: "It looked like one or the other of the men might be killed and *Life* wanted coverage of it. Instead, it turned out to be the gradual destruction of one person by another with all the things that led up to it and made it. I had to establish the personality and the art and the basic differences between the two great artists and then show what happened, and you can't do that in 4,000 words."

This was Hemingway's way of apologizing for having extended the epilogue to 688 typed pages covered with 108,746 words. What had happened was that he turned both the *mano a mano* and the epilogue into a quest for, and a statement about, his own youth, his own heroism, his own art, his own immortality; for he was dying, psychically and artistically, and he seems to have intuited that.

Hemingway had begun his writing career in journalism and though he denigrated it in later life ("Journalism, after a point has been reached, can be a daily self-destruction for a serious creative writer"), he never really left it. The last two books on which he worked so diligently before his death in 1961 were this one and his superb nonfiction sketches of Paris in the 1920s, *A Moveable Feast.*

He lived all his life with his own *mano a mano* between nonfiction and fiction, primarily believing that fiction was supreme. He told George Plimpton that "you make something through your invention that is not a representation but a whole new thing truer than anything true and alive, and you make it alive, and if you make it well enough, you give it immortality."

In an author's note to his 1935 book on big-game hunting, *The Green Hills of Africa*, he also wrote this: "The writer has attempted to write an absolutely true book to see whether the shape of a country and the pattern of a month's action can, if truly presented, compete with a work of the imagination."

His use of the novelist's tools—dialogue, scene construction, interior monologues—in "The Green Hills" was the style that such New Journalists as Gay Talese and Tom Wolfe would popularize so abundantly well in the 1960s. Hemingway's Ego Journalism, wherein the writer's point of view is more important to the reader than the subject matter, would be carried to splendid new heights in a later generation by writers like Hunter Thompson and Norman Mailer.

The Green Hills of Hemingway, however, was only a valiant failure. The book perished in the bush from overkill: too much hunting detail, too much bang-bang banality, insufficient story. By contrast, his two fictional stories of Africa, "The Snows of Kilimanjaro" and "The Short Happy Life of Francis Macomber," were both masterworks.

By 1959, when Hemingway was sixty years old, his plan to write the bullfight epilogue trapped him anew in journalism, and he went to Spain. He followed the *corridas* (afternoons of bullfighting) in which Dominguín and Ordóñez fought the bulls. He worked manically at recording the small and large details of it all, wrote voluminously for five months and in September 1960 published three articles in *Life*.

I remember the articles. I looked forward to them but could not read them. I don't think I finished even one of the three. The great Hemingway had resuscitated all the boredom I'd felt in reading *The Green Hills*. This was also the response of *Life*'s other readers. The articles were a disaster. Nevertheless, plans continued at Hemingway's publishing house, Charles Scribner's Sons, to publish a book from the material.

For many reasons, chief among them Hemingway's suicide in 1961, the book remained a manuscript with elephantiasis until now, twenty-six years after the writing.

The Dangerous Summer is a singular document, as studded with ironies as it is with taurine terminology. What it is also, because of the long hiatus between inception and publication, is the centerpiece of a much larger composite work that readers may put together for themselves. The basic books required for this composite are Hemingway's *Selected Letters*; the autobiography of his widow, Mary, *How It Was*; A. E. Hotchner's peculiar but valuable 1966 memoir, *Papa Hemingway*; Carlos Baker's biography, *Hemingway: A Life Story*; James A. Michener's nonfiction book on Spain, *Iberia*; and a long and sensitive memoir by a Spanish journalist, José Luis Castillo-Puche, called *Hemingway in Spain*.

When they confront the subject of the aged Hemingway, from 1959 until his death and its aftermath, these books together offer a prismatic vision of the dying artist, a complex and profoundly dramatic story of a man's extraordinary effort to stay alive; so that when we come to Mr. Baker's succinct and powerful final sentence in the biography, we have a new comprehension not only of a writer's despair but of suicide as a not unreasonable conclusion to a blasted life. "He slipped in two shells," Mr. Baker writes, "lowered the gun butt carefully to the floor, leaned forward, pressed the twin barrels against his forehead just above the eyebrows and tripped both triggers."

The Dangerous Summer, as centerpiece to Hemingway's final tragedy, does stand alone. It is novella-length, 45,000 words, with an introduction by James Michener that defines terms necessary for understanding the bullfight world as Hemingway describes it. Mr. Michener is reverential to the memory of Hemingway, but as an aficionado of the bulls himself he finds fault with Hemingway's conclusions.

Mr. Michener had access to the entire original manuscript and says it is so excessively detailed that most readers would not finish it. Hemingway knew it was far too long. Mr. Hotchner went to see him in Havana and reported that Hemingway, not trusting *Life*'s editors to cut his work, had labored for twenty-one full days by himself and cut only 278 words.

Hemingway plaintively asked for Mr. Hotchner's help in the cutting but then strangely rejected all suggested cuts with explanations in writing to Mr. Hotchner, who was in the same room with him. Hemingway's mind was out of control and would get progressively worse. His vaunted ability to leave out what was irrelevant, his great talent for synthesis, were malfunctioning.

Mr. Hotchner pressed on, but Hemingway continued to resist. "What I've written is Proustian in its cumulative effect, and if we eliminate detail we destroy that effect," he told Mr. Hotchner.

On the fourth day of talk Hemingway yielded, the editing began, and 54,916 words were excised. These are Mr. Hotchner's figures, and they differ somewhat from Mr. Michener's; but then Mr. Hotchner did the cutting. The residual manuscript went to *Life* and formed the basis for the three articles. Charles A. Scribner, Jr., said earlier this year that he tried to cut the script to publishable size in later years, eventually giving it to a Scribner editor named Michael Pietsch, who reduced it to its present size, "a wonderful job" by Mr. Scribner's lights.

And so here is Hemingway—who derided F. Scott Fitzgerald's "gigantic, preposterous" outline for *The Last Tycoon* and wrote that Fitzgerald would never have finished the book—unable to finish his own runaway journalism. Here is Hemingway—calling Thomas Wolfe the "over-bloated Lil Abner of literature" and saying that if Wolfe's editor (and his own), Maxwell Perkins of Scribners, "had not cut one-half million words out of Mr. Wolfe everybody would know how he was"—psychopathically viewing his own rampant verbosity as sacrosanct.

Nevertheless, I concur with Mr. Scribner that Mr. Pietsch has done a wonderful editing job. Hemingway was very cuttable, and the book is indeed wonderful; but the question remains: Whose wonderfulness is it? Is it half Hemingway? Hemingway by thirds? Should the byline read: "Words Put In by Hemingway, Words Taken Out by Hotchner and Pietsch"? When the same issue was raised with Thomas Wolfe about his reliance on Maxwell Perkins to produce a coherent book, Wolfe left Perkins, even left Scribners, to assert his independence.

The question is not easily answered, for there is another question: Does it really matter, in terms of what the finished book is? And just what is the book? When I began reading it, I felt instantly in the presence of the old Hemingway wit. At the Spanish border in 1953, his first return to Spain since the Spanish Civil War, he expects hostility because he fought against Franco. A border policeman asks: "Are you any relation of Hemingway the writer?" And Hemingway answers, "Of the same family." Instead of enmity he finds warm welcome, and the policeman has read all of his books.

He quickly takes us into the bullring and gives us a lesson in how to cheat at bullfighting. You shave the bull's horns so they are sensitive and he is not so deadly with them; or you use a young bull who does not yet know how to use his horns; or you drop a heavy sack of feed on the small of the bull's back so his hind legs are weakened and he is a diminished threat to the bullfighter. Hemingway accused the managers of the once-great Manolete of shaving horns, and when the articles appeared in *Life*, Hemingway was attacked by Spanish aficionados and idolators of Manolete.

We soon meet Ordóñez, the son of Cayetano Ordóñez, who was Hemingway's friend in the 1920s and the model for the bullfighter Pedro Romero in *The Sun Also Rises*. Hemingway tells Ordóñez he is better than his father. "I could see he had the three great requisites for a matador: courage, skill in his profession and grace in the presence of the danger of death." But in the same paragraph, after Ordóñez asks to see him, Hemingway tells himself: "Don't start being friends with bullfighters again and especially not with this one when you know how good he is and how much you will have to lose if anything happens to him." But Hemingway doesn't heed his own advice, could not heed it. He was in the grip of a compulsion to return to bullfighting, to revisit Pamplona, the setting of *The Sun Also Rises*, where he had become a mythic figure, and to re-create the past when he was living so well, writing so well.

He also meets the capable enemy, Dominguín, and describes him in a fine sentence: "Luis Miguel was a charmer, dark, tall, no hips, just a touch too long in the neck for a bullfighter, with a grave mocking face that went from professional disdain to easy laughter." There is a bronze life-size statue of Dominguín in his own home, and Hemingway finds this odd but uses it to define his qualified vision of Dominguín: "I thought Miguel looked better than his statue although his statue looked just a little bit nobler."

Hemingway returns to Spain in 1959 and very early on establishes the Dominguín-Ordóñez rivalry. Ordóñez emerges as a saintly fighter, who even when the bulls are stupid can work with them until they are brave. "His second bull was difficult too but he rebuilt him."

Dominguín alternates between being brave, noble and talented, and being a cheat: He "really loved to fight bulls and he forgot about being rich when he was in the ring. But he wanted the odds in his favor and the odds were the tampering with the horns."

Hemingway and his entourage traverse Spain by car, and he exults in victory like a great hunter: "We were like a happy tribe after a successful raid or a great killing." Along the way, as always in his best works, he celebrates food and wine and companionship and evokes a vivid sense of place in both present time and in memory.

These moments also serve as changes of pace from the tense reporting on the rivalry, the bulls, the wounds, the pain, the ascension toward the exalted climax. The competition peaks at Málaga on August 14, 1959, with both matadors triumphing over their bulls. Hemingway even approves of Dominguín.

"He made two series of eight naturales [passes with a small red cloth] in beautiful style and then on a right-hand pass with the bull coming at him from the rear, the bull had him. . . . The horn seemed to go into his body and the bull tossed him a good six feet or more into the air. His arms and legs were spread wide, the sword and muleta were thrown clear and he fell on his head. The bull stepped on him trying to get the horn into him and missed him twice. . . . He was up in an instant. The horn had not gone in but had passed between his legs . . . and there was no wound. [He] paid no attention to what the bull had done to him and waving everyone away went on with his faena [work]."

Dominguín goes on also to be overshadowed by Ordóñez in the fourth *mano a mano* at Ciudad Real, and Hemingway ends the chapter on a note of negative suspense: that Dominguín will now go on to Bilbao "to be destroyed."

The final chapter is a triumph—for Hemingway. He throws aside journalistic convention and as novelist enters into the heads of the matadors as they battle to the conclusion Hemingway knew was inevitable.

On Dominguín: "Too many things were piling up and he was running out of luck. It was one thing to live to be the number one in the world

in his profession. . . . It was another thing to be almost killed each time
he went out to prove it."

On Ordóñez: "A bullfighter can never see the work of art that he is
making. He has no chance to correct it as a painter or a writer has. . . .
He can only feel it and hear the crowd's reaction to it. . . . The public
belonged to him now. He looked up at them and let them know, modestly
but not humbly, that he knew it. [He] was happy that he owned them."

So that, in brief, is the book and while I have lived remote from bullfighting all my life, have next to no personal interest in it and tend to
identify with the bulls, I think nevertheless that "The Dangerous Summer" is one of the best sports books I have ever read. Not everyone
could agree. Dominguín, who retired in 1961 and came back to the bulls
in 1971, said in a 1972 book about him by Keith Botsford that Hemingway was "a commonplace bore . . . a crude and vulgar man" who
"knew nothing about fighting bulls." He dismissed Ordóñez as a "cowardly fighter" with "feet of clay all the way up to his brain."

In *Iberia*, Mr. Michener reports on the latter-day Ordóñez, the man
Hemingway said could be one of the greatest matadors of all time. In a
corrida at Pamplona the crowd dislikes his work and so Ordóñez spitefully
kills the bull in a disgraceful way. "It was a shame-filled conclusion to
a shameful performance," Mr. Michener says, and the crowd chants:
"*¡Ordóñez, Ordóñez, sinvergüenza! Ordóñez, Ordóñez, paga la prensa*"
("Ordóñez, Ordóñez, shameless one! Ordóñez, Ordóñez, pays the
newspapers"—to write well of him).

Mr. Castillo-Puche, who was close to Hemingway, argues in *Hemingway in Spain* that the *mano a mano* series was a publicity stunt, that
Hemingway was suckered by the promoters and that Ordóñez used him
to advance his career.

All of that may be true, and in the last judgment by the bulls of
history, Hemingway may be gored in his journalistic femoral artery. But
that is irrelevant to why this is an important and wonderful book. The
value emerges from the subtext, which seems to have two principal
elements: the drive to write this book and the behavior of the writer as
he reports and writes it.

How does a man fight the dying of the light? Is it really with rage?
Mr. Castillo-Puche writes: "I saw [Hemingway] get all confused, tear

up whole sections of his manuscript, rip up photographs or fling them across the room in a fit of temper, swear at those present in the room and others elsewhere, and swear at himself."

Also, while they are at the Pamplona fiesta, Hemingway, Ordóñez and other friends make "prisoners" of two young American women and keep them in thrall for a month. Hemingway writes that "turning up with a couple of prisoners is sometimes ill-received in marital circles." Mr. Castillo-Puche says that Hemingway's relations with all the young women in Spain that year were very chaste, but Hemingway's wife, Mary, was less than thrilled, especially when Hemingway took yet another "prisoner," a young Irish woman named Valery Danby-Smith, who, Mary says in her autobiography, "became Ernest's secretary-handmaiden." Miss Danby-Smith remained close to Hemingway until his death and eventually married his son Gregory.

Mary writes that in the new situation, a "nonstop circus," she became "inaudible" to Hemingway. Soon she "seemed also to be invisible, a worthless quality in a wife," and so returned to Cuba and wrote Hemingway that she was leaving him. He cabled his respect for her views but disagreed profoundly with her decision to leave. "Still love you" he added, and she stayed on until the end.

The pursuit of young women, the vicarious life as a matador, the preening before hordes of autograph-seekers in Pamplona, everything is monkey glandular to Hemingway: "The wine was as good as when you were twenty-one, and the food as marvelous as always. There were the same songs and good new ones. . . . The faces that were young once were old as mine but everyone remembered how we were."

The self-portrait and the portrait-in-the-round from the other books emerge with great clarity. The *mano a mano* is also a story made to order for the dying man's need not to die. He creates Ordóñez as an immortal, for isn't that the status of all the very best dead people?

Hemingway went to Spain searching for youth and found mortality and madness. But what is clear is that this story, these sentences and paragraphs, however truncated from the original, are not the work of a lunatic, and could not have been written by anyone except Hemingway or his spirit. If this work had been publishable, or even conceivable, at this length and with this quality during his lifetime, he might not have shot himself. But that's not how it was.

It is only over Hemingway's dead body that this book could have come to be. And I think it very clever of Hemingway's spirit to relent about the editing and come back to Scribners to tell the folks there how to prepare the text.

1985

J. P. Donleavy:

Captivated by Ginger:
A Non-Interview

> There was a man
> Who made a boat
> To sail away
> And it sank
>
> Grunt and Growl
> Spit and scowl
> You poor pigs
> Are just foul.

The author of the verse is J. P. (James Patrick) Donleavy, forty-two, a hero. He wrote the novel *The Ginger Man*, from which the poems above are taken, and need write nothing else to preserve hero status. Few men make such a contribution. Last week *The Ginger Man* was again out of stock at a local bookstore. Last week you had to get on the waiting list to get the book from the public library.

Last week also J. P. Donleavy made a rare public appearance, at the Poetry Center of the YM–YWHA in New York City, and the youthful people to whom he speaks turned out in a lump to see him, hear him read from his works and hear him deliver a paper on "the tools and traumas of the writing trade." With sideburns, beards, minis and micros, with umbrellas on the wrist and leather boots up to the thigh, with Brooks Brothers vests and Abercrombie and Fitch oversize belts, they came to see Donleavy.

Michael J. Pollard, the unforgettable "C. W." of Bonnie and Clyde's movie gang, was there in his black cowboy hat, long black muffler, black boots and shoulder-length frizzy hair. Young androgynes with horn rims and rounding shoulders, sweet things with cherry-blossom smiles on the wane, knots of unkempt hippies and earnest young creative writing students with weak mustaches, disparate, all of them, all the way to their toenails, militantly individualistic, questers all for that recognizable image that would set them apart—all were joined together in this quiet, anticipatory moment in unquestioning admiration for the hero himself, the man who created Sebastian Balfe Dangerfield, that rogue.

There never has been a rogue like Dangerfield in contemporary literature. He couldn't be put on the screen, not yet, not in America, for he is the most unsympathetic, lying, thieving, drunken, unwashed, brawling, lecherous, foul-mouthed, godless and totally engaging fellow imaginable; and that isn't the mixture that American filmmakers are clamoring to personify in the movies.

But Dangerfield is the totally unrepressed hero to the young people today who spit in the eye of the world as it is, or who would like to. And the man who made Dangerfield come to life—wasn't he, too, bound to be a bit of a rogue himself?

Donleavy strode onto the stage of the Poetry Center in a checkered suit with matching vest, a heavy, Irish-tweedy kind of suit the horsey folk might wear; that, and a solid brown tie and purple pocket handkerchief; all that and thick, powder-gray hair, and dark beard.

> Trust no man,
> Not even your brother,
> If his hair be one color
> And his beard
> Be another.

But should we mistrust Donleavy? He put his sheaf of paper on the dais and acquitted himself of literary pretension immediately.

"Writing," he said, "is turning one of your worst moments into money." The motives for wanting to be a writer, he said, are "women and money, fun and money, and sometimes just money all alone by itself." He said the writer dreams of himself being at home and successful in a beautiful world . . . the author as sailor, "with a gentle breeze and two published novels behind him."

He dreams of girls telling him: "Gee. Your conversation is even more beautiful than your book. . . . Gosh. You're even better-looking than your photograph." Such dreams get dreamt, he explained, at the kitchen table, over peanut butter. But the young, would-be writer knows that writing is antisocial, anticommunity, because it's not a job, and when people ask him: what are you going to be when you grow up, he thinks: "All I can say is rich." But he learns cunning, and says "I'm going to be a doctor."

At length he writes poems, grows up, marries, fathers a baby and discovers that to continue being a writer he needs the first indispensable tool: money—"for the purchase of time, the writer's most important ingredient . . ." He needs time to write the first page and "brood that I will never write a second." But a chord is struck and you're on your way, a writer. "Now you have a desk, typewriter, carbon paper and a vague confidence that what you have written somebody will want to read and will make Mama and Papa die of shame."

As a writer you slip back from the world and your old friends say: "This isn't the same George we used to know who told us he was going to be a doctor." But he writes on, and then one day he's got a manuscript. He looks around for someone to show it to but all his old friends are gone on the way to higher degrees. But there is one old friend who reads it. "He says you're crazy. You pull away the bottle of wine, and he says: Wait. Maybe you're a genius."

Meanwhile, in a big skyscraper in New York sits a guy who majored in English and you send him the manuscript. He is the fellow who feels: "I read Proust in the original straight through one summer on the Cape and I'm sure there is no new Proust budding in the grass." The publisher "finds he is glued to every word and shocked in the bargain. But he is convinced it is not literature."

This, said Donleavy, is an infallible rule: "What is original, vital and offered will be rejected. Everyone is searching for what is new and original, while they're handing over a check to an agent for some imitation of last year's big success."

But then "word gets around that the author looks well in a bathing costume. . . . A girl from Radcliffe said so." And "sex gets whispered about and gets translated into a contract. . . . And then the wind is blowing through the author's hair, making the sound of fresh banknotes."

He discovers after publication that someone wants to film the book, he looks at his contract and finds that 75 percent of such money goes to the publisher, and the author says to himself: "Those dirty rats."

Then the author discovers "the last tool of the writing trade—a lawyer." He also finds that the critics are always his enemy, except through the years they take more and more space to condemn him." And he finds that as he goes along as a published author, he still needs money.

Said Donleavy: "It is a victory to reach the age of forty, be solvent and still love your trade."

The hero smiled, stopped talking and while the audience applauded he took his rather British accent (born in Brooklyn, he now divides his time between London and the Isle of Man) and strode off into the wings. Odd, but this well-behaved fellow seemed not at all like Sebastian Dangerfield. So tidy, so calm, so tailored. Certainly a closer look was in order, a few questions on life-style were in order, a bit of probing beneath this façade was in order.

And so this visiting gawker joined several other visiting gawkers at the stage door and rapped for admittance. A man with a bald head opened the door four inches and said Mr. Donleavy wasn't granting any interviews. Later? he was asked. The man shrugged just as a lovely girl in a purple dress arrived, looking wifely and acting proprietary when she heard Mr. Donleavy being discussed.

"Oh no," said the lovely lady. "He's especially said he didn't want to talk to anyone."

"Would you inquire again, please? We've come a great distance to see him."

The lovely lady smiled, the bald man grimaced and closed the door and the gawkers waited, and waited. Then the bald man reappeared shaking his head. Mr. Donleavy did not feel well.

"No interview later either?"

"Not back here. When he leaves here it's up to him."

And so all gawkers reseated themselves when the lights flickered the end of intermission and the hero reappeared on stage and read from his works—"The Saddest Summer of Samuel S.," "Meet My Maker the Mad Molecule," "A Singular Man" and two passages from a novel in progress:

The Beastly Beatitudes of Balthazar B. He read the final paragraph of *The Ginger Man* and the audience broke into prolonged applause, double the heartiness they gave his other readings.

Outraged
And captivated
By ginger.

The audience asked him two questions. How does a writer continue after he dries up or loses his vision? Donleavy said that was a very American question. He said when troubles pile on, you worry about the troubles and have no time to worry about the impetus to write. So you just write. And a mustached man asked him: you write so much about money, how are you doing financially? And Donleavy said, like an old Irish saying, "I'm like a dog at its father's funeral, neither sad nor glad. So I'd be described as being comfortably off."

And that was the end of the program, and once again the gawkers lined up, with their books and pencils at the ready for autographs, so many of them feeling what J. D. Salinger wrote in *Catcher in the Rye*: "What really knocks me out is a book that, when you're all done reading it, you wish the author that wrote it was a terrific friend of yours and you could call him up on the phone whenever you felt like it."

Touch the Ginger fellow when he comes. Get him to write his name. Take it home and look at it. He's so droll. So witty. Here he comes. With his collar up. In his tweeds. With the lovely. And another fellow who looks like an editor. Who read Proust one summer on the Cape. Taking the pencil. Signing his name as the girlies look.

"Where do you get the money to buy all these expensive books?"

"From my youth," says a girlie.

He moves on. Must keep moving or never get to the street. Remember George Smith, the Singular Man. Remember his philosophy: "Show people you're in command of the situation by not saying much, don't let them get in close, keep everyone at arm's length, stop smiling kindly." And Donleavy moves along, while a young man with Hitler's mustache and thin rims bulls through to say his piece. Mr. Donleavy, he says, I read *The Ginger Man* in law school, but I passed anyway. Hee hee. Smiles all around.

"Excuse me, sir, but would you be available at any time for an interview? Tonight? Tomorrow for a little while? Leisurely interview. Over a few cold beers? At lunch? Any time at all?"

Head down, Donleavy. Look indifferent. Give them the message you're self-contained. But he talks to his chest. He seems terrified by scenes. Won't look. Smiles into his vest.

"Possibly next time. Can't really. Write me in England."

Another pencil, another book. It's over now. All over. No interview. No conversation with the hero. Too bad. Could have told gamy Irish stories. Stayed up till dawn. Strode through the streets in search of additional beer and rashers of bacon. Ah, what might have been. If only the Ginger Man were a terrific friend of ours. But he isn't. So all we can say is.

Ding
Dong.

For Donleavy wrote it himself:

If
There's a bell
In Dingle
And you want to say
How sorry you are
I'm gone
Ring it
And make it go
Ding dong.

1968

James Baldwin:
The Distractions
of Fame

66 6**B**e careful what you set your heart upon,' someone once said to me, 'for it will surely be yours.' Well, I had said that I was going to be a writer, God, Satan, and Mississippi notwithstanding, and that color did not matter, and that I was going to be free."

Today, at the age of thirty-nine, James Baldwin is indeed a writer, one of the nation's most successful and varied. Already accomplished in the essay, the short story, and the novel, he's preparing to enter a new medium, the Broadway stage. His first play, *Blues for Mr. Charlie*, is in the hands of director Frank Corsaro and the Actors Studio Theater.

The Studio reported last week that the drama will open in late February or early March—exact date still unspecified—as its second production of the season. (June Havoc's *Marathon '33* is the first.) Rehearsals begin January 15, and Sidney Poitier is likely to head the cast.

Mr. Baldwin discussed the play in a recent interview conducted in a friend's apartment on New York's Lower East Side. He has his own New York apartment, but he was literally "hiding out," away from the distractions that would ensue if people knew where he was.

During part of the play's creation, in fact, he fled to Puerto Rico. In New York, he explained, memories of violence and misery wreak havoc with his mind. "I'm just going to survive it," he said, "and get out of here. Maybe to Sicily. You could drown in this very quickly."

Exhausted from a day's rewriting of one section of the drama, Mr. Baldwin explained that the play was a year in the creation and five years in the mind. Its genesis occurred when he worked as personal assistant to director Elia Kazan during the Broadway productions of Archibald

MacLeish's *J. B.*, and Tennessee Williams's *Sweet Bird of Youth*. He began work in earnest after finishing his last novel, *Another Country*.

The play, he explained, "pivots on the death of a Negro boy, twenty to twenty-five years old, who left his home in the Deep South, turned into a rock-and-roll singer and a junkie, came home, and was murdered.

"The play is the reconstruction of the crime. I'm not interested in who did it, but in all the forces of the black and white people in the town that made this death inevitable. It is not, I hope, about race at all, but about people in torment who don't know how to liberate themselves from it."

Mr. Baldwin's thirty-two-year-old brother David, an actor for five years, will play the murdered man. The author calls the role "not a major part, but a crucial part."

And after *Mr. Charlie*, what? Mr. Baldwin has plenty of forthcoming projects: a movie version of *Another Country*; a film script of Faulkner's *Light in August*, to star Marlon Brando; a book of essays, *The Beast in the Playground*; a book of short stories, *Come Once Again and Love Me*; a book on Africa; and magazine interviews with Paul Robeson and Ray Charles, the blind singer.

It's evident that Mr. Baldwin has come a long way from the day he vowed to be a writer and to be free, color notwithstanding. But his life hasn't come off entirely as planned. True, he has lost his Harlem chains, and he's well off financially. But he's discovered the world can still be hostile.

"I thought that in becoming a writer I would become safe," he says, "but now I know better."

Further, he is trapped in his status—forced to set up a wall of protective friends to fend off intrusions, forced to keep on the move to insure some measure of privacy. But he moves not merely to keep his life peaceful. He moves to work—the same work he has been doing since the beginning: telling himself (and letting others listen in) what it means to be a highly intelligent Negro in mid-twentieth-century America.

"I started writing when I left home at seventeen," he said. "I wasn't trying to become a writer so much as to save my life. And that is the only way I could do it."

Though he began his first novel in those years, he didn't finish it until ten years later. He was sorting out his rage, trying to understand his misery. "I was in a very bad state," he said. "My whole growing up had been pretty awful and I couldn't get over my father, either in reality or the imagination, and I figured if I was ever going to grow up I would have to forgive him, get past him."

His father was a preacher in Harlem. His son's first novel, *Go Tell It on the Mountain*, had a sensual and egocentric Harlem preacher as a chief character.

James Baldwin has written of his early days of struggle: "When I was about twenty-one I had enough done of a novel to get a Saxton Fellowship. When I was twenty-two the fellowship was over, the novel turned out to be unsalable, and I started waiting on tables in a Greenwich Village restaurant and writing book reviews." He obtained a Rosenwald Fellowship for a second book, which met the same fate as the first. Then: "By the time I was twenty-four I had decided to stop reviewing books about the Negro problem . . . and I packed my bags and went to France, where I finished *Go Tell It on the Mountain*."

The Paris years were the gestation period for Mr. Baldwin's second novel, *Giovanni's Room*. They also were years of escape from a hostile America—and of eventual confrontation with the fact that hostile or not, America was his home. But before that confrontation came the beginning of his essays and a head-on conflict with his hero and early god, the Negro novelist Richard Wright, then a longtime expatriate in Paris.

Mr. Baldwin's first essay was a piece called "Harlem Ghetto," written at the request of the late *Commentary* magazine editor Robert Warshow. He recalled the experience in the interview: "It was very important discipline. I had to say what I meant, and it was very difficult, for I didn't know what I meant. I was so full of rage and pain that I had to find some way of chilling it, controlling it, and the essay worked for that, for I had to be clear about it and get at what I really felt."

His next essay, which caused the conflict with Mr. Wright, was "Everybody's Protest Novel," which he says was a regurgitation of all the thoughts he had while reviewing the "Negro problem" novels. The essay's focus was on *Uncle Tom's Cabin*. Though that book had been of great importance to him as a writer, he was repelled by the spate of novels of similar design that he had read and reviewed. He found them invariably bad, and described them as "fantasies, connecting nowhere with reality, sentimental."

The protest novel, he felt, was a failure because of "its rejection of life, the human being, the denial of his beauty, dread, power, in its insistence that it is his categorization alone which is real and which cannot be transcended."

He felt that Bigger Thomas, the protagonist of Mr. Wright's *Native Son*, however powerful, was merely an opposite portrait from Uncle Tom—"the one uttering merciless exhortations, the other shouting curses"—and that Mr. Wright was guilty of dehumanization in the name of protest.

In Paris, Mr. Wright accused Mr. Baldwin of betraying him and of pursuing "that art-for-arts-sake crap." This disagreement split the two men, and later reconciliations never really healed the break. Mr. Baldwin was further disenchanted with Mr. Wright for his long expatriation ("I had the impression that in order to be able to live in Paris he was able to let a great deal go by the board—his indignation, his impulses") and for what he said was Mr. Wright's desire to be king of the literary mountain.

Now, though, Mr. Baldwin feels the writing he did about Mr. Wright in the early days was "wrong through a certain lack of charity." He made amends, as far as he could, in an essay written after Mr. Wright's death: "Alas Poor Richard." But, he added in the interview: "when you're an idol you're in great danger. The effort is not to become king of the mountain. You're supposed to keep on working. I think if you depend on these other things you inevitably dry up. So, uncharitable as it was, I think that what I wrote about Richard was true. I haven't changed my mind about it."

He quickly admits that changing public attitudes will make part of his own work, as they did with Mr. Wright's, obsolete. But he tried to imbue his writing with the humanity he found lacking in the work of others who wrote about Negroes. He wants his future work, he said, "to be looser, like *Don Quixote*, and stonier, like *Oedipus Rex*—artless, so that it moves the way anything that grows moves.

"At bottom," he said, "it's very hard to tell the truth to yourself. But I think that's the major effort one has got to make. If you do that you are outside the morality you live in, outside the system of values of the people around you. You're suspect because you're examining. You are made to be very lonely, and if you're lonely enough you can perish."

These thoughts are ages away from the time when the Baldwin boy worshipped Paul Robeson and Joe Louis and hoped to grow up like Richard Wright and Charles Dickens. He once defined his early purpose: ". . . To wrest from the world fame and money and love."

He was reminded of this and he commented: "Fame and money— that's always a fantasy. The real drive is to be loved, to be free. I'm not really trying to be famous or even win the Nobel Prize. But I am trying to live."

1964

The Beat Generation:
Ginsberg's Albany Pain
Where Did They Go?
Everywhere.

Ginsberg's Albany Pain

I
Hospital Visitation

> White knees lifting and falling under bedsheet
> Broke-hipped Ginsberg in river of talk
> The words arise
> as from a poet, garrulous spew turning true
> inside nonsense fun exquisitely straying
> out of a stumped body

II
Letter to the Poet

Sent by Mr. Anonymous, A Resident of Thruway Motel.

"OK Beardo. Let's see you write one of your filthy poems(?) based on this picture—Pain In Vietnam? No Pain in Jordan? Make a 'big' statement on Israeli aggression! You don't dare."

III
An Elaboration

The letter came to the poet, Allen Ginsberg, while he was hospitalized at Memorial Hospital in Albany, following a story about him in the newspaper. In the story he talked of his own pain after suffering broken hip in auto accident, then related it to pain suffered by Vietnamese in war being waged by U.S. "We're mass producing this pain for them," said the poet.

Accompanying beardo letter was photograph from newspaper captioned "A Kiss of Grief." It showed Jordanian man kissing his dead child, killed by Israeli bombs during raid at Irbid Eara in Northwest Jordan.

IV
The Poet's First Response to the Letter

"He's right, up to the point where he wants vengeance like Jehovah. And then he gets in the same bag. He's quite right. Pain is everywhere."

V
Accumulation

In the poet's room, 208, friends and strangers had left a spoor: get-well fruit basket. Merry Christmas card in Chinese, photo reprint of Rimbaud as an adolescent, Pastilles—purple anise-flavored candies with 14th century tradition, magazines with Chicago stories, a bottle of Micrin, a scout knife, and books: the Mahatma Letters. Blake. The Gnostics. Teilhard de Chardin. And daisies in a vase.

VI
News of the Poet

He will be on crutches for six months. His book, *Planet News* ($2, City Lights Books), has had 25,000 copies issued in first printing, based on 15,000 advance orders. "Planet News," says Ginsberg-written cover blurb, "collecting seven years Poesy scribed to 1967 begins with electronic politics disassociation & messianic rhapsody TV Baby in New York, continues picaresque around the world globe . . ."

In hospital, poet adds: "It's a chronology. It records all my changes as I went around the world." He adds: "The publication is a very big event for me." He adds: "Two of the poems in the book were dictated into a tape recorder, 'Wichita Vortex Sutra' and 'City Midnight Junk Strains.' " He adds that he changed only about one percent of the dictation in editing. He adds the dictating was made possible through gift of $500 from Bob Dylan. He adds: "Dylan asked me if I needed anything for my work and gave me five hundred dollars to buy the machine. He gave Michael McClure an autoharp and Peter Orlovsky a guitar."

VII
Financial News

"The hospital bill will wipe out my personal bank account."

"There's always driblets coming in."

"City Lights pays once a year."

"I get more from my readings, from one thousand to two thousand dollars, unless I do it cheaper for a smaller school."

(He could ask for more, and probably get it, but doesn't. Why doesn't he?)

"If they had to give me more it means they would not be able to do more that season, like get Eldridge Cleaver. . . ."

VIII
A Poem Is Born

". . . also it gets like a state visit. They think if they're spending that much money that they're entertaining the King of Siam. And the day gets formal. . . ."

IX
A Pause

(To define terms for subsequent clarity)

Microprosopus: From Chapter 25, The Wisdom of the Kaballah: "A human-formed appearance of the Holy of Holy Ones, the Concealed one of All."

Microprosopus: From Ginsberg: "The name of the human manifestation in the image of the formless, unknown god, very self righteous."

X
The Ginsberg-Spoken Poem Begins

Then they want you to come in spats, in a helicopter, an am-
      bulance, with a bodyguard,
They want you to meet the basketball team and have press

conferences and batteries of microphones and TV cameras
Whether you like it or not.
And you're not allowed to get (loved)
And you have to have a prepared speech.

Above $4,000 you have to bring Bob Dylan as accompanist.
Above $6,000 you have to get Shea Stadium and worry about
     assassination.
Over $10,000 you have to be assassinated by a black bullet
          in red and blue spotlight
          by a militant ex-Catholic homosexual
          who wants to draw attention quite justly
               to the starving Biafran Arabs
                    upon whom the Israelis
                         are inflicting
                              physical pain.

So—since I just got ten grand from the Arab League
To play the Mosque in Jerusalem.
I hereby announce the Israelis have trespassed the bounds of
     the Unknown Gods
And that Jehovah is an egotist
          inflicting cruel and mortal pain
               on Palestinian refugees.

I've gone too far.
Stop.
Yes, stop. Everyone's gone too far.

I've been thinking about this. This may be where it all begins.
     Where the earth blows up.
Earth may enter its climactic seizure of grief and
                                        self pity
          and blow itself up out of sheer spite
          of its long, semitic nose.
They're both semites.
They're all worshipping an implacable
     Microprosopus,
          a thoroughly evil creation of the human brain,

that jealous god.
His egotism continually leads to quarreling
   and disputation
      over the justice of his nose.

XI
Title of the Poem
"Pain In Albany, Pain In Northwest Jordan, Pain In Holy Land."

1968

Where Did They Go? Everywhere.

I just read a book called *The Beat Generation* (Scribners), expecting
to be as bored as you probably expect to be when that decade-dead
phenomenon is resurrected as a subject. We've all read all we need to
read about that old bunch of boys, right? Wrong. Bruce Cook has turned
out a first-rate piece of literary journalism that gives us a history of the
Beats in a way that relates them to now—to rock lyrics (through The
Fugs), to LSD (through the Leary-Ginsberg axis), to Woodstock-as-
religion, to the new journalism and much more. The history of the
movement that began in 1955 in San Francisco is woven into Cook's
tour of the world to track down the Beats-that-were: William Burroughs
and Alexander Trocchi in London; Gregory Corso and Seymour Krim
(late-blooming Beat) in New York; Gary Snyder and Michael McClure
in San Francisco; Jack Kerouac, before he died, drinking in his hometown, Lowell, Massachusetts; Allen Ginsberg, everywhere. Cook's book
is not only fine reporting, it is funny and vital in the way Morley Cal-
laghan's *That Summer in Paris* was funny and vital about another generation. And it is written in relaxed American, a prose suited to the
anti-academic stance of the Beats. Cook, book editor of the *National
Observer*, is no Beat, no hipster, no hippie. He passes himself off as a
reporter who looks as square as he shoots, and consequently is suspect.
Trocchi thought he was a CIA agent. Cook's analysis is sharp, occa-

sionally eloquent, as when he psychs out Allen Ginsberg's relationship to woman, based on two poems: "The Change," and the very long *Kaddish*, which Cook thinks is the best poem by an American since World War II.

He is so sympathetic to the Beats that the book is eventually top-heavy with goodwill. Though this is a redemptive counterweight to the antipathy the Beats have always found everywhere in America, a heavy dollop of the kind of antipathy that existed then, and now, would have given the book more balance. The Beats' feud with the academy still bubbles venomously along, which came clear last March at the National Book Awards. Ginsberg, a poetry judge, was the short end of a four-to-one vote for Mona Van Duyn's *To See, To Take*. He was vigorously for Gregory Corso's *Elegiac Feelings American*. After Van Duyn won, Ginsberg stood up and chanted a poem to the press in his best bardic baritone: "Hum, hum, hum / Gregory Corso's genius despised, / Muses bored, / Mediocrity is prized— / [Bleepbleep] the award / Hum, hum, hum."

Poet Richard Howard, also a judge, and Ginsberg wrote on the subject in the April 4 *New York Times Book Review*, an exchange worth reading as a coda to Cook's book. Said Howard to Ginsberg: "You want a poetry of ecstasy and you will not even endure, much less endorse, a poetry of excellence." Said Ginsberg: ". . . it will be dispiriting for the multitude of poets in America and the revolutionarily sensitive-minded youthful readers of poetry if prizes continue to be awarded to poets whose work is not even *exciting*—who methodically denounce inspiration. . . ." The poetry renaissance the Beats generated never really has been taken note of, either by NBA or Pulitzer Prize judges. The poetry the Beats resent being prized was described by poet-playwright-novelist Michael McClure, talking to Cook: ". . . these tremulous little odes about lawn-mowers running over frogs—but neither the lawnmower or the frog they write about are real. Furthermore, they think that what they write is good, more genuine, because it's written in iambic pentameter. *Imagine!* Why, you ought to be able to teach any reasonably attentive twelve-year-old child to *speak* in iambic pentameter in about an hour."

Seymour Krim talks of the same idea, but doesn't restrict it to poetry. He calls it the " 'Dare I eat a peach?' self-consciousness practiced in both the universities and the influential big-little magazines like the *Partisan* and *Kenyon* reviews." Krim's latest book, *Shake It for the World*,

Smartass (Dial), published last year, is another major insight into Beat influence. Especially noteworthy is his essay "The Kerouac Legacy," which provides what Cook doesn't, a long look at the Beat prose style (Cook centers chiefly on poetry) as practiced by the man who named the movement. Krim sees the work of LeRoi Jones, Bob Dylan, Hubert Selby, John Rechy, Norman Mailer, as well as some of the Beats themselves, enriched by Kerouac's freedom of language and imagination. He prizes Kerouac but notes his reservations about Kerouac's spontaneous prose, which at times, he finds, is "only paper-deep and can be blown away by a stiff new cultural wind."

Krim's book, a lively psychological striptease, also extends the Beat canon to journalism. Ginsberg said allegories were so much lettuce, that "A naked lunch is natural to us, / we eat reality sandwiches." Krim says as much about literature (lettuce) vs. journalism (reality). Krim threw his own literary past out the window when the Beats came along, and their reality crush helped him form his new view of what novelists should write henceforth: ". . . now as never before is the time for writing to become direct action and cause things to happen . . . even potentially great novels grow small compared to what I can envision if the novelist puts his power into speaking straight to his audience." Memoir, confessional journalism, factifying: that's the ticket, says Krim. Jimmy Breslin, Pete Hamill, Tom Wolfe, Gay Talese, Nat Hentoff, Jack Newfield, they're the heroes. Forget the novel, that "madeup," that irrelevant writing.

I think Krim is perverse in this, an imp loosed out of all the hells novelists can imagine. The new journalism is all gold; and its practitioners, golden boys of the new age. But I can't believe its limitations, despite the way it opened up the media to innovation, won't eventually become clear. I am not so negative that I view the slap and snarl of relevance, the cult of confessionalism, as fads. They are valuable ways of expressing modern experience. Journalism for years was in bondage to a false kind of objectivity, a revered fustian, just as the Beat generation was the surfacing of a hot life and hot literature that had been long suppressed by puritanism and tepid academicism. The surfacing changed the world dramatically, joyfully, abominably, but boredom went out of style. I can't conceive of *anything* displacing the great achievements the novel allows.

There is more than one kind of relevance. I happened into a meeting of the James Joyce Society last Bloomsday (June 16) at the Gotham Book Mart in New York, an unlikely stop for me; for such gatherings usually have the odor of formaldehyde about them. But not this one. It was full of lively wit, song and story, and I'd say a third of the audience was (surprise) under thirty. The finale was actress Cindy Ames's voluptuous twenty-five-minute abridgement of Molly Bloom's soliloquy, spiced with all those wicked words and thoughts Joyce wrote in the twenties and that the Beats took for their own shock-worthy vulgate thirty years later. Molly Bloom changed the world first with the lewd poetic loveliness of her night-thoughts, and I doubt there is a journalist alive whose confessions and perceptions, even multiplied by nine, or ninety-nine, could produce her equal. This isn't elitism. Krim wants no part of criticism that equates quality with difficulty, and neither do I. But his soulful embrace of journalism-as-salvation does seem to me elitism inverted: the belief that it is now more important to revere Jimmy Breslin than James Joyce. I'm all for Breslin, but this really is gnat-sappery. This isn't even lettuce. It's spinach, and I say the hell with it.

1971

Jerzy Kosinski:

On Still Being There

Jerzy (pronounced Yair-zheh) Kosinski is a supreme artist of The Con, which I define as the art of survival in hopeless climates. "Con" is "confidence" in the traditional definition, but for Kosinski, I would add "control," "confound," "connive" and more. The enemy is any collective that denies individuality and thereby encourages death of the self; a brutal peasantry perhaps, a totalitarian bureaucracy, a mindless television audience, even the cancerous accumulations of a man's own past, which might erode his ability to survive the present. The key survival words are "Endure," "Manipulate." The aim is subversion of the enemy.

To Kosinski, life is relentlessly hostile, and so The Con requires perpetual vigilance. There is no such thing as success, only a benign interlude between failures. Love is the destruction of any love partner's independence, a deep joy at having dominated the other. He writes of existential man, but while the nameless protagonist of his second novel, *Steps*, might admire the arrogant individuality of Meursault, another existential figure from Camus's *The Stranger*, he would really think Meursault naive for not understanding his situation before it became deadly.

Kosinski's education in The Con began in his own childhood in Poland, wildly fictionalized in his first novel, *The Painted Bird*, a masterpiece of horror. A boy, perhaps Jewish or gypsy or neither, is sent by his parents to a rural village to avoid death by the Nazis. He suffers through demons, sadistic abuse, starvation, bestiality, genocide, bodily immersion in water, fire, earth, excrement, all this the work of the peasants for whom harboring Jews or gypsies means death. The boy learns to kill in self-defense, is brutalized into killing strangers to avenge being punished for having black eyes and hair. Kosinski calls the book "trauma personified." But with strange irony, he adds that it is the story of a happy childhood, for the boy survives the war, as millions of children did not.

In *Steps*, the boy grows older. He now relies on no morality, no group, only himself. He quests to understand that self, finds it cunning, murderous, perverse, animalistically erotic, detached from emotion. Kosinski sees his protagonist as the sum total of Western culture, "trauma perceived as a normal condition." "This," he adds, "is how we come to terms with what oppresses us. We assume it's normal." And thus does The Con work on the self: man manipulating his own mind to preserve sanity.

Now, in his new novel, *Being There* (Harcourt Brace Jovanovich), Kosinski moves outside himself and into satire. A man named Chance, perhaps a millionaire's illegitimate grandson, is raised in solitude in the millionaire's garden, fed by a servant, aware of the world only from TV. He grows up, a handsome shell, unable to read or write or think beyond the idiot level. Thrust abruptly into the real world, he is hit by the car of a financier's young wife. Driven to the financier's home, he speaks his truth. His idiocies are taken for pithiness, his talk of the garden, assumed to be metaphoric. The financier marvels at his wisdom, the wife is aroused. Chance, feeling nothing, turns on the TV for sustenance, as the plants in his garden drew sustenance from the sun. What follows is a ridiculous odyssey into fame, culminating not only in survival but perhaps in a Senate seat for this garden-variety idiot whom the world chooses to see as magnificent. Kosinski calls Chance "the Candide of the TV period" and likens his rise to Martha Mitchell being suddenly a household word and Spiro Agnew a part of American history, through TV exposure.

The Kosinski Con is still operative here. Despite his idiocy, Chance intuits a survival truth from TV: "When one was addressed and viewed by others, one was safe. Whatever one did would then be interpreted by the others in the same way that one interpreted what they did. They could never know more about one than one knew about them." Further, Kosinski's aim is still subversion. Mussolini, Hitler and Franco were like Chance, he says; the wishful thinking of the masses was ascribed to them.

Kosinski is thirty-seven, a thin, witty and vital man with thick, dark hair and dark eyes, the man grown from the boy in the cover painting of the *Painted Bird* paperback. We talked at his Manhattan apartment, its walls strikingly abstract with photos he took as a professional photographer in Poland, and with grotesque and erotic sketches by artists for whom *Steps* and *Bird* were the inspirations. Because he has kept himself aloof, this was Kosinski's first literary interview for a mass audience, and yet he is a world figure. *Being There* will be published in twenty countries. Perhaps three million copies of *Bird* are in print in thirty-two languages, and about two million of *Steps* (which won the 1969 National Book Award here) in twenty-seven languages.

After listening to Kosinski for fifteen minutes, you know he would be the last man to suffocate in the bomb shelter. He would know where the extra air was kept. His life seems in unusually tight control, as far as he can control it. He manages his own literary affairs and did so well once, the publisher insisted on secrecy about the terms. He left one publishing house after its lawyers altered his text. He left another that wanted to sell paperback rights before publication to protect the hardcover investment. Kosinski resented this absence of risk, found another publisher in three hours.

He came to the United States in 1957 after conning Poland out of a passport on the pretext that he had a Chase Manhattan Bank Foundation Scholarship. There is no such foundation. He knew Polish, Russian, French and Latin when he came, but no English. He attacked Shakespeare and Byron, saw four movies a day, read mountains of dictionaries (sixty in his apartment, more back at Yale, where he teaches unconventional drama prose and a seminar on death and the American imagination). With English in hand, he wrote two books of anticollective nonfiction in the early sixties, but switched to fiction out of a natural inclination for the abstract. "Nonfiction," he adds, "is outdated by reality. Fiction amplifies reality."

His literary antecedents: Camus, De Maupassant, Kuprin, Sartre, the Malraux of *Man's Fate*, but not Kafka, with whom he is often lumped. "I hate Kafka," he exasperatedly told one European reporter. He sees himself as the opposite of linguistic exploders like Joyce and Nabokov. "You don't need an explosion to get at the oil. A small drill will do." His prose seems the purest possible, life abstracted to the skeletal stage, then its meaning fleshed out by the reader's imagination. "Reduction" is the key word. *Steps*, after twenty-seven reductive drafts, is a marvel of concision, as well as an imaginative powerhouse. *Being There* is Kosinski's first comic thrust, less intense than *Steps*, slight almost, but just as finely wrought and just as insidious with its afterburn. This time out, Kosinski has chosen to write a subtle polemic rather than a work of the spirit. He has now performed the remarkable feat of writing three extraordinary novels in a hostile language and in no way repeating himself. He is a masterful artist. From the exotic weeds in the garden of his own life, he fashions unique arrangements. And by his art he carries the reader well beyond mere literary experience, to ask of himself: How does *my* garden grow?

1971

Postscript: This story on the late Jerzy Kosinski was written for *Look* magazine when *Being There* was published, and was the consequence of my enthusiasm for his first two novels, *The Painted Bird* and *Steps*. There has been revisionism at work on the career of Kosinski in recent years following an exposé by a New York weekly newspaper that accused him of using collaborators to create his novels. Kosinski admitted having people work for him on the books but claimed he was the final arbiter of every line. Later writers have claimed to discredit the exposé, and I am not at all clear on what is true or what isn't on how the books were written. I was less than enthusiastic about most of his later work, and I have cooled a bit on *Being There* (though it did make a great movie, directed by Hal Ashby). But I do know that those first two books still stand as highly original works of literature; and since their importance to me as a writer has not diminished, I see no reason not to reprint my original enthusiasm for them and their author. Regarding these two books the revisionists can go pack salt.

Walker Percy:

Grim News from the Moviegoer

One good thing about the end of the world is that you don't have to take it seriously. That doesn't mean the prospect won't drive you mad, keep you drunk and chasing women in between prayers, explode you with hives and morning terror and turn you into a prophet and redeemer as it did with Tom More. But if you're Walker Percy, who created More as the hero of his new novel, *Love in the Ruins* (Farrar, Straus & Giroux), then you know people tend to accept a story about end times only if it's as absurd as the prospect itself: *Cat's Cradle* by Kurt Vonnegut, for instance, or *Dr. Strangelove*, the Stanley Kubrick film. *Love in the Ruins* resembles both these, but has something beyond them: a fully realized central character living in a fully realized, fantastic, dying country. Vines are cracking the pavement. Nothing works. The auto age passed, since no one wanted to be a repairman. Whites and blacks (Bantus) are armed and ready. Hippies occupy the swamp near Paradise Estates, where the white middle class lives in luxurious anxiety. The GOP is now The Knothead Party. A league of Northern black city-states may secede. Catholics are split in three: the American Catholic Church, whose new Rome is Cicero, Illinois; the Dutch schismatics, who believe in relevance but not God; and the Roman remnant, a scattered flock. Tom More, Catholic descendant of Sir Thomas More, is a physician-inventor, a bourbon-sipping humanist whose wife ran off with a pair of wispy mystics ("the first American to be cuckolded by two English fruits"). He has invented a Lapsometer, which he describes as a "steth-oscope of the spirit," a scientific feat he compares to Newton's and Einstein's. The device diagnoses spiritual ills and, with some help from a diabolical visitor, also treats them. It is the eve of America's racial wars, in Louisiana. Perry Como is seventy, still going strong on TV. Tom More stands ready to press his invention into the service of peace, but . . . well, things fall apart.

Percy says he has tried to include something to offend everybody in his story of America's final grunt: black revolutionaries, white bigots, sex researchers, behaviorists, priests, senior citizens, Rotarians, romantics, flag-wavers, golfers, Rod McKuenites, closet queens, philosophers and other contributors to The End. Tom More, poor, mad genius, is no more stable than anybody else, but his self-appraisals give him unquestionable stature: "I believe in God and the whole business, but I love women best, music and science next, whiskey next, God fourth and my fellowman hardly at all. Generally, I do as I please."

Tom More is obviously a man worth knowing. What I feel for him approaches my reaction to Saul Bellow's Henderson (of *Henderson the Rain King*), but while More is neither as garrulous nor as alienated as Henderson, he's equally thoughtful, equally caught up in the weirdness. I read *Henderson* like an instruction book on psychic survival, underlining those great spasms of received wisdom from All Bellowness. Percy doesn't throttle me that way, but I move sympathetically with More through his messianic flights, his survival tortures, his sexual athletics. More has three women and remembers his wife, but sex, even in the batty sex-research clinic, is conducted on the page with restraint. It is Percy's style to suggest, not wallow. The result is a vast entertainment. I know when More will triumph, when he'll fail, but plot surprises aren't important here. It's the quality of his reaction that matters: ". . . until lately, nearly everyone tried and succeeded in being happy but me. My unhappiness is not the fault of Paradise. I was unlucky. My daughter died, my wife ran off with a heathen Englishman, and I fell prey to bouts of depression and morning terror, to say nothing of abstract furies and desultory lusts for strangers."

Percy, fifty-five, is a very civilized man. I hope I don't insult him by saying this now that he has painted civilization as a bag of demented snakes. We had breakfast together at the Plaza, where he stays when he leaves his reclusive life in Louisiana and comes to New York. The association of the hotel with Scott Fitzgerald is attractive to him, but he has another reason: "The first time my wife and I checked in, we rode up in the elevator with Cary Grant." You'll recall Percy's first novel was *The Moviegoer*. He doesn't go to movies much anymore, won't even let this new novel be filmed. "Movies being what they are," he said, attacking his firmly poached eggs, "I don't think it can be done."

Odd talk from Percy? Well perhaps. But he seems like a vigorously anomalous man. Sitting amid this breakfast elegance and morning sunshine, smiling under his receding white hair, he was a sturdy, treelike father figure, a Norman Rockwell country doc, a font of drawled, folksy wisdom ("The thing that drives Americans crazy is when they become happy"). He even said he likes businessmen, that the savvy ones are the best critics of his novels; and which American writer has stood on that platform lately? Gentleness, kindness, self-effacement are words that Percy-at-Plaza-morning brought to mind. But anyone who writes as randy a prose as he, who is capable of imagining Tom More, has also got to be, somewhere in his head, a bourbon-lickin', good-time honeyman himself. He admits to anomalous origins in a clan of Mississippi planter-politician-writers, notably William Alexander Percy (*Lanterns on the Levee*), his adoptive father. The family career base was the law, and "I knew damn well I didn't want that." He turned reluctantly to medicine, got his M.D. at Columbia in 1941 and interned doing autopsies on derelicts dead of TB. He caught the bug himself, ending that career. His response: "I was the happiest guy ever got TB." Recovering at Saranac, he took up with philosophy, published papers in *Thought Quarterly* and elsewhere. But he wanted more readers and turned to the novel, influenced by Camus and Sartre, who had incorporated philosophy into their fiction. "I saw myself as not leaving the scientific tradition, for the novel can say things science can't. Science can't utter a single word on what it's like to be an individual in a certain time and place, and what it's like to die."

When *The Moviegoer* won a National Book Award in 1962, a cult grew around Percy. It spread with his second novel, *The Last Gentleman*, and now *Love in the Ruins* will intensify the fever. Percy sees the new work as a Christian novel that "by vicarious use of catastrophe" may make himself and his reader "come to themselves," and prevent The End. But I doubt he'll be any more successful with that aim than Tom More was with his Lapsometer. Percy is no prophet, and even if he were, prophecy wouldn't swivel the tempers of any Bantus or Rotarians. But he may be the only doctor-philosopher-honeyman extant, and that is significant, for it has taught him how to reach the musical-erotic area of our brains (his phrase). It's eschatological stuff, all right, but it comes on like love, or fear, like a survival lesson, and turns into a Picasso painting: an American "Guernica" with a woman done in by a shish kebab skewer, a colonel emasculated on the golf course by a sniper. Tom More's psychic defeats in battle have immobilized him on the balcony of a deserted Howard Johnson motel. We drag up a chair beside him, twist open the bourbon, put a Bessie Smith record on the phonograph, our pistols at the ready to keep wandering crazies at bay, and wait for things to improve. The music stops, and then through a crack in a half-open door down the balcony there comes an inviting rustle of silk. We smile. Tom, you old son of a gun, you've thought of everything.

1971

Saul Bellow:

Intellectual Activity: A Form of Resistance

If He Doesn't Have a True Word to Say, He Keeps His Mouth Shut

Intellectual Activity: A Form of Resistance

Author Saul Bellow sat amid the rumples of his dark gray suit, sipped a gimlet, and stared across the lobby of the Algonquin Hotel on West Forty-fourth Street. This was the cocktail hour at the end of a busy day, but he was still working, watching a man bend to a woman at a nearby table and greet her with a kiss.

"Watching people kiss," he said, "I always try to decide what their relationship is, whether they're man and wife or having an affair or what. It's a great game."

The results of a lifetime of close observation of the human species have just tumbled out of Saul Bellow in a torrent of achievement: *Herzog*, his sixth novel and easily the most widely praised work of American fiction in many years; and *The Last Analysis*, a play that recently had a short run at the Belasco Theater here after opening to mixed reviews.

The play was a departure for the author, his first excursion into the theater. But it is *Herzog* that has most intensified critics' efforts to enthrone Mr. Bellow as king of American literature, on the throne vacated by Faulkner and Hemingway.

Saul Bellow is not a reluctant king, but he doesn't take the kingmakers too seriously: "America is a great power. It needs cultural furniture and I'm an article of cultural furniture. I can't pretend I wasn't an ambitious young man when I came to New York in 1939 [he was born in Canada, now lives in Chicago], and I pretty much got what I wanted, which

141

probably serves me right. But this is just a flutter, good for my ego and good for business."

Herzog represents Mr. Bellow's second brush with fame (the first was in 1953, when *The Adventures of Augie March* was published), and most critics have called it the author's most mature creation. Like most of Mr. Bellow's literary figures, protagonist Moses Herzog is engaged in trying to comprehend the vague social and personal forces that plague him. Mr. Bellow says the novel deals with "the person who has lost his direction," and adds that Herzog "finally sees through self-justification and realizes the need for keeping his mouth shut.

"If I were a psychologist," the author says, "I would have written that there is a human instinct for self-justification. Complaining is one of the great secular arts and always has been. People break from a clinch and go off to different sides of the ring, each making his case, calling in the neighbors, crying out to heaven—he was right or she was right. There is a profound human need to be right."

But Herzog and Bellow both frown on too much self-concern: "There are two billion people on the face of the earth," Mr. Bellow says, "and most of them probably suffer more than you do. Why should anyone pay attention to your suffering? Why should any man feel he has the right to claim the attention of any other man for this purpose?" And so it is, at novel's end, with Herzog.

In his triumph over himself and his troubles, Herzog represents what Mr. Bellow calls "a break with victim literature," with the novels in which man is a victim of his environment and his own weaknesses. "But any man who thinks is not a victim," Mr. Bellow insists. "Intellectual activity is not passive, as it is sometimes thought to be. It's a form of resistance. If Madame Bovary, for example, had realized that nobody around her had the power to hurt her, she wouldn't have committed suicide."

This resistance is a key concept in *The Last Analysis*, the farcical story of an old-time comedian named Bummidge (played on Broadway by Sam Levene) who becomes involved in ideas and theories after undergoing psychoanalysis, and begins acting out the principal crises of his life with whoever shows up.

Mr. Bellow views the play as a satire on people who become fanatical about "a system of metaphors," such as the Freudian system of analysis, and relates it in intent to his farcical novel *Henderson the Rain King*. Henderson, outcast from his soul, bedeviled by a want he can neither satisfy nor understand, takes a wild trip to a fantastic Africa to set things right.

"People must either decide to live in submission to the ideas and abstractions which act upon them from outside with such revolutionary force," says Mr. Bellow, "or to take hold and try to free themselves by understanding these abstractions."

Bummidge tried this in *The Last Analysis*, but some critics saw the play as too farcical, too diffuse in intent, and it lasted only twenty-eight performances. Mr. Bellow, nonetheless, found it an education for a literary man to deal with theatrical professionals. A sample difficulty, he said over a second gimlet, was getting to talk to director Joseph Anthony (*Rhinoceros, The Best Man*) about new dialogue when the director was busy with a lighting problem. Mr. Bellow considers lighting problems "superfluous," and was more interested in making meaningful script changes—eliminating dialogue that had gone dead as new dialogue was added. Often the director (for whose expertise Mr. Bellow still professes great admiration) resisted, not wanting to upset the actors.

That gave Mr. Bellow a thought. "Actors," he said, "either have to grasp things intuitively or they don't grasp them at all. They fall back on the way they've done things for years on Broadway, and it's hopeless."

Mr. Bellow views his theatrical education philosophically, for little of his ascent to the top of the literary world has been easy. A learned man, he had to discover a way to write prose that didn't stop dead from erudition on page 3. He began with two highly controlled works, *The Dangling Man* and *The Victim*, and then came the idea to write *Augie March*.

"I was walking along a street in Paris," he recalls, "watching water running along the curb. They were washing the streets, and with the water flowing very rapidly I began thinking about a kid I had known in Chicago back in 1925 who had been a playmate. This was on Augusta Street, which was probably the origin of the name Augie. And I began to think about his family and his life and what might have happened to him in all this time. I had a great deal of childish affection for him, and with thoughts of him came the sort of language he would have used—'Gee, I've got a real peppy scheme.'

"Chicago was full of people who were highly original without knowing it; people who used the public library and talked freely about everything and loved this kind of oratory."

Language flowed through *Augie March* like that Paris street water. Says Mr. Bellow: "I discovered rhetoric." The flood came, he said, "at the end of a depressive cycle in a burst of manic energy."

The burst wasn't unusual. When writing, he says, "I get wildly excited. I'm in a state where I can't eat, can't sleep, or think about other things. If I do think of something else it only leads back to what I'm writing. I'm up in the nighttime with insomnia, but not dull insomnia. It's exciting. In three years with *Herzog* I only slept well when the book was going badly."

He is less than tolerant of much of what he finds in modern fiction, writers who are "very bookish, who get their attitudes from literature. There isn't a contemporary writer I know of offhand who has a curiosity about what civilization is, I mean independent of literary sources."

He rewrote *Herzog* from fifteen to twenty times ("I've lost track"), a rewrite meaning that he reached something like page 250, decided he had gone wrong, and started over at page 1. He explains: "I don't like superfluous things in what I read and I don't think they should be in what a man writes. Wherever I found I was indulging myself, I just stopped and started a new draft to get at what was essential."

1964

If He Doesn't Have a True Word to Say,
He Keeps His Mouth Shut

I'd first met Saul Bellow, the American Nobel Prize laureate, in San Juan in 1960, when he was a visiting professor at the University of Puerto Rico and in the middle of writing *Herzog*. He'd had valuable things to say about what I was then writing and had also made some observations that stayed with me: that character was the single most important element in determining a writer's worth; that a writer shouldn't be parsimonious with his work but "prodigal, like nature," which uses billions of sperm when only one is needed for creating life.

Also, and most memorably, he said that "most American writers don't really know much about American society, for they're used to viewing it from the point of view of the innocent or the underdog. And the sources of real power in American society will never be revealed to innocents or underdogs."

Now here he came with a new book, his ninth novel, *The Dean's December*, anatomizing power and the lack of it: urban decay in a major American city. And so an interview was proposed. I hadn't kept up with all his moves and wrote him at the University of Chicago, where he's been a member of the Committee on Social Thought since 1964. The letter came back marked ADDRESSEE UNKNOWN. I posted another through his publisher and news of his unknownness reached him in Vermont, where he and his wife, Alexandra, a professor of mathematics, have been spending summers. "I'm not what you'd think of as a drifter," he wrote in reply. "But I do drift in a real (i.e., barely conscious) sense— a sort of desert rat with a Smith-Corona instead of a prospector's mule. Not even the Committee on Social Thought fully remembers me. Just as well." He said that he was just finishing the book, "something of a cherry bomb, or a small grenade, I like to think," and that he'd be glad to talk.

And so to southern Vermont; and here, out of an old rented farmhouse, came Saul Bellow, summer squire, in baggy pants and blue-and-white jogging shoes in which he does not jog. How old was he now? "Sixty-six," he said, "but showing signs of decay." His hair is sparse and white, his face lined, but he's trim for a man of these numerals: if he doesn't jog in his jogging shoes, he does stand on his head in them.

"I haven't gone to seed," he said. "But seed is nibbling at my feet. You know it's on you when you've been sitting in a certain position for fifteen minutes and you can't straighten up when you arise. I stopped playing racquetball because I couldn't stay with the young people on the court anymore. There's something humiliating about that. Also women started to ask me for a game."

We ate lunch prepared by Alexandra, then moved to the living room, where his Smith-Corona sat atop a tidy desk, and we settled into facing sofas in front of the fireplace. He began the interview by talking about the new novel.

"I wrote it in a year and a half," he said, "and had no idea it was coming. One of these things that came over me. My wife's mother was dying in Bucharest, and I went with her to give her some support, which in that place one badly needs. The old mother died while we were there. I had been thinking of writing a book about Chicago, and as always when I go abroad I brooded about the hometown.

"The book considers what value a single life has in one of these countries of Eastern Europe," he said. But he thinks its Chicago segments will raise the controversy: "It's a protest about the dehumanization of the blacks in big cities. I'm speaking up for the black underclass and telling the whites they're not approaching the problem correctly. The people [in the book] who stand out in moral stature, who each in his own way tries to do something, are blacks. But it's one of these touchy subjects you know will draw flack. Either the white liberals will be up in arms or the black leadership will disapprove. When I began this book, any discussion of this subject, unless it was framed in the conventional pieties, would have been taboo."

The black condition, he believes, "represents a complete failure of the imagination in the country. We are now in the fourth or fifth welfare generation, people who've never worked, people sealed out, set aside, and they look to me like a doomed population. And from the social organizations, educators, psychologists, bureaucrats—nothing, just zilch. Who's got some imagination about this? Is the city going to turn into a septic tank with people moving out and doing their work by computer and nothing in the city center but the big corporations and the blasted remains? The population is economically redundant. . . ."

He stopped speaking.

"I'm using journalistic terminology. I could kick myself. You can't talk about people being economically redundant." He said that in the novel he quotes the German poet Rainer Maria Rilke, who wouldn't discuss the Great War with anybody. "He shunned all sorts of discussion," said Bellow, "because they could only be held in newspaper language, and he felt this gave him a foulness in the mouth, and you could only betray experience this way."

Bellow has worked journalistically (his own style) in the past, covering Khrushchev's visit to the United Nations for *Esquire*; writing a book on contemporary Israel, *To Jerusalem and Back: A Personal Account*; and a few years ago, he began to face down Chicago for a nonfiction work on his hometown. But that book is dead: "I'll never have any more to do with it. That's a subject for some kind of poetry, not a factual account. The very language you have to use as a journalist works against the true material. To do a piece about, say, the way the criminal courts operate in Chicago, you'd have to write about people on the bench, criminal detention, the conditions that breed crime, and you'd have to do it with a show of objectivity, and in the end it would all be dead."

Bellow turned his energy toward the novel instead and made the protagonist of *The Dean's December* (he's dean at an unnamed Chicago college) a former journalist on the Paris *Herald* who has returned to Chicago to teach. After some years, he writes two magazine articles comparing the Chicago of yore with Chicago today and the articles create a storm, which continues while he is in Bucharest visiting his wife's dying mother. The writing of the novel illustrates Bellow's profound differentiation between journalism and literature: "Although you are reading about it all the time, you can't find out what's happening in this world. You read *Encounter*, *Commentary*, *Foreign Affairs*, books by psychologists, sociologists—and you can't find out what's happening humanly. Unless you pass it through your own soul, you can't understand it. We live in this alleged age of communication, which comes in the form of distracting substitutes for reality. But the reality in our day comes from art. And we live in a country that has ruled this off limits.

"It's hard to interest readers, isn't it? They're not used to following the human motion of character. The motion of the soul is not what they consider to be exciting. The excitement demand has gone sky-high. One week the President is shot, another week the pope. This would have caused a holy war two centuries ago, but now it's only something to titillate the public's appetite for sensation. This causes people to forget human knowledge—knowledge of their own souls. Somewhere they're paying humanly for the lack of reality all this represents. They can always find something to dwarf something else with—Chicago is dwarfed by the Gulag peninsula, which is dwarfed by the Holocaust. There's a totalitarianism in all this, in that it's reductive of human experience."

This loss of the power to experience is a theme Bellow threads through *The Dean's December*. "I felt moved on behalf of the human stuff itself," he said, "and the need to recover the power to experience." As we talked, this feeling translated into an attitude toward the abundance of modern writers who have succumbed to the pop reality and gone to the movies or to thrillers or to nonfiction or to fiction that merely fulfills popular expectations. Bellow feels writers are making themselves superfluous. "They think the game is over, they think we're in a situation where all we can do is prepare for the next epoch by doing more of the same, by repeating the redundancy. That's what heats me up about it. A question that bugs me all the time is, what really is interesting? What is it human beings long to think about, read about, see, or feel? There's some sort of capitalist competition going on about what is interesting. Power is interesting now. Weakness is much less interesting. Sexuality is interesting, or at least people say it is, though they generally mean lust. All this sexual stuff has become practically obligatory, because it's certainly a big deal commercially. And there's a demonism in this sexuality because of the big money that certifies the importance, the social success of this trend. It makes me think of Marie Antoinette: 'Let 'em eat cake.' Now the masses are gorged on all this sexual cake, and everybody's got sexual pimples.

"I have a very simple feeling about this when I'm writing. I don't want to waste people's time. They're gasping for a breath of life and they're being robbed by every con artist who comes along. If I didn't think I was speaking to people's souls, I would not write anything. If I didn't have a true word to speak to them, I'd keep my fucking mouth shut."

Of course, there were American writers who had not succumbed to "pop reality." Which of these writers did Bellow value?

"I like [John] Cheever very much. . . . I have a weakness for writers of my own generation—Wright Morris, J. F. Powers, Ralph Ellison, Eudora Welty, Flannery O'Connor among the novelists. Bernard Malamud is extraordinarily good. I liked *The Assistant* very much, and I like the stories immensely.

"I admire Norman Mailer quite a lot. I think he's a writer of immense talent, but he's lacking in originality. I know his originality takes American readers by storm, but I find him crowded with clichés. I like the improvisational ones—writing about prizefights. He's a man of remarkable talents, but his seriousness is impossible to take seriously."

What did he mean about Mailer's clichés?

"Take the recent one about the knifer [*In the Belly of the Beast*, in

which Mailer introduces the letters of the convict Jack Henry Abbott].
Malraux was giving the world shudders with this kind of stuff fifty years
ago, and even then it was old hat. It came from an earlier French
generation of syndicalist wild men—Sorel's *Reflections on Violence*—
and tons of supporting hooey way back into the nineteenth century.
Wyndham Lewis is awfully good on this when he looks into Sartre and
Malraux and points out how all these admirers of criminal violence came
from the middle class and had the best education France could give
them.

"It's literature in the worst sense of the word because it's only writing
about the knife. But then comes the knife, and a life is taken [Abbott
was convicted of a fatal stabbing while free on parole and was returned
to jail.] The good old *New York Times* writes an editorial that blames
the prison system. Rebecca West says that men see things in outline,
silhouettes and nothing else. Women see the human details. So when
there is a threat to the community or to the state, the men go for
armaments and the women say these terrible things wouldn't happen if
there were decent bathrooms for everybody. So *The New York Times* in
this case takes the feminine attitude that this wouldn't happen if our
prisons weren't so bad.

"And there's another point to be made about writers enveloped in
sexual charisma—that they are drawn to violent criminals who are also
sexually charismatic. Now, the criminals, I suppose, are knifing in real
earnest. But the writers are in the sexual game with their violence. There
is a kind of flattery of women in it."

He'd praised Cheever, now and also publicly. What was it in Cheever's
work that moved him?

"He's one of the few American writers who have undergone a visible
development. Take a writer like [James T.] Farrell. He wrote *Studs
Lonigan* first and he wrote *Studs Lonigan* last. Most of them are that
way. But here's Cheever—you read those stories and you see his power
of transformation, his power to take the elements given and work them
into something new and far deeper than they were at the outset. I think
you can truly judge the importance of a writer by his power to transform
the original given."

He'd translated Isaac Bashevis Singer's short story "Gimpel the Fool"
from the Yiddish. What did he think of Singer?

"I think he's written a couple of first-rate books and some marvelous stories. He's very prolific, and sometimes he hits the target and sometimes he hits a spectator or two."

Which books of Singer's did he think were really first-rate?

"*The Magician of Lublin, The Spinoza of Market Street*, and *Gimpel the Fool*, the book of stories with that title. I don't think my praise will cut much ice with him. His opinion of himself is so high he doesn't need anyone else's certification."

He noted an egregious fact of American literary life: that good readers are hung up on Hemingway, Fitzgerald, and Faulkner. "It's very strange that serious readers think this country has made so very little progress since then. That they formed a standard around themselves is something to wonder at. It's as if people were saying, that's when we were still okay—before the fall. Funny they should all be considered so American when they were so nihilistic. But they gave Americans an image they wanted to be known by. The Fitzgerald stereotype alternated with the Hemingway one—in ball parks, in newspapers, and among the younger people in universities, though not so much there anymore."

Bellow considered all that he had said to me and explained that he didn't usually make these sorts of statements. "I've never been so outspoken before about people like Mailer. It's an exhibitionistic thing to do, which amuses the public, but I'm getting old enough now not to care. I could have named lots of people. They'll never know how much they've been spared."

This talk of American writers led naturally into talk of writers of world stature. Whom did he judge to be of the first rank?

"One reads less as one grows older," he said. "You realize your time is limited and that you have to ration yourself. I may mention some strange birds to you. The late Nadezhda Mandelstam, for one [she was the wife of the Russian poet Osip Mandelstam]. Her two volumes, *Hope Against Hope* and *Hope Abandoned*, are very important modern books. They have a kind of personal, human, intuitive, intelligent, and cultivated response to what has happened in Russia since 1917, through life and death, through war and peace. A fragile little old woman in her sixties and seventies wrote these books, which seem to me to contain the complete answer to Communist totalitarianism.

"Solzhenitsyn is a wonderful writer but a kinky one. He's chock-full of old Slavophile ideology, religiosity, to which I have no objection. Among the Russian dissenters, he belongs to the right wing, which I find fascinating but not especially sympathetic. Anyone who could stand up to the regime as he did needs heroic virtues and all kinds of special powers, and he clearly has them. But I'm not deeply moved by his novels, except the first one, *One Day in the Life of Ivan Denisovich.*

"There's a Russian writer, Varlam Shalamov—his collection of short stories about the concentration camps, *Kolyma Tales*, is worth reading —and Andrei Sinyavsky (Abram Tertz is his pseudonym) is also an admirable writer; I think that he's a writer of genius.

"I like Rebecca West, a marvelous old broad. She's wrong about a lot of things but incomparably right when she's right." He picked up the twenty-fifth-anniversary edition of *The Paris Review*, which he'd been reading, and quoted a passage from an interview with West. She was talking about writing multiple drafts of a book and said to the interviewer: "I've never been able to do just one draft. That seems a wonderful thing. Do you know anyone who can?" And the interviewer responded: "I think D. H. Lawrence did." To which West answered: "You could often tell."

Bellow roared and took off his glasses. "A marvelous one-liner," he said. "I can tell with Lawrence where he didn't revise. There's a certain repetitiousness and silliness, even in his very best things."

We talked about other writers.

"There's another old girl," he said. "Christina Stead. Her novel *The Little Hotel* I recommend strongly. I think you'll love it."

And what of Samuel Beckett, who certainly belongs in the first rank?

"I just met Beckett in Paris," Bellow said. "He's very gentle. Indrawn rather than withdrawn."

What did "indrawn" mean to him?

"He shows the physical tension of having removed himself inwardly to some deeper location inside. He's physically an old man, worth looking at, worth studying. There's an odd twist to him. The color of the eyes is like nothing I've ever seen. Even the growth of the hair expresses some kind of torsion—there's a twist of sorts to his constitution. It's very appealing, most attractive. His constitution has its own sort of grain."

What did Bellow and Beckett talk about?

"Literature, his life, and Joyce and Pound and Hemingway and Wyndham Lewis. He was willing to talk about them, but not enthusiastic about those conversations. He spoke with reverence of Joyce but not of many others. We met in the lobby of the Pont Royal Hotel. The bar downstairs was the headquarters of Sartre and Company all through the highest moments of existentialism, and I said: 'Do you want to go downstairs to the bar?' And he said no. He wouldn't have anything to do with that stuff. In fact, he wouldn't have anything to do with anybody's stuff, and I rather like that about him because there's something in me that's similar—the dislike of being one of the pack, any pack."

What did Bellow think of Samuel Beckett as a writer?

"He's an extraordinary writer. Not my sort. I'm not his sort either. He interests me. He doesn't stir my soul deeply. But it was a friendly meeting in which the tones counted more than what was said. The vibes, as the children would say. I was satisfied with the vibes. I can't speak for him. He's too mysterious to be spoken for."

Last spring, on the wall of an English department in an upstate New York university, and presumably on college walls everywhere, a document appeared announcing the creation of the *Saul Bellow Newsletter*, a publication that will pursue "Bellow materials"—bibliographies, reviews, interviews, conferences, probably gossip on the private life as well. This thrusts Bellow into the company of Joyce, Hemingway, Fitzgerald, and other writers judged by academe to be newsletter-worthy icons. How did the new icon feel about this newsletter?

"I don't get it," he said. "And if I got it I wouldn't read it. Somebody told me about it, but I just stay in my foxhole."

How did he feel about books by academics analyzing his work?

"I've read few of the critical works," he said. "I don't pay too much attention to them. I always think, the end is not yet, and when I see these things I think: 'Don't announce the results of the election or the people on the Coast will walk away from the polls.' Also, it is sometimes depressing to read what educated people think I'm doing, and I feel downcast for days. It can be very distressing to see how wrong people are. And then they invariably translate what you do into the modern intellectual vocabulary, which itself is depressing."

He teaches and lectures at universities but sees himself apart from academic life.

"I went back to Chicago in the sixties because I didn't want to get caught in the literary life and its rackets. There were gangs organized in those days—the New York poets, the *Commentary* group, The *New York Review of Books* group, the people around Stanley Kunitz and Cal [Robert] Lowell—and I thought I might just as well go back to Chicago, where a spade is a spade and a philistine is a philistine. I really do prefer the untroubled vulgarity of Chicago, where, when my wife gives her name to a department-store clerk, the clerk asks, 'Bellow? Doesn't your husband swim in the Olympics?'

"As you grow older as a writer," he said, "you become more and more accustomed to talking to yourself. In what the punks like to call the literary milieu you'd think you'd find some milieuvniks to talk to. You'd think there were heaps of people to attach yourself to. But you have to pick yourself through heaps of no-goodniks, casts of thousands in the literary world who don't know what the hell I'm talking about."

We arrived, finally, at the subject of the Nobel Prize. It came to him in 1976, and the Swedish Academy praised his work for these reasons: first, because it represented an emancipation of American writing from the "hard-boiled" style that had become "routine" in thirties literature; and second, for its mix of "exuberant ideas, flashing irony, hilarious comedy, and burning compassion."

Bellow's initial response to the prize was viewed by the press as casual, and I asked him about this.

"How should I behave?" he inquired.

I had no suggestions but noted that Jean-Paul Sartre, for instance, had rejected the prize in 1964, partly on political grounds.

"I don't feel it incumbent on me politically to do one thing or another," Bellow said. "I don't think the world is waiting to see how I line up. Part of me thinks back to the streets of Chicago and says, 'Who, me? Don't be silly.'

"What it is, is one of those greatest-show-on-earth things, and why should I be too good to take part? So I clowned a bit and turned a few somersaults."

What has been his international role since the prize?

"I just sign more manifestos," he said. "My name has to be ignored by Brezhnev more and more often.

"I would have been quite happy without the Nobel Prize," Bellow added. "I know it upsets some men not to get it, but actually it's better to write a marvelous book than to get the prize. It's easy for me to say that, but what I mean to say is, I still go on doing my damnedest to write the best book that's in me."

Will that be difficult, now that he's become an industry?

"I don't mind becoming an industry," he said. "In Japan people go to the Buddhist temple and buy a long strip of paper with their horoscope on it, and with Japanese efficiency they roll the papers up and tie them to shrubs by the temple door, so the shrubs have more horoscopes than they do leaves. And I suppose the Saul Bellow industry makes a shrub of me by the temple door. It's all right as long as they don't come and tear off my blossoms."

He had earlier, in passing, mentioned a vague Hollywood interest in his books. Had he ever thought of writing for the movies?

"I concentrate on the form of unreality I know best," he said. "When I was young and pretty I was fingered by a talent scout who asked me to come to Hollywood. *Dangling Man* had just come out, and I thought he wanted to buy the book for the movies. He was a member of the Goldwyn family, not a very famous member, and he hadn't even read my book. He saw my picture on the jacket and thought I could make it as an actor. Write for them? Hell, I could've acted for them."

Now, would he, as a way of concluding this talk, compare the Bellow who wrote *The Adventures of Augie March* with the Bellow who had just finished *The Dean's December*?

"One of the things I said in the new book," he said, "was that the dean lived a very quiet life. And the reason was that he had made so many mistakes that he had a lot to think about. He had his work cut out for him. You remember when you took elementary chemistry? You were handed a lump of stuff and the professor said, 'By the end of the semester I want you to tell me what's in this.' And you had to sweat over it in the lab for what elements were in it. Well," said the author with an unfinished smile, "I haven't gotten to the bottom of my lump."

1982

E. L. Doctorow:

A Strong Voice in the Universe

Shimmering
Loon Lake

A Strong Voice in the Universe

The prevalence of talk against the novel, and of its supposed relegation to a position behind nonfiction in our age, has gained much of its real momentum from novelists. Philip Roth, some years ago, gave aid and comfort to the reactionary legions of nonfiction supremacists by suggesting that the novel had trouble keeping pace with modern life, that today's theme was swiftly superseded by tomorrow's newspaper. Soon thereafter, Roth wrote The Great American Bathroom Novel, which is not likely to be superseded by any newspaper. Also, Truman Capote and Norman Mailer, out of some cancerous boredom with their previous interior literary landscapes, turned to nonfiction. Though their work has been nonpareil, has had an ennobling effect on magazine and book journalism, and has made them culture heroes on the basis of their artistic vision of events, their elegant or boisterous public syntax and their self-regenerative TV personalities, it has also demeaned novels in the public mind. Capote and Mailer stand as ex-novelists turned relevant fact-mongers, and highly successful because of that. Novels, by contrast, are made to seem irrelevant fantasies, the doodlings of cloistered freaks, read chiefly by hefty androgynes and English majors who still smoke meerschaum pipes.

Wrongheads who think like this should read E. L. Doctorow's new novel. *The Book of Daniel* (Random House), which imposes an eminently relevant perspective on the past four decades of America by imaginatively reenacting a tortured moment: the case of Julius and Ethel Rosenberg, who were electrocuted in 1953 after being convicted of conspiracy to steal U.S. atomic secrets for Russia.

Only one nonfiction book on the notorious case is still in print. But even if a dozen were in print, none would be likely to convey what Doctorow's does; for nonfiction's virtue is providing a *cerebral* comprehension of events through an authentic marshaling of facts (even if the facts are the workings of Mailer's matchless mind); and Doctorow gives the fact fetish a swift kick in the slats. He did not research the private lives of the Rosenbergs (he told me), he invented them. He did not know them or their children or anyone who did. Yet his people are convincingly real (he calls them Paul and Rochelle Isaacson; their children, Susan and Daniel), and his book achieves authenticity at a level closed to nonfictionists, that is, the province of the novelist—the creation in the reader of an *emotional* comprehension of history. This is fodder for inexhaustible argument. I only suggest that the difference between the impact of nonfiction and fiction on the psyche is the difference between enjoying stimulating new vistas with an old flame whose limits we understand, and falling in love with a voluptuous stranger.

"The novelist," Doctorow said in a phone conversation, "has to break through the facts to get at the truth. And if he feels constrained by the facts, to that extent he'll fail."

Doctorow doesn't fail. His book is a stunning success. It is only ironic that its weakest points are those where he imposes too much historical data on the story and slows the action in order to re-create the eras through which the characters move, and the philosophies (1940-ish communism, the Truman Doctrine, last year's Yippieism) that undergird them.

The book purports to be the doctoral dissertation of Daniel Isaacson, a young man whose human, political and literary savvy are equal to Doctorow's, which is to say, very high. As such, it is a curiosity shop of styles, moving back and forth between first and third person, in and out of essays (on capital punishment through history, and a brilliant conclusion on Disneyland as cultural totalitarianism). The eccentric Daniel includes his sudden surreal impressions (violin spiders), a moving conversation with his grandmother after her death, Joycean foolery (if this bee is tristante make the mort of it).

The book is ultimately less about the parents than about Daniel and Susan, whose relationship is the great achievement of the book: two children who must rebuild a life after an entire nation turns its full hatred on their parents and executes them. Doctorow has written that he sees this as a metaphor for a current condition in which "all children discover that their parents are murdered by the system, and that murder is what they have to build their lives on." That seems too general a burden for such a specific book to carry. But it does reflect, as Doctorow also said when we talked, "the essentially sacrificial function of Left politics, the peculiar and bitter kind of career it offers; but also its humanity."

For black writers today, such social themes are everything, but for white American novelists, black and dreck humor are still the vogue, along with studies of cultural alienation, neurotic introspection, sexual emancipation, suburban desiccation. Doctorow's book is a throwback to the concerns that moved the young Steinbeck and Dos Passos.

"I don't see how our name novelists have been able to remain absolutely silent about the Vietnamese war," Doctorow said on the phone, "and I think that's one reason why people talk about the death of the novel."

Doctorow, forty, worked as a literary editor for a decade and is now a teacher (next year, at Sarah Lawrence). He wrote two early novels, *Welcome to Hard Times*, an allegorical Western, and *Big as Life*, a fantasy in the science-fiction vein. He's writing a new novel, and a children's book on comparative revolution.

"When I went to college," he recalled, "the general view of the artist might have been expressed by a Henry James remark to the effect that life is hot but art is cool. That can be a terrible burden if the artist believes it too thoroughly. Pablo Neruda's inspirations were not cool at all. Dostoevsky was not a cool guy. . . . My own view is that there's no reason for the novel except to convey your own imaginative vision of the life of society, bits and pieces of everything and everybody. And all sorts of strange voices in the universe."

1971

Shimmering *Loon Lake*

Two-thirds of the way through this stunning new novel by E. L. Doctorow, a failed poet by the name of Warren Penfield, watching a puppet play in Japan, has this thought:

". . . when I speak I hear someone else saying the words when I decide to do something someone else is propelling me when I look up at the sky or down at the ground I feel the talons on my neck how true what genius to make a public theater out of this why don't we all stand up and tear the place apart what brazen art to tell us this about ourselves knowing we'll sit here and not do a thing"

The narrator then adds: "The puppet play told the story of two lovers who, faced with adversity, decided to commit suicide together and so at the intimate crucial moment there were eight presences onstage."

The implication here from the narrator is that it takes a composite of four psychic stances to create one individual, a sort of Jungian concept. Jung wouldn't have limited the number to four and in fact neither does Doctorow. A case can be made that he creates at least five significant males and five significant females who shape the psyche of his hero, a wanderer he calls Joe from Paterson (New Jersey).

One of the novel's great achievements is the way in which Doctorow has those five, or ten, resonating constantly in Joe's consciousness. What he achieves is the creation of a truly complex man functioning in a truly complex society—the 1930s Depression years in America.

Much of the book is set in the Northeast. Albany, Utica are evoked by name. The Adirondack wilderness at Loon Lake (where five presidents vacationed in the late nineteenth century as America discovered that wilderness too could be luxurious) is a major presence and symbol in the novel.

The social view is from the top, in the person of a millionaire named F. W. Bennett who has a fifty-thousand-acre estate on the lake which he shares with his elegant, hoydenish Amelia Earhart–type wife, Lucinda.

The view is also from the cultural wasteland that the poet Penfield (a wonderful character) inhabits; and it is from the world of a traveling carnival, where Joe works as a roustabout for the teeth-sucking owner, beds his larcenous wife and grows protective of the moronic fat lady who is a sex object for the yokel customers.

It is the view from an assembly line in Bennett's Autobody Works in Jacksontown, Indiana—Heart of the Hoosier Nation—where Joe finds a job, and where he unknowingly befriends a company spy and inherits both the spy's treason and his wife. It is the view from below in the person of the gangster Tommy Crapo, who breaks heads for Bennett, and Clara Lukacs, Tommy's moll, who becomes Bennett's doxy and Joe's woman.

Early in the story Joe takes off from the lower-class life in Paterson, rides the freights, wends his way north and one day sees the beautiful, blonde Clara, naked in a private railroad car. On impulse he follows the tracks and ends up on Bennett's estate, where he is attacked by a pack of wild dogs, and after being nursed back to health by sullen servants, becomes part of Bennett's domain and begins his erratic rise in the world.

Here Joe meets Penfield, who is a roly-poly lap dog for Bennett's wife. He becomes friends with Clara (and eventually runs off with her) and he also stands up to Bennett himself by rejecting him.

Unlike Bennett's servile servants, Joe has no use for the self-anni-hilating security they find in Bennett's employ. What he runs on, he tells himself, is "the force of self-distinguishing," which he found com-mon among hoboes. "When you are nobody and have nothing, you depend on your troubles for self-respect."

And so he tells Bennett he won't work for him and will go back on the road. Bennett, amused, implants his capitalistic wisdom in Joe's brain (with strange effect) with a remarkable speech:

"Well, I say why not, if that's what you want. Just be sure you've got the guts. So that if you have to steal or take a sap to someone's head for a meal, you'll be able to. Every kind of life has its demands, its tests. Can I do this? Can I live with the consequences of what I'm doing? If you can't answer yes, you're in a life that's too much for you. You get on the bread line. If you can't muscle your way into the bread line, you sit at the curb and hold out your hand. You're a beggar. If you can't whine and wheedle and beg your cup of coffee . . . why, I say be a poet. Get in, get into the place that's your nature, whether it's running

a corporation or picking daises . . . live to the fullness of fit, become
what you are, and I'll say to you, you've done more than most men. Most
men—and let me tell you, I know men—most of them don't ever do
that. They'll work at a job and not know why. They'll marry a woman
and not know why. They'll go their graves and not know why."

What happens to Joe, the voices he hears, the wisdom he swallows,
the crises he survives, is the novel's story. It is told with a pervading
sense of strangeness, with obliquely rendered interior monologues which
seem irrelevant to the story and yet prove eventually to be the soul of
it. There are computeresque reports on the characters, there are excerpts
from Penfield's wretched poetry, and yet there is poetry in the book
which is clearly Doctorow's and which is full of haunting imagery.

Some critics have noted echoes of Theodore Dreiser and John Dos
Passos in the book, especially the latter's use of innovative devices and
poetry to give a wider social ambience to his story. True enough; and
some of his stylistic debt is also to William Faulkner's novel *The Sound
and the Fury*, which taught a whole generation of writers how to tell a
story as a puzzle. One of Faulkner's notable devices was the use of the
biographical sketch to enlarge and complete the story; and Doctorow
does this on the book's final page with great effectiveness.

This single page forces the reader to reconsider all that has gone
before, but in a new light, and it thumbnails the character forward with
both economy and high significance.

On first reading some sections seemed irrelevant to the main thrust
of the book; but Doctorow insists by his willful style that when he says
that something is relevant, it most definitely is relevant.

Not every reader will agree. Those who buy *Loon Lake* expecting a
repeat performance of *Ragtime*, his phenomenal best-seller of five years
ago, will be in for a twelve-dollar jolt.

I think this is Doctorow's best novel, which is saying a great deal,
for *The Book of Daniel*, his third novel, was a work of great power.
Nevertheless, I think *Loon Lake* is better, more shimmering as a work
of art and an example of the contemporary American literary imagination
at its very best.

1980

Norman Mailer:

An Eavesdropper at the Lotos Club

On November 13, 1991, Norman Mailer was formally invested with his most recent laurel by Governor Mario Cuomo, who conferred upon him the title of New York State Author. It is an honorific position that lasts for two years, and carries a few obligations—some formal speeches around the state, and serving on the committee to choose the State Author who will succeed him.

At Norman's investiture I gave the introduction, and because no one here at the Lotos Club tonight, except Norman, my wife, my son, and myself heard that introduction, and because Norman taught me many years ago that the mark of a serious man is that he can always reconstitute his mood, I thought I would repeat my speech and its mood.

Back in 1967, when Norman had just published his tenth book, and his fifth novel, *Why Are We in Vietnam?*—plus a lengthy magazine essay on film, literature, politics, and American culture—and was also writing, directing, and acting in his first movie, I decided to write a piece on him for my Sunday column in the *Albany Times-Union*. For me Mailer was—and still is—a great innovator, a writer with extraordinary control of the language and an outlandishly inventive mind. He was an unpredictable citizen of multiple worlds, a man who didn't seem to repeat himself, who was anxious to create new forms of fiction, journalism, and self-communion. Like most of the American literary community, and long before I was a part of it, I relished Mailer's debut in 1948 with *The Naked and the Dead*; for although he'd taken a major cue from John Dos Passos, a hero of innovation in the American novel (he has also said the biggest influence on that novel was *Moby Dick*), Norman had

161

moved the form forward into territory—explicit sexuality, for instance —where Dos Passos had never trod. Norman was twenty-five years old, a wunderkind, and he reaped the rewards that go with such an incarnation.

The Deer Park came along in 1955, and maybe it was and maybe it wasn't Jack Kennedy's favorite among Mailer works, but it became mine; the best Hollywood novel—though it was much more than that—since Nathanael West's *Day of the Locust*.

The year 1959 saw the publication of *Advertisements for Myself*, a paradigmatic work whose form was so viable that it is still being emulated today. *Advertisements* was a vital, funny, wacko, nasty, talented, and enormously readable work, a roundup of fiction, poetic, dramatic, and polemical fragments from all points of Norman's literary compass. It was in this book that Norman began collecting his opinions. He probably has not yet published his opinion on everything, though it does *seem* that he has: strong opinions, provocative opinions, offensive opinions.

It really isn't unreasonable to say that throughout his long and judg-mental career as a writer, Norman has offended just about everybody worth offending. He has made enemies of Presidents, clerics, conser-vatives, liberals, prizefighters, sportswriters, militarists, oncologists, feminists, blacks, birth-control advocates, sexual purists, gays, voters, readers, plastic manufacturers, publishers, critics by the boatload, and, of course, other fiction writers.

One of his non-ideological traits that usually offends the self-effacing wallflowers among us has been his willingness to talk to himself about himself. Early on he found, in his own internal conversation, a bountiful supply of ideas of notable substance, and, working as an aggressive and scholarly journalist of the ego, he relentlessly explored them. In the process he delivered unto us that memorable literary form, "The Self-Interview." I'm not sure Norman invented this form, but he certainly elevated it to new significance.

I came across it when I was writing about him in the sixties, and I thought of using it myself. But that seemed slavishly imitative. Surely there was one more form waiting to be invented. And so with some pleasure, back then, I gave voice to myself, and to Norman, by selectively quoting what he had written or said, and offered my readers a form I called "The Self-Interview, with the Absent Subject as Occasional Commentator."

I'd like to return to that form now, but, since Norman is not absent tonight, it's only proper to give the form a new name. And so here we present, for the second time anywhere, "The Self-Interview with the Eavesdropping Subject as Occasional Commentator."

INTERVIEWER: Could you explain why Norman was chosen as State Author this year?

KENNEDY: The judges unanimously agreed that his lifetime achievement in literature, journalism, and letters was extraordinary, and that his literary ambition was even beyond that. Consider his new novel, *Harlot's Ghost*, which runs 1,310 pages.

INTERVIEWER: How did Norman react when you told him about the award?

KENNEDY: He wondered if the governor really would show up to present it. He also mentioned all the presidential clamor being heard in Albany, and said if this had happened to him when he was running for mayor of New York City he certainly would have known how to handle it.

INTERVIEWER: What does he think about this award business?

NORMAN: Your speaker is here to state that he likes prizes, honors, and awards and will accept them. . . . We are entering a world in which the value systems of the stoutest ego will spin like a turning table, the assertions of the inner voice go caroming through vales of electronic rock. So it is nice to have awards and to accept them. They are measures of the degree to which an Establishment meets that talent it has hindered and helped.

INTERVIEWER: A friend of mine suggests that Norman has hindered himself as much as anyone has; that he has been his own worst enemy. My friend sees Norman as an imp of the perverse, the universal id.

KENNEDY: That's not an unreasonable judgment. Norman likes to place himself in jeopardy. As the critic John Leonard pointed out, during a lightning storm you can count on Norman to put up a kite instead of an umbrella. Isn't that true, Norman?

NORMAN: As one of my characters says, "If you are afraid, don't hesitate. Get right into the trouble if that is the honest course. . . . The natural condition of men's lives [is] the fear of tests. . . ." I admired men who were willing to live day by day with bare-wire fear even if it left them naked as drunks, incompetent wild men, accident-prone.

INTERVIEWER: Will Norman go on writing fiction?

KENNEDY: He's writing a book on Picasso, but he's also already at work on a sequel to *Harlot's Ghost*. No matter what else he might do, fiction is where he lives. Am I right, Norman? Tell me I'm right when I'm right.

NORMAN (smiling): I believe the novel has its own particular resource, which is almost magical. If you write purely and your style's good enough, you can establish a communion between yourself and the reader that can be found in no other art. And this communion can continue for hours, weeks, years.

INTERVIEWER: We could continue for hours with this discussion, but it is now time for Norman to speak for himself not only in his own words, but in his own voice. And so with great pleasure I now turn this microphone over to our State Author, and one of the best and most vital writers on the planet, Norman Mailer.

1992

Robert Penn Warren:

Willie Stark, Politics, and the Novel

In 1946 Robert Penn Warren published *All the King's Men*, the novel that would make him an international literary figure. It was the story of Willie Stark, a Southern governor not unlike Louisiana's Huey Long, whom Warren had observed from a distance in the early 1930s at Louisiana State University. The book became a critical success, a bestseller, won the Pulitzer Prize, and was translated into at least seventeen languages.

Warren conceived Stark's story first as a verse play, *Proud Flesh*, then wrote the novel, then wrote a new play with the same title as the novel. The U.S. film version of the book won an Academy Award, and a Russian version also won a best-picture award. The book has been the subject of a vast amount of scholarship, and has been called the best political novel of the century.

Robert Penn Warren was sixty-eight, not all gray yet, tall, trim, and tweedy when we talked at his home in Fairfield, Connecticut, on February 14, 1973. I was writing the first of what was to be a series of interviews for a national magazine with writers on their masterworks; but the series never materialized and this interview was never published until now.

Warren had moved to Fairfield in the early 1950s, converting two old seventeenth-century barns into a spacious rustic-modern home with eighteen-foot ceilings. He had published nine novels up to this time, plus nine volumes of poetry, and had won a second and third Pulitzer (both for poetry; he is the only writer ever to win the prize for both fiction and poetry), a National Book Award, the Bollingen Prize, the National Medal for Literature, the National Humanities Foundation's Thomas

Jefferson Award, and much more, all these for his poetry. In 1986 he would be named the first official Poet Laureate of the United States.

Warren's wife, the writer Eleanor Clark (*The Oysters of Locmariaquer*, a National Book Award winner), prepared lunch for us all in the midst of our Fairfield conversation. The Warrens both work at home, each with an office in one of the two converted barns. To reach Robert Penn Warren's office you walked past garden implements and fertilizer and then you arrived at what he called his boar's nest.

But we talked in tidier surroundings, a living room of the main house with a picture window that looked out onto a meadow with tall pine trees that Warren had planted in the 1950s. His Kentucky twang was difficult to understand at first, but then you quickly tuned in, and you noticed how often he laughed when he talked.

KENNEDY: When you look back, does the book have a special place among your works?

WARREN: It's a hard question. I don't think any of the novels had the intimacy of the poems, but putting the poetry aside, if I'm just rating the novels, I think it's one of the three I have to rest my case on, feel closest to.

KENNEDY: And the other two?

WARREN: *World Enough and Time*, the novel that came after it, and then *Flood*, which came out in '64. The first two were extremely well received, and *Flood* had, you might say, a controversial press. Lot of savage attack, and praise too. Those three, I think, are the novels with the most weight in them. Of course I always say the next one's going to be it.

KENNEDY: In some ways it's not political at all, but it's been called the best political novel of the century. Why are there so few memorable political novels?

WARREN: I don't think of novels in categories like that, novels about horse racing, about crapshooting, and lovemaking. I think of them in terms of the emotional tone or the thematic issues they propose, categories which are more inside.

KENNEDY: But when you think of novels of substance with political content, what comes to mind?

WARREN: I guess you could call *The Gilded Age* by Mark Twain a

Robert Penn Warren makes a literary point, orally and digitally, to
interviewer William Kennedy, at the Warren home in Fairfield, Conn.,
in February, 1973.

political novel and that's a memorable thing; it involved politics. *De-
mocracy* by Henry Adams is an unreadable novel but a fascinating book.
He sure couldn't write novels but as a commentary on politics it's fascinating. *Under Western Eyes* by Conrad is political in one sense; revolutionary psychology is what it's about rather than the practical
applications of it. Of course there's Shakespeare's plays, some intensely
political, and they're quite memorable; but it isn't the first thing you
remember about them.

KENNEDY: Or your book either. Maybe in retrospect it's Willie Stark's
story but when you're reading it it's Jack Burden's dominance, and the
structure of a society.

WARREN: When I was in Italy in '48 Berenson wrote me. I went to
see him and he said, "Your book's not about Stark," and that surprised
me a little because I didn't think it was about him either. And he says
"Stark's not very interesting. The book's about Burden and that's what
I like. That's your book." I hadn't thought of it so baldly, total dismissal
of the Stark story.

KENNEDY: But Stark did dominate your first work on the subject, the
verse play.

WARREN: Yes. I began that play in the shade of an olive tree in a
wheat field outside Perugia in the fall of '37, finished a first draft just
before Christmas in 1939. I rewrote it but then put it aside and started

another novel, and when I looked at it again in early 1943, my whole feel for it changed. And I decided there were more things involved than I was able to get into a play. I began to see that one thing that caught my interest originally had not been the notion of a man of power, obsession of power, riding against the obstacles in his way to success and then disaster—but the context—his relations to other people. More and more I had felt more than a personal story here. The man of power is only half of the matter—the other half being the context in which power is achieved. The man of power achieves power only because he fulfills the needs of others, in both obvious and secret ways. In its most obvious form in my novel this appears in Sugar Boy, the little stuttering gunman, whose devotion to Stark comes from the fact that Stark "can talk so good," is an orator. And so on up to Jack Burden, who having lost a grip on his personal life, only comes alive when he identifies himself with the man who can act. The pattern that finally emerged—emerged because it was not according to a scheme but by a development, a slowly growing envisagement—was that Stark fulfilled some need in every person around him. And this, of course, has implications for politics, or history.

But who could tell the story? It had to be somebody who was intimately involved in the process, who had a deep personal stake and who was intelligent and detached enough to understand his own predicament. Then Burden came in almost as an accident. He had been in the original play as merely a technical device in the assassination scene. He didn't have a name even. He came in to distract the audience and in a sense distract the assassin, before the victim comes on and is shot. A newspaperman, an old friend of the assassin, Adam Stanton, they talk and Adam is caught at the moment of murder and suicide with one backward look to boyhood, to the other world, the unspoiled world.

Then two years after I finished the play I saw Burden as the key to the context I was after. The first morning I sat down with pencil and paper and started to write the novel, Burden started talking.

KENNEDY: Would you explain why you decided to write the Cass Mastern section [a long flashback to a pre–Civil War episode].

WARREN: I was jammed. I'd gotten to the point where I was going to have a flat, straightforward story. I couldn't see how I could give a new dimension to it. You know you don't think about things in these abstract terms at the time. You feel it rather than think it. At that point the story was going in a straight line to a preconceived climax. I had to have a new dimension to put the whole story against. The Cass Mastern story gave that. It came in a kind of flash.

KENNEDY: How far were you in at the time?

WARREN: At the exact point where the story is interpolated (about one-third in). I was reading a lot of stuff about Kentucky history at that time.

KENNEDY: I wondered about your research on that.

WARREN: It wasn't research, it was reading. I don't research a novel. I did no research at all for the Stark side of the thing, not a damn minute of it, didn't even read a newspaper. What I didn't have in my head I didn't have. I was not following Huey Long; I never did one minute of research on Long. I didn't care what Long was, in that sense. I was trying to make a character. But I was reading a lot of Kentucky history, just reading, at the time I was writing the novel and this character [Mastern] began to take shape.

KENNEDY: You've credited your editor on that book, Lambert Davis, with changing it. What did he change?

WARREN: He was an extraordinarily able editor at Harcourt Brace, my editor and friend. He was not much older than I but was farther along in the world than I was. The big thing was he said the novel is starting wrong. Cut that out and start right here, where I start now.

KENNEDY: What was wrong about it,

WARREN: Too wordy, too abstract.

KENNEDY: Was it nonrealistic?

WARREN: No, it was realistic, but rhetorical rather than specific. Abstract in that sense. I remember in that opening description, when Burden meets Stark the first time in a saloon . . . it was like Caesar described by Plutarch. The young man standing on a street corner of Rome, delicately scratching the top of his scalp with one finger; who would've thought he had any harm in him? That kind of crap. Now Lambert said, "This is where the thing begins, on this road, going to Mason City. And this [other] is all preparatory and obviously preparatory, and a lot of bad writing here too, inflated writing." And so I tried what he suggested. In the car going to Mason City the scene comes alive, something happens and you get into Stark's world immediately. Lambert was right. You had to take the author's promise that [the original opening] was going to mean something later. That's a very poor way to start a book.

KENNEDY: How did the Elizabethans influence the book? You've written about that but without being specific.

WARREN: Let me take an indirect approach to that question. Back then—and now—I was much more soaked in poetry and Elizabethan drama than I was in fiction, and that fact, no doubt, made me think of a novel in much the way I think of a poem. I think of a story, sure, but I also think of it as a metaphorical structure going at the same time as the narrative and other structure. And frequently this feeling I'm driving for seems to come as an image, even a scene, that is floating there, not tied to narrative yet. It's there ahead of me. It couldn't be dramatized directly yet it is somehow in the background. That's related to the Elizabethan stuff. The literal plays behind the novel were two Shakespearean political plays, *Julius Caesar* and *Coriolanus*; they were there consciously. And then, less consciously, Webster's *White Devil*. Flaminio, a character in *White Devil*, was in the back of my mind in some sense, I'm sure. I did not realize it at the time but I now see it was. He was somehow behind Jack Burden. Flaminio is a man of blankness gone evil, who's taken refuge in evil to find meaning.

KENNEDY: Did you consider Willie evil?

WARREN: I wanted to make him a good man, a decent man. . . . He's gone so far into making the means defile his ends that there's a horror he can't dig out of in the end.

KENNEDY: Have you ever written about a totally evil figure?

WARREN: No, I have no desire to. This thing came to a head when they were making a movie from the book. There were two movies made in this country, one by [Joseph] Mankiewicz, a two-shot TV thing I never saw, I was out of the country; and Robert Rossen did the other, made a damn good movie of it. But about two-thirds through he left my character entirely and made a total villain out of Stark: the fascist brute. My man, you see, gets some redemption out of the novel . . . dies repentant. Now Bob had four or five endings and ran them all off and said "Now, Red, which do you like?" I picked one but said none of them represent what I said in the book. "Son," he said to me, "when you come to Hollywood you've got to learn one thing—there's not going to be anything called irony in the end of an American picture. It's gonna be cops and robbers, cowboys and Indians." And so Willie died muttering the last line from the Horst Wessel . . . tied right into the Nazi-Mussolini picture. Bob and I got along fine because we understand each other. It's his movie, not mine.

KENNEDY: Did the book and movie make a big financial difference to you?

WARREN: After the book I felt I could eke out a living without teaching. I'd tried it before but it didn't work out.

KENNEDY: Part of the success of the book, its wide appeal, seems at least in part the Huey Long element, the politics, the feeling people have that they've got a window on something authentic. You've written about this but I wonder if you'd take it now into the question of fiction versus nonfiction, the appeal.

WARREN: A lot of fiction from the start has been based on the fact that it must claim authenticity. . . . *A Journal of the Plague Year* . . . the manuscript found in the chest, the bottle, the thing being authenticated. This is the appeal to journalistic interest, in the best sense of that word. We want the facts of the case. . . . With the rise of modern journalism, in terms of the Civil War, the rise of big newspapers, the country put tremendous new weight on the fact, and this, associated with the rise of pragmatic philosophy, not only William James but the whole sense of the state of mind you associate with James's philosophy: the open-endedness of moving in to see what action means—this is all mixed up with it. By the time you get to the 1880s and the nineties, with the rise of protest journalism, organized muckraking, you have a new urgency about the handling of fact, fact as meaningful politically, in another spirit: we are exposing the hideous underside of life. You get a person like Stephen Crane as a young boy going down in the mines, standing in soup lines and sleeping in flophouses to see what it was like. He was saying the fact is better than the story. Now this became so acute that one of the reigning novelists at that time, H. B. Fuller, who is recognized by Dreiser as the father of American realism, said that the novel is dead, that novelists should become biographers, writers of fact; there's no reality in fiction anymore. Now in another aspect of the romance of fact you get Richard Harding Davis, this handsome, well-mannered, adventurous youth whose life is more interesting than fiction—war correspondent par excellence. He became an arbiter of taste and the model for young men to follow in their lives, the pre-Hemingway model. Davis was so famous it's hard to believe it. The old Oliver Wendell Holmes, the great autocrat of the breakfast table, the dictator of taste, would make a personal call on Davis. Now these two impulses [that Crane and Davis represent] are very strong and we've had them with a vengeance. But Crane is very mixed, on one hand in the flophouses to capture the sensation, to say the imagination can act, and on the other hand his most famous book [*The Red Badge of Courage*] is about a war he never saw, pure imagination. Interviewing a few old men down around Frederick and then reading the official record of the Civil War and thinking about it, imagining it, he gets a masterpiece. He made a very fruitful blending of these things, the technique of fact in the world of the imagination. The point I'm getting at is you find a world now hailing this as a new discovery.

KENNEDY: What work are you referring to?

WARREN: Capote, say. *In Cold Blood.* Touting this as new. It's an extremely effective book but there's no novelty to it. It's what Fuller was pulling for and others have practiced for a long, long time. . . . People read for a number of reasons. They want to find out how beet sugar is made or how to give a dinner party, or what's the best practice in bed. These are all marvelous know-how books, and they also tell about people, gossip books. But the immediate appeal is the newsworthy element. Fitzgerald's fame was based on his bringing news from the underworld of youth. That's big, and why shouldn't it be? . . . But one thing the fact novel or journalistic essay cannot do is give the inside, because only the imagination can do that. You believe the inside of Hamlet, or Marcel in Proust, or Ishmael more than you believe the inside of Henry Adams in the autobiography, or the inside of the *Cold Blood* killers. The killers you know a lot about, but you don't know them. You know Clyde Griffiths, though. You know him only because he's not factual, only because the fact of creation has made him credible. This is not saying better or worse, it's saying different. The fact novel is fine for decor, the milieu. When the real crisis comes it's always the thing seen from the inside that sticks.

KENNEDY: But people don't seem to value that truth these days. Talk to publishers and they say, "What are you going to do about fiction, it doesn't sell."

WARREN: One reason we can say is that there are not enough good novels.

KENNEDY: But why is that?

WARREN: I'm just making a guess, and I don't mean well-crafted novels but ones that take bold risks of imagination. Maybe too much depends on documentation. The novel approaches too close to journalism and forfeits its powers of imaginative creation to be more convincing at the level of reportage. And you can't compete with reporting.

KENNEDY: You wouldn't think it was because of the absence of interest in the interior of the human being?

WARREN: It may very well be that. At the same time the notion of the interior is news too. But [you find] people interested in inner life as treated by generalizations, by experts, by Kinsey researchers, by God-knows-who dealing with inner life. But they're not talking about individuals. They're talking about patterns. And it may be that the notion of individualism is in decay, that your mass culture isn't interested in individuals at all.

KENNEDY: What does this mean for fiction?

WARREN: I don't know, but you find people as far back as Valéry saying that journalism and movies give you immediacy of fact and impact you don't get in a novel, and so literature can only become more abstract, move toward the patterns more or less like abstract painting. So you get the pattern in the art itself rather than art as related to life. And this is a very elite, very difficult kind of art which is not related to the meat and potatoes of living. Now this [move to abstract literature] is hailed today by some as new, but it's not new at all, it's an echo of Valéry. It's important to remember there's a history to these things. It gives a different feeling about the future of the novel. Maybe a more pessimistic one, or optimistic, I'm not saying which it'll be. We're in a process that's been going on a long time, and to gamble it has to be a long-range gamble. Meanwhile, I'm writing another novel, and I have to try to individualize it.

1973

Damon Runyon:

Six-to-Five:
A Nice Price

There's really only one question to ask about Damon Runyon: is he, or isn't he, back in town? We all know he's back on Broadway, ever since the spring of 1992, when the remarkable revival of *Guys and Dolls* opened. But there is also something else going on. I have been approached twice in the past month about writing a movie about his private life, something in which I have a minus-twenty-seven-percent interest; and now here comes Al Silverman (Viking out of Penguin) saying he has snatched up the rights of 125 of Runyon's short stories that have been lying doggo for a number of years and is looking for somebody to handicap two and a half dozen of them and see if there is enough left in the old guy to justify a wager that he can still wow them not only on Broadway but also in Albany.

When I was eleven years old I thought Runyon was the funniest man alive. He was a great newspaperman, which is how I first came to know his name; and then I discovered his short stories and found he could make me laugh three times in one sentence. That was maybe 1939. Now it is 1992 and I laugh four, maybe five times in a paragraph, like this one about a character named Feet Samuels:

"He is a big heavy guy with several chins and very funny feet, which is why he is called Feet. These feet are extra large feet, even for a big guy, and Dave the Dude says Feet wears violin cases for shoes. Of course this is not true, because Feet cannot get either of his feet in a violin case, unless it is a case for a very large violin, such as a cello."

Feet Samuels is a relatively peaceful citizen, but Big Jule (usually pronounced Julie), who made a comeback by being the crapshooting villain of *Guys and Dolls*, is something else. He came on the scene long ago in the Runyon story "The Hottest Guy in the World." Big Jule is considered hot because he is wanted for robbery or safecracking in such locations as Pittsburgh, Minneapolis, Kansas City, Toledo, Spokane, San Francisco, and Canton, Ohio, and there is, as Runyon puts it, "also something about a shooting match in Chicago, but of course this does not count so much as only one party is fatally injured."

But the tally makes Big Jule very hot indeed, about as hot as John Gotti, the Mafia chieftain who in early April of '92 was convicted in Brooklyn of racketeering, which included five murders, a murder conspiracy, extortion, and such things.

Mr. Gotti, visited in the courtroom by movie stars, his wardrobe written about as a fashion trend, was, at the moment of trial, a celebrity of serious note, although having been sentenced after trial to life in prison, the note stands some chance of being muffled. But there are always appeals to higher courts, and John Gotti may make a comeback like Big Jule. What is certain is that if Damon Runyon had been alive in '92 he would have covered the Gotti trial and probably would have been a sometime dinner companion of Mr. Gotti also, as he was with Al Capone before Mr. Capone's trial for tax evasion; such was Runyon's fascination with gangsters and his need to know what made them what they were.

In his younger years Mr. Gotti served prison terms for attempted burglary and attempted manslaughter. But thereafter he avoided conviction on assault and racketeering charges in widely publicized trials. Incriminating tape recordings were used in his 1992 trial, but Mr. Gotti's lawyers argued that these were not evidence of criminality, much as Big Jule says of himself in *Guys and Dolls*: "I used to be bad when I was a kid but ever since then I have gone straight as I can prove by my record—33 arrests and no convictions."

Many of Runyon's characters are viewed at times as romanticized gangsters, defanged and cuddly, when they are really deadly citizens; and this sugarcoating of evil is said to be responsible for the popularity of his tales.

Some consider this to be a knock on Runyon, but such a knock isn't worth anybody's time. Crime and criminals in any form are a given in literature, movies, and theater, and this fact antedates Runyon by centuries: in John Gay's *The Beggar's Opera* of 1728, for instance, from which the Brecht-Weill *Threepenny Opera* of 1928 derives, and where that engaging scoundrel Macheath, or Mack the Knife, was born. It was Jonathan Swift who suggested that a Newgate prison pastoral "might make an odd pretty sort of thing," which it did in Mr. Gay's hands, and it has continued to do so on Broadway and also in Hollywood, where sixteen (at least) of Runyon's short stories have been turned into movies, some terrific, some dreadful. God must have loved gangster movies, he made so many of them.

Criticism of Runyon that is more to the point of argument here was reported in a biography, *A Gentleman of Broadway*, by Edwin P. Hoyt, published in 1964. Mr. Hoyt wrote that in the early 1960s, 150 academics, mostly literature teachers, decided that Damon Runyon, in the biographer's dismissive synthesis, "stood and stands nowhere."

This was the man, two of whose short-story collections in the late 1920s and early 1930s had sold more than a million copies each in paperback; who was translated into French, Dutch, Italian, Indonesian, and British. Lord Beaverbrook published him at length in the *London Evening Standard*, and the *Standard*'s literary critic called Runyon (according to Clark Kinnaird's preface in the Modern Library treasury) a genius as authentic as Laurence Sterne or James M. Barrie, saying Runyon had "invented a humanity as new and startling as Lewis Carroll did."

(In his story "The Lily of St. Pierre," Runyon makes balanced mention of a Lewis Carroll work: "Lily talks English very good," says the speaker, Jack O'Hearts, while he is recuperating from pneumonia in Lily's house, "and she is always bringing me things . . . and sometimes she reads to me out of a book which is called *Alice in Wonderland*, and which is nothing but a pack of lies, but very interesting in spots.")

Runyon being embraced by the British prompted John Lardner to conclude that "very plainly . . . after a long, slow pull, by way of Poe, Whitman, James, Twain, Cather and Hemingway, our culture finally hit the jackpot with Runyon."

But Runyon died in 1946, his reputation faded, and at the time when he was standing "nowhere," only two of his books and the Modern Library treasury were in print (the treasury is now out of print), and the man did seem to be going the way of yesterday's newspaper.

Today eleven, perhaps twelve of his collections of stories and journalism are in print, which is pleasant news for Runyon fanatics, of which there are several. Also, three more biographies have appeared: *The World of Damon Runyon*, by Tom Clark (1978); *The Men Who Invented Broadway: Damon Runyon, Walter Winchell and Their World* (1981), by John Mosedale; and *Damon Runyon* (1991), by Jimmy Breslin. These and the Hoyt book complement each other, filling in gaps in the life and the work and the age, and so we have a detailed overview of the maestro in his own time.

Jimmy Breslin, whom some regard as the Runyon of his own era (but far more politically sophisticated), is the revisionist, bringing us into the Runyon private life, and finding the famous writer mu~h more wanting as a human being than we previously thought. Mr. ᴮ⸗ ᴵ also offers this evaluation of the man's achievement as a writer:

"Damon Runyon," he writes, "invented the Broadway of *Guys and Dolls* and the Roaring Twenties, neither of which existed, but whose names and phrases became part of theater history and the American language. . . . He made gangsters so enjoyable that they could walk off a page and across a movie screen. . . . He stressed fine, upstanding, dishonest people who fell in love, often to the sound of gunfire that sounded harmless. . . . Many of his people and their actions in real life were frightening to temporal authorities, but what does this have to do with the most important work on earth, placing merriment into the hearts of people?"

This Runyon merriment was, and is, chiefly an achievement of language—the language of gamblers, hoodlums, chorus girls, and cops, that he acquired by listening, then used in his stories, and is therefore credited with inventing. It is a nonesuch argot, and he uses it like no other writer who came before or after him. In the best of his short stories there is a comic fluency in this invented tongue, an originality of syntax, a fluidity of word and event that is a relentless delight.

In a story called "Broadway Incident" he tells of the suffering love of Ambrose Hammer, a Broadway drama critic, for a beautiful doll named Hilda Hiffenbrower, whose husband, Herbert, will not give her a divorce. Runyon writes:

"Well I happen to know Hilda better than Ambrose does. To tell the truth I know her when her name is Mame something and she is dealing them off her arm in a little eating gaff on Seventh Avenue, which is before she goes in show business and changes her name to Hilda, and I also know that the real reason Herbert will not give her this divorce is because she wants eight gallons of his heart's blood and both legs in the divorce settlement, but as Herbert has a good business head he is by no means agreeable to these terms, though I hear he is willing to compromise on one leg to get rid of Hilda."

This is a bit of serious character building through language; but Runyon's asides are often what ring the gong, for instance in that St. Pierre story again: "The first time I see St. Pierre I will not give you eight cents for the whole layout, although of course it is very useful to parties in our line of business [smuggling whiskey]. It does not look like much, and it belongs to France, and nearly all the citizens speak French, because most of them are French, and it seems it is the custom of the French people to speak French no matter where they are, even away off up yonder among the fish."

Far more serious writers than Runyon have fallen on their faces and other parts because they lacked what he had: a love and mastery of his language, a playful use of its idiosyncrasies. His plots, on the other hand, were usually convoluted exercises in simple irony—O. Henry reversals, frequently predictable, sometimes zany, with resolutions often sticky with treacle—and will not stand up in court.

And yet he salvaged these stories, more often than not, with his rhythmic street idioms, his indefatigable wit, and his peculiar acceptance of the paralegal rules of this world that he chronicled. If he'd been a moralist among the grifters, goons, and golddiggers, he'd have remained an outsider, without the privileged insights that have made his work so singular.

The Runyon method was to be the nameless narrator, the detached observer, the reticent sponge, taking it all in, but not even asking questions; for, as he pointed out, when you start asking questions, people are liable to think that you are perhaps looking for answers. He knows everybody and has formed cogent opinions on them all. As to Judge Goldfobber in the story "Breach of Promise," the narrator points out that he is only a lawyer, not a judge, "and he is 100 to 1 in my line against ever being a judge, but he is called Judge because it pleases him, and everybody always wishes to please [him because he] is a wonderful hand for keeping citizens from getting into the sneezer, and better than Houdini when it comes to getting them out of the sneezer after they are in."

The chance of any writer's work surviving his own death for very long is always a longshot. I used to quote Runyon as saying "All life is nine-to-five against." But Peter Maas, the writer, countered my numbers and said that the true quote was as follows: "All life is six-to-five against, just enough to keep you interested." It turns out that Peter is somewhat correct. The quote comes out of the story "A Nice Price," in which Sam the Gonoph hears that the odds on a boat race between Harvard and Yale are one-to-three, Yale, and Sam the Gonoph, who is handy at making odds, says, "Nothing between human beings is one-to-three. In fact I long ago come to the conclusion that all life is six-to-five against."

And so, confronting the question of whether Damon Runyon is back in town, we must consider the catalytic effect of the *Guys and Dolls* revival, and then all these old Runyon films turning up regularly on cable TV—like *Lady for a Day* and its remake, *Pocketful of Miracles*, both of which I always watch all over again. And I think of how I was convulsed many years ago by the movie made from the Runyon–Howard Lindsay play, *A Slight Case of Murder*; and I think of the vibrant journalism Runyon wrote—*Trials and Other Tribulations*, for instance, which was the book he was preparing for publication when he died.

And I think, most of all, of the short stories in this book, which I have just been rereading for the past week as a way of challenging my most significant values, such as, can I still read these things? And half a century after I discovered them I am delighted to report that I find myself tickled silly by them still, all of them, and want to pass them on to my grandchildren. I already passed them on to my children.

Like a second-story man who can't stand heights, I don't want to get too lofty about all this; and, what is more, I have predicted comebacks in the past for John O'Hara and William Saroyan and I am still waiting for their trains; and I know the thinning ranks of modern readers will be put off by Runyon's antique argot, and by the prehistoric hipness (hepness in those days) of his world; and yet I am willing to take a little of that six-to-five that Damon Runyon is back, not quite settled in yet, a little unsteady on his pins after the journey, but definitely here: our literary equivalent of his contemporaries, the Marx Brothers (does anybody ever knock them because of their plots?), which is to say that his work has not turned into dusty dingbats but has proven to be enduringly comic, thoroughly original, and that he ranks as one of the funniest dead men ever to use the English language. Six-to-five, a nice price. Bet me.

1992

PART THREE

Thirteen Reviews, One Review Rebutted

Samuel Beckett:

The Artful Dodger
Revealed

We thought we knew how it is with Samuel Beckett—maestro of the reclusive act, translator of spiritual angst into the mysterious, convoluted novels and plays that have made him the most written-about writer of the century. But we didn't know. Now we know, from Deirdre Bair's new biography. It is difficult to imagine a more revealing work of literary scholarship being published in this age than this stunning tale of the horrendous and admirable life of one of the world's most important writers.

Bair, who teaches at the University of Pennsylvania, was working toward her doctorate in 1971 when she blithely wrote Beckett, asking if she might do his biography. To the surprise of all, including very likely Beckett himself, a lifelong artful dodger of questions about his private life, he said what amounted to yes, but with peculiarly Beckettian ambivalence. (The word he perhaps most prefers in the world is "perhaps.")

"He would not help me, he said, but he would not hinder me, either," Bair writes in a preface. She met Beckett in Paris and he introduced her to some of his friends and wrote letters to foundations and libraries on her behalf, telling them all the same ambivalent yes. Bair, a former journalist, then spent six years reporting on and piecing together this tissue of agonies, miseries and pyrrhic triumphs that constitute Beckett's life.

The result, says Bair, is not definitive, for she left out certain information on the private lives of Beckett and people close to him. Lack of time also kept her from seeing others with much more to say about the man. Even so, the book bears comparison to Richard Ellmann's great biography of James Joyce, to which it is a companion piece, just as Beckett's life is companionate to Joyce's.

Ellmann refused to be interviewed by Bair for this work, very likely because Beckett so strongly disapproved of Ellmann's treatment of Joyce ("He did not need to pry, to publish all those letters," said Beckett vitriolically of Ellmann). So much more wondrous, then, is the Bair achievement, which extensively uses some three hundred letters Beckett wrote to an Irish scholar, Thomas McGreevy, in which Beckett detailed the whole inner core of his suffering, isolation and occasionally large, but more often small, joys over several decades. Without these letters, Bair admits, the biography would hardly be what it is. In Chapters Nine and Eleven, for instance, ninety-one out of 154 footnotes cite the McGreevy letters.

The book is probably full of other revelations, but one would have to read the hundreds of books about Beckett to be certain. One revelation of which this book's advance publicity boasts is the story of his winning the Croix de Guerre for his years in the French resistance in Paris during World War II. He was also in the maquis in unoccupied southern France, which is also partially documented. "Boy Scout stuff," Beckett said of these involvements, a typically modest attitude toward his own achievement. Only his wife and a fellow resister knew of his award, until it became public knowledge in 1975.

But we must believe that in spite of disdaining it, Beckett also valued it, as he valued his honorary doctorate of letters from his alma mater, Trinity College in Dublin (which he accepted in person), and the Nobel Prize (which he accepted in absentia). He yearned mightily for recognition for two and a half decades, even as he refused to court the marketplace. He yearned, too, for popular success, even as he wrote the most inaccessible works of any modern novelist except, perhaps, the author of *Finnegans Wake*.

Such a curious polarity helped keep him ill for a lifetime: hating his mother, the prime source of his trouble, at the same time he felt almost psychotically guilty for being separated from her. His relationship with his wife, Suzanne, whom he married in 1961 only to insure her inheriting his wealth, is comparable. They have been together since 1938, but have lived bizarrely separated lives (two telephones in the one house, with separate listings; her quarters furnished with the effulgence of a *haute bourgeoise*, his with the sparseness of a Trappist monk).

A major weakness of the Bair book is its delineation of Madame Beckett, who seems far more complex than the admittedly abundant detail makes her out to be, and clearly of extraordinary importance in Beckett's life. She and he, Beckett admits, are the prototypes for Hamm and Clov in *Endgame*, and she floats significantly through the works he wrote after the war. But in the biography she is elusive, and we know there is more to her, a feeling we do not get, say, from Ellmann's treatment of Nora Joyce.

But Madame Beckett is as private a person as her husband, and perhaps as idiosyncratic, and vulnerable. She refused to partake of his social life very early in their relationship, living only to care for him as a mate, rankled when she could not, passionately resenting his success, envying his fame, and also obsessively loyal to his every need.

But if the book fails to confront her fully, it deluges us with data and insightful appraisals of him. He was an isolated person from childhood (he felt he was not fully born, and his first memory, he claims, is prenatal). His family never understood him, or his overpowering drive to be a writer. They were ashamed of his early work (*Whoroscope* and *More Pricks Than Kicks*), on the basis of the titles alone. He exiled himself from them as best he could, living only off their meager dole.

Their Irish puritanism was as alien to him as their mercantile brains, yet he loved his father, and loved and hated his mother, and maintained a horrible but enduring, and in its own way loyal, relationship to them until they died. But his suffering for it all was equally enduring: he generated psychosomatic boils on his genitals, cysts in his anus, constipation, night sweats, nightmares, insomnia, colds, flu, pleurisy and mental breakdown. He had lifelong trouble with his teeth, mouth, heart and lungs. He had choking fits, and withdrew into the fetal position.

Psychoanalysis in London helped bring him partway out of his misery; distance from the family helped at other times. But even at the pinnacle of his success—winning the Nobel Prize—for months he was so physically debilitated by so many ills that his doctor could not operate on the glaucoma that was keeping him all but blind.

His works have always treated of prolonged and profound suffering, but not until the revelation of this biography have we been fully able to understand that that old bum Molloy, that nameless protagonist of *The Unnameable*, that sexless figure in *How It Is*, the Hamm and Clov of *Endgame*, and the Vladimir and Estragon of *Waiting for Godot*, who cannot go on, but who go on, are not only Beckett's psychic projections, but the full, transported actuality of this extraordinary man's extraordinary burden.

His subjects are failure (*Murphy*, his first novel, was rejected by forty-two publishers and sold six copies during its first year of publication in France), agony, despair and suffering. He has lived all his life in hell, and it steams up from the brimstone of every line he ever wrote.

Writing these lines has been his whole life. Women were conveniences; love didn't exist, only sex. Friends were important but resistible, whiskey was invaluable, isolation essential. Yet only writing really sustained life for him, writing of a kind that came from a spelunker in the deepest caverns of the soul and the unconscious. Beckett was from the beginning an intellectual, a Proust and Dante scholar, a Joyce explicator, a student of Descartes and Schopenhauer. But he devalued intellectual writing all his life, once dismissing an Aldous Huxley novel as "unremittingly smart."

He became famous in 1953 as a playwright (after a quarter century of struggle), but he plays this down, thinks of himself primarily as a novelist, and of theater as the therapy that helped him out of his fiction-writing block. He considers *Godot* a poor play that was written for money, and *Endgame* his masterpiece. He has a trunkful of unpublished and unfinished manuscripts which we may or may not have access to in time, and he continues to write even now, minimally, but significantly.

Bair closes her book with Beckett's eloquent remark about this continuation of work: "I couldn't have done it otherwise. Gone on, I mean. I could not have gone through the awful wretched mess of life without having left a stain upon the silence."

We learn from the biography that Beckett's work was an obsessive piling up of failures, which in time came to be viewed as qualified successes, or perhaps masterpieces. But one also derives from the story of this generous, self-denying, long-suffering, willful man that the final triumph is much more than exemplary compulsion, that it is a writer's victory on that moral plane where we venerate the special few who never confuse obligation with commitment.

1978

The Lime Works:

Thomas Bernhard's Citadel

Knowing it isn't what it seems to be will help you penetrate Thomas Bernhard's formidable novel *The Lime Works*. What it seems to be at first is a perverse, self-indulgent anti-novel. But it becomes a masterfully dense set of aesthetic, social and political metaphors about contemporary life, about art, about obsessive commitment to any thing—metaphors that open up to reinterpretation on second and third readings.

The novel is 1973's Christmas present to literary exegetes and to readers in search of something besides narrative sweep. It is, to suggest a few interpretations, a parable about the death of archaic romanticism at the hands of soulless modernism, an attack on anarchy as ultimately self-destructive, an exposé of the bankruptcy of inhumane scholarship, a study of failure, a treatise on the imperfectibility of art, a probe of the symbiotic relation between the analytic and the poetic, an anatomy of an artist's madness, a diagram of a marriage of inimical opposites— spirit and intellect, revolutionist and reactionary, Communist east and capitalist west—and a cautionary tale of the impotence of life stripped of sweetness. The book is none of these above. Neither is it a gothic horror tale that can stand independently of them, though it sometimes seems that. The metaphors are too frequently and obviously intrusive for any conventional story to survive. The book is a jungle of meaning, the opposite of simplistic allegory, and a major achievement because of this.

Set in rural Austria, the book's central figures are Konrad (no other name), and Mrs. Konrad, his wife, no first name; her maiden name was

Zryd. Konrad means bold or wise counselor, an irony, for his boldness
and wisdom are revealed as negative examples of how to live and work.
I don't know what Zryd means.

Konrad has long since rejected his know-nothing capitalist family and
its fortune and chosen a life of the mind. He turned autodidact and fixed
on a book, *The Sense of Hearing*, as his life work. After much haggling
with a nephew who controlled them, Konrad finally buys the defunct
lime works, which has been in his family for centuries, and moves in.
Designed as a lordly manor, with every architectural detail "the result
of a thousand years of calculations," the lime works are immense, with
a vast number of subcellars, every decade seeing a new addition, "a
superstructure tacked on, some part of it torn down."

Each description of the place adds to its strangeness. Visitors approach
it, then run from it. Its grillwork represents two centuries of bad taste.
It is surrounded by ornamental shrubbery which Konrad removes as he
installs new and heavier bars and locks. It stands as a citadel of privacy,
of Spartan commitment, a prison, a dungeon of solitude few men could
endure. It is hidden, accessible only from the east. It has been the scene
of numerous murders.

As the novel begins, Konrad is still writing his book, as he has been
for two decades. He has nothing to show but notes and false starts, for
he is neurotically waiting for his distractions to end and the gush of final
inspiration to begin. He has the entire book in his head and believes
premature shaping through words will destroy it.

He has also just blown the head off his crippled wife with the Mann-
licher carbine she kept strapped to her wheelchair. (The killing was
done Christmas Eve. Konrad dragged the corpse through several rooms
while planning to throw it out a window into the lake, but finally dragged
it back to her bedroom and propped it up in the wheelchair. He then
hid himself in a pit where police find him, his shoes "bloated with liquid
manure.")

The novel then becomes the oblique revelation of how and why Konrad
and wife came to the lime works, how they lived there, why she died,
what Konrad told several of the townsfolk. The story is a free-associated
mass of hearsay, told by an unidentified life-insurance salesman who
keeps quoting people he calls Fro, Wieser, the public works inspector

and others. He often qualifies the sources of his story with comments such as "Konrad is supposed to have said," and so there is doubt as to the accuracy of everything.

Bernhard deliberately keeps us emotionally distant from Konrad and willfully avoids traditional narrative style. The reader must endure Konrad-like distractions and suffer Konrad-like boredom, along with confronting Konrad's long, sometimes brilliant, sometimes mad disquisitions on the masses, the individual, truth, violence, food, sounds, music, death and on—in order to get at Konrad's deceptive character and the story behind the murder.

At first Konrad seems a despotic monster: "He recited to [his wife] a series of sentences with the short *i* sound, such as 'In the Inn district it is still dim,' a hundred times slowly, then a hundred times rapidly and finally about two hundred times as fast as possible in a choppy manner. When he was done he demanded an immediate description of the effect his spoken sentences had on her ear and her brain."

He does this exercise regularly, sometimes for seven hours, giving his wife chronic earache, driving her into apathy. He makes notes on her responses but destroys the notes so no one can deduce his method.

His wife is equally batty. She sends him down every five minutes from her second-floor room to the cellar for a glass of cider, but insists he bring only one glass at a time, never a jugful that might save him a few trips. She also has been knitting him mittens for years, but unravels them as soon as she finishes them. Konrad loathes mittens and she knows it. But on she knits.

The wife, who is Konrad's half-sister and was once a great beauty, is the embodiment of moribund romanticism in the austere modern age, the aristocracy left over after the revolution. She longs for the elegant life she had with her family in the town of Tolbach. Konrad loathes Tolbach. She yearns for the poetry of Novalis, the nineteenth-century German romanticist, but Konrad force-feeds her the politics of Kropotkin, the Russian anarchist, who is his hero.

The two have traveled the world together, accumulating thousands of heirlooms and treasures, which have all (icons too: good-bye religion) been sold for survival money. But Konrad can't bring himself to sell his wife's maternal grandmother's sugar bowl (receptacle of the sweet life, long gone) nor can he part with the Francis Bacon painting, for Bacon is another of his models.

"One had to be more than a mere medical man or a mere philosopher," Konrad says elsewhere, coveting Baconian diversity. "To do this [his own book] it was absolutely necessary to be a mathematician and a physicist as well, that is to say, one should be a master of all natural science, as well as a prophet and a superlative artist." His wife, awash in her anachronistic dilemma, doesn't know whether her husband is a superb artist or a crackpot.

Thomas Bernhard is surely an artist. He is forty-two, Dutch-born, now Austrian, a poet and recipient of several literary prizes in Europe. His three earlier novels are *Frost, Amras* and *Gargoyles*, the latter published here in 1971. *The Lime Works* invites comparison with the run-on novels of Beckett. After page 12, the 241-page book consists of one solid paragraph. One sentence runs thirty-seven printed lines. Yet nothing is impenetrable or even syntactically obtuse, thanks to Sophie Wilkins's always lucid and fluid translation from the German.

The comic element of Konrad's mad commitment is rarely heightened by her, however. The verbal wit, the subtlety and dexterity of language that gives a Beckett paragraph a life all its own, is missing, and so Konrad's behavior can be comic without being very funny. But wishing Bernhard and Miss Wilkins had Beckett's gifts in addition to their own is greedy. What they offer in *The Lime Works* is more than enough for anybody: a Byzantine work of art.

1973

Players:

DeLillo's
Poisoned Flowers

"So where are we?"
"Who knows?"
"We're inside," Lyle said.
"That's for sure."
"It's obvious."
*"It's obvious because if we were outside the cars would be climbing
up my back."*
"The outside world."
*"That's it," McKechnie said. "Things that happen and you're helpless.
All you can do is wait for how bad."*
Lyle didn't know exactly what they were talking about . . .

What we have here is homage to the vapid ironies of Beckett and
Pinter, but we are also in the middle of Don DeLillo's remarkable new
novel of menace and mystery, *Players*, a fastidious rejection of the
modern age. The rejectors and rejectees are one and the same, Lyle and
Pammy, a couple so hip they wonder if they're too intelligent to stay
functional; and they are—in the world their hipness mocks. "Modern-
stupid" is Pammy's view of it all.

She works for the Grief Management Council in the World Trade
Center ("It Ends For Him On The Day He Dies—But You Have To
Face Tomorrow"). Lyle is a broker on the floor of the stock exchange,
loathes it, and amuses his friends with comedy routines he learns from
records. The theater bores him (but not movies) and at home he has fun

quick-flipping the television dial. They order dinner from Dial-A-Steak and argue over whose responsibility it is to buy an extra battery for the Italian clock. When Pammy gets angry at Lyle she cleans the apartment.

The book opens with an allegorical prelude DeLillo calls "The Movie," which collects all the story's principal characters, none of them named yet, on an airplane, watching a movie of a band of terrorists slaughtering several golfers on a fairway, a vicious scene accompanied by tinkly piano music suitable for a Buster Keaton movie. The contrast of blood and piano steeps the scene in "gruesomely humorous ambiguity, a spectacle of ridiculous people doing awful things to total fools."

When the scene ends we are thrown into the real story—Lyle's and Pammy's empty lives—and the book threatens to become another witty send-up of hard-core sophistication. But on page 76, while Lyle is seducing a secretary from the office, he sees in her apartment a photo of her with a man who was recently shot on the stock exchange floor. Also in the photo is the man who shot him. The story instantly assumes a tantalizing new dimension in keeping with the prologue. The killing was connected to terrorists, and so, clearly, is this girl.

Lyle is enthralled and anoints himself as a double agent, initiating contact with the CIA and urging the girl to connect him to the bombers. "I'm out," he tells her. "Let it all come down. Don't you think everybody, nearly, feels that way about their work, where they work all those years?" The bombers take him in with vague talk about plans to bomb the stock exchange. Or do they take him in? It feels like a play to Lyle. Is J. Kinnear, who may have had connections to Oswald, a terrorist? A double agent himself? And what of Marina Vilar and her brother? Did they really dynamite the embassy in Brussels? And Burks, is he CIA, or what?

Lyle feels intelligent conning everybody, but he doesn't know exactly what they are talking about. Again.

Pammy, to rid herself of the stench of up-to-date boredom, flies off to the pure air of Maine with a pair of homosexuals, one of whom she makes her lover. Pammy has no more awareness of what's going on in her life than Lyle has of his, but it's a nice change in Maine, the sex is different, and the talk is amusing. It is certainly some shock when her lover immolates himself at the garbage dump, a simulated Buddhist monk, self-sacrificing in protest against the war this life wages against vulnerable people like himself. Pammy comes back to the city and discovers the meaning of the word "transient."

When we last see Lyle he is in a motel in Canada with the girl who connected him to the terrorists. She is sleeping and he is propped up in bed beside her, awaiting a call from J. Kinnear as to his next move. He has joined the players in the play, he has undergone a transformation. DeLillo writes: "The propped figure . . . is barely recognizable as male. Shedding capabilities and traits by the second, he can still be described (but quickly) as well-formed, sentient and fair. We know nothing else about him."

DeLillo is a spectacular talent, supremely witty and a natural storyteller. (He has written four other novels: *Americana*, his first; *End Zone*; *Great Jones Street*; and *Ratner's Star*.) From his first book it was also clear that his control of the language was of a high order. The difference between that first book and the latest is what he leaves out. *Players* is half the size of *Americana*, but just as dense with implication of the meaning of the lives it presents to us.

Lyle and Pammy are hastily defined, sketches really. But unforgettable sketches, like Lautrec's. How did they get the way they are? Who cares? There they are. Dig them. The entropy of bumblebees. And the flowers are all poison.

1977

Something Happened:

Joseph Heller's Great Monologue

Joseph Heller's new book is exhaustive and exhausting, a major contemporary novel. It maintains him in the first rank of American writers, in the niche he never abandoned after *Catch-22*, but which skeptics were denying him, thinking him a one-book phenomenon. It's been thirteen years since *Catch-22* was published, but it was a worthy gestation period if *Something Happened* is the result. If it had turned out to be a mediocre work, Heller would have been kicked to death by the grasshoppers. But he leaps over multiple heads, let's name no names, primarily because of the scope of the new book and the endlessly fascinating monologue he puts into the mouth of his main character, a son-of-a-bitch named Bob Slocum, a contemporary corporate cipher, a man incapable of producing *Something Happened* or anything so meaningful, but out of whose mouth it all rolls. The book is 569 pages long. I was often bored and exasperated by it, the way we are bored by so many of our unpleasant friends. But I would have kept reading for as long as he kept talking, the way we keep listening to those same awful people spill out their trouble and bile. The fascination of the abominator.

Bob Slocum is no true friend of anybody's. He is a woefully lost figure with a profound emptiness, a sad, absurd, vicious, grasping, climbing, womanizing, cowardly, sadistic, groveling, loving, yearning, anxious, fearful victim of the indecipherable, indescribable malady of being born human. Heller goes the Beckett route (the novels) in creating Slocum. The book is a monologue with remembered dialogue, almost static in terms of time, but with some progressions eventually. It reads like a self-analysis and memoir dictated nonstop over a few weeks, but it covers a longer, not quite definable span in which Slocum has a family disaster at about the same time he is promoted in his job and gets to do what he wants most to do in life: make a three-minute speech at the company's convention in Puerto Rico. His former boss, Jack Green, vicious and sadistic but without Slocum's redeeming weaknesses, has denied him the chance to make the speech in previous years. But when Slocum is promoted and succeeds his best friend in the company, Andy Kagle, whose lame leg Slocum wants to kick and whom he immediately betrays, he has power independent of Green's and he makes his speech. Nobody remembers what he said.

The speech is the metaphor for everybody's immediate, pressing but meaningless goal, the way the company is the framework for the society we live in, the way the combat group in *Catch-22* was the framework of the war society. Heller is a big metaphor man.

Slocum has a sizable metaphorical family also, an aging, unlovable wife, an insecure and nasty sixteen-year-old daughter whose shins he wants to kick, an idiot son he is sick of and would like to unload, another son, aged nine, who is the principal joy of his life and whom he ruins by allowing the company's values (get to the top, don't give your money away, compete, compete) to smother the boy's wondrously selfless and noncompetitive good nature.

Slocum also has a mother whom he refused to bring into his home when she got old and feeble ("You're no good" were her last words to him), a father who died young and whom he yearns to have known, twenty-three girls he periodically screws, a special mistress of long standing whose abortions he pays for whether he's been responsible or not.

He also, and most remarkably of all, has the ever-fresh memory of the twenty-one-year-old secretary he knew when he was seventeen. Her name was Virginia Markowitz and she gassed herself while he was in service during the war. They used to talk dirty to each other and love each other in a frustrating way, meeting furtively and frantically for neurotically (her neurosis) brief sexual gropings in the stockroom or a back staircase at an automobile casualty company. That company was where Bobby Slocum was introduced to corporate life and values in the technological age, also to sexuality and sexual craziness, to desire, and to the chief delusion of innocence: the belief that what we want so badly now will come to pass one of these days. The days of innocence are the time of his life Slocum most fondly remembers, now that everything has come so anticlimactically to pass; everything, that is, except Virginia, whom he never made. Her name is the name of his virginity, not hers.

What he wants now is to want something the way he once wanted Virginia. "Is this really the most I can get from the few years left in this one life of mine?" The answer is yes. His job has no meaning that can nourish a man. He can't find romance anymore. When he says things can't get better for him and his wife he means not that things are great but that the low ceiling on their happiness will probably only get lower. He talks of divorce and imagines his wife's suicide; but he can't leave her.

He loved his wife. She was pretty and vital but now she drinks during the day and flirts embarrassingly at parties. We change, Slocum says, and we don't know how to change back. Sad. Why can't some things other than stone remain always as they used to be, he wonders. Sad. What happened is that something happened. To everybody; and Slocum knows how it is now, but he spends the whole book trying to re-create what was and what is, speculating endlessly on what caused the ruin of such glorious innocence, such exciting desire. He has no more desire, only a stale, processed lust.

The book is a baring of what Heller thinks is everybody's soul: at least everybody who shares the values of the corporate state, the company scramble, the family debacle. It will be a rare man anywhere, but especially in America, who doesn't see something of his own soul in Slocum's disastrously honest confession. Egocentric, selfish, cruel, conniving, obsequious, hypocritical and cravenly intelligent, intermittently likeable, he never spares himself in his tirade against the unfathomably dispiriting condition of his life. "I wish I were part of a large family circle and enjoyed it. I would like to fit in. I wish I believed in God."

He admits he has adjusted "contemptibly" to his culture, environment, past. He knows he's a cheap egotist. "I find it harder and harder to feel sorry for anyone but myself," he says. "My wife is stronger than I am, and better, too," he says, "but I must never let her find that out." He admits he wants to be rid of her before her health fails.

As to the company, everyone there fears everyone else. "In my department," he says, "there are six people who are afraid of me and one small secretary who is afraid of all of us. I have one other person working for me who is not afraid of anyone, not even me, and I would fire him quickly, but I'm afraid of him."

Call reports are meaningless but must be filed by the staff. Andy Kagle is demoted because his name is only half right. Andrew is okay, but Kagle? Also his clothes are wrong. "He shows poor judgment in colors and styles as well as fabrics. . . . He moves to madras and paisley months after others have gone to linen or hopsack. . . ." Also, and most unforgivably, he wears "terrible brown shoes with *fleur de lis* perforations." Says Slocum, "Kagle has ability and experience, but they don't count anymore. What does count is that he has no tone. . . . I suspect it is no longer in his power (if it ever was in his power) to change himself to everyone's satisfaction."

Heller voluminously details Slocum's attitudes on everything: whores, underwear, the female and male sex organs, divorce, men's garters, his wife's bad breath, his fear of death and aging, teenage drug habits, money ("I love money better than ice cream," Slocum's daughter says), jocks and faggots, incest and oedipal frenzy, the fear of losing as the key to so much trouble in the world. Slocum on America:

> I am a broken waterlogged branch floating with my own crowd in this one nation of ours . . . with liberty and justice for all who are speedy enough to seize them first and hog them away from the rest. Some melting pot. If all of us in this vast, fabulous land of ours could come together and take time to exchange a few words with our neighbors and fellow countrymen, those words would be Bastard! Wop! Nigger! Whitey! Kike! Spic!

Perceiving decently, his actions are usually mean and obscene.

There is no way to sum up all Heller has put into this book. It is as rich in wit, social and psychological insight, American irony and memorable conversations as it is devoid of story, plot structure, tidy continuity and other accoutrements of the conventional novel. His chief stylistic tool is repetition. The Virginia Markowitz story, for instance, he seems to tell a dozen, maybe two or three dozen times. I lost count. But every retelling is from a different angle of memory, with another nuance. The accumulation makes the relationship between Bobby and Virginia a remarkably original fictional creation. It is peculiarly Heller's and it echoes the repetition that gave *Catch-22* such an original tone.

The new book will doubtlessly be compared to *Catch-22*. The double-bladed wit so peculiar to Heller ("She wants me to tell her I love her. I won't. A reason I won't is that I know she wants me to") is here, but this work is so unlike the first that similarities are important only because of their irrelevance.

Heller has learned from Beckett, but he is clearly himself, one of the world's most interesting writers.

1974

Ionesco's Remarkable
Irreducibility

I'm writing this not long after talking with C., a good friend and a newspaperman, on the value of the printed word. He argues that nobody reads, that literature has been passed by, the trend is to the visual, etc. He is coddling his own taste and presumes he is being hip. I explain I'm also a movie nut, but that if anybody thinks movies, or any visual media now available, can convey the complexities literature does, then they are mad. He says I'm print-oriented, which carries the onus of being passé. We are listening to long-playing records that he is taping. Billie Holiday comes on. Who can argue that she has been made obsolete by the Jefferson Airplane? Who can be that mad? C. reveals that he is leaving America for a European island, where he will open a bar, play jazz tapes for the customers and write a novel.

I have discovered the nontheatrical writings of Eugène Ionesco, the best thing that has happened to my reading in years; also a reinforcement of all I've said above. The new book is *Present Past, Past Present* (Grove Press), which appeared in France in 1968. It is a journal Ionesco wrote first in 1940–1941, then again in 1967, commenting on the early entries, with new perceptions, dreams, children's stories added; an eclectic work that resembles the diaries of Franz Kafka, whom Ionesco reveres. I've also read *Conversations with Eugène Ionesco* (Holt, Rinehart and Winston) by the French critic Claude Bonnefoy. It is literarily informational, in an old-fashioned *Paris Review*–interview sort of way, but it has none of the memoir's zap. The reason? It's a transcription, a mechanical achievement that allows us to confront only a fragment of the artist. To reach any man, we must get past his public self, his speech, and reach his thoughts. With rare exceptions (a film like Bergman's *Persona,* for instance), the visual media offer an exterior view of man. It's not possible for any film to convey what Ionesco's memoirs give us—the complex nature of one man in crisis for three decades with the same unchanging problem: how to keep his essential self intact.

Ionesco writes that "One must be oneself," a hoary cliché, which, coming from the great cliché-exploder, is provocative and is the core of everything that he writes and is. *Rhinoceros,* his most popular play, was inspired by his resistance to the spread of Naziism in the 1940s, but stands also for resistance to any movement that destroys individuality. In the play, everyone but the hero turns into a rhinoceros. Ionesco today resists the political Left in the way he resisted the political Right in his youth. He likes to think of Jean-Paul Sartre as a petit bourgeois tyrant. "All armies are armies of rhinoceroses," he wrote in 1940, long before he wrote the play. "All soldiers of just causes are rhinoceroses. All holy wars are the doings of rhinoceroses. Justice is the doing of rhinoceroses. Revolutions are the doing of rhinoceroses. . . . Humanity does not exist. There are men. Society does not exist. There are friends. It is not the same thing for a rhinoceros."

These memoirs, as well as Ionesco's earlier *Fragments of a Journal,* published here in 1968, prove to be inspirational works, for they demonstrate a lifelong commitment to discovering the point beyond which the self is irreducible. "One must look at things from a great height," Ionesco writes. "One must not let oneself be caught in the trap of ideologies, the ephemeral clichés, the circumscribed truths of the day, those who would have it, for example, that individualist literature is out of date; that it is necessary to write in a 'collectivist' spirit. . . ." I read this soon after reading Jerry Rubin's new book, *We Are Everywhere* (Harper & Row), in which he proclaims: "All great art today is revolutionary," "Close down the universities" and other slogans of the moment. Rubin would like to be a great Yippie ideologue, but he is only a comic celebrity peddling iconoclastic clichés. Eric Hoffer, the Lawrence Welk of American philosophy, writes in a collective vein in *First Things, Last Things* (Harper & Row), a new essay collection: "We must deflate the pretensions of self-appointed elites." His "elite" list includes intellectuals, the rich, the young, the militant poor and militant blacks.

Hoffer dreams of the day when "the common people"—i.e., middle Americans with money—will "kick up their heels and trample would-be elitists in the dust. . . ." Rubin and Hoffer are both appealing to mobs. They are an unmatched pair of rhinos.

"Only those who have something to say should speak and write," says Ionesco. "Everybody has something to say," but: "those who are only everybody have nothing to say since everybody says the same thing they would say." He concludes: "It is necessary to be personal. Myself is what is opposed to others; others are those who oppose my self. It is this opposition, this balance that constitutes the personal." This is yet another Ionesco exploration of his own individuality, which he confronts everywhere. His authoritarian father turns him into an antimilitarist. But he also finds trained fleas instructive: "The fleas are put under glass. The fleas try to jump, bump against the glass, and fall back down again. . . . The glass can be taken away. And the stupid fleas now walk slowly around . . . they will no longer jump." He writes of the chameleon who turns every color, one after the other, but remains a chameleon. He inquires: "What is the I? It is the consciousness of being me." Every facet of the book reflects this man's quest to be singular.

Ionesco in the Kennedy family: I took my daughters to a show of short films, one of which was the cartoon *Rhinoceros*, a short version of the story the play tells. When we came home, the younger one drew a cartoon about it, showing two men greeting one another. Both have identical hats. Both have green shirt buttons, green cuff buttons, green shoelaces, green eyes. One has a horn coming out of his head, one does not. My daughter said she didn't understand the film, but that seems not to be true.

"We are all looking for something of extraordinary importance whose nature we have forgotten," Ionesco writes. "I am writing the memoirs of a man who has lost his memory." He says he finds only "pale glimmers from a world that was once dense, intense, brightly colored." Certain images now cause him pain, but he can no longer say why. He says he has the key to happiness: "Remember, be profoundly, profoundly, totally conscious that you are." Yet he keeps losing the key. This book is a documentary of his continuing struggle to find it again, and guard it. It is not a casual struggle. Treating the idea of "being oneself" as a cliché can be perilous. A character in Ionesco's play *The Bald Soprano* comes to think of the week as consisting of three days: Tuesday, Thursday and Tuesday. The self can become equally unreal if not attended to. Ionesco, dreading this, tells himself: "I will not let myself dry up; I will not grow older. I will risk being vulnerable."

1971

Far Tortuga:

Peter Matthiessen's Misteriosa

Peter Matthiessen says that he worked on this virtuoso novel about a sea turtle fishing voyage in the Caribbean for nine years, put it aside many times but never tired of it. He pared the work down, he said, made it "so simple that metaphors, stream-of-consciousness, even such ordinary conventions of the novel as 'he said' or 'he thought,' seemed intrusive, even offensive, and a great impediment, besides. . . ." The author opened the book up to white space, "more air around the words." Some pages carry only one or two words. Small sentences sail across the page like flying fish. Men's deaths are lonely splotches of ink at the bottom of a page. All this accumulates in a design that is handsome, unusual and welcome.

The writing style is that of a poetic screenplay. Characters have no thoughts, they only speak; and there are no quotation marks around the speech. Quotes are indented. Asides and whispers are printed in small type and there is no attribution of remarks to anyone by the author. The characters all speak in Caribbean dialects, which are presumably varied but sound similar on first reading, and which have a melodic and implicitly comedic element to them on the printed page:

> So I'm telling you dat a bad memory is a disasterish thing to a person in life. With no remembrance, a mon cannot learn. To me—I'm not makin bragado or anything—but I know every rock out on de banks, like my own dooryard. It were Copm Andrew Avers dat taught me, and come to pilotin, he were the island's best.

We must discover the identity of the speaker from internal evidence. Matthiessen helps us out by having his people call one another by name fairly often, but this is a substitute form that obtrudes more than would a phrase like "the captain said," which we barely notice because of its familiarity.

Matthiessen, interviewed in *The Paris Review* briefly about this novel, admits that in the early pages (the first hundred at least), you are not always sure which man is speaking, but later on you are. This is true enough, but three-quarters through, though he has defined all his characters, there is still occasional confusion, and the method finally proves more vexing than Matthiessen suggests. Aesthetic consistency triumphs, but with a certain expense of comprehension.

The book's form has impelled James Dickey to suggest that it points the way "that the English-speaking sensibility must and should go, from this book on . . . the way of passionate impressionism." Matthiessen, says Dickey, "is creating our new vision."

Dickey's enthusiasm is shared by a slate of well-known writers who, taken together on the book's jacket, surely comprise the heavyweight blurb round-up of the year. Eleanor Clark, Stephen Becker, Lillian Hellman, William Styron and even our foremost literary hermit, Thomas Pynchon, all wax rhapsodic over the novel—not, like Dickey, on innovative grounds, but about the power of the story.

Matthiessen's writing and structural styles do set the book apart. But French experimenters in recent years have offered more radical stylistic departures from fictional conventions. Joyce did away with quotation marks an age ago. e. e. cummings, Dylan Thomas and a whole generation of modern poets have diddled with linear irregularity, the line as sculpture, as impression. Steve Katz sculpted a novel with type. Ronald Sukenick was ahead of Matthiessen in the prodigal use of white space.

Where Matthiessen is truly strong and most original is in his command of detail. This is not a book that could have been written by a young man, not even a precocious one. It is the work of a mature writer with a poetic bent who has lived with the sea for much of a lifetime. He knows the nomenclatures and moods of its wave, its spray, its temper, its skies, its winds, its creatures, its birds. He knows the Caribbean sailor's fears, superstitions, jokes and dreams. He knows the lore of turtle fishing, the stories of wrecks and wrong decisions by captains. His achievement is, foremost, in the realm of experience—vast experience—transformed.

He illuminates brilliantly the vanishing profession of turtle fishing as well as the land and sea life of the turtles themselves. The turtles have been so ravaged by greedy men, one of Matthiessen's characters says, that they are going the way of crocodiles, seals, snipes and iguana, and are now a declining species in the sea off Nicaragua, where this doomed fishing expedition takes place.

The crumbling craft is the schooner *Lillias Eden* out of Grand Cayman, and it has a bent shaft, no running lights, no fire equipment, no chronometer, no life jackets. Its lines are frayed, its food is dismal and there is no cook. One of its two small boats leaks, its radio receives but cannot send messages. The nine-man crew, with the exception of one ambitiously good worker who yearns to work the land, not the sea, is ragtag: a garrulous drunk, a drifter in love with violence, a teenage innocent, a Jonah figure with second sight who reads the multiple omens and perceives the disasters to come, and other assorted lechers, thieves and malcontents of black, brown and white skins.

The captain is Raib Avers, the one truly complex figure in the story, who like Ahab is the reason the voyage is undertaken at all, and who will make many crucial decisions. But unlike Ahab, Raib is not questing but maniacally pursuing the only life he knows, refusing to be reduced to an anachronism.

Raib knows it is late in the season for turtles. He knows the craft is sick, the crew scum. But he says he will make a real crew of them and to a degree he does. Even the worst try to perform well when trouble strikes, and when the arduous turtling finally begins.

Through the boring sail south toward the turtle cays (the reader may follow the voyage on an endpaper map) the crew members tell one another tall tales of mirth and tragedy. They rag each other, complain about Raib, fight, sing sea songs, report on duppies and other ghosts, such as a notable talking hen with teeth, and, through the conflict this closeness generates, they all slowly individualize under Matthiessen's hand.

None, however, achieves the personal density of Capt. Raib Avers, who is mercurial, intelligent, likeable, feared. He is partly mysterious. Was he a pirate? (The book is finally a superb pirate story.) Did he burn a ship once for insurance? Is his enemy—Desmond Eden—really his half-brother? The family relationships are a strong point of the story—Raib and his son Buddy, the teenage innocent who is always seasick; Raib and the vicious Desmond; Raib and his father, Captain Andrew, who comes aboard the *Eden* from Desmond's boat in one of the book's most memorable scenes—tied to a chair and swinging from a boom in midair between Raib's and Desmond's vessels. The old man has suffered a stroke, been struck silent, and Desmond no longer wants him. He presents a problem to Raib as well, since the voyage of the *Eden* has only half begun. And so old Captain Andrew spins in the chair, white hair flying, awaiting his fate.

Perhaps this is one of the passionate, impressionistic moments that so impressed Dickey. There are others: the refugees from Jamaican poverty who inhabit certain cays, going wild with hunger, rum and the absence of civilization (and who ultimately play such a significant role in the story), racing in skiffs toward the *Eden* as it passes, anxious to trade rum for food. But Raib, knowing what they're like, slings their line away when they toss it to the *Eden* and screams at them:

"Pan-headed niggers! Get de hell away!"
Raib has already explained his coldness of heart in this matter:
Modern time, mon.

The people in this book are all victims of the modern time, whether they be headed for savagery or ruination, really two sides of the same coin; for the conflict is between the used-to-haves and the never-hads, a prevailing struggle in so much of the world; and in this sense the book is a modern parable.

There is also the deft, realistic delineation of the people, all very vivid. And yet there is a strange one-dimensionality about them all, except Raib. He alone makes the decisions, acts capriciously and is thrust into an internal conflict made truly visible—conflict with his father, son, crew, his enemy, with the sea, the winds, the aged ship. The other people are subordinate to him, but also victims, partially, of Matthiessen's restrictive style of storytelling. However vivid the impressionistic strokes, the people exist, like the customers in Harry Hope's bar in O'Neill's *Iceman*, as types, each with diverse function, but never transcending that function the way Hickey transcends, or Raib transcends. What they are at the outset they remain at the end. There are hints of change, but since Matthiessen's style is to enter no one's head, we can see only behavior, the manifestation of internal conflict. The result is what even good cinema so often is—memorable but uncomplex.

Raib is different: Matthiessen gives us a long look at the man in transition and conflict and also lets him periodically explain himself with crude eloquence:

> . . . I tellin you now, boy, dat I bitter. Dere are days when I very, very bitter. Cause I wore myself out to get to de place where I de best dey is in the main fishery of de island, and now dat fishery don't mean nothin. No, mon. De schooners all gone and de green turtle goin. I got to set back and watch dem ones grow big on de Yankee tourist trade dat would not have amounted to a pile of hen shit in times gone back. I got to swaller dat.

And a crewman answers:

Modern time, mon.

The turtles are scarce for Raib and his crew, and so he heads his ship for the uncharted Misteriosa reefs, where, they say, the green turtle abounds. But it is far out to sea. Bad reef. Heavy tides. Far Tortuga, it is called, and maybe it doesn't really exist, that abundance. Maybe Far Tortuga really is only a myth.

But Raib has a theory that it does exist, and so the story that had begun slowly, and in a seemingly disjointed way, finally comes together in a spectacular, fully earned finale at Far Tortuga, where the destiny of Raib Avers and the men of the schooner *Lillias Eden* is resolved, not by caprice but by dint of their own acts, their own needs, their own decrepit condition. And Matthiessen's art prevails.

1975

O'Hara's Letters:

A Quest for Celebrity

John O'Hara voted for Richard Nixon in 1960, which at first seemed to one reader to be hard-core proof that his previous seven years of sobriety, and three decades of success, had done him irreparable brain damage. But a reassessment of O'Hara's life, as seen through the words that gush all but visibly out of his mouth in this collection of wonderful letters, reveals him to be a figure permanently warped by the untimely and all-but-penurious death of his father. The family's subsequent insolvency frustrated John's social and educational ambitions, made him a bellicose, vainglorious scrambler after celebrity and other emptiness, an Irishman who would always view himself as superior to other Irishmen (including Nixon's 1960 opponent), and a compulsive writer of a high order who at times seemed to think that writing fast and fatly was as important as writing well.

Whatever his faults, O'Hara was a vital, witty maverick in twentieth-century American literature, a man whose writing talent was obvious even when he was fired from the *New York Herald Tribune* in 1928 for being drunk—and city editor Stanley Walker cried at having to show him the door. O'Hara by then had already connected himself to *The New Yorker*, and became one of that magazine's most prolific contributors for the next four decades (except for the years 1949–1960 when he sulked after feuding with the editors).

He is inseparable really from the history of *The New Yorker*, having almost singlehandedly set the style for its elliptical short stories of the early years. And yet we don't think of him as a permanent part of that *New Yorker* circle—Thurber, White, Gibbs, Benchley, Parker—even though he was; for he went on to write larger things: the novels and films and plays that made him internationally famous, a millionaire at his death, and appraised by some as the American Chekhov.

Reappraisal time is here for O'Hara, a new biography is under construction, and some critics are at work sifting the quick from the dead in his work. The odds offered from this corner are that his critical reputation will wing up from the grave now that he's not around to demand from the world what it always refuses to give to importuners.

O'Hara's own sifting of his work, as revealed in this collection of letters edited by Matthew J. Bruccoli, put his novel *From the Terrace* at the top of his preferred list. Everybody else's favorite, *Appointment in Samarra*, he placed in a favorite-but-flawed rank. He put himself on a level with Steinbeck, Hemingway, and Faulkner in 1949 (giving Faulkner the edge) but few others have ever rated him so high.

O'Hara had to contend with negative visions of himself and his work all his life. One in particular rankled. Alfred Kazin called him "a social sorehead from the other side of the tracks" in 1962. O'Hara retorted publicly and also said in letters to friends that his lineage in America predated the American Revolution, that his name in Ireland was one of a few that dated back to the tenth century, and that his father had graduated from an Ivy League school (Penn) "when the Ivy League was known as the Big Four." He added: "I grow weary of the efforts of people like Kazin to squeeze all Irish-named people into a Studs Lonigan mold."

Instead of viewing assaults as irrelevant to the artist in him, O'Hara let them curdle his days. He wrote obsessively and vituperatively, and probably accurately, about many of the critics who punished him for his popularity and overlooked his achievements. He was vitriolic about the way they turned on Steinbeck after he won the Nobel Prize. O'Hara himself yearned desperately for the Nobel and wrote often and candidly of how many times he'd been passed over for it.

His social climbing never ended. He assuaged its fury with club memberships. Scott Fitzgerald put him up for The Brook but he was blackballed and at the time of his death he was lobbying with insiders for membership in two English clubs, The Garrick and The Savile. His unrequited love for Yale (which he couldn't afford) was a lifelong cliché he couldn't abandon either. He preened when his daughter Wylie married a Yale man, and two years before his death in 1970 he thought of entering his newborn grandson into Yale's class of 1992, but decided this was impertinent.

O'Hara's refuge against isolation and rejection was his work, as he said over and over, which explains his compulsion but not his talent or imagination. He wrote much that is belabored and overstuffed, but at his best there was no one who could equal him in putting the spoken language of so many varying Americans on the printed page.

In a letter to John Hersey, when Hersey's novel *White Lotus* was being panned, O'Hara explained his own record of literary Purple Hearts and pointed out to the freshly wounded Hersey that critics had destroyed James Gould Cozzens and Fitzgerald, had hurt many other writers, and that the only American writer who really escaped them was Faulkner.

"But he was made invulnerable by his genius," O'Hara wrote Hersey. "You cannot hurt a genius, even with a silver bullet."

O'Hara all but relished his own vulnerability: "To go through life as Faulkner [has], untouched, like Sunshine Biscuits, by human hands, is not my desire."

And he always touched back. He touched his enemies, his critics, he touched his editors, his publishers, those who snubbed him and those he needed to snub in order to prove his own worth to his contentious and long-wounded self.

These letters form an epistolary novel which coalesces these and many other high and low truths of his life that O'Hara had put into the mouths of so many fictional people. The letters are wonderfully amusing and revealing, often shallow and oddly bumptious, deliciously vindictive, painfully wrongheaded and self-inflating, but thoroughly real and honest and intelligent in an anti-scholarly, wilfully bad-boyish way.

They are a record of a singular writer, a singular man, who tried to be aware of all his faults and almost made it. He wasn't Faulkner's equal in literature and he knew it. But he wrote better letters.

1978

The Grapes of Wrath at Fifty: Steinbeck's Journals

I told a friend of mine, a writer, that I was rereading John Steinbeck's epic novel, *The Grapes of Wrath,* on the occasion of its golden anniversary—it was published April 14, 1939—and my friend said he wouldn't dare reread it. "That was my great book," he explained. "I couldn't bear to find that it doesn't stand up."

John Steinbeck had a similar problem. He was choking with trepidation about the novel as he was writing it: "No one else knows my lack of ability the way I do. . . . Sometimes, I seem to do a good little piece of work, but when it is done it slides into mediocrity"; "Got her done. And I'm afraid she's a little dull"; "My many weaknesses are beginning to show their heads"; "My work is no good, I think—I'm desperately upset about it . . . I'm slipping. I've been slipping all my life"; "Young man wants to talk, wants to be a writer. What could I tell him? Not a writer myself yet"; "I am sure of one thing—it isn't the great book I had hoped it would be. It's just a run-of-the-mill book. And the awful thing is that it is absolutely the best I can do."

He wrote the book in five months, beginning in May and ending in late October 1938, writing in longhand and producing two thousand words a day, the equivalent of seven double-spaced typed pages, an enormous output for any writer, and ultimately a daily tour de force. But he was flagellating himself for this also: "Vacillating and miserable. . . . I'm so lazy, so damned lazy"; "Where has my discipline gone? Have I lost control?"; "My laziness is overwhelming." This novel would be his ninth work of fiction in ten years, and he would be thirty-seven years old at its publication.

These remarks of his are culled from the diary he kept daily while writing *The Grapes of Wrath*, that diary now published for the first time under the title *Working Days*, with a long, informative commentary and voluminous notes by Robert DeMott, a Steinbeck scholar who teaches English at Ohio University, and some newly discovered Steinbeck letters. It will provide a field day for Steinbeck aficionados, but for its insights into the creative mind it is also a valuable book for writers, aspiring or arrived. The struggle to create an original work is an everlasting one with most writers, and it is well anatomized here. "I've always had these travails," Steinbeck reminds himself halfway through the book. "Never get used to them."

The book also has the fascination of privacy invaded. Steinbeck said he had often been tempted to destroy it, yet he sent it to his editor at the Viking Press, Pat Covici, obviously aware of its worth. He requested first that it not be published in his lifetime and also that it be made available to his sons, so they might "look behind the myth and hearsay and flattery and slander a disappeared man becomes and to know to some extent what manner of man their father was."

The fiftieth-anniversary edition of *The Grapes of Wrath* itself includes a strong and moving introduction by Studs Terkel, who makes the case for the novel's relevance to the lives of Chicano farm workers in California today and to Midwestern farmers who, in recent years, have lost their farms to the banks.

The novel is also, it seems to me, a vivid fifty-year-old parallel to the American homeless: a story of people at the bottom of the world, bereft and drifting outcasts in a hostile society. Here is Ma Joad, the greatest of all the characters in Steinbeck's densely populated story, talking to another Joad family member, Uncle John:

"We ain't gonna die out. People is goin' on—changin' a little, maybe, but goin' right on."

"How can you tell?" Uncle John demanded. "What's to keep ev-er'thing from stoppin'; all the folks from jus' gittin' tired an' layin' down?" . . .

"Hard to say," she said. "Ever'thing we do—seems to me is aimed right at goin' on. . . . Even gettin' hungry—even bein' sick; some die, but the rest is tougher. Jus' try to live the day, jus' the day."

I can't go on, I'll go on. It's Samuel Beckett's theme before Samuel Beckett. It's the Joads' as well as it is that of thousands now sleeping on heating grates and in cardboard boxes all over America, who somehow survive subzero temperatures and move on to the next ordeal—modern migrants in a nation that has created an urban class abysmally more hopeless than the fruit-picking peon class to which the Joads belonged. That peon class, one soulless corporate farmer said (and Steinbeck noted this), was necessary to the survival of California agriculture.

Mr. DeMott cites Steinbeck's witnessing of such people in a flood at Visalia, California, in March 1938, an event so heartbreaking to Steinbeck that the objective reporting he had planned to do for *Life* magazine seemed inadequate. And so he was driven to give it the greater power of his fiction.

Of the sight of thousands flooded out of their shelters and starving to death, Steinbeck wrote: "The water is a foot deep in the tents and the children are up on the beds and there is no food and no fire, and the county has taken off all the nurses because 'the problem is so great that we can't do anything about it.' So they do nothing." And he later said: "They starved to death. They dropped dead."

We now see that the flood that swamps the Joad family at the end of the novel was in Steinbeck's mind from the outset. And no more vividly pitiful scene has ever been written in American fiction.

The book went through four stages of creation, the first, following on Steinbeck's intense focus on the desperation of the migrants, being seven articles in *The San Francisco News*, originally published between October 5 and 12, 1936, and republished last year in paperback as *The Harvest Gypsies: On the Road to the Grapes of Wrath*. This is a straightaway documentary: flat narration of dismally depressing detail on the lives of the migrants, coupled to Steinbeck's informed and sensitive plea for change.

By the end of 1937 he was at work on *The Oklahomans*, what he termed a "rather long novel" and which he abandoned, perhaps at an early stage, and probably destroyed, since it has never been found. From February to May 1938, he wrote what Mr. DeMott calls a "vituperative satire" with the ungainly title of *L'Affaire Lettuceberg*, attacking a cabal of power figures who organize terrorist vigilantes to destroy a migrant workers' strike. Steinbeck finished *Lettuceberg*, decided it was a "bad book" that focused on the wrong end of the problem, junked it and immediately began writing *The Grapes of Wrath*.

Briefly put, this novel is the odyssey of the Joads of Oklahoma, who after a great drought lose the family farm. The landless Joads set out in a dilapidated truck, across the desert, to find work picking fruit in the promised land of California, a pipe dream that turns into a nightmare.

The story opens with Tom Joad returning home from prison, where he did time for killing a man who knifed him at a dance; and Tom becomes the catalyst for much of the story's action and movement. He is its intellectual center and, with Ma Joad, carries the principal weight of the book.

Lesser Joads move on and off center stage: Pa, who loses his authority in the family to the wiser and more decisive Ma; Uncle John, summed up in a brilliant paragraph by Steinbeck, but who remains a Johnny-one-note character thereafter; Rose of Sharon, pregnant child bride (who becomes the centerpiece of the unforgettably poignant final scene), and her worthless groom; brother Al, who loves to fool with cars and women; Noah, a simple cipher in the family; Winfield and Ruthie, the children growing wild without a home; Grampa and Granma, the comic elders who fail to survive the family's transplanting; the former preacher Casy, a staunchly moral, honest and godless man; and an assortment of secondary figures like Muley Graves, who loses his farm but won't leave, and lives on, with fugitive, gun-toting hostility toward banks and sheriffs. "I like Muley," Steinbeck wrote in his diary. "He is a fine hater."

When published, the novel became the top best-seller of 1939 (430,000 copies sold) and also one of the top ten best-sellers of 1940. It won the Pulitzer Prize in 1940, and to date has sold close to four and a half million copies in the United States, and it still sells 100,000 paperback copies annually. And it has sold more than fourteen million copies worldwide.

All well and good for the publisher, but does the book stand up?

It does indeed.

It stands tall.

I read and relished much of the Steinbeck shelf in the 1940s and 1950s and yet wasn't impelled to go back to him the way I go back always to Faulkner and Hemingway, the two writers Steinbeck claimed to admire most. Reading this book, you can see the influence of other peers of his generation: Thomas Wolfe, in the spasms of overblown rhetoric and impersonalized overview of the national life; and John Dos Passos, in the interchapters Steinbeck called "generals," which is to say, general American subject matter that exists outside of, but parallel to, the continuing story of the Joads.

In the generals Steinbeck writes of the dust bowl as phenomenon; the tractor—which plowed the land mechanically and knocked down farm homes—as enemy; the Far Western states as state of mind; the roadside lunchroom; thieving used-car salesmen and much more. These generals get in the way of the story in the same way that the lore of whaling gets in the way of the story of Ahab and Moby Dick. But just as it was Melville's obsession to present the totality of whaling, so was it Steinbeck's obsession with the migrants' plight that led him to excess.

Here's how he saw it at the time: "Better make this scene three pages instead of two. Because there can never be too much of background"; the book "will take every bit of experience and thought and feeling that I have"; "Afraid of repetitiousness. Must watch that."

But he didn't.

He repeated in the generals what he had embodied in the story, an obvious mistrust of minimalism. Even some of the Joad chapters go on past their effectiveness.

Throughout, the Joads personify Steinbeck's ideas of what is and what should be, but he exceeds the dramatic limit at times and force-feeds the dialogue, as when Muley Graves bemoans the takeover of land and farm by the banks: " 'Cause what'd they take when they tractored the folks off the lan'? What'd they get so their 'margin a profit' was safe?" Maybe Muley always talked about margins of profit, but I doubt it; and so for a moment he lost credibility. But only for a moment. Otherwise I bought him. Whole hog. Whole Muley.

Even Tom Joad's now classic farewell speech, when he's on the run after killing a vigilante, is loaded with Steinbeck's idealism: "Wherever they's a fight so hungry people can eat, I'll be there. Wherever they's a cop beatin' up a guy, I'll be there" and more. Steinbeck's rage pushed Tom beyond seemly boundaries.

Then again, how valuable, really, is the seemly? This novel stood the critics of its day on their ear (with a few exceptions). They saw it had flaws, but they gave it their huzzahs anyway. One wrongheaded critic for *Newsweek*, Burton Rascoe, who endures as a naysayer in Steinbeck lore, found it not well organized and added witlessly: "I can't quite see what the book is about, except that there are 'no frontiers left and no place to go.' " Two weeks later he was back, now a full-throated philistine: "Some of my colleagues in criticism have gone into such jitterbug ecstasies over [the book] that I feel I should be more specific." And he then denigrated the novel: "silly propaganda, superficial observation, careless infidelity to the proper use of idiom, tasteless pornographical and scatological talk . . . a bad book by a man whose work I have so greatly admired."

But hindsighted Rascoe-love doesn't take him off the hook. He marches at the head of those anti-Steinbeck vigilantes about whom the novelist Jim Harrison said: "Where's their 'Grapes of Wrath'? They didn't even write 'The Grapes of Goofy.' "

Six months after his great novel was published, John Steinbeck wrote in his diary: "That part of my life that made the 'Grapes' is over. . . . I have to go to new sources and find new roots." He changed the subject matter and the style of his writing, and also broke with his wife, Carol (a radical who had typed and edited the *Grapes* manuscript, had also chosen its title, a phrase from the "Battle Hymn of the Republic," and to whom Steinbeck dedicated the book).

Steinbeck's second marriage didn't work for long and ended in divorce. Much of his later writing didn't work well either, though there was *Cannery Row* and *East of Eden* (which he undertook after rediscovering this diary of *The Grapes*). Then in 1961 he published *The Winter of Our Discontent*, and the Swedish Academy the following year awarded him the Nobel Prize in Literature. At a press conference the day the prize was announced, a reporter asked Steinbeck if he deserved it. With characteristic self-deprecation he replied: "That's an interesting question. Frankly, no."

Anders Osterling, the secretary of the academy, said the award was based on *Discontent*, adding that it marked a return after more than two decades to the "towering standard" Steinbeck had set with *The Grapes of Wrath*. As reported in *The New York Times*, Osterling described the author as an "independent expounder of the truth with an unbiased instinct for what is genuinely American, be it good or bad."

Not everybody would agree that *The Winter of Our Discontent* and *The*

Grapes of Wrath are of equal weight. I am one who would not. But I look back at that long list of John Steinbeck's achievements—*Of Mice and Men, The Long Valley, Tortilla Flat, Cannery Row, East of Eden* and *The Grapes*—and then I look around and try to find other American writers whose work has meant as much to me, and I count them on one hand. Maybe one and a half.

John Steinbeck had the power. And if at times he lacked the language and the magic that go with mythic literary achievement and status, he had in their place a mighty conscience and a mighty heart. And just about fifty-one years ago this time, that man sat down and put pencil to paper; and in five miraculous months he wrote a mighty, mighty book.

1989

Malcolm Muggeridge's
Wasted Life

Malcolm Muggeridge, the career curmudgeon, has started to reveal how he got that way in this first of a three-volume autobiography. Here he writes of his first thirty years and the elements in them he was later to reject: liberal journalism, the intellectual Left of Britain, his agnostic, Marxist upbringing, the pernicious and fatuous nature of colonial rule and of Soviet Russia.

A life of vitriolic rebellion against fools and assassins, through the written word, began in hero-worship of the writer, any writer. "To compare a writer with some famous soldier or administrator or scientist or politician or actor was, in my estimation, quite ludicrous. There was no basis for comparison; any more than between, say, Francis of Assisi and Dr. Spock."

Muggeridge is probably best known as onetime editor of *Punch*, but he had set his sights much higher than magazine editing. He wrote plays, had one produced, also wrote fiction. He succeeded in neither realm but did produce "a Niagara of words" for newspapers and magazines and adds with poignancy: "I confess they signify to me a lost life."

He offers a disclaimer to bitterness over literary failure. No regrets for masterpieces unwritten or genius unfulfilled, he says. Why not? Because he was born into a civilization already dying, maybe dead. Art and literature have definitely expired. The contemporary genius is technological and the arts are in the hands of charlatans and drunks. Hemingway hit the mark only when he blew his brains out. Maugham was a pederast celebrating the lost bourgeoisie in the century of the common man. Shaw, when he criticized Muggeridge's only produced play, misunderstood it, just as he misunderstood Shakespeare, Caesar and everything else. Eliot was the death rattle in the throat of a dying civilization.

Muggeridge is another Miniver Cheevy: "At the beginning of a civilization, the role of the artist is priestly; at the end, harlequinade. From St. Augustine to St. Ezra Pound, from Plainsong to the Rolling Stones, from El Greco to Picasso, from Chartres to the Empire State Building, from Benvenuto Cellini to Henry Miller, from Pascal's *Pensées* to Robinson's *Honest to God.* A Gadarene descent down which we must all slide, finishing up in the same slough."

Muggeridge's corner of the slough turned out first to be teaching English to blank-minded Indians and Egyptians in colonial schools, later working among pusillanimous, queasy liberals on *The Manchester Guardian* and at length fulfilling his early leftist dream of living in Russia. The last section forms the richest segment of this sassy book.

Serving as *The Guardian*'s man in Moscow removed Muggeridge's leftist verve. When his editor refused to print his exclusive exposé of the Russian famine, which was to kill millions, Muggeridge separated himself from moderate men as well. He left Russia, equating it with Germany under Hitler, and seems not to have changed his views much since then. He ridicules transient pundits like Shaw, who came to Moscow during the famine and reported no one going hungry, and H. G. Wells, who won a rare confrontation with Stalin and then tried to interest him in the P.E.N. Club. He is very tough on other Moscow newsmen of that era, among them Louis Fischer, Maurice Hindus and especially Walter Duranty, *The New York Times*'s man, ". . . a little browbeaten boy looking up admiringly at a big bully," whose dispatches, Muggeridge claims, were often "evidently nonsensically untrue" but whose exalted status helped shape FDR's Russian policy. Muggeridge blames *The New York Times* for having "spared no expense or effort to ensure that capitalism will not survive."

Acidulous portraits of Bertrand Russell, Ramsay MacDonald, Beatrice and Sidney Webb, Winston Churchill ("something malign and disagreeable, as it seemed to me, behind the image-mask of high living, low thinking and general amiability") and many more spice Muggeridge's summaries of his own and the century's early years. He is not all acid. He loves his wife, loves love, covets humility but says it probably will elude him, admires a few, a very few, friends along the way, says he cherishes life and wishes no man ill.

He is particularly fond of Jesus and says the New Testament was "the key to how to live" for him. He is now a repentant carnalist, admits cultural fraud (carrying books for show) and treachery to employers and lovers; frequently he wears his memoir like sackcloth.

He talks of his belief in immortality and of being not far from the beyond (he's seventy). So this repentance begins to sound like a confessional soliloquy just before the curtain. His rage against almost all he once accepted smacks of facile rebellion and professional grouching.

But we can't accuse the complex Muggeridge of being cowardly, expedient or facile, not after a life dense with the pursuit of knowledge and wisdom; at least not yet. He makes a serious effort to balance the book with marginal positive thinking, but obviously he's far more at home gutting somebody with his edgy syntax and letting them bleed all over his paragraphs.

Writers as heroes? A few helped him learn, but they're dead, and now he doesn't even value this long, triadic memoir he's writing. Despite his disclaimer, the impression thus far in the Muggeridge story is that the protagonist failed to create himself as an artist, settled for journalism, an inferior alternative, and has been taking it out on everybody else ever since.

1973

Frank Sullivan:

Serious Only About Humor

How sad. It's no longer a funny world. At least it's no longer a world in which there are writers who believe that being funny is the only thing worth doing.

Such as Robert Benchley, for instance, writing: "While rummaging through my bureau one day I came across some old snow." Or P. G. Wodehouse ending a chapter with this: " 'Bah!' said Mr. Waddington. It was not much of a last word, but, such as it was, he had it."

Both lines are cited by Frank Sullivan, Saratoga's first citizen, in a letter he wrote in 1959 explaining to a friend that on reading the Wodehouse line he laughed so hard that he woke up somebody who was sleeping in the house. The letter is from a new book, *Frank Sullivan Through the Looking Glass*, and has any number of lines guaranteed to make you laugh your bedmate into wakefulness, such as the time Aunt Sarah Gallup caught a two-and-a-half-ton salmon at Niagara Falls just to dry the salmon eggs to use as croquet balls. Or the fairy godmother who turned a wicked king into a past participle. Or Sullivan's discovery of a man in Syracuse who had a pet boa constrictor named Julius Squeezer.

Sullivan's book, his twelfth since 1926, comes along the eve of his seventy-eighth birthday (September 22), when most writers have long since uttered their last word. It is a collection of some of his best comic pieces, dating to the early thirties, but it also includes many letters (from the twenties to the late sixties) that are new to everybody except those to whom they were originally sent.

"They're even new to me," Sullivan said in an interview this week.
"I'd really forgotten most of them."

Sullivan is known mainly as the fellow who writes the Christmas poem
in *The New Yorker* magazine every year (he's done it since 1932) and
who dashes off occasional pieces on the state of things in Saratoga, his
hometown. But his writing days are pretty much ended. He may not
even do the Christmas poem this year. "I've banged that typewriter for
a long time," he says. "I think I'll give it a rest."

Born in Saratoga a block from where he now lives on Lincoln Avenue,
Sullivan went from Cornell to the army to the old *New York Herald* to
The World, the most famous newspaper of the 1920s—the Pulitzer paper
that had Herbert Bayard Swope as its editor and such famous names in
journalism as Heywood Broun, F. P. Adams, and Sullivan.

"I was a lousy reporter but meant well," he recalled in 1967. "The
motto at *The World* was, Never let Sullivan within a mile of a fact. That
suited me fine. I drew down what was then a princely salary for covering
the Atlantic City beauty parades and the shad-boning contests held
annually at Hartford, Conn. It was fine until they gave me a goddam
column, which spoiled everything."

Sullivan went to *The World* in 1922 and in 1925 was given the job
of filling in as a columnist during F. P. A.'s vacation. It was the beginning
of a daily grind that made Sullivan famous but also nearly drove him to
quit writing altogether. He wrote in 1927 of his task that "the 'modern
daily feature' idea is the most stultifying killing factor the brisk mind
of the American editor has invented. The last two years, since I was
torn from a very comfortable, happy and cloistered sinecure as a reporter,
have made a neurotic out of me. . . . One simply hasn't got something
to give every day—especially not 1600 words. . . ."

Nevertheless, Sullivan persevered and when *The World* died in 1931,
it was more than sad. "It was an awful disaster in my life," he said last
week. He wrote a piece in 1931 called "Thoughts Before the Undertaker
Came," and he closed that out saying: "When I die I want to go where
The World has gone, and work on it again."

In 1931 he went to *The New Yorker* magazine. He'd been dabbling
with the magazine since it started in 1925, but in 1931 became one of

editor Harold Ross's regulars, and a member of that company of Great White Humorists that included Benchley (the funniest of them all, says Sullivan), and James Thurber and Dorothy Parker and E. B. White and Perelman and Ogden Nash and more.

White Humor is an easy opposite of Black Humor, the favored style of some serious writers who leaven their seriousness with generous doses of wit. Sullivan and Benchley might have had a cutting edge to their humor, but basically, it was as non-serious as they could make it.

Thinking about the subject last week, Sullivan reaffirmed something he said in 1967.

"I think the humor is still what they call black—sick—most of it," he said, "and very few are writing humor. Art Buchwald is one, and Sid Perelman is still writing—the only one of the old guard of my generation active now. Black humor doesn't get me. Of course it's understandable in these times—the times are not carefree now, not like the days when Benchley and Thurber were writing."

He appraised Woody Allen, a frequent *New Yorker* contributor, as "rather funny," and Russell Baker, humor columnist for *The New York Times*, as having "a nice quiet humor. He belongs on *The Times*."

When Edna Ferber died he wrote to a mutual friend recalling a night at Saratoga with her and George Kaufman when "Ferb" was trying to interest Kaufman in doing a play about old Saratoga. Kaufman never bought the idea, and instead of a play the idea became Miss Ferber's novel *Saratoga Trunk*. But the event was made memorable to Mr. Sullivan by a Kaufman remark about death: "Well, I've decided to kill myself when I reach sixty," he said. Miss Ferber inquired deftly: "What with, George?" And he said: "Kindness."

The Sullivan character and taste emerge sideways from the letters, telling a friend, for instance, about the new Thornton Wilder novel: "It is such a pleasure to read a book by Thornton; he believes men and women have some innate decency and dignity through every tribulation, and reading him is like a cool drink on a hot day; he's utterly free of all the atrocities you are up against in the trash that passes for today's novels filled with drunkenness, perversion, drugs, incest, and despair.

The letters are to Howard Lindsay, Nunnally Johnson, Thurber, Corey Ford, Ferber, Robert Sherwood, Wilder, Russell Crouse, Will Cuppy, Alexander Wollcott, Ross, and dozens more.

They provide a portrait of an era, obliquely seen to be sure, sandwiched in sideways between Sullivan's endless stream of jokes, but there nevertheless. And Sullivan also emerges as the very nice gent that all his friends apparently thought he was. Who else but a nice gent could have written this to James Thurber after Thurber dedicated his book *The Years with Ross*, to Sullivan:

"Well I never had a book dedicated to me before but if by some occult arrangement I could have picked the book I wanted dedicated to me, this would have been the one. I would have turned a deaf ear to Proust, Shaw, Maugham, Hemingway and all such when they begged me to let them dedicate books to me, and I'd have said to them, 'No, I'm sorry, but Jim Thurber is going to write a book along about 1958 which he will dedicate to me, and I prefer to wait for that, thank you.' "

1970

The Fan Man:

Kotzwinkle's Buddha as a Saint of Dreck

Here it is only March, man, and we already have the funniest book of 1974. It's the story of Horse Badorties, man, a fellow who says man a lot and who has a lot to say to any man.

Who is Horse Badorties? He's an avatar for our time, a filthy, hippie dope fiend and dealer who lives in what he calls an ever-shifting shit pile, who plays the moon lute and chases fifteen-year-old chicks, man. And catches them. But has trouble making it after the catch, man, because he's so busy. And so is his pad. Take that Chinese chick who went up to the filthy, stinking, horrible, soaking-wet Horse Badorties pad with Horse, there to confront reality:

> We struggle around in the junk, man, trying to find a place to lay down, but it is not safe on the floor, even the roaches are going around in little paper boats. "We'll have to do it standing up baby." She reaches for my Horse Badorties pants, man, and I am knocked off balance, and we topple, down into the unknown impossible to describe trash pile. We are rolling around in the dark contents—old loaf of bread, bicycle tire, bunch of string in peanut oil, bumping weird greasy things and slimy feelings and sand and water, lid of a tin can floating by on a sponge. There's my book on telepathy with a roach on page 12 reading about the Dalai Lama.

Horse's beloved trash thwarts Horse's lovemaking, Chinese chick splits, but Horse is sanguine and considers how chick will perhaps return tomorrow to ride with him in old yellow school bus he is going to buy with rubber check at a New Jersey junkyard; also buys old air raid siren, old minesweeper, braking mechanism from old subway car and ten-dollar greasy dog covered with slime and ick and so rotten when he brushes against you you have to throw your clothes away. Horse piles all equipment and dog into bus and drives off:

> Listen to that engine purring. It handles like a tank, man. I can hardly steer it, what an advantage. Turning it around man, in the junkyard practically tears my arms out of the sockets. . . . Maestro Badorties is wheeling along at last, man, 40 miles an hour in his own valuable vehicle.

Horse Badorties is obviously an unusual person. So also must be William Kotzwinkle, who has invented Horse in this short, artfully structured, supremely insane novel about a freaky quasi-Hindu-shmindu brahman who is one with the ridiculously filthy, worn-out world. It is Buddha's story turned inside out, glopped up and set in Manhattan, notably the East Village where Horse's ever-shifting shit pile is situated.

Kotzwinkle's artistry is such that you take the allusions to Buddhism and Hinduism for granted as merely arcane tidbits from the weird, eclectic Horse Badorties speech pattern. But the fan obsession, man, begins to form a religious pattern of its own. It hums. Horse is deep into fans, carries several $1.95 battery-powered Japanese fans with him in his also eclectic satchel, buys more fans, gives them away, orders one for each member of the Love Chorus he is organizing at St. Nancy's Church in the Bowery, where Horse is at home among the bums, where many fifteen-year-old chicks show up to sing medieval harmonies to the accompaniment of the sound of the fans, the one sound in which all other sounds are contained, the sacred note OM, which when blown forth through Horse's fans, or past his sphincter, or especially through the huge fan in the Museum of Natural History which Horse visits, sounds like this: B R A A A A A A A A A A A A A A A A A-AAAUUUUUUUUUUUUUUUUMMMMMMMMMMMMMMNNNNNNN. This is brahman as well as OM, or, as it is broken down, A-U-M, a trinity of syllables that embodies the creator, the preserver and the destroyer, all of which Horse simultaneously is. He is into samadhi, man, the identification with all worldly objects, so that he is, as any halfway decent avatar ought to be, tuned into a thousand things at once. Consider his state of mind as he plays his moon lute:

> It is an incredibly weird sound, man, the likes of which no one in Tompkins Square Park has ever heard. It is so weird, man, it is driving me crazy to play it, but at the same time it is so perfectly beautiful, man, because I am master of every opening and closing rhythm pattern known to the mind of man, and in moments like these, man, when I am playing them all, I know man, that music should be the only thing I ever do. Which is why I am going to become a used car salesman instead, man. . . . Fingers going man, fifty fingers, all over the strings . . . how I wish I was eating a clam sandwich . . . this is so beautiful man, I have to split over to my pads immediately, someone might be trying to phone me about some carrots.

And so as Horse gallops along through his densely packed realm we perceive him not as another Ginger Man, which at times he seems to be, but as a lowest-level saint of dreck and yecch, a holy man climbing up from the oily, filthy bottom muck of Central Park lake, following Buddha's path, lugging a red, white and blue hot-dog umbrella to protect himself, moving toward a cosmic consciousness of all things—stinking hundred-year-old Chinese eggs, wild saxophones and trombones, piña colada and Forty-second Street rubber hamburgers, merging into the pure white grease of this and every other historical and precognitive phase of life, tuned into dinosaurs and elephant dances, the Egyptian piano, the Etruscan bagpipe, the Babylonian police, which he remembers running from.

He is moving toward the rekindling of first enlightenment, like Buddha remembering the bo tree. Horse finds his tree in Van Cortland Park in the Bronx, the one beneath which he balled his first chick. He sits in the park while his Love Chorus gathers in front of NBC cameras, a miracle of oneness arranged by Horse alone, avatar of unifying music and the collective social consciousness.

> I have the missing centuries in my grip, man, brought back into consciousness through musical discipline. I've studied it all, man, I know the music of the ages. A memory like this is a great power, man, to be used for the good of the world. I will have to open a special

Memory School, man, and train people to remember all of their life-times, or money back.

Horse is probably destined for another life, avatar or not. He is purifying himself but has not yet learned to love violins or Ukranian folk songs and he is racist on Puerto Ricans who he fears are taking over the world with their chicken rhythm music, which he keeps out of his mind by wearing his soundproof Commander Schmuck Imperial Winter Hat with anti-Puerto-Rican-music earflaps, man. We all have our failings and prejudices, even Horse.

Wearing one Japanese, one Chinese shoe, uncoding the Tibetan Book of the Dead and dealing Acapulco produce via Colorado, Horse walks into American literature a full-blown achievement, a heroic godheaded head, a splendid creep, a sublime prince of the holy trash pile. Send congratulations to William Kotzwinkle, also a hero, man.

1974

Nathanael West:
The Stink of Life and Art

When Nathanael West gave his mother a copy of his first novel, *The Dream Life of Balso Snell*, it was her pride to anticipate that she could now brag about her son who had gone to Paris to write a book, and then prove it by showing the book. But, she told her son, she couldn't show it because "all it says is 'stink, stink, stink.' " She thought it was a dirty book.

Life treated West like that over and over again, which is the same way life treats the characters in West's novels. He was destiny's literary tot, just as Miss Lonelyhearts, the lovelorn columnist in West's novel of the same name, is the fateful victim of his own Christian heart. Miss Lonelyhearts weeps for the girl with no nose who writes him a sad letter, and for all the other letter writers "all of them alike, stamped from the dough of suffering with a heart-shaped cookie knife."

We could almost weep the same way for West, reading of his life in Jay Martin's splendid biography, *Nathanael West: The Art of His Life*. But only "almost," because West, victim though he was, also had a counterbalancing sense of hope, and of the importance of the day to day life. Robert Coates, the writer-critic who was a close friend of West's, said of him, "He was about the most thoroughly pessimistic person I have ever known. . . . But though this colored all his thinking, both creatively and critically, it had no effect on his personality, for he was one of the best companions I have known, cheerful, thoughtful, and very flexible in all his personal attitudes."

Not pitiable, then, but certainly West was a writer whose career was cataclysmically awful, and worth studying by prospective writers of originality and talent, for the world that did in West hasn't changed much.

Miss Lonelyhearts and *Day of the Locust* are both major achievements, *Balso Snell* and *A Cool Million* less successful artistically. Yet West's fame is secure if only because of *Lonelyhearts*, a perfect piece of work only ninety pages long. It took him four years to write, always condensing, paring, throwing out chunks and phrases alike. Martin captures West the artist—reading the sentences of *Lonelyhearts* aloud, trying them out in speech until he perfected them. "He had to read it to know what it sounded like," said another writer who was in the next room while West was writing.

He was influenced variously, but Martin singles out the work of Flaubert as most significant to West, for it crystallized his own desire to achieve perfection in style. Someone wrote that *Miss Lonelyhearts* might have been another work like Dostoyevsky's *The Idiot* if West had not been so concerned with understatement. But he himself had once said that he felt he could have improved Dostoyevsky—with a pair of shears. *Miss Lonelyhearts'* intensity cannot be improved upon.

Liveright published *Miss Lonelyhearts* at the approximate moment that the firm went into bankruptcy. Some two thousand of the 2,200 printed copies were held by the printer, who refused to release them until he was paid. Despite some astute blurb gathering by West for the dust jacket—heavy praise by Edmund Wilson, Dashiell Hammett, Erskine Caldwell (all of whom West had given free rooms when he was manager of the Sutton Hotel in New York), and despite rave reviews with almost no negative comment, the book could not be bought. West eventually signed a contract with Harcourt, Brace two months after the original publication, but too much time had elapsed, and the public no longer was thinking of *Miss Lonelyhearts*. The novel was remaindered.

Similar sad tales are told of the rest of West's career as a novelist. As a screenwriter he was prolific, but only in service of movies even film buffs have forgotten. As a playwright he was a flop. He was killed stupidly, passing a stop sign—his own characteristically bad driving—and crashing with another car. His wife, Eileen, died with him, on December 22, 1940.

He populated his novels with grotesque people and events, and in *Day of the Locust* he wrote the most powerful novel ever written about Hollywood without ever depicting anyone of higher status than a screenwriter. The grotesques at the lower level of life were what he had observed closely and written about so compellingly—the locusts who came to California to die. And the accuracy of his vision Martin points up in a paragraph telling what happened in the West home after the Wests were killed: "Acquaintances moved in and divided West's books and Eileen's wardrobe among them; one person laid claim to the furniture in the bedroom."

Martin, professor of English at the University of California (Irvine), has done justice to West's grotesque life. His book is easily the best source of information and insight into one of the best American writers of the twentieth century.

1970

Nothing Happens in Carmincross:

Benedict Kiely's Deathly Variety Show

The main character in Benedict Kiely's new novel is a man named Mervyn Kavanagh, and when he is asked by a publisher to write a coffee-table history of Ireland, he thinks: "I'll do it and welcome: anything to oblige and the money's good. I'll send them my plan here and now. Begin with the latest atrocity."

He conceives of the dust jacket of the book depicting a man rushing madly out of a freshly bombed building, arms wide and on fire from head to toe, a flaming cross on the run. Happily printed underneath the picture would be the old Irish saw: "Health and long life to you, land without rent at you, the woman of your choice at you, and death in Ireland."

We might think of the new Kiely novel, *Nothing Happens in Carmincross,* as the surrogate for that book, in the same way that we might think of Mr. Kavanagh as the surrogate for Mr. Kiely. The novel brims with fire, bombs, and dead men, much to the pain and woe of Mr. Kavanagh, who was born in the North of Ireland, like Mr. Kiely, but who has grown up as an Irish-American (Mr. Kiely is widely known in this country for his short stories). At book's opening Mr. Kavanagh is returning to Ireland to attend the wedding of his favorite niece at Carmincross, a composite town in the North created from Mr. Kiely's memory of such peaceful small communities, and from his latter-day perception of what has happened to those places as the result of the presently rampant insanity that is usually referred to, with enormous understatement, as "the troubles."

Mr. Kiely's novel is linked in subject matter to his book of short

stories, *The State of Ireland*, published here in 1980. Most particularly
it is linked to the novella in that collection, "Proxopera," which is a
small masterpiece about a bombing in a small town. But whereas "Proxopera" was constructed with great attention to plot and suspense, *Carmincross* is written as if plot and continuity were as inimical to the author
as are the depredations of the British army and the murders by the
Roman Catholic and Protestant fanatics of the North's political war.

Mr. Kiely creates Mervyn Kavanagh as a fat, bald, middle-aged storyteller, incapable of not interrupting himself. Kavanagh, "a reading
man cursed with a plastic memory, who also goes to the movies, and
watches television," has a mind that "is a jumble sale, a lumber room,
a noisy carnival. . . ." Add the fact that Kiely-Kavanagh is a man of
great and curious erudition—in literature, history, myth, song, and
barroom folklore, and what you end with is an incorrigible archivist, a
manic associationalist.

Now he's with Fionn MacCumhaill, tracking Diarmuid and Grainne
through mythic mountain heather, now with Helen of Troy and Olivia
Newton-John; now with the MacDonnells of the Isles, foreign mercenaries
with double-headed axes, hacking their way through medieval Ireland;
now with Leila Khaled, wreaking havoc for Palestine; now with a half-
dozen blacks setting a white girl on fire in Boston. At a oneness with
all the violence of history, he finds vicious twists to the Irish-American
ballads—"I'm dreaming of thee, dear little isle of the West, sweet spot
by memory blest . . .": this after the bombs go off.

This style is the novelistic stream-of-consciousness writ large, the
work of a man with a godlike view of history, and the didactic urge of
an angry citizen for whom the tidiness of art (like "Proxopera") is not
enough. This man needs to sprawl cosmically, for how else can one tell
the story of a heavenly garden decomposing into a backyard of hell?
How else can the reader be made to see not only consequences but
causes?

Mr. Kiely has succeeded so often as an artist that he needs no further
consecration; but I sense that this work will be viewed as something of
a tract, a political argument in which the politics are not only implicit
but also imposed. The thin plot is Kavanagh's odyssey to the North from
New York City, onto an airplane bound for Shannon, then to a nearby
hotel where he will be reunited with an old mistress and a childhood

pal, and where he will also meet people with whom he will eventually rendezvous at Carmincross.

But the people, with the exceptions of a priest and a garrulous Fenian "hero," who exist only to be satirized for their solipsistic immersion in Irish irreality, and the ex-mistress who is Kavanagh's partner in sex and bedroom banter on their way to Carmincross, are chiefly complements, or contraries, of the Kavanagh point of view. When the book is not an argument it is a monologue, or a collage of actual, violent news stories, or a tissue of legendary or mythic tragedy, remembered in that plastic mind.

John Montague, one of Ireland's major poets and an old friend of Kiely's, has described him as one of the most beloved of Irish writers who is "almost overcome by the variety of life." This book is testimony to the truth of that observation.

None of this lessens the book's achievements, especially for Americans for whom the news of Ireland is always insufficiently reported, except when the roof is blown away. What is here, along with the bomb and the gun, is the madness behind them both—the eleven Protestant women, members of a militant organization in Belfast, who took a blindfolded fellow member, who had fallen from favor, into a room and, while wearing masks, beat her to death with bricks. When finished, some of the murderers went off discoing. Kavanagh observes that the women were rough types from the gutters of Belfast, but as the police noted, "they would never have gone so far if it had not been for the surroundings of political violence."

He cites two presumably Catholic teenage girls in Belfast "fighting for the possession of a pump-action shotgun so that one of them could take a crack . . . at a soldier," and he appends to that the old women in Derry city who "on good evenings used to take their armchairs out of doors, so that they could sit in comfort and, from their grandstand seats, look down on all the lovely rioting."

Benedict Kiely loves the North, but, despite his great wit and exuberance of language, he must surely be one of the saddest men in Ireland because of what is going, and gone. No man not weighted with loss could summon the anger that is behind this book. He gives us the natural world, the evolutionary history, and the society that is in shreds within them.

He also knows that Northern Ireland isn't the worst place in the world. Lebanon's violence is worse, Mexico's earthquakes produced more corpses. But one good man killed in his innocence, one family bombed away by inadvertence, one town smithereened by men who derive meaning only from death, all deserve scrutiny and reverence.

Just before Carmincross goes up, a young IRA bomber tries to give warning by alerting a young woman in a nearby town, telling her to call the police and spread the word. The woman assumes the man is a robber and does nothing. At length she senses the truth, but too late for Carmincross.

"So," writes Kiely, "are great deeds done or perpetrated in my homeland . . . in the name of God and of the dead generations." And in these lines he fuses both his own sadness and the heroic, revolutionary rhetoric to whose cadences so much innocent blood is now blowing in the Irish wind.

1985

Freedom of the City:

Clive Barnes Is Wrong About Brian Friel

Clive Barnes's recent review of Brian Friel's new play from Ireland, *Freedom of the City*, spoiled my breakfast. I don't know why I should be upset at an Englishman failing to understand an Irishman, but in this case we are talking to Americans, or at least Friel is, since his play is here in New York. Barnes was, and now I am. And Americans are so meagerly informed of the Irish situation that even one small puddle of misinformation, such as a particular paragraph by Mr. Barnes, which we will quote in due course, is too much to bear in silence.

In the play, a woman and two young men seek shelter after their peaceful civil rights demonstration in Derry is broken up by force. They find their way, by chance, to the Lord Mayor's quarters in what corresponds to city hall. One youth is a radical, one a naive liberal, and the woman, Lily, is a simple citizen, mother of eleven, who makes the protest march every week on behalf of her mongoloid child. Really she doesn't know why she protests. She is not political, only angry.

The trio is doomed, dead from opening curtain, a tactic Mr. Barnes did not like, suspense being foiled. But since we do not waste a lot of television energy wondering what is going to happen next, we are free to speculate on the why of their deaths, which seem to me Friel's purpose; and a purpose fulfilled.

But I am not really talking about the play, or about failed or successful dramaturgy, but rather about the reality on which the play is based, and Mr. Barnes's grasp of it. I was in Ireland last year, Dublin and Belfast, doing some reporting, and saw the Friel play at the Abbey Theatre on the day I returned from the North. The play did not reflect the whole of the Northern situation; nothing short of an Irish *War and Peace* could begin to do that. But it was so close to certain fragments of the conflict that it often seemed like a transliteration of Northern actualities to the stage; and no bones broken in the move.

Mr. Barnes, however, finds it an unlikely play—farfetched in its conclusion. The play's Irish director said during a short chat that London's critics did not take to Mr. Friel's new work either. Since it is a harsh critique of English domination, this is not a surprise.

Mr. Barnes points to the play's irony and advises Mr. Friel that "Irony is much strengthened by likelihood. Can we really be expected to believe that the British Army would mobilize, against these three people, 22 tanks, two dozen armored cars, four water cannon and 'a modicum of air cover'? The finding of the court (which exculpates, with notable finesse, the British Army for murdering Lily and the boys as they exit unarmed and with hands up) is far-fetched, indeed, impossible."

So Mr. Barnes has already explored the limits of possibility in the behavior of people who live in, or militarily occupy, Ireland. Splendid. He must know, then, that the British army has used police-state tactics in dealing with prisoners suspected of IRA leanings—held them without trial, kidnapped them out of their beds without charge. (It is ironic— everything in the North is ironic—that the presence of the army is also a buffer between Protestants and Catholics, a pogrom preventive. "If only the bloody British army hadn't come in," a (Protestant) Unionist senator complained after one riot, "we'd have shot ten thousand of them by dawn.")

But the army did come in and some of its tactics have been a shame on Britain, as Mr. Barnes must know, since he understands the limits of possibility in Ulster. I refresh his memory of a book he has undoubtedly read, a first-rate piece of work called *Ulster* and put together by the Insight team of reporters from *The Sunday Times* of London. The book notes several examples of overreaction by the army, a phenomenon which, Mr. Barnes must know, from his readings in comparative American possibility, does crop up from time to time during military action: Attica, for instance, and Kent State.

The Insight team summarizes the Compton report on British army atrocities committed on Irish Catholic prisoners this way:

In sum, the Compton report left a number of questions unanswered and a number of anxieties unstilled. It nevertheless confirmed that citizens of the United Kingdom—innocent citizens because not proved guilty—who were also Northern Ireland Catholics, had been made to prop themselves against a wall by their fingertips, and to wear black hoods, and to hear frightening and deafening sounds, and to go without food and sleep, all for long periods. Whatever that meant for the moral health of the United Kingdom, its meaning for Northern Ireland Catholics was clear. Internment had been a grave injury: this was an irredeemable outrage. There could be no forgiveness for a state which did these things to their people. Its rulers could never be trusted again. For the great majority of Ulster Catholics, the State of Northern Ireland was dead.

The courts, the police, the entire government structure in the North has been dominated by Protestant hierarchies for centuries and their bias in favor of things Protestant and English, at the expense of Catholics, is a given. This bias is at the heart of the Heath government's efforts to make power sharing work—give the Catholics a share in deciding what happens to them, that is. A new government has been organized on this basis, but everyone seems to agree that its success is the least likely thing in Ireland's future. Harmony never! Both Catholic and Protestant extremists are working diligently to see that no peaceful political solution interrupts their respective quests for mutually exclusive demands.

The Catholic argument against legal injustice, which is one of Mr. Friel's points, is supportable (in contrast to the internment) by a case which made the papers while I was there: the arrest of sixteen Protestant men in a "darts club." This club was a front for a segment of an illegal Protestant army. The arrest turned up four handguns, three submachine guns and six thousand rounds of ammunition. The sixteen were promptly charged, tried, and acquitted.

Nothing is really impossible in the North, particularly in the realm of violence, which is the only topic really well reported in the U.S. press coverage of the North. A Catholic senator was killed by a Protestant murder gang while I was there, as was his woman companion, a Protestant. She was stabbed twenty times, he thirty times, and his throat was cut. Newspapers dredged up comparison cases from the files: the man who was stabbed 110 times; the man who was beaten with a hammer on the head, the chest, the arms, the legs, each finger; the woman who was stabbed multiple times in the shape of a cross and her broken rosary beads stuffed into each wound.

"The only thing that hasn't happened yet," a Belfast editor wrote in an editorial, "is the eating of the dead."

Protestants have no shortage of bizarre tales of the possible. The depredations of the Provisional wing of the IRA are endless; the bombing of Coleraine's shopping district, for instance, was perhaps a miscalculation by the IRA, which was too ashamed to take credit for it. Yet random death is merely another kind of terror weapon in the North, and in Coleraine, six people died, all of them over sixty; thirty-three were injured, children among them, a living quotient of lost limbs, melted faces. The Provisionals have also given the army continuing reason to hate Catholics, the main point of their campaign being the killing of British soldiers, around four hundred the last count I heard.

Though the Provisionals are representative of only a small minority of Northern Catholics, this, to hostile eyes, is a distinction without a difference. This too, is Mr. Friel's theme: that you die for the wrong reasons in the North, are vilified for the wrong reasons, are mythicized or canonized in death for the wrong reasons; that the North, with a history that is an endless tissue of bigotry, malevolence, psychopathy, opportunism and stupidity, is a supreme bastion of wrongheadedness, a classical study in what a nation should not be.

Mr. Barnes, finding Mr. Friel's play "perhaps too luridly fictionalized," would tone down the drama of overreaction and viciousness. He would prefer the North be made a more "likely" place.

So would just about everybody in Ireland.

1974

Postscript: This was written as a letter to the editor in 1974, when Mr. Barnes was working as drama critic for *The New York Times*. The Friel play had a short run on Broadway, and the *Times* chose not to print the letter. It is published here for the first time. Mr. Friel's latest play on Broadway, *Dancing at Lughnasa*, has been a great critical and popular success.

PART FOUR

Ten Latin Writers, Plus Translator

Gabriel García Márquez:

One Hundred Years of Solitude

The Yellow Trolley Car in Barcelona: An Interview

One Hundred Years of Solitude

*O*ne Hundred Years of Solitude is the first piece of literature since the Book of Genesis that should be required reading for the entire human race. It takes up not long after Genesis left off and carries through to the air age, reporting on everything that happened in between with more lucidity, wit, wisdom, and poetry than is expected from a hundred years of novelists, let alone one man.

That man is Gabriel García Márquez, an Argentine of incredibly magical imagination.* His novel is an always accessible, surreal fable

---

* When I wrote this review for the *National Observer* it carried the headline "All of Life, Sense and Nonsense/ Fills an Argentine's Daring Fable." The only biographical information I had on García Márquez was from the book's jacket copy, which identified him generically as a Latin American writer. Why no mention was made of his Colombian nationality I don't know. Perhaps it was an effort to internationalize him as the author of the Great Latin American Novel, which is what he became with the publication of this book. The one identifying element in the book was its copyright note: "The book was first published in Argentina in 1967 by Editorial Sudamericana, S.A., Buenos Aires, under the title *Cien Años de Soledad*." And so I called García Márquez an Argentine in print. Two years later I went to Barcelona and interviewed him, in part to discover who he was, which was even then an irrationally well-kept secret; and the story, *The Yellow Trolley Car in Barcelona*, became the first biographical report on him in both the United States and England. When we talked in Barcelona I told García Márquez about my goof and he said: "Ah, so *you're* the one."

about the town of Macondo, situated somewhere in a Latin America that doesn't exist, yet existed always. He tells the town's story from founding to burial, centering on the lives of three generations of the Buendía family.

Patriarch and founder of the town is José Arcadio Buendía. Once settled, he becomes mesmerized by the magic that the gypsy Melquíades periodically brings to Macondo—alchemy, magnetism, a magnifying glass, false teeth, ice—and spends his waking hours failing with a frenzy to invent anything of substance. He's a fool, yet he concludes in isolation, aided by a sextant from Melquíades, that the world is round. The discovery is of no use to him or to anyone else in Macondo.

Melquíades brings flying carpets and wears a hat like a flying raven, which a great-grandchild of José Arcadio Buendía remembers without ever having seen it. The patriarch and his wife, Úrsula, the eternal mother of all generations, who lives to be 122, produce children whom they name Aureliano or José Arcadio, and these beget more Aurelianos and more José Arcadios, who form a clan. The clan endures from the time that Macondo is merely an oasis between the sea and the great swamp, through the advent of the gypsy miracles, the arrival of the first pianola, the rise of Christianity, the futile wars, the first train, the first telephone, the first motion picture, the sellout of liberal idealism, the rise of the banana plantations and the ensuing banana plague, the massacre of three thousand workers, the deluge, the dust storm, and the cyclonic wind that buries the town and the last of the family forever.

The solitude of the title is the solitude of all men but also of Macondo, which never bridges its isolation from the great world except briefly, when a boat arrives, a caravan arrives, a train runs for a time. But these connections are always momentary, just as the solitude of each character is relieved only for a moment by the intrusion of another person, usually bringing love or death. But then time passes, as mother Úrsula alone seems to truly understand, and the pox of solitude once more settles.

Mr. García Márquez's Spanish is translated to English by Gregory Rabassa with such fidelity and sensitivity to the imagination of the author that the two are like the twins José Arcadio Segundo and Aureliano Segundo who were so alike that even their mother could not tell them apart, especially when they secretly decided to call each other by opposite names.

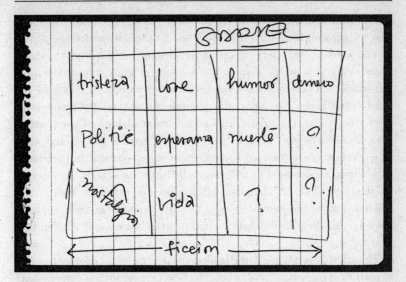

Gabriel García Márquez's list of the ingredients of fiction (*ficción*) from left to right: sadness, love, humor, money, politics, hope, death, nostalgia, life, and at least three elements unknown to the fiction writer, whoever he may be.

The book is like *Finnegans Wake* in its ambition to suggest all of man's life on earth, but it is written in simple and beautiful prose, without the incomprehensibility of the Joycean portmanteau puns. It is like Thornton Wilder's *Skin of Our Teeth* and *Our Town* in its reduction of all civilization to the family level, but without Mr. Wilder's sentimentality and with infinitely larger scope and far more toughness. It is like *Pilgrim's Progress* and all the morality plays, fused with a modern tongue and a horizonless surrealism.

The magic of this grand book is in its strangeness. From the outset, when José Arcadio Buendía and his men wake in the middle of the jungle to find a Spanish galleon that is covered with petrified barnacles, embedded in stones, and adorned with orchids, life abounds with the inexplicable. In time people rise from the dead; ghosts grow old; a man is born with the tail of a pig; a plague of insomnia strikes the town;

Arabs, Turks, and the wandering Jew pass through; and Buendía learns how to increase his weight at will. When he dies, it rains flowers.

The book is the story of the seven deadly sins, the mysteries of Christianity and black magic, the wisdom of man that somehow is transmitted to others even when civilizations vanish. It concerns the lives of the harlot, the saint, the general, the beauty, the glutton, the fairy, the priest, the aristocrat, and all the mad nuts of every stripe who are everywhere always. Every myth, legend, fable, and fairy tale, every piece of revered dogma and received wisdom and scientific fact, seems represented or at least implied in some way that is relevant to the Buendías. A daughter, Remedios, is assumed bodily into heaven, taking two bedsheets with her. Men remember their origin in the sea. An illegitimate child is said to have been found floating in a basket.

Though told as allegory, the book gives the reader an enormous sense of reality, of a genuine family saga. Mr. García Márquez has done nothing less than to create in the reader a sense of all that is profound, meaningful, and meaningless in life. His success is one of the best things that has happened to literature in a long, long time.

1970

The Yellow Trolley Car in Barcelona: An Interview

"**D**o you speak English?" I asked him.

"Nada," he said on the phone. "Nada, nada."

Well, it isn't true, but he likes to insist that it is, and so I dug up some rusty Spanish and asked when we'd get together and where he lived. "In a house," he said, and added he'd pick me up at five at my hotel on La Rambla, the great thoroughfare of Barcelona's old city. I told him my wife, Dana, was a *puertorriqueña*, so we could get through the fine points of language in either direction and he said *bueno* and that was that.

Ten minutes later he'd changed his mind and said he'd come by at noon. And at precisely noon on the Day of the Book, Gabriel García Márquez came down the crowded, noisy Rambla in a double-breasted navy-blue sports jacket, gray slacks, an open-collared blue shirt with a brown and white paisley design, a full head of curly black hair, and with a less than lush goatee, begun recently when he'd gone away for a month and forgotten his razor.

Hallo, hello, greetings, how are you, *cómo está*, a pleasure, handshakes, and then he asked: "Have you bought a book yet?"

"Of course. Yours."

His book means his big book, *Cien Años de Soledad* (*One Hundred Years of Solitude*), the semi-surreal saga of a hundred years of life among the Buendías, a family of mythical achievements and absurdities in the mythical South American town of Macondo. García's dramatic comedy of Macondo's century, acclaimed a masterpiece again and again, seems to suggest every human high and low point from post-Genesis to the air age. The *Times Literary Supplement* described it as "a comic masterpiece and certainly one of Latin America's finest novels to date." It won the Prix du Meilleur Livre Étranger in France in 1969 and won Italy's Premio Chianciano the same year. It has been published in twenty-three countries, has sold a million copies in the Spanish language during twenty-one printings since Editorial Sudamericana in Buenos Aires brought it out in 1967. It has been translated into eighteen languages, sold sixty thousand copies in Brazil, fifty thousand in Italy, thirty thousand in Hungary, 18,650 in hardcover and 46,650 in paper in the United States, where it made the best-seller list. All of this gives him the economic and literary freedom he long sought, but also burdens him with what he now sees as a "persecution" by newsmen and editors.

In a letter to a friend he bemoaned the waste of two hours of self-revelation to reporters who reduce it to a page and a half of copy. As for the editors, one came and asked García's wife, Mercedes, for his personal letters. A girl appeared with the idea for a book called "250 Questions to García Márquez." Wrote García to his friend: "I took her for coffee and explained that if I answered 250 questions the book would be mine." Another editor asked him to write a prologue to the diary of Che Guevara in the Sierra Maestra and García answered he would gladly do it but it would take him eight years, because he wanted to do it right.

And so when any outlander calls, he does not invite him home but meets him elsewhere, in front of a hotel on Las Ramblas, for instance, stays long enough to be civil, then excuses himself. If the interview goes well, he might keep it going. His problem, he says, is to see as few people as possible. Even friends are a complication at times. He accepts a luncheon date with a friend and finds twenty strangers invited to meet him.

"Then I can't make jokes," he said. "I have to be intelligent for them. This is horrible."

But life in Barcelona is not out of control, despite these pressures. "I have accomplished one thing," he said. "I have not become a public spectacle. I know how to avoid that."

As we walked inconspicuously along the crowded Rambla, seeing flowers everywhere, García had another question: "Did you buy a rose when you bought the book?"

Dana showed him a rose to prove we had. It is the custom on the Day of the Book for the city's publishing houses and bookstores to sell books in temporary wooden stalls on the main streets. By tradition, you buy a rose for your lady and she buys you a book.

"We ought to go someplace where it's quiet," I said, barely able to hear García above crowd noises.

"It's hard to find a place like that in Spain," he said, but then he pointed. "Look, we could go to that bar. It's American. Nobody goes there."

So at a Formica-topped table in a bar-restaurant memorable now for its plainness and near emptiness, García ordered coffee for himself and red wine for the visitors, specifying Imperial 1956 to the waiter so that our taste would not be offended by the ordinary *tinto*, which he does not drink. He apologized for not having wine himself. Too early. He likes to drink when it's dark. Also, he had only one coffee in the two hours we talked. Weight-watching. And balancing values.

"Coffee now," he said, "less whiskey tonight."

I told him the last writing I had done before leaving for a European trip was a short review of his last book published in the United States, *Leaf Storm* (*La Hojarasca*), actually his first short novel, published in

Colombia in 1955. I explained that even though another short novel and many short stories had been published in the United States, very little personal information about him was available. He agreed.

Moreover, despite a critical reception in this country that for a Latin has been second only to the Borges boom of the 1960s, the literary magazines have been rather unconcerned with the man who wrote a masterwork. This is less strange than it seems. I remember a conversation in an Irish bar in Albany, New York, some years ago, when revolutions were erupting in two Latin American nations. The bored bartender ended a discussion of both upheavals with the observation that "neither of them countries is worth a cat's titty," and this has stood ever since in my mind as a most lucid summary of United States attitudes—literary, political, military, it doesn't matter—toward the lands and people of the subcontinent.

It has been suggested that this less than enthusiastic reception of García as a literary personage has a political basis: the consequence of his work as a Communist newsman from 1959 to 1961 for Fidel Castro's *Prensa Latina* in Bogotá, Havana, and New York. He left the United States in 1961, and not until he was given an honorary degree by Columbia University in 1971 was he allowed to return. But if his Communist past ever did percolate down to the level of assignment editors, which is doubtful, it is likely that the Cat's Titty syndrome, rather than anticommunism, was the dampening agent. Another literary Latin leftist. Ho-hum.

The Spanish-speaking literary world behaves differently toward García. At Columbia University last April, Pablo Neruda referred to *Cien Años* as "perhaps the greatest revelation in the Spanish language since the *Don Quixote* of Cervantes." García is already the subject of an excellent critical biography, *Historia de un Deicidio* ("The Story of a Deicide") by Mario Vargas Llosa, published in 1971 by Barral Editores, Barcelona. Vargas, a teacher and novelist (*The Time of the Hero*, *The Green House*), wrote the book with García's full cooperation, and García says it is the best book about him to date; and there are several. But he vouches for the authenticity of only the first eighty-four biographical pages, paying Vargas the compliment of being afraid to read the rest.

"Mario's book may have the key to me," he said.

Why should he be afraid of somebody else's analysis?

"It's a gamble," he said, "a game. It's possible I would not be harmed by change if I read it. But why should I take the risk?"

There are instructive literary ironies in García's becoming both a critical success and a best-seller. ("If I hadn't written *Cien Años*," he said, "I wouldn't have read it. I don't read best-sellers.") He had given up writing and for more than five years did not write a word. This was overreaction to his negative feeling about his early books, to a disorienting change he'd made in his style and approach to his material, and to the influential but frustrating hold that film had on him.

He says he was always a writer, for as long as he can remember. He was born on March 6, 1928, in the small northern Colombian town of Aracataca, which is the prototype in García's imagination for the mythical village of Macondo, where life rages and sighs for one hundred years in his masterpiece. His first published stories did not appear until 1947, when he was at the University of Bogotá, studying law and hating it. Political violence closed the university and he transferred his studies to Cartagena and continued writing. Then during a visit to Barranquilla, he became involved with a small group of other writers and newsmen who knew his work. He quit law school, moved to Barranquilla, and took a job as a newspaper columnist. In 1954 he returned to Bogotá as a film critic and reporter for *El espectador*.

"As a reporter," he said, "I was the lowest on the paper and wanted to be. Other writers always wanted to get to the editorial page, but I wanted to cover fires and crime."

His biographer compares his career as journalist-into-novelist to Ernest Hemingway's, and there are similarities. But there are also substantial differences. Hemingway was the realistic, impressionistic, serious-minded reporter. García, much less solemn about his job, more inclined to see it as a source of experience rather than as an outlet for opinion, seems to have had as much Ben Hecht as Hemingway in him. At least that is the impression one gets after reading a letter García wrote to a friend, recollecting a story he once covered in the Colombian town of Quibdó. An *El espectador* correspondent had cabled reports of wild fighting in Quibdó, and García and a photographer traveled far and with great difficulty to reach the action, only to find a sleepy, dusty village, and no fighting whatsoever. They did discover the correspondent beating the heat in a hammock. He explained that nothing ever happened in Quibdó and that he'd sent the cables in protest. Unwilling to go back empty-handed after such an arduous trip, García, his photographer, and the correspondent, with the help of sirens and drums, gathered a crowd and took action photos. García sent back action stories for two days, and soon an army of reporters arrived to cover it all. García then explained the Quibdó scene to them and directed the creation of a new and even larger demonstration they could report on.

A high point of his newspaper career came in 1966 when a sailor named Luis Alejandro Velasco came to *El espectador* with the offer to tell the whole story of his famous survival at sea.

Velasco had lived ten days on a life raft after a Colombian naval destroyer, en route home from New Orleans, was struck by a storm. Eight sailors were lost overboard and only Velasco survived. This had already made him a national hero, and quite wealthy. But only the newspapers favored by Colombian dictator Gustavo Rojas Pinilla had been allowed to talk to him. His offer to *El espectador* to tell the tale anew, long after public interest had peaked, was first received, says García, as "una noticia refrita"—a rehashed story—but one editor had second thoughts, and turned Velasco over to García.

The result was a fourteen-chapter, first-person narration, signed by the twenty-year-old seaman, which revealed that the destroyer had not encountered a storm at all—and meteorologists verified this—but had been carrying contraband cargo, badly packed on the deck. The vessel almost keeled over in some high winds, the cargo broke loose, and the eight crewmen were knocked overboard. The public found this story delicious and *El espectador*'s circulation climbed. The embarrassed dictatorship denied all, but the paper subsequently proved its case with photos from other crewmen, showing men standing on the destroyer's deck alongside clearly labeled boxes of TV sets, refrigerators, and washing machines from the United States. The Rojas Pinilla government initiated reprisals against the paper and months later, when García was in Paris as *El espectador*'s roving European correspondent, closed it down.

The articles were republished in paperback in Barcelona under García's name in early 1970, the first time he was publicly connected with them. He entitled the book: *The Tale of a Shipwrecked Sailor who was*

*adrift ten days on a life raft without food or water, who was proclaimed
a hero of the nation, kissed by beauty queens and made rich by publicity,
and then loathed by the government and forgotten forever.* In a prologue
to the unaltered reprint, García credits Velasco with a natural gift for
narrative and an astonishing memory for detail, and adds: "It depresses
me that editors are not interested in the merits of the text as much as
they are in the name of the author, for much to my regret, this makes
me out to be a fashionable writer. Fortunately, there are books that
belong not to those who write them but those who suffer them and this
is one of those." And he states that the rights of the book belong to
Velasco, not García.

It was Hemingway who argued against journalism, adjudging it a good
training ground if you get out in time, but one that could spoil a writer
who stayed at it too long. García could not accept such a dictum, for
he was writing journalism to live, and he stayed at it from 1948 to 1961.
He was much more in tune psychologically with William Faulkner, who
felt that nothing could destroy a good writer. Like so many serious writers
at mid-century, García was deeply influenced by the work of Faulkner,
and so much has been made of this that he now draws the curtain on
extended talk about the relationship. Nor can he read Faulkner anymore,
perhaps because of this, although he ascribes it to the effusion of Faulknerian rhetoric that put him off when he went back to him in 1971. But
in the late 1940s, when García was writing *Leaf Storm*, Faulkner was
of major importance to him.

Leaf Storm was finally published in 1955, the same year as the shipwreck articles, after almost seven years of searching for an editor who
would accept it. One critic rejected the book for an Argentinian publisher, advising García that he was not talented as a writer and ought
to dedicate his life to something else. The story of *Leaf Storm* is told
alternately by a father, his daughter, and his grandson, who are the only
mourners at the burial of a doctor who once lived with them. The doctor
later became a recluse and by a single act earned the enmity of the
whole town, which now wants to humiliate his corpse. Faulknerian phras-
ing is evident and the doctor bears some resemblance to Reverend Gail
Hightower of *Light in August*.

But despite Faulkner's influence, *Leaf Storm* is not a derivative work. Its own language is rich, dense, but without the difficulty that goes with much of Faulkner. It is occasionally surreal in a way that Faulkner's work is not. And though it establishes Macondo in emulation of Faulkner's Yoknapatawpha County, it does so with such originality and relevance to Latin American life that by the time Macondo matured into the fully appointed village in *Cien Años*, multitudes of Latin readers recognized it as the dwelling place of their communal spirit.

The world García imagines is always solidly grounded in the real world, but it is deceptive, for the real is also frequently surreal.

In *Leaf Storm*, the old doctor sits down to a pretentious, bourgeois dinner and startles everybody by saying to a servant: "Look, miss, just start boiling a little grass and bring that to me as if it were soup." "What kind of grass, doctor?" the servant asks. "Ordinary grass, ma'am," the doctor says. "The kind that donkeys eat."

Surreal? Not to García. "A man said that in my house," he said.

He believes that Faulkner differs from him on this matter in that Faulkner's outlandishness is *disguised* as reality.

"Faulkner was surprised at certain things that happened in life," García said, "but he writes of them not as surprises but as things that happen every day."

García feels less surprised. "In Mexico," he says, "surrealism runs through the streets. Surrealism comes from the reality of Latin America."

About two weeks before we talked, a newsman had called to ask García for his reaction to an occurrence in a rural Colombian town. About ten in the morning at a small school, two men pulled up in a truck and said, "We came for the furniture." Nobody knew anything about them, but the schoolmaster nodded, the furniture was loaded onto the truck and driven off, and only much later was it understood that the truckmen were thieves.

"Normal," says García.

"One day in Barcelona," he continued, "my wife and I were asleep and the doorbell rings. I open the door and a man says to me, 'I came to fix the ironing cord.' My wife, from the bed, says, 'We don't have anything wrong with the iron here.' The man asks, 'Is this apartment two?' 'No,' I say, 'upstairs.' Later, my wife went to the iron and plugged it in and it burned up. This was a reversal. The man came before we knew it had to be fixed. This type of thing happens all the time. My wife has already forgotten it."

García likes the principles of surrealism but not the surrealists themselves. Given a choice, he prefers the painters to the poets, but he does not think of himself as being like any of them. And it is true that his work is based more in the anecdote than in the symbolic or random flow of events so important to the surrealists; true also that his aim is to be accessible, not obscure. And yet, a surreal quality, a rendering of the improbable and impossible as real, pervades his work. And its importance to him has obviously intensified since the tepidly surreal grass-eating of *Leaf Storm*. In *Cien Años* he made the leap to earth-eating, to a plague of insomnia, to ghosts that grow old, to a young woman who ascends bodily into heaven and takes two bedsheets with her. His improbability usually extends an everyday reality. In *Cien Años*, for instance, José Arcadio, son of Úrsula, enters his bedroom, closes the door, and a pistol shot is heard. Then:

> A trickle of blood came out under the door, crossed the living room, went out into the street, continued on in a straight line across the uneven terraces, went down steps and climbed over curbs, passed along the Street of the Turks, turned a corner to the right and another to the left, made a right angle at the Buendía house, went in under the closed door, crossed through the parlor, hugging the walls so as not to stain the rugs, went on to the other living room, made a wide curve to avoid the dining-room table, went along the porch with the begonias, and passed without being seen under Amaranta's chair as she gave an arithmetic lesson to Aureliano José, and went through the pantry and came out in the kitchen, where Úrsula was getting ready to crack thirty-six eggs to make bread.
>
> "Holy Mother of God!" Úrsula shouted.
>
> She followed the thread of blood back along its course, and in search of its origin she went through the pantry, along the begonia porch where Aureliano José was chanting that three plus three is six and six plus three is nine, and she crossed the dining room and the living rooms and followed straight down the street, and she turned first to the right and then to the left to the Street of the Turks, forgetting that she was still wearing her baking apron and her house slippers,

and she came out onto the square and went into the door of a house where she had never been, and she pushed open the bedroom door and was almost suffocated by the smell of burned gunpowder, and she found José Arcadio lying face down on the ground on top of the leggings he had just taken off, and she saw the starting point of the thread of blood that had already stopped flowing out of his right ear.

We talked of this passage in connection with the surreal aspect of the book, but García all but dismissed the improbable quality of it, saying only: "It is the umbilical cord." And we moved on to something else.

After *Leaf Storm*, García encountered some heady influences that would change his fictional style and bring him as close to socialist realism as he would ever come. The Communists in Bogotá wooed him after *Leaf Storm* was published; but while they wanted him as a writer and a mind, they rejected his style as too artistic to convey the stringent socialist realities. On this point Mario Vargas Llosa writes: "Although he never fell into the coarse conceptions of socialist realism, García Márquez nevertheless reached a similar conclusion about his narrative language some months later, at the beginning of his second novel." The change in his writing that followed could hardly be adjudged a bad one, for working in his new style García produced three highly regarded works. But he was not satisfied, because the change restricted his imagination.

He had a flurry of party militancy in Bogotá, but it faded quickly and he then went to Europe for *El espectador*. He found himself in Rome covering Pope Pius XII's hiccups, and he enrolled at the Centro Sperimentale de Cinematografía, with plans to become a director and film his own version of *Leaf Storm*. After some months of study, he moved to Paris and learned there that the Rojas dictatorship had closed his paper and that he was out of a job.

He stayed in Paris, beginning a short story about some violence he remembered from childhood, changing the locale from Macondo to "El Pueblo" (the town), a shift which has generated confusion about the settings of his various works. His language became more staccato, with dialogue playing a larger role. The short story he had begun expanded quickly and took shape as a novel, then two novels. The last offshoot he completed first and it became *El Coronel No Tiene Quien Le Escriba*

(*No One Writes to the Colonel*), the story of an old military man who waits endlessly for his military pension, long after he and the war that he fought in have been forgotten by the government.

"He had written a small masterwork," Vargas Llosa writes, "but not only did he not know it, he also experienced the same sensation of failure as when he finished *Leaf Storm*."

He then completed his novel about violence in the same small town, the violence provoked by *pasquines*—anonymous signs that appear mysteriously on the walls of public places. The book is called *La Mala Hora* ("The Evil Hour").

García's life in Paris while writing these works was memorable but not happy. He lived, he said, on "daily miracles," deeply impoverished, as a foreigner not allowed to work, unable to speak the language very well, at one point turning in empty bottles for cash. When his money ran out, his landlord let him live in an attic, where he wrote steadily. When he returned to Paris in 1968 as a success and looked back on his three years of poverty, he concluded: "If I had not lived those three years, probably I would not be a writer. Here I learned that nobody dies of hunger and that one is capable of sleeping under bridges."

My wife and I had just come from Paris to Barcelona, and we told of the extraordinary time we'd just had in the city.

"I had money when I went back there," García said. "I wanted to eat all the things I had not eaten, drink all the wine I could not afford to buy. And I hated it. I hate Paris."

He lifted himself out of his poverty there in 1957 by selling newspapers in Bogotá and Caracas on the idea of a series of ten articles about the Iron Curtain countries. A newsman who went with him on that tour, Plinio Apuleyo Mendoza, later in the year became editor of *Momento*, a Caracas magazine, and hired García immediately. It was in Caracas, confronting his fictional world only on his days off, and reporting meanwhile on the last days of the Pérez Jiménez dictatorship, that he wrote some new short stories. These he called *Los Funerales de la Mamá Grande (Big Mama's Funeral)* when he published them in Mexico in 1962. These, too, have the staccato quality, except for the title story, which is written in dense language that satirizes Colombian political and editorial-page rhetoric. It is the only story set in Macondo, another point of confusion. The others in the collection, all set in El Pueblo, make no mention of Macondo.

The assumption by many casual readers of García's work is that all his fiction is set in Macondo. But when he broke with the lush style of *Leaf Storm* and took up with the Communist party realists, he not only adopted a kind of Hemingway realism but he also left his fictional hometown. He returns to his natural style, an exalted but not overblown prose, only in the title story, in which he returns to Macondo.

García said he has a problem convincing people about El Pueblo. "*Leaf Storm* and *Cien Años* are in Macondo, nothing else," he said emphatically of his books. "The other three [*Colonel, Mala Hora, Mamá Grande*] are in El Pueblo." He opened the United States edition of the *Colonel* to page 42 and cited internal evidence where the Colonel remembers Macondo and mentions when he physically left it, in 1906.

"But some people," he said, "do not accept any evidence, and I leave them so I don't have to discuss it."

Another rumor is that he is through writing about Macondo, but of this he says, "It is a lie. I don't tamper with the future." During the past year, in fact, he completed a short novel which develops the lives of characters he created in *Cien Años*. It is called *The Incredible and Sad Tale of Innocent Eréndira and Her Heartless Grandmother*, and is now being translated into English by Gregory Rabassa, who translated both *Cien Años* and *Leaf Storm*.

García's career as a fiction writer remained publicly static during his time in Venezuela, but journalistically he took an odd turn: he left *Momento* and went to work for *Venezuela Gráfica*, a magazine commonly called *Venezuela Pornográfica* in Caracas. Solemn fictionists might be put off by such work, but García accepted it then and still accepts it.

"I'm interested in personal life," he said, explaining that at the moment in Barcelona he was reading the memoirs of Jackie Kennedy's chauffeur. "I read all the gossip in all the magazines. And I believe it all."

The Cuban revolution lifted him, for the first time in his life, out of journalistic fluff and fun and into advocacy. He opened the Bogotá office for *Prensa Latina*, went to Havana later, and in 1961 became assistant bureau chief in New York. He quit in mid-1961 during a wave of revisionism, in solidarity with his disgruntled boss; and with his wife, Mercedes, the Barranquilla girl who had waited for him for three years until he married her in 1958, and his two-year-old son, Rodrigo, he left New York, but not without a tropical memory of the city.

"It was like no place else," he said. "It was putrefying, but also was in the process of rebirth, like the jungle. It fascinated me."

The Garcías headed for New Orleans by Greyhound, passing through Faulkner country. García duly noted one sign advising DOGS AND MEXICANS PROHIBITED and found himself barred from hotels where clerks thought him Mexican. He had planned to return to Colombia, but Mexico, being a film capital, lured him, and on the urging of Mexican friends he changed plans and began slowly, and with much difficulty, a new career as a screenwriter. He wrote one short story in Mexico and then lapsed into a silence that lasted several years.

The screenwriting was partially the cause of the silence, but so was what he considered his failure as a writer of fiction. He wrote film scripts, some in collaboration with Mexican novelist Carlos Fuentes, and several became movies, memorable now mainly because he worked on them. In dry periods he worked again as an editor and at one point did publicity for the J. Walter Thompson office in Mexico City.

"It was a very bad time for me," he said, "a suffocating time. Nothing I did in films was mine. It was a collaboration, incorporating everybody's ideas, the director's, the actors'. I was very limited in what I could do and I appreciated then that in the novel the writer has complete control."

His friends remembered him as being blocked and in a period of severe self-criticism, dissatisfied with all he had done, not wanting to return to anything like it.

It was in January 1965, while driving from Mexico City to Acapulco, that he envisioned the first chapter of the book that was to become *Cien Años*. He later told an Argentinian writer that if he'd had a tape recorder, he could have dictated the entire chapter on the spot. He then went home and told Mercedes: Don't bother me, especially don't bother me about money. And he went to work at the desk he called the Cave of the Mafia, in a house at number 6 Calle de La Loma, Mexico City, and working eight to ten hours a day for eighteen months, he wrote the novel.

"I didn't know what my wife was doing," he said, "and I didn't ask any questions. But there was always whiskey in the house. Good Scotch. In that respect my life hasn't changed much since those days. We always lived as if we had money. But when I was finished writing, my wife said, 'Did you really finish it? We owe twelve thousand dollars.' She had borrowed from friends for a year and a half."

At one point, he said, his wife was given the option by the butcher shop, where she was a good client, to pay by the month. She refused, but later, when getting money every day was more difficult, she accepted the offer and paid monthly installments to the butcher. At another point there was no money for the rent, so she told the landlord she couldn't pay for six months and somehow he said all right; so they didn't have to worry about that.

"She is stupendous," García said.

We had been talking in the Rambla bar for almost two hours and now García had to leave for an appointment. But he said we should come to his home at five and continue the talk, and we did.

He and Mercedes both greeted us. She is a slender, serene beauty, her dark, shoulder-length hair parted in the middle, an Indian quality in her face that is reminiscent of some of Gauguin's Tahitian women. She speaks softly and said that the Spaniards tell her she speaks a sweet Spanish, as contrasted with the cacophonies of Castilian. She employs a day maid to help with the housework, in notable contrast to the time when García was writing *Cien Años*. She lived those days, she said, trying not to dwell on the precarious quality of their life, for when she did, she became very nervous.

"I would not want to go through that again," she said.

It is not at all likely she will have to.

The Garcías' apartment is modern in its furnishings, with wall-to-wall carpeting, floor-to-ceiling drapes, the color scheme beige, brown, and orange. The hi-fi, which García, and no one else, operates, is a significant object in the room, and in García's life. He treats his records as if they were fine crystal, wiping each one after use. His sons Gonzalo, ten, and Rodrigo, now twelve, have their own phonograph, so that Papa's will not be disturbed. Reading as he listens to music forms the second part of his day and regularly follows his morning work period, which usually begins at ten and lasts until about two. (One page a day, of twenty-four lines, is his average output, five pages his record.) Apart from the records—he played Leonard Cohen for the visiting North Americans— a large and orderly collection of classical works on cassettes occupies a shelf beside the sofa.

"There were no records where I grew up," he said, "and now all this on cassettes. Imagine!"

A discussion of some of García's literary tastes was prompted by the living-room shelves which held some of his books.

"He left most of his books in Colombia when he moved to Barcelona," Mercedes said, "but the Conrad, Plutarch, and Kafka he takes with him wherever he goes. And the Virginia Woolf he always buys when he gets there, if he can find it."

The shelves had all of these, plus the complete works of Stefan Zweig and A. J. Cronin, fourteen volumes of Borges, Rabelais's works, and among other items, *The Day of the Jackal* by Frederick Forsyth. Ah ha! A best-seller.

"Literarily," García said, "it is of no importance. But things happen. It is good false reporting."

From the blue he asked: "What do you think of Graham Greene?" His manner implied that I would be judged by my response. I said I had a high opinion of Greene.

"He teaches you how to write," García remarked. "His technique of narration is so good. He also taught us to see the tropics in books like *The Power and the Glory*, *The Comedians*, and *A Burnt-out Case*, which is set in Africa, but which is like Latin America. People think of life in the tropics as being exuberant, happy, rich. But Greene shows its elements—the heat, the plants, the rain, the animals, the sea. And he shows life is poor and sad. And that is the truth about that place."

Greene brought to García's mind one of his prejudices. "The intellectuals would like to like Greene," he said, "but they don't think they should. He writes a good book like *A Sort of Life* and then confuses them by writing *Travels with My Aunt*. The intellectual is the worst thing there is. He invents things and then he believes them. He decides the novel is dead but then he finds a novel and says he discovered it. If you say the novel is dead, it is not the novel. It is you who are dead."

He talked of liking Ray Bradbury, but selectively. "There are two

Ray Bradburys. One writes the science fiction and one is human. I don't like the science fiction."

He said that he has read no great American writers since what he called "the Lost Generation"—meaning Faulkner and Dos Passos, and Erskine Caldwell and Hemingway for their short stories. He liked none of the Hemingway novels. *"The Sun Also Rises* was a lengthened short story," he said. Of the Faulkner works, he was most captivated by *Absalom, Absalom!*, but added, only half facetiously, that he thought *The Hamlet* was "the best South American novel ever written."

"Until you're about the age of twenty," he said, "you read everything, and you like it simply because you are reading it. Then between twenty and thirty you pick what you want, and you read the best, you read all the great works. After that you sit and wait for them to be written. But you know, the least known, the least famous writers, they are the better ones."

Of contemporary Latin American novelists, two in particular, and both of them known in the United States, were early boosters of *Cien Años:* Carlos Fuentes and the Argentine, Julio Cortázar. García sent his first three chapters to Fuentes, who was so impressed that he wrote for a Mexican magazine:

> I have just finished reading the first seventy-five pages of *Cien Años de Soledad.* They are absolutely magisterial. . . . All "fictional" history coexists with "real" history, what is dreamed with what is documented, and thanks to the legends, the lies, the exaggerations, the myths . . . Macondo is made into a universal territory, in a story almost biblical in its foundations, its generations and degenerations, in a story of the origin and destiny of human time and of the dreams and desires by which men are saved or destroyed.

Cortázar, one of the first readers of the completed book, and equally enthusiastic, said García's imagination had redeemed the South American novel from its boring ways. Cortázar's novel *Hopscotch* had won the National Book Award for its English translator, Gregory Rabassa, in 1967. García was dissatisfied with the English translation of *No One Writes to the Colonel* and, after reading Rabassa's version of *Hopscotch*, he asked his publisher to have Rabassa, a professor of Romance languages at New York's Queens College, translate *Cien Años*. The publisher found Rabassa tied up for a year.

"I'll wait," García said, a decision for which anyone attuned to the English translation must be grateful.

Rabassa describes García's Spanish as "classical, very clear. He doesn't fool around with syntax. Certain local words do creep in, in dialogue, but he is not an experimenter. He uses the right word in the right place. I would compare his language to Cervantes'."

Rabassa will doubtlessly translate García's next major work, which Vargas has said has the title of *El Otoño del Patriarca ("The Autumn of the Patriarch")*. García has been working on it since before *Cien Años*, inspired by his exposure to the Jiménez dictatorship in Venezuela, and strengthened by what he learned of the Batista dictatorship during his time in Cuba, and the Rojas dictatorship in Colombia. The central figure is a Latin dictator who lives to be 270 years old.

García's alienation from right-wing politics raises the question of why he now lives in Spain under the Franco dictatorship. I asked how he felt about Spanish politics. He groaned and put his head in his hands as a reaction to a question whose public answer could jeopardize his residency in Barcelona, where he lives in apolitical peace.

"If I were to choose a country which had politics that I like," he said, "I would not live anywhere."

"A clever answer," I said. "I won't press the point."

"You are a gentleman," he said.

We talked of Barcelona as a place to live and I expressed my short-term admiration of its magnificence and the vibrancy of its life. I also told a trolley-car story: that when we crossed into Spain at Port Bou, we asked at the tourist window for some literature on Barcelona and were given a brochure which, among other things, detailed the trolley lines in the city, by number and destination. At Columbus Plaza we tried to get a trolley that would take us to Antonio Gaudí's Sagrada Familia church, one of Barcelona's wonders. A vendor of fresh coconut at the plaza explained that there hadn't been any trolley cars in Barcelona for fourteen or fifteen years. Why, then, were they still mentioning them by name in the tourist literature? The coconut vendor had no answer and so we boarded a bus instead of a trolley and rode toward Gaudí's monumental work. We stood at the back of the bus and watched the mansions and apartment buildings make splendid canyons out of the street, at times looking like I imagined Fifth Avenue must have looked in its most elegant nineteenth-century moments. And then I said to Dana: "Look, there's a trolley."

She missed it, understandably. Its movement was perpendicular to our own. It crossed an intersection about three blocks back, right to left, visible only for a second or so, then disappeared behind the canyon wall.

"What trolleys still run in Barcelona?" I asked García.

He and his wife both said there were no trolleys in Barcelona. Mercedes remembered a funicular that went somewhere.

"This one was yellow," I said, "and old-fashioned in design."

"No," she said. "The funicular is blue."

García called his agent, Carmen Balcells, on the phone. "Is there a yellow trolley car in Barcelona?" he asked. "I'm here having an interview with Kennedy and he saw a yellow trolley."

He listened, then turned to us and said, "All the trolleys were yellow in the old days."

He asked about the blue trolley, but Carmen said it was outside of town, nowhere near where we had been. In a few minutes she called back to say that about two years ago there was a public ceremony in which the last trolley car in Barcelona had been formally buried.

What had I seen? I have no idea.

"To me," García said, "this is completely natural."

Then he told of hailing a taxi in Barcelona not long before this, but when he saw someone in the back seat he pulled down his arm. The cab driver stopped anyway and García then saw no one in the back seat. He explained this to the cabbie, who was outraged. "People are always seeing somebody in the taxi with me," he told García.

We had been drinking Scotch carefully for about five hours, lost in small talk and the free-form interchange of two languages. What had begun as a meticulous quest for the translation of phraseology through the intermediacy of Dana had loosened to the point where I was asking Dana questions in Spanish and she was talking to García in English. García was popping English phrases at me more and more, and I was fluently pidgin in Spanish. There was no comprehension problem. We praised the liberating effect of whiskey, but I downgraded it as a tool for writing. García agreed but hesitated: "There is a point where it works," he said.

It was a quarter to eleven, the theater hour in Barcelona, when García decided we should go to dinner. He drove, soberly, through the old streets, parked near an alley, and then led the way to what he called "the best secret restaurant in Barcelona." I put on my steel-rimmed glasses to read the menu, but García said, "I have better glasses than those," and took out a pair of steel-rimmed half-glasses.

"Are you blind without them?" I asked.

"Not quite," he said, holding the menu as far away as he could. "My arm is still long enough."

I ordered baby squid in garlic and acceded to García's choice of *perdiz*, which we finally figured out meant partridge. He ordered French wine, Côtes du Rhône, I think, which came in a dusty, crooked-necked bottle. He chewed a piece of bread, clearing his taste buds of old Scotch, before tasting the wine for approval.

We had one more literary discussion at dinner. We had talked of politics and fiction earlier and he had mentioned a writer who, he felt, had hurt himself by overemphasizing politics, and whose work had changed. García considered this a loss. I then asked what he thought the proper place of politics was in fiction. He borrowed my pen and drew some intersecting vertical and horizontal lines in my notebook, creating twelve boxes. Beneath the boxes he wrote the word "*ficción*" and drew arrows to the left and right vertical borders. Then he wrote "*politic*" in the left central square. He paused. The vacant squares impelled him to further statement, and randomly, in two languages, he filled them in: "*tristeza*," "*love*," "*humor*," "*dinero*," "*esperanza*," "*muerte*," "*nostalgia*," "*vida*," and three question marks.

There is another García drawing in my notebook; it shows a flower blooming atop a two-leafed potted plant and an open-mouthed fish about to bite on a dangling fishhook as a one-eyed sun rises, or perhaps sets, behind an undulating horizon. In homage to Kennedy, he included in the drawing a two-wheeled trolley on a track, off to the left, denoting it

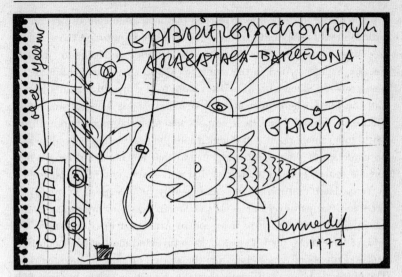

Gabriel García Márquez writes better than he draws cartoons, but the fish is not half bad. Top line is his signature, beneath that is Aracataca-Barcelona (his home cities in Colombia and Spain), and the "old yellow" trolley car is what Kennedy (lower right-hand corner) did or did not see in Barcelona in 1972.

---

as "old yellow," and he signed it in two places and included my own name with the year mentioned, 1972.

We eventually left the restaurant, around one-thirty. I discovered I'd left my copy of the Vargas biography at the García apartment, but I was told not to worry, that there would be bookstalls open on La Rambla where we could get another copy. García drove to one but it was Mercedes who leaped out and bought the book; for how would it look, García said, for him to go out and buy his own biography at one-thirty in the morning?

There was a conversation whose site I do not remember. Maybe it was the American bar, or maybe the apartment, or the best secret restaurant in Barcelona. But it has to do with García and his going back to Colombia every two or three years, and returning to Aracataca.

"Each year less," he said of the hometown, meaning each year the world he knew vanishes a little more. But there is a renewal. For each year, as the fame of *Cien Años* grows, Aracataca becomes more and more a place where tourists who have read the book go to compare its reality with the reality they have in their heads. They want to see the chestnut tree where José Arcadio Buendía, the founder of Macondo, died in beatific madness, tied to the trunk for years, seeing the ghosts of his past grow old along with him. They want to see the old Buendía house, and the plaza where thousands of striking banana workers were massacred by the army and their corpses taken on the longest train in the world to a remote point and dumped into the sea, so that not only would no evidence of their deaths remain but that the lie would be given to anyone brazen enough to suggest that a massacre had taken place.

Years later that massacre would merely be a legend, its reality as accepted, yet as unverifiable, as the Trojan horse, or my yellow trolley car. García overheard it as a legend in Aracataca when he was young and he later reinvented it, just as he reinvented most of Macondo from bits and pieces of Aracataca, from the storied or merely imagined past. The Macondo he created barely exists in Aracataca today, but that does not stop the enterprising small boys of the town from reinventing, with *their* imaginations, what the tourists want to see. For a few coins they will find José Arcadio Buendía's tree and the place where the ants devoured the last newborn in the Buendía line, the infant that had been conceived incestuously and born with the tail of a pig. The cycle of the imagination is not dependent on any reality that can be bought at the hardware store like a seventy-eight-cent screwdriver.

Writing fiction today, a friend once advised me, is about as significant as playing bridge. Possibly this is true for those who dwell in the Land of the Cat's Titty. Possibly, for them, other things have replaced it. But in the face of a primordial event like the creation of Macondo, the argument is not worth rebutting. Whatever the numbers, and the numbers never mattered, there are still those who would rather dwell there for a time, and ride the yellow trolley car that may or may not exist, and thrive on the heat of a one-eyed sun, and draw sustenance from a book full of verities and question marks. Those who feel this have no need to justify their preference.

A Bogotá journalist went to Aracataca in 1969 and found that the home of García's ancestors was being eaten to dust by ants, just as García had predicted the dust storm that would bury the Buendía house and the town forever. The journalist found ruins and solitude in the town, no doubt what he went to find, and which always exist everywhere if you look closely. But the fading of Aracataca was not the consequence of a cursed, fateful prophecy. It had been predicted by García Márquez not because he had chosen it to be that way in his godlike role as novelist, but because—like the gypsy Melquíades, who in *Cien Años* had written in the coded parchments that "The first of the line is tied to a tree and the last is being eaten by the ants"—he deciphered the key to history, and he knew that events occurred because they had to, that the turn of time was cyclical and that the vital, bloody warmth of every life held in itself not only its own dusty eventuality, but the seeds of regeneration as well.

García's nickname is Gabo, and the diminutive of that is Gabito. And in an Aracataca bar the Bogotá journalist heard a song being sung which was really a song of the rebirth of this novelist, this man:

> It was in the land of Macondo,
> Where little Gabriel was born.
> All of the people knew him,
> By the name of Gabito. . . .

1973

Gregory Rabassa:

Keeper of the Golden Key: An Interview

"**H**eaven-sent or hell-bent, according to the critic," writes Gregory Rabassa, "translation is really something apart from the other arts. But it is, indisputably, an art. Too often people have defined it in terms that only partially apply, for it has never received the massive attention given to other aspects of literature. It follows, it serves, it is the squire of the arts, but it was Sancho Panza who made Don Quixote possible."

And it has been Gregory Rabassa who has made Gabriel García Márquez possible in the English language, and Julio Cortázar, and a long list of other superior writers from Latin America and Spain during the past fifteen years. The works of these writers are widely appreciated in English today because Rabassa is a chameleonic stylist, a master of language, and a superb writer himself. The Rabassa shelf includes his own 1965 book on Brazilian fiction, written in Portuguese as an expansion of his doctoral dissertation, and, since 1966, twenty-four translations of novels and short-story collections from the Spanish and Portuguese, one translation of Brazilian literary criticism, five plays, and, in progress, two works of fiction and a volume of letters and sermons.

Rabassa has been formally recognized for some of his work. For Julio Cortázar's *Hopscotch* he won the National Book Award for translation; and for Gabriel García Márquez's *Autumn of the Patriarch* he won the P.E.N. Translation Award. *Hopscotch* gave him recognition, but it was his translation of García Márquez's novel *One Hundred Years of Solitude*, one of the great fictions of the twentieth century, which, though it won him no prize, earned him the fame few translators ever realize.

García Márquez became an international celebrity with that great novel, set in the mythical town of Macondo—a book that seems to embrace the history of mankind from Genesis and alchemy through the age of the biplane and aluminum foil. García Márquez's Spanish is, in Rabassa's opinion, classical on the order of Cervantes. But when one reads the English version there is no hint that this work was not conceived by a literary maestro working in English, such are the bright rhythms of the sentences, the surprises trapped by the transformations Rabassa makes in the author's ebullient Spanish. "He doesn't translate phrase by phrase," García Márquez said of him. "I have the impression he reads the whole book and then writes it."

"He has such energy, and he's covered such a range," comments Rabassa's longtime colleague, Frank MacShane, director of the Translation Center (retiring in summer 1981) at Columbia University. "His name appears on so many books whose quality is very high. He's been sensible to have done the very best. He was lucky to translate *One Hundred Years*, but it's a two-way street. He helped to make it accessible."

Rabassa's connection to *One Hundred Years* was a direct result of *Hopscotch*. Cortázar advised his friend García Márquez to have Rabassa do the English translation, but Rabassa was busy with *Bomarzo*, a long novel by the Argentine writer Manuel Mujica-Lainez. "Julio advised him to wait," Rabassa recalled, and García Márquez waited a year. Then Rabassa attacked the novel and finished his remarkable translation in four months. It was published in the United States in 1970.

Rabassa had already been courted by publishers after *Hopscotch*, but now the books began to pour into his office from publishers and Latin writers, "so many I haven't been able to read them all," he says in his office on the Queens College campus. The walls of the office reflect his ties to the Latin world and its languages: a poster announcing his lecture at Dartmouth on "Solitude as Failure in García Márquez," a map of Brazil, a photo of the soccer wizard Pelé, a lapel button with the message *Tentamos sempre fazer melhor ainda*—the Portuguese translation of the Avis slogan, "We try harder"—and a poster from the Basque nation that looks vaguely Cyrillic but is wholly Basque and reads: *Euskadi Ta Askatasuna*, whose precise meaning Rabassa is unsure of. "I put that up to baffle people," he says.

Sitting there in his rumpled corduroy suit, and exuding a wickedly comedic mind—made manifest through his steady laughter and the crinkling of his eyes when he relishes a memory—Rabassa talks of how he works with his authors, and of his ties to them. He is close to Cortázar, who occasionally visits the Rabassa seaside home on Long Island, New York, and listens to old jazz records. And he is close enough to García Márquez to call him by his nickname, Gabo.

"I understand Gabo and Fidel Castro are great friends," Rabassa chuckles. "Fidel calls him up at two o'clock in the morning. I'm waiting for the day when some wild piece of news comes out of Cuba, some absurd thing Fidel has done, and you'll know he took Gabo's advice."

How does Rabassa differentiate the style of a García Márquez from a Cortázar and not impose his own syntax on the work? "I let them lead," he says promptly. "I just sit down and let it go and if I get to a hard spot I stop and think about it. If you get too conscious about it you get self-conscious and that kills it. Do what comes naturally and García Márquez will sound like García Márquez and Cortázar will sound like Cortázar."

Was this wisdom the consequence of having a maestro whom he emulated? "I think it was the other way around. I wanted to avoid the artificiality you notice so much. Take Constance Garnett, for instance. Though I admire her very much for what she did, I don't admire how she did it. I got suspicious when I was reading Dostoyevsky and he sounded just like Tolstoy. You could tell by the content they were two completely different people and wrote in different styles, and yet they came out sounding like Constance Garnett, a genteel English lady."

Rabassa came late to translation but the study of language was an early passion, stemming, he feels, from his perusal of his father's late-nineteenth-century classic edition of the *Encyclopaedia Britannica*. "If you picked up the article on Germany," he recalls, "they'd have pages and pages of the German language, and the same on China and so on. I got to collecting words."

He was born in Yonkers in 1922; his mother was an American, his father an affluent Cuban in the sugar business in New York. Young Rabassa had no need to learn his father's Spanish, since the elder Rabassa was fluent in English. But he absorbed culture from him ("my father was a fine piano player who played with Casals, his contemporary, in Barcelona"). The family moved from New York to New Hampshire when the sugar market collapsed not long after Gregory was born; there his father opened a small country inn near Dartmouth.

"I suppose it was foreordained I would go to college there," he says. He majored in Romance languages, joined the armed services in 1943, and, through an O.S.S. recruiter, was sent to Europe, where he became a translator and "paraphraser"—confusing the enemy by translating the English coded message into different English. A remnant of the war years, a well-worn red military beret given to him by a British intelligence group, is still a sartorial trademark.

After the war he earned a master's degree in Spanish literature at Columbia, then a doctorate in Portuguese literature, and taught there until 1968, when Queens College made him an offer Columbia failed to match. He began his translation work in 1960 when he, along with Saul Galin and some colleagues at Columbia, started a short-lived magazine called *Odyssey Review*, which translated little-known foreign authors into English (Jorge Luis Borges and Nobel Prize–winner Miguel Ángel Asturias were early choices, before they became well known here). Rabassa took on minor translation chores as the magazine's work load mounted, and in 1964 Sara Blackburn, then an editor at Pantheon Books, asked Rabassa to try a translation of *Hopscotch*. He worked on a sample; everyone, including Cortázar, liked it. That was the beginning of a new career.

His translations—although abundant, lauded, and in great demand —do not earn him a living. When he began, the going rate was around fifteen dollars for a thousand words; now it's up to forty dollars, although he commands fifty dollars plus sometimes a small percentage of the royalties. "Even if I worked my tail off I still wouldn't make twenty thousand dollars a year," he says.

Translating technical nonfiction bores him, and not all fiction by fine writers sustains him. He regrets choosing *The Green Pope* and *The Eyes of the Interred* by Asturias. "After I got into them I said, 'I should never have taken this on.' I didn't realize how imperfect they were. You could eliminate a lot of scenes that didn't serve much purpose. It was a good example of how a writer shouldn't be too hasty."

His translation of Demetrio Aguilera-Malta's *Seven Serpents and Seven Moons* was a labor of love. He knew the author, and his wife, Clementine, now a professor at Medgar Evers College in Brooklyn, was writing her dissertation on him. Rabassa saw a manuscript copy of *Seven Serpents*, read it, decided "it was time Demetrio got some recognition," and began the translation, which was eventually published by the University of Texas Press.

He has translated works by Mario Vargas Llosa of Peru, Brazilian novelists Osman Lins and Clarice Lispector ("She looks like Marlene Dietrich and writes like Virginia Woolf"), and Spaniards Juan Goytisolo and Juan Benet, whose novel *A Meditation* is forthcoming.

The translation that gave him the most trouble was *Paradiso* by the late Cuban writer José Lezama Lima. In its original version the novel was vast and sprawling. Rabassa valued it highly, yet the publisher cut it and pruned it "much too strongly," he feels. "They simplified it. It had a complicated syntax, and it gave me a lot of wonderful problems. With some writers you have to be inventive, but with Lezama Lima you had to be reconstructive. You knew what he was saying but damned if you could say it in English. You had to rewrite the sentence to make it fall into place."

But he insists there is a limit to how far a translator should rewrite: "The translator is not in the silk-purse business; when the novel is inadequate, how can the translation redeem it? Yet, there are exceptions: Poe is a better poet in French than in English because of Baudelaire."

To illuminate the problem a translator faces, Rabassa cites the language of a rooster. English-speaking roosters say "Cock-a-doodle-doo," but in Spanish they say "Ki-ki-ri-ki."

"There is a difference between a substitution and a replacement," he has written. "Nabokov would speak of translation as a kind of eclipse: the two words are represented by circles, but the new word almost never covers the old one completely. Each word has a portion that it doesn't share with the other. These parts that lap over are what make substitution impossible. This is the stuff that puns are made of. What can we do with George S. Kaufman's masterpiece, 'One man's Mede is another man's Persian'?"

Rabassa is working slowly on a book on translation that Yale University Press wants to publish. It will not be a theoretical work, for he feels George Steiner's *After Babel* is the last word on that matter. His will be a memoir about his life and work with his remarkable authors.

There is so much more he wants to translate, such as the work of the

Brazilian writer Dalton Trevisan, for example, whose collection, *The Vampire of Curitiba*, he translated in 1972. "He's a mystery man," Rabassa says, "not quite as extreme as J. D. Salinger. He was a devil to work with. He would make changes that had nothing to do with the translations. He keeps sending me his books. What I've got to do is translate some short stories and get them published individually. His last book didn't do too well and yet it's a good book."

Rabassa is solicitous not only of his own authors but also of the translator's survival problems. He talks of the need for a clearinghouse, an idea pushed by the American Literary Translators Association in Dallas, which would match publishers with competent translators of valued foreign works; not an easy task, as the abundance of unreadable translations obviously proves.

It stands, then, as a marvelous gift to English readers that Rabassa flourishes. One is grateful not only for the masterworks that have filtered so magically through his remarkable mind, but also for the little-known works that he has been instrumental in bringing to light—including his most recent revelation, the wild and frenetic *Macho Camacho's Beat* by the Puerto Rican writer Luis Rafael Sánchez. The response to all this work at first encounter is enormous surprise and pleasure, and then gratitude for its accessibility. And in an age when consciousness of Latin America is exploding in this country, one looks hopefully to the other extraordinary writers standing outside our literary gates, waiting for more benefactors like Rabassa to come along with the golden key and let them in.

1981

Carlos Fuentes:

Distant Relations

Carlos Fuentes creates two families, both named Heredia, in his Byzantine new novel: a ghost story, a gothic trompe l'oeil, a perplexing but fascinating plunge into historical and literary allusions he calls *Distant Relations*.

The title (it was *Una Familia Lejana* when published in Mexico in 1980) reflects the link between the Heredia families, the ties of the past to the present, the old world to the new, France to Mexico, Alexandre Dumas to Carlos Fuentes, and much more, of which we will add another matched pair not equated in the text: José María Heredia, Cuban journalist and poet, born in 1803, exiled in 1823 for his role in a failed revolution, and who died in Mexico in 1839—and José María de Heredia, born in Cuba in 1842, but who became a French poet, a member of the Parnassian poets and whose fame rests on a single collection of sonnets and poems, *Les Trophées*.

The latter Heredias were cousins and stand as a near-perfect inspiration for Fuentes's novel: existing resolutely in separate worlds, on separate continents, products of separate cultures, linked by common birthplace, common blood, a common name, and by poetry that is perfectly polarized for Fuentes's use—one the product of a passionate revolutionary mind, the other classical in origin, method, intent and achievement.

Fuentes doesn't need these Heredias, and whether they actually did inspire him is only relevant as a literary footnote. His own life really inspired this book, which he says is the novel of his for which he cares most. "It says the most about me as a writer and my interests in literature," he told Alfred MacAdam and Charles Ruas in a *Paris Review* (Fall 1981) interview. "It is about writing, the only novel I have ever written about writing."

He adds: "It also deals with the influence of France on the Caribbean nations, the ghosts of French writers who came from Latin America, like Lautréamont or Heredia. The novel deals with the origins of fiction, how no story can ever be fully told, how no text can ever be fully exhausted."

To this end he has written a novel which can never be fully understood, his meaning not only deliberately incomplete at novel's end, but leading perhaps into a novel yet to be written.

It begins reasonably enough in a Jamesean sort of situation and setting, the Automobile Club de France overlooking the Place de la Concorde, where two men sit, one talking, the other listening. Talking is the Comte de Branly, eighty-three, a French aristocrat. Listening is a younger man, who is not identified until the novel's late pages and who proves to be the narrator of the novel we are reading, a man named Fuentes.

"You are afraid to be the narrator of this novel about the Heredias," Branly tells Fuentes, "because you fear the vile devil who may take revenge against the last man to know the story. But you are forgetting something I have tried to tell you more than once. Every novel is in a way incomplete, but as well, contiguous with another story. Take your own life. In 1945, Fuentes, you decided to live in Buenos Aires; you became a citizen of the River Plate region, and then in 1955 you came to live in France. You became less of a River Plate man, and more French than anything else. Isn't that so?"

Fuentes says it's so, but he ultimately identifies with both branches of the Heredia family of the story, overcoming any free-floating fear of the devil which may be hovering about, telling us his story, and seeking—in and also outside this novel, it would seem—to heal the ambivalence he feels within his psyche: a man pressured by the influences of Parnassian France as well as the *mestizo* life of Mexico.

Branly tells Fuentes that his Mexican friend, Hugo Heredia, an archaeologist more enamored of Toltec stones than of men, was characteristic of the polycultural Latin American intellectual. He had, says Branly, "the passion to know everything, to read everything, to give no quarter, no pretext to the European, but also to know well what the European does not know and what he considers his own . . . above all, to demonstrate to the European that there is no excuse not to know other cultures."

This looks very like a mirror image of Carlos Fuentes as we have come to know him, an omnicultural figure who interprets for his readers and listeners not only the life, literature, politics and history of Mexico, but of Latin America, France, Spain and the United States. He is clearly a literary hybrid: a manically acquisitive intellectual, compulsively analytical, yeasty victim of the temptation to elaborate, and a manic storyteller as well, creator of a tale so convoluted and contradictory that it requires the novel's full length just to state its mystery. Resolution of the mystery Fuentes leaves to the soothsaying literary critics among his readers.

Let me add that in spite of this, *Distant Relations* is not difficult to enter, and it is translated with very readable fervor by Margaret Sayers Peden, Fuentes's regular translator. Once within the story, though you barely hold on to the plot as you acquire it, you cannot help but listen, for Fuentes holds you with his formidably surreal imagination.

He dedicates his novel to the great surrealist filmmaker Luis Buñuel, and adds a quotation: "What is frightful is what one cannot imagine." Fuentes has also said: "Nothing astonishes me, because the world has bewitched me."

His story is so bewitched that it is unsummarizable. But in part it goes like this: the archaeologist Hugo Heredia has lost his wife and his son, Antonio, in a plane crash (they were en route to Europe). A second son, Victor, did not take the trip, and Victor and Hugo develop an unusual closeness.

Victor and Hugo become Branly's house guests in Paris, and as is usual with them when they visit a new city, they play their name game and look up other Heredias in the phone book to make connections. They call another Victor Heredia, then visit him (taking Branly along) at his chateau, a literary creation Fuentes says was somewhat inspired by a chateau once owned by Gustave Doré, and which Fuentes rented.

"The house," he told MacAdam and Ruas, "brought back all my yearnings for form and terror. Doré's illustrations for 'Little Red Riding Hood' for example: they're so incredibly erotic! The little girl in bed with the wolf! Those were the signs under which . . . *Distant Relations* was born."

At the chateau Branly and the Mexican Heredias encounter the Parisian Heredias—father Victor, son André. The son is equal in age to the Mexican boy, Victor, and an affinity is struck which peaks in one of the book's most bizarre scenes: when Branly comes upon the two boys in the back seat of his Citroën, which, three days after he'd been in an accident in it, had become a "foul smelling cave . . . a depository for rotted vegetation, swirling temperatures, and detritus. . . ."

In this cave of a car the boys, Victor and André, are copulating. But this is far more than what it seems, though Branly will be a while discovering that.

Branly tries and fails to break up this union, unaware it exists on a plane of mystery he will never really understand. What this generates in him is a series of memories of two of his own lost playmates, one a boy who will turn out to be the French Victor Heredia, the other a girl who will be the wife of Hugo Heredia, and also be a girl perceived by Branly's specter in a park 180 years ago. Branly encounters these phantoms in the chateau, where he remains inexplicably bedridden while the ghosts are incarnated.

Branly reports on his response to all this as the book winds down: "I did, it is true, finally see the relationships among certain objects. What I still do not know is why those relationships exist [. . .] Perhaps one of my ancestors in the fourteenth century, with no difficulty, understood the homologous relationship among God, a hart with burgeoning antlers, and the hunter's moon. By the sixteenth century, another ancestor would not have known this; he could not see the correspondence among these things. Art, you see, and especially the art of narration, is a desperate attempt to reestablish analogy without sacrificing differentiation. This is what Cervantes, Balzac, Dostoevsky accomplished. Proust was no different. Surely no novel can escape that terrible urgency."

Branly tells Fuentes that they too are "bound together by a shared rejection of the death of the past" and that by some incomprehensible juxtapositioning of time and event, they all came together, all of the Heredias, Branly, now Fuentes, to create, to perceive, an angel. That angel turns up on the iron catwalk which spans the swimming pool in the Automobile Club.

The angel is a waiter with an empty tray, and he is singing the last lines of a madrigal, "So beautiful were its waters that in them I did drown." He has a face like a wildcat, curly bronze hair, golden skin, and parts of his head and body appear to belong to different creatures. He is, of course, the fused being created through that copulation in the Citroën. Isn't he?

Branly is swimming in the pool's tranquillity and then, as the angel-waiter hovers, the pool erupts in violent waves, almost drowning Branly, who is saved by Fuentes. The waiter vanishes. Branly is weakened and returns to his bed.

Later, Fuentes returns to the pool and as he approaches he smells freshly cut pineapple, ripe plantains, "the butter red flesh of the mamey." He hears a Mexican woman singing a melancholy ballad, finds the pool obscured in a tangle of lush plants, ivy-covered trees. He startles parrots into flight, dislodges the nests of tiny hummingbirds, finds himself facing a monkey with the face of Fuentes. His feet sink into the moist earth, the yellow mud of the swimming pool's edge.

He climbs to the catwalk, looks below into the now-scummy pool to see two bodies, embraced, floating, "two fetuses curled upon themselves like Siamese twins, joined by their umbilicus, floating with a placidity that repudiates all past, all history, all repentance. . . . These are preternaturally old fetuses, as if they had swum nine centuries in their mother's womb . . . the faces of two boys become old men. . . ."

"Heavy of heart," says Fuentes, "I retreat, never turning my back, as if bidding a last farewell to an imprisoned hero, to a god interred in life, to drowned angels. . . ."

With five more lines the book ends, the puzzle begins.

1982

Osman Lins:

*Avalovara**

What we have here is a nonesuch, a great curiosity of the age, an eloquent, maddening puzzle for literary cryptographers and cabalists, a novel of dazzling intellect, sublime and ridiculous poetry, surreal explosions, brilliant excess, and vast stretches of magniloquent boredom. It is a work of almost scientific precision, geometric in design, arithmetical in growth, mythical, mystical, humorless, and high camp to the thirty-second degree.

The novel, first published in 1973, is one of the major works of a Brazilian writer, Osman Lins, who died in 1978 at age fifty-four, and it introduces Lins to American readers. The translation from the Portuguese is a tour de force and reconfirms the preeminence of Gregory Rabassa in bringing a canon of modern Latin American masterpieces to the English language.

Avalovara is masterful not because of what it reveals about human behavior, which is questionable and minimal, but because of how that minimality is grandiosely imagined and structured.

"Prose is architecture," said Hemingway, "and the baroque is over." Lins gives half of that dictum the old heave-ho and creates an architecture of a most baroque order, structuring the kind of novel Jorge Luis Borges might have written, if he'd only had the inclination to write a novel, and if he'd had a sexier mind.

Sex, lubriciously poetical sex, is central to the book. It's not an

---

* This review was written for *The New York Times Book Review* but not published. It is printed here for the first time.

arousing sort of sex, never pornographic, content (with one small exception) with talk of vulva and glans. Whenever it threatens to go over the edge into down-home salacity, Lins switches to images of chariots, lanterns, birds, and rugs. The sex, an assignation in a Brazilian hotel between the two principals, begins on page 1 and climaxes spectacularly on page 332. In between may well be the longest case of coitus interruptus on record.

The principals are Abel, son of a whore, now a writer (with a life itinerary that seems similar to Lins's), and a married woman named only by an ideogram, which looks like this:

For purposes of typographical ease, she will be henceforth referred to as O. Apart from the sexual element implicit in the letter, she bears no resemblance to the protagonist of the well-known *Story of O.* "O" refers additionally here to the perfection of a circle, the spirality of this love affair, O as a mystical letter combining the angelic and the carnal in man, etc. The two horns may represent the other two women in Abel's life, whom he now finds reembodied in O. The dot in the middle of the ideogram might be for the bullet wound where O shot herself on her wedding night, after her bridegroom raped her with his icy glans. (The bridegroom, Olavo Hayano, is a yolyp, about which more later.) The dot might also be for O's second vulva, or her second being, or her second perfection, for she is twice-born, has four eyes, and has been a double, a Janus, an amphibian, etc., ever since she fell down an elevator shaft on her tricycle at the age of nine. She is 32 during the assignation. Also she is 23.

Abel, as might be expected, is questing for Paradise, and he finds it in O, literally. When they fuse, the mystical bird, the Avalovara, which is inside both of them, and which is really made up of a swarm of tiny birds, takes flight, and O and Abel become one to the point of sexual duality and even interchangeable ownership of the immediate vulva.

But I'm getting ahead of the story.

From the outset, the work is staggeringly episodic. It is composed of eight books, each with a separate theme, subject, form, and style, each broken up into numbered and lettered segments (two books have 10 segments, two have 17, one has 24, etc.). The segments of each book grow progressively larger (probably in some prefigured arithmetical progression which requires scrutiny beyond my patience) and the books are all interwoven, a method of presentation which can derange even a careful reader, especially since Lins is diabolically clever at withholding any information that might lead to clarity.

To avoid derangement I read four of the sections separately; and read this way they are accessible set pieces. In one of these, "The Spiral and the Square" (the spiral being an equivalent to time, the square to space), Lins, through a parable of a merchant and slave in Pompeii, explains the theme and the geometry of the overall work, which is a spiralling palindrome within a square. The palindrome, in Latin, is: "SATOR AREPO TENET OPERA ROTAS," which has a mysterious double meaning: "The farmer carefully maintains his plow in the furrows" and "The Plowman carefully sustains the world in its orbit." Since we are also talking about sex here, I suggest a third meaning; but since Lins didn't spell it out I won't either.

A second discrete section is "Julius Heckethorn's Clock," and I found this the most satisfying section in the book: mysterious, as Lins likes it, but also complete. In it Julius builds, in the 1930s, a clock of almost miraculous complexity, equivalent, in the author's intention, to this novel. "Julius is aiming at this," writes Lins: "to place people, as they face the sound systems of his clock, in the same attitude of perplexity that they undergo before the universe."

The clock is so complex (it plays the introduction to a Scarlatti sonata) that it stands "as a symbol of the astral order." By the time it finds its way to Brazil, three decades after its creation, no one alive has heard the full phrase from Scarlatti, though the clock, presumably, has chimed continually. It will reveal the full phrase, full complexity, perhaps, when O and Abel climax; just as an eclipse of the sun will take place about the same time, and U.S. rockets will be fired from Brazilian shores in a great public sabre-rattling.

Both the spiral and the clock sections are Borgesian in style and relate only metaphorically to the O and Abel story.

The other two separable sections are "Roos and the Cities" and "Cecelia Among the Lions," and are the stories of the two women, other than O, in Abel's love life.

The Roos section is Abel's chase of the ethereal Roos (she quotes

Anacreon verbatim) through several European cities, Abel panting heavily, Roos generally giving him the back of her frosty neck. Yet he loves her, wants her, sees in her face the mystical city for which he is questing. But he never scores, and he wonders if he should have shown her his sexual equipment as a persuader.

The Roos section is essential to Abel's mystical quest, but this does not keep it from being boring and absurd. Roos as a character is as thin as an interface, and the dialogue at the pair's anguished farewells is so fatuous it's hard to believe Lins wrote it: "Thanks for the lakes" . . . "If you can, send me a postcard at Ravenna . . ." . . . "I will" . . . "I'll never be able to thank you enough for coming to Milan." Or: "Goodbye. Send me a postcard." . . . "Roos . . . I was happy this afternoon! I feel as if I'd been inside a drum. A loud drum. As if I were surrounded by a rhythm. A roll. The drum."

"Cecelia Among the Lions" is much more vital, almost naturalistic at times, with abundant and vivid dialogue as it sketches Abel's early, lower-class life in the city of Recife. But its earthy realism also mingles with wild surreality as Lins tells the story of Cecelia, the social worker and hermaphrodite, and of Abel's passion for her—his embrace of contraries, as the author neatly puts it.

Lins at one point calls this novel an imitation of an ancient morality poem. An inkling to at least part of his moral intent emerges in the Cecelia section, where Abel views the people of Recife as being lost privately within a lost nation. He sees Brazil as absent of meaningful focus, moving chaotically, erratically, the Recife people possessed of an "incapacity . . . for any permanent effort of continued obligation." Abel sees himself as one of these, unable to commit himself to any revolutionary action, writing for reasons he cannot understand, questing for the ungraspable, but questing artificially through dreams and hallucinations.

The theme of oppression looms over the work, as it looms over modern Brazil, and Lins embodies this oppression in Olavo Hayano, a lieutenant colonel in the army, and also a yolyp. Lins defines the yolyp at considerable length, but piecemeal, before he connects it to Hayano, typical of his narrative method. Only six yolyps ever exist at one time in the world in any generation; all are male, born with a spiny placenta which wounds the mother so grievously that she never reconceives or even fully recovers; the yolyp's face is visible in the dark; he is sterile, and brutal; and he's also O's husband.

Living with a yolyp, living with Brazilian political oppression; these themes (among others) merge throughout the four remaining sections of the book, some of which will put you to sleep. All four concern either the assignation or the histories of O and Abel—even though we never find out how they met, or became lovers, or what they are truly up to in this assignation. Is it a suicide pact? Just another moment in the affair? Will they confront the yolyp? Follow the spiral to Paradise and find out. Maybe.

Abel-Lins spells out his views on the yolyp question in an essay which he serves up, as usual, piecemeal, in the last quarter of the book. A major point—articulated—is that "an artist can remain faithful to the questions that absorb him most intensely and still do his work, ignoring sordidness and brutality. . . ." The writer who thinks this way is contaminated, Abel argues; but in so behaving he also "rescues an anomaly . . . that the expansion, purity and sovereignty of spiritual life are not incompatible with oppression."

Lins's novel stands as an argument favoring this view. But whether he proves or negates the same point with the story of O and Abel as they ignore the yolyp and pursue their spiritual ends, is arguable. But then almost everything in the book is arguable, for Lins creates Abel as a man who can rationalize any issue, who accepts the world's mysteries as existent and worthy of scrutiny, but is unable to translate them into graspable metaphors. Abel's imagery is forever shifting, fantastic, confounding, and his quest is built on this imagery.

Lins tells us his own attitude early on when he speaks of this book as the "tracing out . . . of a trajectory of which the protagonist is ignorant and the meaning of which has still not been defined for the author."

In this authorial confusion, as well as in the story's maddening obliquity, the book evokes comparison with the work of Robbe-Grillet, and Alain Resnais, separately, and most particularly in their collaboration: the great non-sequitur film, *Last Year at Marienbad*, on whose meaning they disagreed. Also, many sections of Avalovara are voyeuristic in the way of Robbe-Grillet's anti-analytical novels; only Lins extends the voyeurism to Abel's surreal imagery, whose meanings are as moot as those of Robbe-Grillet's furniture. Also, Julio Cortázar's *Hopscotch* comes to mind as a precursor of any novel written in numbered sections. And in the Paradise sequences, when lubricity is at flood, Lins drops much of his punctuation and moves nonparodistically into the style Joyce gave to Molly Bloom's soliloquy.

Lins, like Abel, began as a banker with a degree in economics and finance. He published his first novel in 1955, and three more novels thereafter, plus two books of stories. His works won prizes and some were published in France, Spain, and Germany, but until now, nothing has appeared in the United States. At his death his work-in-progress was a novel.

Lins also wrote for theater and television, published several collections of essays, wrote a travel book with his second wife, Julieta de Godoy Ladeira, also a writer, who survives him. He taught Brazilian literature, and won his doctorate at age forty-six. But fiction writing was the work of his life, and *Avalovara* the book of his life. Whatever its flaws, echoes, and excesses, *Avalovara* is a nonpareil work.

1980

Lygia Fagundes Telles:

The Girl in the Photograph

Lygia Fagundes Telles, little known in this country, is one of Brazil's most popular serious writers, a novelist and short-story writer who has been publishing since 1944, when her first collection of stories appeared. She has published ten other books since then, among them *The Girl in the Photograph*, the novel which appeared in 1973 under the title *As Meninas*. This publication is the first of several works by and about Latin American women in the Avon/Bard paperback series of fiction originals.

The novel is obviously the work of an accomplished writer, and has had exceptional popularity in Brazil—a best-seller given eleven printings. I assume the book's success is the result of its appeal to an audience of young women, plus the author's substantial reputation—she published two other novels and five collections of short stories prior to this work. The three books which followed it were two collections of stories, and a book of fragments called *The Discipline of Love*, her most recent work, published in 1980.

Her preference, clearly, is the short story, which is without doubt one reason this work is not as satisfactory as it should be, given her stature, her obvious talent, her insight into human behavior, her subject matter, which is rich in social detail, and her courageous views on political repression. The translation of the novel by Margaret Neves is clear and accessible, even when the author is being elliptical. Language is never a problem, but the form in which it is packaged most definitely is.

The story concerns three young women, all living in Our Lady of Fatima Boarding House, run by Catholic nuns. The boardinghouse is perhaps a metaphor for Catholic Brazil in the 1960s, a time of social upheaval, torture of political prisoners, and radical resistance to fascism. The author seems also to use her three principal characters metaphorically, isolating them as types—components of contemporary Brazilian womanhood.

One of the principal characters, the lovely Ana Clara, is a model who has dropped out of college, a child of loveless squalor now become a heroin addict, deeply into pathological promiscuity. The second is Lorena, child of wealth, militant virgin endlessly fantasizing her defloration by a married man, about whose life and love she speculates monomaniacally. She spreads her wealth magnanimously among her friends, who use her for their own ends, her largesse again metaphorically linked to a family of dynastic wealth (her brothers are named Romulo and Remo). The third girl is Lia, mulatto daughter of a Dutch Nazi (disaffected from Naziism). She is an intellectual, a sexually liberated young woman, a committed revolutionary.

All three are linked to men who never appear in the story, the point being their obsession with insubstantial maleness. Ana Clara craves money and so has a rich fiancé whom she loathes. She loves, without really being able to give or accept love, Max, another addict, who gives her nothing she can use in life. Lorena throughout the book awaits the call from her lover, Dr. Marcus Nemesius, but the call never comes; he is less than serious about her. And Lia thinks only of Miguel, her radical lover, jailed for his revolutionary activity, but freed in exchange for a kidnapped ambassador. Lia prepares to go to Algeria to join Miguel and live a revolutionary life. She will crawl to him if necessary, yield her body to strangers to get to him.

Of the three women, the most appealing is Lia the revolutionary, because she at least is an active figure in this world, a woman who, however subordinate to the male, is nevertheless aware of the need to be done with the victim status; and this is something the other women do not understand. The most satisfactory scene in the first half of the book comes when Lia confronts a young man in whom she has no interest, and takes him on sexually in the way one might feed a stray cat. It is a *Tea and Sympathy* encounter, taking place in a grubby and dirty office where revolutionary students talk about Malraux and Rosa Luxemburg and scheme about changing the world, which means raising their own lives an inch or two up from squalor through their intellectual visions of a better world.

We are grateful for this scene on page 111 because it is at last a scene, and until this point Fagundes Telles has been giving us character. God, does she give us character.

Her choice of storytelling method is a fatal error in the design of this book, although I cannot forget all those readers who put the novel through eleven printings in Brazil. Why was I so bored with it up to this point? I do believe it was because the author chose to go the Molly Bloom route, and Molly the wondrous sometimes gets heavy, even for Joyce fanatics.

Fagundes Telles does not eschew punctuation as Joyce did, but she eschews action. She chooses to define her characters by what they think, chiefly of themselves, and sometimes of one another. We come to know the specifics of Ana Clara's addiction from her friends, Lorena and Lia (who are very easily confused until the book is well along, merely because of the "L" element and because of the switching of internal monologues from one to the other when they are talking together).

The internal monologue is a tool, but only a genius can use it to the degree Fagundes Telles uses it. It becomes repetitive and obvious here, an unpleasant thing to say about a writer of her quality.

If the reader is concerned only with an excursion into female ideology, the analysis of the three types through this method may present no problem. Fagundes Telles is obviously satirizing upper-middle-class vapidity, Catholic sexual repression, as well as the lethal joys of the drug culture. She also loads the cannons against men in all particulars: there isn't a worthy one on or off camera in the novel, as far as we can tell. This may be hateful to the macho supremacists among us, but it really isn't important. Her point is the females' acceptance of subordination, the psychological rape and exploitation that they agree to without any comprehension of what is really happening to them.

This is no doubt important, but as a story it all palls, until about three-quarters of the way through, when the author opts for action. Her story then is vitalized—Ana's encounter with a Valentino freak; Lia's class encounter with Lorena's ridiculous and neurasthenic mother (another victim of male exploitation, but again the men are absent, the women are the problem); and finally, the turning of the virginal worm, when Lorena the child grows up to face the tragedy at hand, and behaves with love and wisdom and courage and foolhardiness.

By ending the book on an active note, a most satisfying piece of behavior, the author unites the three principal characters meaningfully, and creates in them a dimension none of their interior meanderings had been able to convey.

A final point on the storytelling: the sections are discrete, and sometimes effectively so, but this works against the novel's coherence. The author appeals to that in us which reveres small detail, private insights contributing to the epiphany; but she lacks the quality that vivifies such detail in a narrative and compels us to read on.

The self-concern of the three young women is discouraging. Even so we would follow them willingly if we knew the intertwining of their lives was leading us somewhere. But there is no plot, there is only self-referential character, and then the fusing of the isolated lives in a climactic moment.

Three flawed lives, three sad young lives, three lives that sputter along, each in an emotional wasteland of its own unique design: this is what the book comes to. It is an important spectacle but its presentation is tedious. The book should have been shorter. Fagundes Telles should trust us to understand behavior without marathon introspection. The monologue may work on the analyst's couch to exorcise the demon, but on the printed page it turns the demon into a sleeping pill.

1982

Jorge Amado:

Tereza Batista:
Home from the Wars

If we were back in the 1940s Jorge Amado's new novel would be a
great vehicle for Dorothy Dandridge, or maybe Rita Hayworth in brown-
face. His heroine, Tereza Batista, is a lithe and loving copper-colored
saint, a glorious nonesuch from the subcontinent, a fantastic beauty with
a bod of bods, a prism of strength, a champion prostitute, a magnificent
concubine, the personification of selflessness, a martyr to charity, a
paradigm of virtue and fidelity, a cop-kicker and leper-licker, but also,
sad to say, rather a bore, and a literary joke.

Amado has written a sensual, comic work this time out, again about
Bahia in Brazil, again with all the lavish detail of life as it is lived in
the torrential spew of his imagination. Amado has his champions in this
country, after his success with *Gabriela, Clove and Cinnamon, Dona
Flor and Her Two Husbands* and other work published here since 1962.
He has been publishing novels in Brazil since 1931 and is a respected
artist at home and elsewhere. Perhaps there are abundant readers in the
United States who will value this new work as they valued his others,
who look to him for diversion from the North American landscape, and
who revel in the small details of life in the provinces, the slums, the
brothels and the aristocratic and bureaucratic degeneracies of Brazil.

Perhaps also, in his own language, the book is different from the
product at hand. The translation of this new work is by Barbara Shelby
and it is fine English. Yet it has the same quality to be found in the
translations of Isaac Babel, another regionalist whose dialect and slang
are not entirely lost in translation but arrive here like a package that
has been too long at the bottom of the parcel-post truck. It's not the

same as it started out. Babel is a giant of concision. Amado is logorrheic, repetitious and in quite another literary dimension from the Russian maestro. Yet their language comes at us from the funhouse mirror, and that distortion—once the art is missing—may be at the heart of why Amado makes it in Portuguese but not English.

Or is it simply that the art is clearly missing, even in Portuguese? Amado believes not only in repeating himself four, five, six times, but also in summarizing each of Teresa's adventures in advance, so that we not only drown in verbosity but we are also denied the surprise that even rotten fiction usually dangles before us.

He maneuvers us through the "wars" of his subtitle—all but one of the wars wholly involving Tereza, the yonic saint. We see her at the outset, in the full bloom of womanhood, falling in love with a sailor who sails away and leaves her forlorn during her time as a singularly sensual samba dancer. We flash backward then to her being sold as a child bride to the rich, vicious, sadistic, lecherous, one-dimensional brute, Captain Justo, and we carry along through the war she rages (and wins) against the captain's bizarre abuse of her body and soul.

On then we go to a smallpox epidemic when Tereza, like nurse Edith Cavell and other female bastions of grace under pressure, single-handedly stands up against the raging plague, while the whole town cowers in fear. She is the power who organizes the local whores to isolate and treat the sick, haul away and bury the putrefying corpses. She and the girls do not get the plague, lucky for them, and her doctor lover runs off like a cowardly dog to save his worthless self. Does the world reward Tereza for her selflessness? Nix.

Tereza earns a respite from whoring, sadism and other poxy fates when she is taken in by the wonderful, thoughtful, refined, wealthy, intellectual, loving and kindly old aristocratic whoremaster, Dr. Emiliano Guedes. The randy old doc turns Tereza into a lady and is just about to write her into his will when, oops, he succumbs in the saddle. Amado then takes us back through the idyllic six years in which Tereza and the doc made sweet pudding together. And, in the words of Red Smith as he once watched a yacht race, Amado here opens up great new vistas of boredom to us.

The final fragment of this book—which is really a series of independent novellas entwined with recurring characters—is the best part of the work, a low-level spin-off from *Never on Sunday*, in which the whores of the town go on strike against an evil cartel of cops and real estate opportunists, just as the American fleet pulls into port. Tereza plays a minimal role in this section, for which a reader must be thankful. A statue comes down off its pedestal and gods materialize to save the whores and give the evildoers their ironic justice; in all an entertaining social farce is played out with more suspense than Amado heretofore saw fit to generate.

Tereza does have a small hand in this war and at the victorious end she is reunited with her sailor, who sails home from the sea just in time to save sweet Tess from a loveless marriage to a baker with plenty of dough. Our heroine is about to be mounted again at fadeout, but this time she likes it because it's for truly true love, the truest she's ever known.

Amado has made his book dense with superficiality, and in doughty Tereza he has created an affectionate, affronting literary icon for these times of multi-angular sexuality: a composite of Wonder Woman, Mary Magdalene, Lola Montes, Lupe Velez, Melina Mercouri, Clara Barton, Foxy Brown and Little Annie Fanny. *Ms.* magazine will probably not print an excerpt.

1975

Carlos Castaneda:
Tales of Power

Carlos Castaneda's new book, his fourth, should transport him once and for all out of the land of anthropological rationality and into the mysterious realm of fiction. The debate on whether the elusive little Latin from California really did turn up a turned-on Yaqui Indian named Don Juan Matus in the Sonora region of Mexico, there to be instructed in the ways of sorcery by this wise old man, has been part of the literary, philosophical, anthropological and head-culture dialogue of America since Castaneda's first book, *The Teachings of Don Juan: A Yaqui Way of Knowledge*, came out in 1968. The mystery attenuated in 1971 with the follow-up volume, *A Separate Reality*, in which, as with the first, the way to self-knowledge under Don Juan's tutelage was gained in part through peyote and the magic mushroom. In his third work, published in 1972, *Journey to Ixtlan*, Castaneda (known in the books as Carlitos) forwent the drugs and began the task of seeing the world with only an apprentice sorcerer's undrugged eye.

Now in *Tales of Power*, which Castaneda says is his last book on Don Juan, his instruction is completed, again without drugs. The sorcerer's apprentice graduates into his "totality" on dream and guidance only, and sets off at book's end alone, with his two teachers, Don Juan and Don Genaro, receding from his life to become what they used to be, "dust on the road" of his life.

The new book is the capstone of the tetralogy, wrapping up the teachings of Don Carlitos so completely that the other books are not really necessary to an understanding of what he's been up to. One of the teachings for us all is that you can get away with literary grand larceny, even peddle your dreams, fantasies and fabrications, if you orchestrate them under the label of nonfiction. Norman Mailer knows this. Clifford Irving knows this. Hunter Thompson knows this.

The nonfiction maneuver does not diminish the meaning of the work but it unquestionably enhances its marketability in an age when fiction struggles for a place on the shelves of the nation's bookstores.

Castaneda told a *Time* interviewer in early 1973: "Oh, I am a bull-shitter! Oh, how I love to throw the bull around!"

Why didn't we believe him? A more genteel way of putting it would be that the man revels in his imagination. This new work is so clearly a product of Carlitos's very special imaginative process that it is difficult to see why there has ever been any doubt about the fakery of his pose as a nonfictionist.

But really, it isn't entirely fakery, only a rare man's way of hedging the bet of his life. Carlitos, who once thought he was a student and wrote his first book as a doctoral thesis, is unquestionably a teacher. His books are as didactic as Plato's and just as fat with instructional dialogue. His Don Juan, who constantly tells Carlitos to end his own internal dialogue, is as garrulous as Jonathan Winters and just as fractured by his own jokes. And yet if Castaneda is not about to inseminate Western culture with a vision of how it really is, he is at least on the cusp of twisting its head a few millimeters. He is a cult figure now, especially with the young but not exclusively so, approaching Hesse, Vonnegut, Golding and Salinger. You think he's popular this year? Wait till next.

Remember *Franny and Zooey*? That finely honed little pair of short stories was as didactic as anything ever wrought by an American writer, including Dale Carnegie's and Norman Vincent Peale's combined oeuvres. Salinger was setting us up for a guru, the noted but still unfulfilled Seymour Glass, who according to his siblings had all the answers to how to get on in this world and maybe the next half dozen too. Jesus, Epictetus, Emerson, Zen. Put them all together you get Jeez, Seymour.

Salinger fattened his bundle and both enhanced and diminished his literary reputation with his *Franny and Zooey* self-help didacticism; and Carlitos, so says his agent, either is or will be a millionaire from his books. Such is the contemporary addiction to random wisdom.

What wisdom does Carlitos come to in this final episode of the quartet?

First he goes out to one of those notable "power spots" where things happen, finds a murmuring shadow that looks like a man but turns out to be a moth and is really only his opening encounter with the "nagual," a presumably Mexican word for all the unknown and indescribable elements of life. Getting to know the nagual is the key to sorcery, for it is the means of controlling the "tonal" (another presumably Mexican word), which is all that is rational and knowable in life. The point: most of us live and drown in the tonal's rationality. But if we can divide ourselves, if we can visit the nagual without being killed by its terrors or seduced by its sublimity, we will then be able to move in and out of dreams and fantasy, and the surreal phase of our existence will balance the oh-so-deadly real stuff. This will, in time and with practice, and with the opening of the bubble of perception, permit us to achieve the totality of ourselves.

We get there, says Carlitos, by seeing in a special way what few others see, by dreaming, by will, by stopping our internal dialogue. We get there by learning to end our self-pity and by taking responsibility for what we have done. We get there by eliminating our past as a source of anxiety and by living in the present, by being in touch with all the fine detail of life that those who wallow in their own grief or exhausted past histories never can appreciate.

The message is at times very like Thornton Wilder's in *Our Town*. It is also like Salinger invoking Zen to urge us not to seek rewards for our work. The direction is blessedly free from moral stricture (we are admittedly dealing in the black magic of the spirit), free also from sex (there are no significant women in this book), and free from any worldly temptation except that of slipping back into the muck and dreck of reason. Reason alone, says Carlitos-Juan, is slow death. Of course death, if we only knew it, is the way to life. Death is that solitary set of headlights behind us on the highway, always following us. The only way we'll ever know we're alive is if we realize death is going to overtake us at any moment.

Being so full of such bromidic salvation, it would seem the book is useless. But Castaneda has the skills of a superb but flawed novelist. He has structured his philosophy novelistically and structured it with great care. For instance, before he fully advises us how to split ourselves, and how to dream ourselves into the nagual, he conjures up a "magical" event for Carlitos to experience—seeing himself sleeping in two different places, witnessing two separate sets of events. He is thus able to transcend space and time, which his teachers, Don Juan and especially Don Genaro, are so adept at doing. Don Genaro leaps up and down canyons, walks upside down on trees.

By book's end it is clear that Carlitos is not really talking about magic at all; that the whole work is, like that dual sleeping scene, an elaborate and admirably detailed metaphor with the aim of guiding the reader out of the humdrum and into self-awareness. The magical events are no further out of our reach than our next willfully weird daydream.

It has been said that Castaneda has dressed out his Mexican spirit world as thoroughly as Faulkner detailed Yoknapatawpha County, a ridiculous thing to say. Castaneda's strength is in pictorializing his philosophy with surreal metaphors. But when he begins to detail a man, or a real cabin, or a city park, he is as ill at ease as a brick mason trying to point up gold leaf on the Taj Mahal. His dialogue is fluid but often gawky, acceptable finally because you don't believe he's even trying to simulate reality. The behavior of Don Juan and Carlitos is so thinly and repetitiously imagined when they are not involved in dialogue or dream, that it would earn the author a revoked passport to any decent creative-writing class. Don Juan does almost nothing but laugh at all that Carlitos says. Carlitos spends his time taking notes or dropping his notebook or pencil. Don Juan laughs when he drops it. Carlitos takes notes on Don Juan laughing. Don Juan then laughs at that and Carlos drops his book again. Don Juan doubles up in glee. Carlos picks up his book and makes a note of the glee. Don Juan slaps his thigh and chuckles.

This is a serious drag until you stop faulting him for inadequate anthropological definition and let him carry on with his plot. That plot, wherever it began in his personal life, whether on some mushroom orgy in a Los Angeles apartment or a spooky walk along some dusky chaparral in Mexico, has turned into something nifty for a great many people. Who can object to wising up the human race? If Richard Nixon had read Castaneda he'd know that not all artists are Jews. Too late for that, but Carlitos is still here for all the unborn and not-yet-undone.

The way to his secrets is not easy. You have to wade through a lot of silly prose. But when you get there you like Castaneda for all his effort. He is as welcome as any other novelist who gives his whole being to his books. He really doesn't know any more than any of the other would-be wise men among us, but he thinks he does. And that determines what winds up on our bookshelves.

1974

Ernesto Sábato:

On Heroes and Tombs

In an author's note to his second novel, *On Heroes and Tombs*, Ernesto Sábato talks of a fictional narrative "whereby the author endeavors to free himself of an obsession that is not clear even to himself." He says that he has written countless "incomprehensible" stories but put few of them in print.

He published, in 1948, his first novel, *El Túnel* (translated into English by Harriet de Onís as *The Outsider* in 1950), and in the thirteen years between that novel and his second, "I continued to explore the dark labyrinth that leads to the central secret of our life. I tried at one time or another to express in writing the outcome of my research, until I grew discouraged at the poor results and ended up destroying the majority of my manuscripts."

He says friends persuaded him to publish what survived, and *On Heroes and Tombs* is among the survivors. It is a very remarkable survivor, a book which derives its main motive power from incest, and which at the same time aspires to be a work of national significance: the Great Argentine Novel as of 1955, perhaps.

Helen R. Lane's translation does high justice to Sábato's prose, which ranges from syntax that is lush and fluid and baroque to dialogue that is irreducibly spare.

Sábato, born in 1911, has been active politically throughout his life: an early Communist, disillusioned; an editor, a polemical essayist, anti-Perónist; and so it is natural that politics plays a role in his fiction. In this novel politics is metaphorically central. He focuses the modern segments of his tale on the first Perón era (1946–1955) and also saves his most elegiac prose for a historical section set in 1841—the story of rebel soldiers in terminal retreat toward the Bolivian border, which powerfully and movingly captures the manic spirituality that in spite of temporary defeat eventually freed the nation from tyranny and shaped its democratic future. But tyranny returns under Perón, and Sábato explores its effect on the soul, but in a way which is open to myriad interpretations.

Principally the novel is the story of a young man named Martín del Castillo and his love for Alejandra Vidal Olmos, a young woman from a decadent aristocratic family which has been a part of the Argentine oligarchy that opposed Perón. Alejandra is living a secret life as a high-level prostitute for affluent Perónists. Her father, the third figure of significance, is a paranoid anarchist–bank robber named Fernando Vidal Olmos, with whom Alejandra seems to be having a prolonged incestuous relationship. A fourth character is Bruno Bassan, all but faceless, a childhood friend of Fernando, who narrates three of the novel's four sections and is Sábato's opinionated surrogate.

The novel, through Bruno, is a discursive, distracting, sometimes fascinating pastiche of Sábato's attitudes toward Buenos Aires as Babylon, toward Peronism, Marxism, the *Reader's Digest*, graffiti, Don Quixote, Jorge Luis Borges, the Argentine oligarchy, football, Patagonia, Italians, Jews, blacks, fascism and much more.

Sábato reveals in a prologue that Alejandra shoots and kills her father in June 1955 (the year of Perón's overthrow) and then commits suicide by setting fire to herself and to the decaying Olmos mansion. He then opens the book with the young Martín encountering Alejandra at a public park. There is an immediate spark and after they talk and start to separate she says to him: "You and I have something in common, something very important. . . . Even though I think I shouldn't ever see you again. But I'll see you because I need you."

This meeting all but destroys Martín's young life. Lovesick, he moons insipidly after Alejandra, who keeps him at arm's length, tells him that she is "garbage" after she reluctantly makes love to him. Passion has nothing to do with why she likes him; neither he nor we ever learn precisely why she does, though he seems to be her lone link to innocence, to a healthy relationship with the male sex.

Martín follows her, begins to understand something of her secret life, but only dimly, then sees her with a man who seems to be her lover. "The man was cruel and capable of anything . . . reminiscent of a bird of prey." Martín suspects this is a cousin of whom she has spoken, and he confronts her with that notion. She is horrified at what Martín has seen (has he uncovered her incestuous passion?) and she angrily shakes him and tells him the man is Fernando, her father.

Sábato abruptly intrudes on this story with a discourse on the turbulent condition of Argentina under Perón, linking it to Martín's continuing quest for an absolute to cling to, "a warm cave in which to take refuge." But Martín, he concludes, had neither a home nor a homeland, "or what was worse, he had a home built on dung and disillusionment [he thinks of his mother as a sewer], and a tottering, enigmatic homeland." He had flung himself, like a shipwreck victim, on Alejandra: "But that had been like seeking refuge in a cavern from whose depths voracious wild beasts had immediately rushed forth."

Sábato follows this with an episode from June of 1955, when the Argentine navy rose against Perón in a coup d'état that failed, but led to Perón's overthrow three months later. In reprisal for the uprising, Perón's troops burned Catholic churches, since the church had sided against him. Martín moves through the debacle of church burnings, with Perón, in absentia, created in the image of a cruel Antichrist.

This concludes the first two sections, or half the novel. Sábato here imposes a novella, his 139-page, first-person *Report on the Blind*, written by Fernando, and recounting his paranoid fantasies about a conspiracy of blind people ruling the world "by way of nightmares and fits of delirium, hallucinations, plagues and witches, soothsayers and birds, serpents . . ." (Birds play a major role in the book; Fernando as a child put out the eyes of a bird with a needle, then released it inside a room.)

The *Report* is a tour de force which is brilliant in its excesses, a surreal journey into the depths of Fernando's personal Boschian hells, which, in their ultimate landscapes, are provinces of a "terrible nocturnal divinity, a demoniacal specter that surely held supreme power over life and death." This ruling specter is a faceless goddess with the wings and head of a vampire and a single gigantic phosphorescent eye shining where her navel would have been. Her realm is a charred museum of horrors. I saw hydras that had once been alive and were now petrified, idols with yellow eyes in silent abandoned dwellings, goddesses with striped skin like zebras, images of a mute idolatry with indecipherable inscriptions. It was a country where the one rite celebrated was a petrified Death Ceremony. I suddenly felt so hideously lonely that I cried out in anguish. And in that mineral silence outside of history my cry echoed and reechoed, seemingly down through entire centuries and generations long since gone.

Fernando realizes he must enter the giant vampiric goddess and he does enter what is clearly the vulva of the goddess:

Something hideous happened to me as I ascended that slippery, increasingly hot and suffocating tunnel: my body gradually turned into the body of a fish. My limbs slowly metamorphosed into fins and I felt my skin gradually become covered over with hard scales . . . powerful contractions of that narrow tunnel that now seemed made of rubber squeezed me tightly but at the same time carried me upward by virtue of their incredibly strong, irresistible suction."

The consequence of this rising is a transcendent orgasm:

I saw . . . afternoons in the tropics, rats in a barn . . . dark brothels, madmen shouting words that unfortunately were incomprehensible, women lustfully displaying their gaping vulvas, vultures on the pampas feeding on bloated corpses, windmills on my family's *estancia*, drunkards pawing through a garbage can, and huge black birds diving down with their sharp beaks aimed at my terrified eyes.

He awakens in the room of the Blind Woman, whom he has met almost at the outset of his descent and he perceives her to be the instrument conceived by the sacred Sect of the Blind to punish him. He anticipates the "most infernal of copulations" with her, which he senses will be the end of his lifelong quest for an unknown destiny. He imagines himself a centaur attacking the Blind Woman outside time and space, he becomes a lustful unicorn, a serpent, a swordfish, an octopus attacking her insatiable maw again and again, a giant satyr, a crazed tarantula, a lewd salamander. Excessive?

And again an orgasm:

> . . . men and beasts alike were swallowed up or eaten alive. Mutilated beings ran about among the ruins. Severed hands, eyes that rolled and bounced like balls, heads without eyes that groped about blindly, legs that ran about separated from their trunks, intestines that twisted round each other like great vines of flesh and filth, moaning uteruses, fetuses abandoned and trampled underfoot . . .

He awakens in his own room, finishes writing his *Report on the Blind*, hides it, and goes to meet his fate, "to the place where the prophecy will be fulfilled." He goes to his daughter's home where she shoots him and then immolates herself.

What is one to make of such events? A sizable body of criticism and analysis of the novel, and of Sábato's other work has appeared in the Spanish language since the book was published in 1962. Sábato has also discussed its meaning in a dialogue with himself included in *El Escritor y Sus Fantasmas* ("The Writer and His Phantoms") in 1963, but critics disagree on precise meanings. Sábato's own ambivalence contributes to the confusion, for instance his prefatory note about his "obsession" not being clear even to him. He has said that his questions to himself in the 1963 book were the synthesis of what many journalists and readers had asked him. Was the conflict in the novel representative of the actual conflict going on in Argentina? Was Alejandra an image of the country?

Sábato has said that this was "a curious hypothesis," and that such an idea about Alejandra had never occurred to him. But perhaps it is a valid idea, for he sought to create a "very Argentine woman," one for whom he had a passion: "A woman with whom I myself could have fallen in love."

One suspects that Sábato is being somewhat disingenuous here, for he has relied heavily on overt symbolic statement: the dates of Fernando's death and Perón's overthrow coinciding; and Martín saying after his first meeting with Alejandra that she was "a being he seemed to have been waiting a century for." The author has also seen to it that Alejandra looks like not only her own mother, Georgina, who was Fernando's cousin, but also Fernando's mother, who was an object of Fernando's pubescent passion. Alejandra is thus the personification of womanhood in three generations (all targets of Fernando's lust) and the last female member of the aristocratic Olmos line.

But she also stands for Sábato's definition of the feminine principle. In a work called *Heterodoxia*, a collection of brief essays on life and literature, he wrote the following, under the title "Feminine-Masculine":

> The principles coexist in each human being.
> Feminine: night, chaos, unconsciousness, body, curve, softness, life, mystery, contradiction, indefiniteness, "corporal" feelings—taste, touch. Origin of the baroque, the romantic, the existential.
> Masculine: day, order, consciousness, reason, spirit, rectitude, hardness, eternity, logic, definition, "intellectual" feelings—hatred, vision. Origin of the classical, the essential.

These feminine attributes apply perfectly and repeatedly to Alejandra, and the masculine attributes are parceled out, although sparingly, to the young, conscientious and intellectual Martín, who in the final section of the book transcends his despair over Alejandra's death and becomes the spiritual inheritor of the future.

Further, Sábato links both male and female archetypes to Fernando and his unity with the demonic female goddess. The author has made Fernando a gangster, a cruel and violent child who grows into a cruel and violent man, a shrewd manipulator of people, power and money, an anarchist, an autocrat, a tyrant and ultimately a maniacal solipsist. Does the description fit Perón?

In 1956 Sábato wrote an open letter titled *The Other Mask of Perónism* and in it defined "Perónist" as a person whose basic doctrine was "the elevation of Colonel Perón by any method." He saw Perón as an "empiricist without scruples, an aeronaut disposed to throw any ballast overboard, any person, any theory, any promise, any system that obstructed his unbridled ascent."

He theorized further that Perón's ascent was not explainable by reason but by the passion of the masses who backed him. And the masses, he added, are feminine—that is to say, in his view, illogical, romantic, sentimental. Sábato feuded publicly with Borges in 1956 on the role the masses played in elevating Perón to power and maintaining him there, and at several points throughout his work he seems both accuser and apologist of the masses for what they did to the nation. They were wrong, but I understand them, is his tone.

His imposition of femininity on the masses has a historical counterpart, for Perón broke with Argentine political tradition, embraced feminism (however self-servingly), won for women the right to vote, and in 1951 they voted overwhelmingly for him. His wife Evita though heavily dependent upon Perón (a pussycat feminist herself) was also a powerful influence in attracting the masses to his cause. And as a postscript, when he returned to power in 1973 only to die a year later, his wife Isabel ran the government for two years.

Victoria Ocampo, the grand dame of Argentine letters, took exception to Sábato's views of women when he published an article, "On the Metaphysics of Sex," in her magazine *Sur*, in 1952. She argued convincingly that he was stereotyping women; he countered that she was a "furious priestess of Bacchus, ready to tear me apart alive and eat me raw," and insisted that feminism was really masculinism.

Whatever one thinks of Sábato's views of women thirty years ago, the point here is that they fused with his political views and his unconscious (which he felt was also feminine) and formed the ideological and phantasmagorical basis for *On Heroes and Tombs*. The politics are transformed into a paranoiac's incestuous cravings for his daughter, and hers for him; their coupling becomes a nightmarish trip into the vulva of the goddess, and the cloacal wasteland of Fernando's personal, private hell is a reflection of the tyranny, tortures and killings of the regime.

Incest as the spiritual metaphor for politics is a striking invention, but Sábato is doing more than this. He has said that the novel's four main personages, Bruno, Martín, Alejandra and Fernando, are all phases of himself. Their dialogue, he says, represents his own internal struggles. Martín is his innocent young manhood, Fernando his dark side. He is a strong proponent of a "national literature" which expresses the fundamental problems of the nation, but the fundamental problems of the human heart have equal primacy for him.

He believes a novel should reflect the fact that life is not explicable, that it is full of overheard whispers, fleeting visions, incomprehensible facts; and so he stocks his work with such characters, who pass through only to make a speech and move off to oblivion. The incest is never confirmed, only alluded to by Martín's glimpse of the passionate hand-holding by Fernando and Alejandra. Is Alejandra the Blind Woman of Fernando's paranoid fantasy? That would explain a great deal. But Sábato does not confirm this.

His aim, he wrote in *El Escritor y Sus Fantasmas*, is to create "beings who can never decide from within if the changes in their destinies are the consequence of their efforts, their failures, or the course of the universe."

Why, for instance, should a spiritually cunning and promiscuous woman be drawn to an innocent like Martín? And why did Martín begin to behave like a paranoiac himself when speaking of Alejandra to Bruno, spewing out a flood of minute details as only madmen do? Was it because Alejandra's mind was ensnaring him as it had presumably ensnared Fernando's? Says Bruno: ". . . the pain born of a passion constantly confronted with obstacles, especially mysterious and inexplicable obstacles, is always more than sufficient reason . . . to cause the most sensible man to think, feel, and act like someone out of his mind."

The book, then, is a psychological melodrama as well as a work of politics, a cultural history as well as a bizarre dream of infernal order; and not least in Sábato's aesthetic priorities, it is a book of hope.

El Túnel was a cornerstone for *On Heroes and Tombs*, the story of a painter who falls in love with a married woman and then murders her when he discovers she has betrayed him. Prefigured are the paranoia, the love which becomes obsessive, the blindness (of the woman's husband), the violence. This book earned Sábato the praise of Thomas Mann, Graham Greene and Albert Camus, and gave him instant international status as a novelist.

But Sábato saw *El Túnel* as a work of his youth, a work that embraced only the negative side of his personality, his "black and hopeless side."

Martín comes to this sense of hope in the depths of his gloom after Alejandra's suicide. In an alcoholic stupor he stumbles onto Fernando's hellish terrain—"a vast swampy plain, amid filth and corpses, amid excrement and mire that might swallow him up . . . repellent landscape crawling with worms, running with his little crutch toward the place where the face seemed to be waiting for him . . ."

The face belongs to a woman, Hortensia Paz, who brings Martín to her home and helps him sober up from his despair. She is the mother of an infant, is living alone, is very poor and struggling, but insistent to Martín about the positive values: ". . . there are so many nice things in life." There's the baby, music, flowers, birds, dogs. "It's a shame the cat from the café ate my canary. It was such good company. . . . It's so beautiful to be alive!" Hortensia (her name means "Garden of Peace") succors Martín, draws him instantly up from the dismal swamp. He gives her his grandmother's ring as he leaves.

This lapse on Sábato's part, this ascent into the empyrean realm of Norman Vincent Peale, is repellent not in its Pollyanna hopefulness but in its absence of imagination and its facile reduction of 465 pages of dire complexity to a barrage of pop sloganeering. But Sábato means for Martín to come out of his depression alive and with a complete skin, and he recovers his stride effectively by giving Martín a ride to Patagonia with a trucker named Bucich.

This scene is largely dialogue and resembles Hemingway in its pithy understatement. Bucich, who has been on the Patagonia run for years, and who values the stars, wishes he'd been an astronomer. He's a realist, Bucich; he remembers his father's futile search for gold as far south as Tierra del Fuego, remembers an Englishman who told his old man: "Why don't you settle down here instead of wandering all over looking for gold? What's gold around here is sheep-raising, and I know what I'm talking about."

The message, of course, is not lost on Martín. The air on the southern pampa suddenly seems more decent to him. He feels useful. He is up from the sewer now and he sits by the fire waiting for the meat to cook. "The sky was crystal clear, and the cold intense. Martín sat there staring thoughtfully at the flames."

Counterpoint to Martín's Patagonia excursion is what I judge to be the best writing in the book, the conclusion of the final days of the retreat of General Juan Galo de Lavalle (an authentic figure) and his rebel forces, defeated in 1841 by the allies of Juan Manuel de Rosas, the caudillo who ruled Argentina from 1829 to 1852. An ancestor of the modern Olmos family rides with Lavalle, not only maintaining the historical thread, but also serving as a juxtaposed figure to Martín—two youths whose powerlessness in the face of oppressive life is told in parallel stories.

Lavalle dies a hero to revolutionary fervor, but Sábato wants us to see also his mundane side, and he ends the book with Lavalle's mythic figure appearing to an old Indian. Lavalle rides a white charger and wears a cavalry saber and a high-crested grenadier's helmet.

"Poor Indian," the narrator concludes, "if you only knew the general was only a man in rags and tatters, with a dirty straw hat and a cape that had already forgotten the symbolic color it once was. . . . If you only knew he was simply a miserable wretch among countless other miserable wretches!"

Wretches all, we read Sábato and we shudder, we exult, we are bewildered, fearful, mesmerized.

1981

Julio Cortázar:

A Manual for Manuel

This is Julio Cortázar paying his dues—his first effort at a political novel, the obligatory genre for Latin American writers. It is willfully experimental, the author tells us, with authentic political clippings from newspapers interwoven with an absurdist's tale of leftist intrigue and kidnapping. Cortázar half apologizes for the concoction: "Proponents of reality in literature are going to find it . . . fantastical while those under the influence of fiction will doubtless deplore its deliberate cohabitation with the history of our own times."

Cortázar has had a reputation as an avant-gardist since the publication (in Spanish in 1963, in English in 1966) of *Hopscotch,* a do-it-yourself novel in which, with the help of an author's road map, one may read chapter 73 first, then travel back to chapter 1, then on to 2, then to 116, then to 3, then 84 and so on. The novel was highly regarded throughout the world and earned Cortázar a reputation as one of the principal, if elder (he was born in 1914) figures in the so-called Latin literary "boom"—which includes Carlos Fuentes, Gabriel García Márquez, Mario Vargas Llosa, Jorge Luis Borges, Alejo Carpentier and a dozen or two others. This sort of listing (used here to make the point) is always unfair, for it reinflates the best-known Latin names, who are not necessarily the authors of the best new Latin novels. Cortázar's new one is not one of the best. He wants it to be important, and at times, excruciatingly, it is, mainly for what it tells of political torture, violent punishment of innocents, murderous fascist depravity and casual cruelty toward social nonconformists.

The English-, French- and Spanish-language clippings about these topics, strewn through the novel, are the real power of the book, and have an impact reminiscent of John Dos Passos's accumulations of authentic 1930s tidbits in his trilogy *U.S.A.* Cortázar's clips go beyond Dos Passos's in their singlemindedness: which is to touch the open nerve of political oppression in contemporary Latin America, and to point the finger at the United States for its expedient morality in defending, training and funding the multiform sadists in Brazil, Argentina, Chile, Nicaragua and so on. With these antifascist clippings he is creating a scrapbook for the Manuel of the title—an infant at the time of the novel's events, who will presumably grow up to learn the truth of his era from this data. What the author is also doing is documenting the defiant, self-sacrificial and not quite hopeless (or so it seems) gesture a handful of manic Marxists make toward the oppressor.

He moves in and out of the mind of a number of too thinly defined characters. But, owing to the nature of his absurdist approach, we never inhabit the psyche of any of his people, not even of his intermittent first-person narrator, Andrés, who is the most developed character of all. And without the intimate connections to his people, Cortázar delivers up to us only literary and socialist artifacts. Puppets. And who really cares whether a puppet laughs or cries?

The novel's dramatic frame is the kidnapping, in Paris, of a Latin bigwig—the so-called "person in charge of the coordination of Latin American affairs in Europe," whom Cortázar calls the "Vip."

It doesn't matter that there is no such cosmic person, that he is a caricature, for almost everything in this novel is a caricature, including the author himself, who appears as "the one I told you." Late in the novel he confesses: "At a certain point in the disorder the one I told you begins to realize that he's gone too far in spontaneity. . . ."

Whether he has or not depends on the loyalty and pertinacity of the individual reader. I admit to agreeing with the author. He is taking a leaf from Pirandello and Flann O'Brien in letting author and character carry on dialogues, Platonic and otherwise. But he uses pronouns whimsically and with unnecessary obfuscation, intent on being original even if it kills us. Worse, his avant-garde forays too often drag us backward in time. He plumps, in one section for instance, for the use of candid sexual language.

"A man's sex is so strange," says one of the book's women. And her bedmate retorts that "calling it a sex is silly, anyone would think you'd learned Spanish through a correspondence course."

Cortázar then delivers up a set piece (as he does repeatedly in the book), this one on the sexual vulgate, and how it varies from Chile to Cuba to Argentina. We must, the argument goes, avoid using banal, lifeless sexual language; for "that type of vocabulary links us to the Vip."

If this warmed-over sexual boldness should be confused with an avantgarde position, then someone please page Norman Mailer immediately. Mailer was arguing on behalf of dirty talk ten years ago as the way toward a funky new world, and even then we were hip-deep in the verbal crustaceanisms of Henry Miller and William Burroughs, and catching up belatedly with the waning clandestinism of De Sade's stuff, and Frank Harris's. After all that, can anyone still believe that foul-mouthery (or long hair, or blue jeans, or rock, or dope) will hasten the revolution? Can Cortázar?

Well maybe he doesn't. Maybe his story of this handful of socialist plotters and their groupies is meant to satirize zealot as well as villain, for a dumber bunch of kidnappers you're not likely to come upon in a hurry.

Yet, despite such disparagement, despite Cortázar's recidivistic intellectuality, the book is a work of high seriousness in service of a higher morality—the use of excellent language, sex and silliness to carry us a few inches closer to socialist nirvana. It is translated with great panache, as usual, by the wizard Gregory Rabassa.

Anyone who values Cortázar's previous work should certainly confront this new novel for historical similarities, anomalies and mutations. Anyone looking for literary effusions, or for meditations on the new social and political realities, will have to test the water and decide privately what has been revealed. Anyone looking for a good novel should keep looking.

1978

Pedro Juan Soto:

Spiks

To What Extent Was Enrique Soto the Creation of Pedro Juan Soto?: An Interview

Spiks

This is a landmark book, the first published work of one of the best modern Puerto Rican writers of serious fiction, Pedro Juan Soto. It is Soto's second book to be published within a year, a breakthrough for Puerto Rican literature. Much high-quality Spanish-language fiction from the island remains dammed up behind him, victim, like Soto's work, of this country's longstanding linguistic and political prejudice toward Puerto Rican writers, many of whom are leftists and active workers for Puerto Rico's political independence from the U.S. It is also a blatant case of literary myopia in which a rich cultural achievement on the American landscape has been totally ignored.

Soto's first language is Spanish (he also has taught and written in English) but he is unquestionably an American, not a Caribbean, writer. His subject is the U.S.—the scene in New York and Puerto Rico, the interplay of the two cultures, the exploitation of the island, of the island in the city, of the islands of the Puerto Rican heart.

Spiks was pure gold as subject matter—the anguished spirit of New York's Puerto Rican ghetto—when it appeared in Mexico in 1956 under the Los Presentes imprint. Other writers mined the same material much later, Piri Thomas in *Down These Mean Streets*, Oscar Lewis in *La Vida*, both nonfiction, both in English, both successful. Soto, in Spanish, remained invisible.

But Soto's collection of seven short stories and six miniatures was never invisible in Puerto Rico. It was a cult work from the time its pre-publication fragments began winning literary prizes in the early 1950s. It is a tiny book of short works whose concision has the excitement of poetry because of the enormities suggested in so few words.

Unfortunately the book was also a feat of language that the present English translation doesn't reflect. Soto worked with the Puerto Rican Spanish vulgate in New York. Victoria Órtiz, who did the translation and a preface locating Soto in the literary framework of the island, doesn't echo that vulgate with her Studs Loniganese: ". . . you think yer king or somethin. Geddoudahere, you miserable. . . ," an archaic American street idiom that has nothing to do with the language of Soto's spiks.

The ghetto as prison, daily life as agony, that is what the world has come to for the people in these stories; a place where the innocent fail easily, love turns into hallucination or nightmare, violence erupts in the peaceful soul and mockery is the lot of the slut who finds God in her own belly. The people are pool players, lonely women, a would-be artist, a pushcart peddler, a barber. The mood is one of depression realism, but Soto is a skillful ironist who can turn a value inside out with the flick of a wrist and who sees well beyond the street problem. The street is only the now of these lives. But there was a garden. "In Puerto Rico in my day you didn' see such things. . . ." And in the lost island garden, life was possible, even when the palm trees were fake and the moon was made of paper.

The chief influence on *Spiks*, according to Soto himself, was a book of stories in Spanish, *El Hombre en la Calle* (*The Man in the Street*) by José Luis González, which Soto read in New York in 1948. González looked on his own work as a break with the dominant tradition of "jibarismo," the romanticized literature of Puerto Rico's rural peasantry, and the beginnings of a realistic literature of the city. Soto, stunned by its powerful simplicity, vowed to match it. *Spiks* was the result.

González is now the big dad of the generation of writers that came to flower in the 1940s and 1950s and is enjoying a republishing renaissance in Puerto Rico after twenty years of exile in Mexico. Another of that generation, Emilio Díaz Valcárcel, won much attention in Spain and Latin America in 1971 with his avant-garde novel, *Figuraciones en el*

Mes del Marzo (*Figurations in the Month of March*) and was accorded by some critics at that time a place in the current so-called boom of quality Latin fictionists.

(Among other members of the forties–fifties generation in Puerto Rico—Rene Marqués, Edwin Figueroa, César Andreu Iglesias, Abelardo Díaz Alfaro, and Luis Rafael Sánchez—only Sánchez is widely known in the United States in 1992.)

One of Soto's novels is available here. Dell published *Hot Land, Cold Season* (*Ardiente Suelo, Fría Estación*) as a paperback original in early 1973, but disguised it as a juvenile for the high-school market in Puerto Rican studies, assuring it of no serious attention.

But the odds against the novelist have always been longer in Puerto Rico than elsewhere. Soto recalled in a conversation at his home in San Juan that until his generation, Puerto Rican writers published their own books at their own expense. "We felt this was not honorable," he said, "a hobby. I didn't find any seriousness in them."

Since Puerto Rico had no book publishers, the new generation went to Mexico and Spain for recognition. Los Presentes accepted *Spiks* but charged Soto $200 to help with the printing. It was his first and last bit of self-subsidy.

His second book was *Usmail*, a novel which won him a literary prize and became a Puerto Rican book club selection. All this earned him $500. *Ardiente Suelo* followed and earned $300. *El Francotirador* (*The Sniper*), a novel, was a coup: $800. But times changed. Puerto Rico in the sixties mushroomed as a literary market. This has been largely because of the concern the 30,000 students and faculty at the University of Puerto Rico are suddenly showing for Puerto Rican literature.

"Professors who haven't read a book in twenty years have begun to recognize Puerto Rican writers," said Soto, who has been teaching literature at UPR.

The current English version of *Spiks* is the book's fifth edition. The second, of 6,000 copies, was to be for distribution to high schools by the Puerto Rico Department of Education, but the Grundys thought it a bit salty and all 6,000 books are now somewhere in a closet. Soto doesn't know where. The third and fourth editions were 3,000 each, for general distribution.

Soto has more novels, a story collection, and criticism coming and will try to publish it all off the island as a way of resisting insularity and also proselytizing abroad for the unsung Puerto Rican literature. When Soto talked of that literature being ignored for so long his bitterest word was for the Latin critics and writers who have come to live on the island but have written nothing about its books.

"I've asked myself if it's the poor quality of our literature," he said, "but I don't find that true at all. I say it's politics. They're afraid that if they elevate a Puerto Rican book they'll be attacked for selling out to a colony of American imperialism. American writers and critics who come here usually don't know the language, but for the Latins to be so ignorant and ungrateful, that's really sad. Every time I talk about this, people think I'm expecting it for myself, but that's not true. I don't mean people should praise the hell out of everything, but they should read whatever is on hand and comment on it. They seem to me to be mainly tourists."

If there were any literary fair play such as Soto hopes for, *Spiks* would have been recognized and published in English in the late fifties, when its bleak realism would not have seemed dated. But then this is a work of protest as well as compassion, the kind of writing that has almost ceased to exist in the U.S., and whose role is partially filled here now by nonfiction. Puerto Rico exists in a different literary time zone from the mainland. Nonfiction does not yet have such a vogue on the island and fiction, old and new, is in flower, as it is throughout Latin America. *Spiks*, in 1974, must therefore be judged not as a creation from yesterday afternoon but as an artifact of precious metal lifted from a time capsule.

1974

To What Extent Was Enrique Soto
the Creation of Pedro Juan Soto?:
An Interview

*Carlos Enrique "Quico" Soto Arriví, the eighteen-year-old son of famed
Puerto Rican author Pedro Juan Soto, was one of two young men gunned
down by police thwarting an alleged terrorist attempt near Villalba Tuesday noon.*

*Soto Arriví and a man identified as Arnaldo Darío Rosado, twenty-
eight, were gunned down reportedly during a half-hour battle with twelve
police agents, allegedly when the two were trying to sabotage federal and
Commonwealth communications towers in Cerro Maravilla in the central
mountains. . . .*

—San Juan Star, *July 27, 1978*

In a story in Pedro Juan Soto's new short-story collection, "Un Decir
. . . (de la Violencia)," a young man strips himself naked and runs
across an area guarded by armed police in order to explode a plastic
bomb on the door of a university chancellor's office, a symbolic bombing
to affront what he feels is repressive authority.

He places the bomb on the door, puts his fingers in his ears, sees
the door blown away. He waits for reprisals, but no one comes after
him. He looks out toward the area where he had run the gauntlet of
police steps. Panting, he throws himself on top of his own naked body,
which lies on the lawn, a bullet through the forehead.

The explosion in the story proves to be only imagined by the young
man in the instant before his death, and in this respect seems extraordinarily prophetic of the fate of the author's son Carlos Enrique Soto
Arriví, eighteen.

Young Soto was fatally shot during what police have said was to be
a terrorist attack on a communications tower at Cerro Maravilla, near
Villalba, on July 25. He and another man, Arnaldo Darío Rosado,
twenty-eight, were shot to death by a squad of police, in mufti, who had
been anticipating the attack for more than a day.

A police undercover agent, Alejandro González Malave, who was with Soto and Rosado, and who has been described as an agent provocateur, was wounded by his fellow police in the shooting. The three had kidnapped a público driver and taken him and his car to Cerro Maravilla with them. The driver, Julio Órtiz Molina, has described the event as a massacre.

The case of young Soto is singular for he is the son of one of the best-known independentistas in modern Puerto Rican history. Pedro Juan Soto has published seven works of literature—novels, short stories, theater pieces—in which his characters are often politically motivated, or are victims of oppressive social conditions. This is hardly the full range of his work, which is ambitious in intellectual and psychological as well as social and political dimensions. His works have received international attention and acclaim and made him one of Puerto Rico's most famous writers.

But because of the political element in his writing, and because Soto has associated himself publicly with the cause of Puerto Rican independence, with the Cuban revolution, and with other leftist causes, the question arises: to what extent was Enrique Soto the creation of Pedro Juan Soto? What does his father think of what he was, and of what he planned to do at Cerro Maravilla? What does this father now plan to do as a consequence of his son's killing?

Soto was interviewed at length last week and addressed himself candidly to these questions. He spoke entirely without emotion, as if his son were a character he had created in a novel. His friends are intrigued by the obvious personal control which Soto maintains over his emotions, though his wife, Carmen, who fills with tears at the mention of her stepson Enrique, says that Soto does not sleep at night now. "He lies awake with his eyes open, thinking it out, thinking everything out," she said.

Soto neither looks nor talks like a sleepless man. He writes and speaks fluent English (in which this interview was conducted), and his responses could in no way be considered the responses of a fatigued or confused person.

He believes that his son was entrapped by a provocateur and that he was ripe for entrapment.

He thinks he himself failed with his son because his son is dead.

He thinks he himself has been a failure because he has been too much a literary man and insufficiently a political activist.

He believes political violence is on the rise in Puerto Rico.

He believes there is a concerted effort by the enemies of Puerto Rican independence to commit a kind of psychological and social "genocide" on the young generation of independentistas.

Enrique Soto, the second of Soto's three sons (Roberto is twenty-six, Juan is thirteen), became politically conscious about 1974 when his father and stepmother, Carmen Lugo Filippi, were both studying for their doctorates in literature at the University of Toulouse in France. (Both Soto and his wife teach at the University of Puerto Rico in Río Piedras.) Enrique was with them in France, and learned to speak French well; and later was with them in Zaragoza, Spain, where they wrote their theses. This was a period before and after the death of Franco, and Enrique became absorbed in both French and Spanish politics, and talked often with his father about such matters—journalism in a dictatorship, the discovery of America as a capitalist endeavor, the workers' movement.

"In Spain he was of course against Franco," said Soto. "And he also complained about his fellow students there. They had all been born under this dictatorship and it was really amazing to him to find them so docile . . . nobody even contradicted a teacher."

Enrique was a consistent reader, often of books suggested by his father. Soto says his son also read several of his fictional works and liked *Spiks* best, a collection of short stories about Puerto Ricans in New York City.

"He also liked *Usmail* [a novel], but *El Francotirador* [*The Sniper*, another novel] he had doubts about," said Soto. "The technique was too advanced for him. When he died he was reading *Un Decir . . . (de la Violencia)* [*A Saying About Violence*]."

The young Soto had many friends in Spain and had a girlfriend there with whom he corresponded after he came back to San Juan. They exchanged clippings of articles on politics. Back here, said his father, he eventually found a new girlfriend. But he was not quite as gregarious here as he had been in Spain.

"I found that he didn't have many friends here," Soto said. "Two or

three, maybe. He had acquaintances. He was gregarious as a child, but
by aging he got more particular. I noticed he was staying up late in
recent times and I used to wait for him and give him hell. He said he
was no longer a child, that he could no longer get home by ten o'clock.
He wanted to stay until eleven. But even then I'd have to wait half an
hour or forty-five minutes longer."

"Were you a strict parent?" he was asked.

"Yes, I think I was very strict."

The younger Soto was, of course, not wholly political. He was a fan
of films, science fiction particularly, and he had seen and talked much
about *Star Wars* and *Close Encounters of the Third Kind.* He was a fanatic
for rock music, and particularly for salsa. His father gave him records
by such traditional salsa groups as Ismael Rivera and El Gran Combo,
but he preferred the more modern, and wilder, music.

"He was obeying the fashions of his time," his father said. "I told
him all this babbling, no lyrics at all, was just shouts, music made by
mutes. Well, he said I was out of his time. He said he couldn't blame
me, but then I should not criticize his taste."

Writing was a part of the young man's life also. He wrote and enjoyed
writing on social studies at the high school he was attending, República
de Colombia in Río Piedras. "He liked his teacher and spoke often about
him. Enrique said he was a good teacher because he dealt with facts,
with personal observations, not with suspicions, about what was right
or wrong."

He also wrote a short story before the family went to Spain, when he
was in Osuna High School in Baldrich.

"It was about drug addiction," Soto said, "and he won a second prize.
I told him I would not read it before he handed it in because I thought
he was going to be questioned about whether I had influenced his writing.
I eventually read it and found it so-so and told him. But he was interested
in doing something creative."

The elder Soto now censures himself for what he told Enrique about
school. Teachers often chided the boy for occasional slackness in a
subject, saying, 'You're a shame to your father, a famous writer.' What
I told my sons to say was, 'Look, my father has his own job to do and
I have to do other things. I am not going to be attacked because I am
my father's son. I am me. My father is my father.' "

"Are you censuring yourself now," he was asked, "for encouraging too much independence of mind?"

"No," said Soto, "I don't think you can ever go too far in that. I'm all for independent thinking and independent being for all my sons. But perhaps he thought that that [the Maravilla episode] was a way of saying I am my own man."

"Rebellion against parents, was that in his makeup?"

"He was pretty rebellious."

Lately Enrique had been trying to find summer work, and had applied at Manpower, the employment agency, but nothing came of it. "He said nobody wanted to give the nonskilled worker a chance to gather some experience," his father recalled. The elder Soto had told his son his doubts about gaining employment through Manpower, since he had no skills. "He just had to go someplace and work, and there acquire some skills. He was confident he would get a job. He spent his time reading a lot, and playing chess—he was a good chess player—and talking to his friends."

Then in the last three or four months Soto noted a change in his son.

"In terms of politics we had several conversations, some of which I wish I had continued with. His belief was that something should be done, he didn't know what. We talked about the Nationalist Party, the Socialist Party, and he was, I found, growing rather desperate. We never talked about violence but I suspect he was looking at that. We talked about the history of France, Spain, and other countries, and he found there was no use in parliamentary proceedings. He once told me: 'Can you mention a single country which has become liberated by this parliamentary thing?' I told him about several countries in Africa. Then he posed this thing about having, for instance, Great Britain write your constitution for you. And that any government like that was really a lukewarm nation."

"How did he respond to such things beyond parliamentary proceedings as peaceful protest?"

"We talked about Martin Luther King a lot. He said that the black movement was going to be successful, but they cut off the head of the movement. And what is happening now? We talked about Gandhi and that once you do something—threats—you're going to be branded and you're going to be dead sooner or later. He agreed with that, and I think he concluded that we have a problem—there is no solution ever through voting, and what else is there? He was against the Populares and Estadistas. The Populares had been in power for such a long time and had done nothing for the liberation of Puerto Rico. And of course he knew the annexionist attitude of the Nuevo Progresista Party was just awful. And of the independentistas, some things he applauded and others he resisted—going back and forth before the U.N. He said that would take ages. He was happy over the decolonization committee, and of course the attitude of the Cuban ambassador to the U.N. Other than that he didn't see much of a way out. He was also discouraged by the PSP and the PIP participation in the 1976 elections."

"You say he was impatient and wanted some kind of action. Did he express a specific form the action should take?"

"No, but I recall his commenting on the takeover of the Statue of Liberty [by twenty-eight independentistas, in October 1977; they unfurled a Puerto Rican flag across Miss Liberty's brow]. Enrique was confused by that. I told him, well, what does it mean? It's a simple gesture. He said he found history was full of gestures, some good, some not. My position was that it was a publicity stunt and he didn't agree. He said there should be more publicity like that."

"What is your view of the violent gesture, such as the bombing of the Fraunces Tavern in New York City?" Soto was asked.

"There is not much thought behind that. You're really limiting your strength by those means. You become an easy target. I talked with Enrique about the Nationalists and he was very much in favor of the Nationalist assault on Congress and all that. Yes, I respected that gesture, but it has done very little for Puerto Rico. And I told him, if you were going to do some violent action, or going to undergo some violent passion, you have to think about it very well and do it well."

"You said you had a conversation with him about shooting a cop and that someone else would kill you immediately, or catch you very swiftly."

"Sure. And what's a cop's death worth in terms of politics? You have to pick better than that when you kill. You have to value human life enough to know when to kill."

"Did he ever own a gun?"

"He had a pellet gun. He told me he was going to hunt in the forest behind our house in Naranjito but he never went there with it. He was going to hunt the fat iguanas there."

"Could this pellet gun hurt you seriously?"

"No. They call them cat chasers."

"He had no interest in weapons, as far as you know?"

"He had no interest in weapons at all."

"How do you see yourself as different from what he became?"

"I think of myself as a rather moderate man. I don't think much of myself as a political activist. I find that in that way, I have failed. I have concerned myself with writing. I wish I had been a man of action. I'm sorry I'm not."

"How do you define man of action?"

"As an author is an actor, a politician is also an actor."

"You're talking about running for office, that sort of thing?"

"Yes."

"You're not talking of extremism."

"Oh yes. I'm holding that in mind. I wish I had been able to do something for my country other than write. Try to be as heroic as possible to do something to change circumstances here."

"Are you moving toward extremist thinking?"

"No, but let's say participating more in politics. That would mean sacrificing my writing, but if that's it, let's try to do both things, or to do one well. I don't know which right now."

"The question arises of your attitude toward violence as a political weapon."

"I believe there is a way out through violence. I've come to believe it. I've been a dead man."

"Did you ever, at any point in your life, consider violence as the proper behavior and then reject it?"

"Yes, I've considered it several times. I think it is the most convincing argument in any struggle for liberty. You don't gain liberty by dealing with whatever papers are at hand. It's not been done except for a few African nations. Other states have been creations of violence. After [Governor] Romero falls in 1980 we'll go back to what—the Populares, who are now demanding more autonomy. They say we have autonomy, we want more autonomy. They'll probably die talking about it."

"You are critical of publicity stunts and gestures. What sort of action is it that you admire?"

"I would say the Tupamaros in Uruguay. They were not successful, but they shook up the government enough to show that it was not really the Switzerland of South America, as it had been commonly known. Everyone's eyes were turned toward Uruguay, and that was because of the Tupamaro actions. The movement ended two or three years ago when the leader, Raúl Sendic, was jailed. But I found them intelligent. Everything was well executed—so well that to me they were an exemplary movement."

"Do you think yourself capable of violent political action?"

"I think so. I'd have to educate myself to that."

"Is the death of your son instrumental in this, or is it something you've been thinking all your life?"

"I think the death of my son has affected my sense of balance, if you want to call it that. I think it has been a very unjust year. In order to correct things I don't think you can wait, as this will just float away in the memory of the people. Puerto Rican people tend to forget too soon."

"What are you proposing to do?"

"Something I started several months ago—essay writing. That and another thing. I don't know what the other thing is."

"You're also undertaking lawsuits against the government."

"Yes. And also my main concern is the Committee against Repression. I don't think this case will really be cleared up ever, not by the government, unless we move, and I mean independentistas, Populares and even statehooders. We are convoking people to meet at 10:00 A.M. on August 20 to march from Condominio Quintana [where the Sotos live] to police general headquarters. We intend to pose several questions concerning the case and demand complete presentation from their part."

"How do you respond to the suggestion that the work you've done led your son into violent ways?"

"I don't think so. My opinion of this particular case is that he was just led into it. He was trapped. Even though in a way he was well read, he was to me an illiterate in the political sense. His feelings were pretty flimsy about politics. He got seduced by this agent, Alejandro González Malave. I blame everything on him. But Enrique was ripe for him. He had all of a sudden developed a thing I disliked. He was buying at least two papers every day. He said he wanted to keep in touch with their differences. I told him it was all repetitious, that the facts you want aren't there and if you know how to read you see this. He read the statehood paper every day, and *El Vocero*, the sensationalist paper. He didn't like *El Mundo* or *The San Juan Star*, even though he used the *Star* for several things concerning civil rights and human rights. He was also being fed these anti-intellectual theories—stop reading, that will damage your brain. You have to do something, it's about time. Alejandro González Malave."

"Do you know how he got involved with this agent?"

"No. According to what I hear from Quico's friends, Malave showed up about three months before this [Maravilla], just floating around Quintana. He just came in from time to time. I hear they had meetings at Darío's house" [Darío Rosado, who was killed with Soto].

"Your estimate is that this agent came in to collect a couple of likely candidates?"

"Of course. You can see that he was in every one of the so-called subversive activities—the shooting at former Governor Múñoz's house, the U.P.R. police raid, and the Maravilla thing. Malave was a fisherman. He just looked around to see what he could catch."

"Why was Enrique susceptible to this? Why did he move into such a desperate position where he thought action was necessary?"

"I find you get gradually into that. And that depends on who the leader is. Once you're faced with alternatives—you do this or you're chickening out—what it is is an appeal to his machismo. Then he developed a theory they could do something effective for independence through sabotage—this plan they apparently had for Cerro Maravilla if they had a plan, I don't know. Malave probably told them he was linked to other subversive groups and therefore he could justify offering them all kinds of weapons—whatever they needed. They were going to Guanica, and Enrique had asked permission to go, for the PSP and the LSP were going to hold a congregation. He'd been there before and I told him to go if he had transportation, and he told me he did. I didn't ask whose. I have great respect for the intelligence of Enrique, and that's what amazes me. He being so intelligent, so full of questions on everything, how could he be led into this trap? If the agent tells him, look, I have transportation, I have the weapons, I have everything we need—did they get to inspect what he said he had? I think they were working under pressure—that they were convinced on the way to Guanica, and that they took off for Ponce (where the hijacking of the público took place). Now why did they kidnap this público driver? That's another person you're carrying with you as a witness, so it's silly. They did the kidnapping because González Malave was the kidnapper really. He pointed the gun and all they had to do was follow the leader. But it's foolish also. What they were attempting to do I don't know."

"Do you think there is a climate here now for political violence?"

"Oh yes, it's definitely going that way."

"How do you see Enrique as part of this?"

"I think of him as a good child who grew up and became a good man who thought he could do things for his country in ways I haven't tried. I believe that he grew more serious, and got into complications of thought and actions. I believe there may be more young men like him who think they have to do something their elders didn't get to do, a generation already showing such complete frustration and discouragement that they tend to find what they think is a way out for the country, a way out for themselves. That condition is being taken advantage of by the opposition, by the annexionists. They think they can stop the continuity of thought pertaining to freedom beliefs. They have gotten the country into this polarization and now they want to do away with the opposition. I would even accuse them of genocide."

"Genocide? Two people are dead."

"There are two dead men in one case, six under arrest in another, and three or four in another. They are trying to get them at least afraid. If you don't, as a young man, shut up and stop thinking in terms of independence for Puerto Rico, they'll shoot you, or get you where they want you in order to be shot. This is called political seduction, entrapment. Or once you are accused of something you put up bail and are apparently free. But your reputation is dead from then on, and how do you get it back? You are a dead man or a dead woman in Puerto Rican society. If they get away with this, no one here will be sure he can walk the streets, or be sure he can even defend his rights before a policeman."

"When was the last time you saw your son?"

"I saw him on my birthday on July 11 in Naranjito and then took him back to Quintana, because he didn't like the country. We talked several times about Quintana and I told him I didn't like the place for several reasons, among them the fact that it has become drug-infested; and that attracts narcotics agents, police agents. And by tracing the drugs they could easily build up cases against the many independentistas living there. Enrique didn't like the place either and he wanted to move someplace else. The trouble is I didn't have the money to move into a new condominium. But Enrique was very aware. He said he knew about it all, that he was watching his step in making friends and all that. But I find he failed in that respect. He had been advised. Anyway about Saturday [July 15] I came back to give him some money and said I might be back from the country the next Friday, but we didn't come back until rather late on July 25 to see how things were and we found this note of his saying he had left for Guanica, and not to worry."

1978

Postscript: The Cerro Maravilla case became the "Watergate" of Puerto Rico—not the cover-up of a burglary, but of two murders; and carried out on a grand scale that involved the Justice and Police departments of Puerto Rico at numerous levels; contributed heavily to the defeat of Governor Romero Barceló, who was in power during the entrapment and killing of Soto Arriví and Rosado; and also generated three federal investigations, along with allegations that the FBI withheld information relevant to the prosecution. It was conclusively proven that the young men had been executed by police while unarmed and on their knees in front of their captors. It was also proven from photographs that came to light in public hearings in 1983 that Soto Arriví and Rosado had also been viciously beaten before their execution, their battered bodies visibly refuting the allegation that policemen had killed them in self-defense. In October 1992, the case was still ongoing, awaiting the final results of a Puerto Rican Senate investigation, the conclusion of which had been repeatedly delayed. To date, ten police officers have been convicted of perjury in the cover-up, and sentenced from six to thirty years in jail. The chief of Police Intelligence, who headed the Maravilla investigation, was sentenced to twenty years but is now out on parole. Six policemen, in plea bargains, pled guilty to second-degree murder and went to jail for periods of six to eighteen years. Rafael Moreno, the policeman who pulled the trigger on Soto Arriví, was found guilty of perjury and second-degree murder and was sentenced to thirty-year and twenty-five-year sentences, to run consecutively. Two Puerto Rico Justice Department officials who carried out two of the failed investigations were disbarred for life, the Puerto Rico Supreme Court's having concluded that they pressured witnesses to give false accounts and conspired to hide the truth. A Puerto Rican district attorney was suspended from the practice of law for suppressing evidence to protect police who argued they acted against Rosado and Soto Arriví in self-defense. Two other district attorneys were also suspended from practicing law because of their behavior as prosecutors.

Two *San Juan Star* reporters, Manuel (Manny) Suárez and Tomas Stella, played significant roles in opening the case to official investigation, and were nominated for a Pulitzer Prize for their work. Suárez has written the best book on the case to date: *Requiem on Cerro Maravilla: The Police Murders in Puerto Rico and the U.S. Government Cover-up* (Waterfront Press, 1987).

Pedro Juan Soto started to write a novel about the murder of his son and its cover-up, but abandoned it, and has all but finished a nonfiction work on the case. It awaits only the final chapter of the Senate investigation. Eight years and two months after the murder of their sons, the Rosado and Soto families settled, out of court, their lawsuits against the police and Governor Barceló, and each family received $575,000. In the years since Cerro Maravilla, Soto has published two books: a critical study of the Puerto Rican novelist José I. deDiego Padró, and a collection of short stories, *Memoria de Mi Amnesia*. Asked what he thought of the whole investigation, Soto replied, "Shit. Only the men who pulled the trigger have paid for what they did, but not their bosses."

Mario Vargas Llosa:

Aunt Julia and the Scriptwriter

And now for something entirely different from Latin America: a comic novel that is also genuinely funny. This is a screwball fantasy on the workings of the imagination that stands also as Mario Vargas Llosa's confession to the world that he was weaned on soap opera as a writer, and that he made the leap out of adolescence by marrying his very delectable aunt.

A main element of the book is an excursion into a vast comic landscape populated by soap-opera heroes, victims and villains, and at first glance this seems to be the same manic world a hero like Garp inhabits. But Vargas Llosa is as interested in naturalistic fiction as he is in fantasy, and so he creates a parallel landscape, a pastoral place where tender romance thrives. He then fuses both worlds to shape a reality far more complex than either could represent by standing alone.

Vargas Llosa is one of the most widely known Latin American writers of this age, a scholar, a critic, a playwright, a novelist (*The Green House, Conversation in the Cathedral*) whose work has made him a progenitor of the so-called boom in modern Latin American literature, even though he is only forty-six.

He has lately become a talk-show host as well, and his book under discussion here, originally published in Barcelona in 1977, has been made into what his publishers say is a "top-rated television series in Colombia." This is a tidy little recycling that belongs among his novel's nest of ironies. Out of soap it came, back to soap it goes. But in its intermediate stage as a novel, it functions as a most accomplished work of comic art.

The book has three principal characters: Aunt Julia, a lovely, intelligent coquette, a thirty-two-year-old divorcée with a splendid lack of common sense about love; Pedro Camacho, a small man, not quite a dwarf, fastidious in threadbare suit and bow tie, who comes to Lima from Bolivia to write, direct and act in radio soap operas; and Mario Vargas, a young radio newsman, age eighteen, whose life in the early 1950s intersects with Julia's and Camacho's.

The realistic sections about Mario's life, which he narrates amiably in the first person, are pleasant, suspenseful in a small way, but too often tedious and overlong in their willful reconstruction of the ordinary. Yet they ground the tale with their low-keyed realism; and within them, as well as in the histories of most lives, lurks the snappy stuff of soap opera; and Vargas Llosa takes pains to uncover all of that.

Mario's romance with the flirtatious Julia is an idyllic story fraught with the perils of a 1940s Hollywood romance: as if Greer Garson went suddenly mad for Donald O'Connor. The lovers meet secretly to avoid a scandal in their upper-class family, for incest is in the air as a social evil even though Julia is not Mario's blood relative; she is the sister of his uncle's wife. They hold hands, coo, sit in the last row of the movies so they can kiss; and in time they pet. They eventually get on to some serious improprieties, but only when marriage is imminent, and what they do then is rather chastely narrated by the author.

Even so, some consider Vargas Llosa's treatment of the romance and the family as rather scandalous exposure, for it is heavily autobiographical. Real names are used, and Julia was the author's first wife in real life. He dedicates the book "To Julia Urquidi Illanes, to whom this novel and I owe so much." The novel recounts only the story of their courtship and marriage. They remained together eight years, which is revealed in a few sentences at book's end. When they separated, says the family-oriented Mario, he married his cousin.

Pedro Camacho is little more than a cartoon in the first half of the book, but as the story progresses, Mario the newsman views him with increasing awe; and as Vargas Llosa imposes his own formidable imagination on Camacho's soaps, the man becomes a cartoon of substance, a brain worth scanning.

Camacho is as solemn as a totem pole. When Mario remarks that he seems to be an early riser, Camacho explains: "Clock time means nothing where art is concerned." His inspiration for writing, he says, "dawns with the sun and gradually grows warmer along with it. I begin to write at first light. By noon, my brain is a blazing torch. Then the fire dies down little by little and around dusk I stop, inasmuch as only embers remain." He won't read other writers, fearing influence on his work. His long companion is a book of quotations, subtitled, "What Cervantes, Shakespeare, Moliere etc. have had to say about God, Life, Death, Love, Suffering, etc. . . ."

He writes ten half-hour installments a day for his serials, one an hour, then works seven more hours rehearsing and recording them. "The scripts," Mario recalls, "came pouring out . . . each of them exactly the right length, like strings of sausages out of a machine. . . . I once told him I was reminded of the theory of the French Surrealists with regard to automatic writing, which according to them flowed directly from the subconscious, bypassing the censorship of reason." Camacho replies: "Our mestizo Latin American brains can give birth to better things than those Frogs."

Camacho lives monastically, loathes money, snubs the fame his serials give him. When he writes he assumes roles physically, wearing false mustaches, a fireman's hat, the mask of a fat woman. Mario finds him at his enormous typewriter, writing about the birth of triplets. He is in a white smock, surgeon's skullcap and long, rabbinical black beard. "I'll do a Caesarean on the girl," he tells his visitor, "and then I'll go and have . . . tea with you."

Camacho's soaps are written as narratives in the novel, not as scripts, and they alternate with the realistic story. In the first one I encountered I faulted the translator for a rush of clichés, not yet aware this was the work of Camacho and not of Helen R. Lane, whose formidable translating skills are equal to both the manic tone of Camacho's madness and the ruffled normalcy of Mario's daily life.

The Camacho serials start simply and grow in complexity. His first is an ordinary, everyday story of incest and marital deceit; his second the tale of a policeman who discovers a starving, naked, Stone Age African savage muttering gibberish in a deserted warehouse, and arrests him for burglary. When nobody knows what to do with the savage, the policeman is ordered to take him to the dump and murder him. Will he do it? A boy whose sister is reduced to a pile of bones by hungry rats takes up rodent genocide as a career and brutalizes his family, which turns on him and beats him to the edge of death. As he lies unconscious, a mouse with sharp teeth comes out of its hole and studies him. An aspirin salesman kills a child with his car and grows phobic about vehicles, but is cured of his guilt by a psychiatrist who teaches him to hate children. An industrialist raises a son, stupid beyond belief, who nevertheless grows up to be Peru's most famous soccer referee. The father puts the son in charge of a factory, which he swiftly bankrupts, ruining the father, who develops a humiliating tic: sticking out his tongue and trying to lick his ear.

The stories grow progressively more confused, the aspirin salesman becoming a psychopathic rapist-killer in another story; a policeman dying in a fire and then turning up in a different serial in order to drown. Camacho imposes his own psychic ailments, some of them revealed in his chats with Mario, on the characters in his soaps: his niggling comic hatred of Argentines (he was married to one), his constipation, his championing of masturbation for priests. But his memory boggles under the strain of juggling ten soaps, and he finds himself uncertain as to who is who. To solve this he kills off everybody in assorted apocalypses—an earthquake, a sinking ship, fires, massacres—as a way of starting fresh. But it's too late. He snaps and is carted off to the madhouse. Will he remain there? Can this be the end of Pedro Camacho? No.

What Vargas Llosa has done in this book is to diagram myriad levels of the writing life, and chart the arcane, volcanic reaches of a writer's psyche. His early self, Mario, is writing unpublishable short stories all during Camacho's hegemony over the Peruvian air waves, and the young man begins to wonder:

Why should those persons who used literature as an ornament or a pretext have any more right to be considered real writers than Pedro Camacho, who lived only to write? Because they had read (or at least knew that they should have read) Proust, Faulkner, Joyce, while Pedro Camacho was very nearly illiterate? I felt sad and upset. It was becoming clearer and clearer to me each day that the only thing I wanted to be in life was a writer. . . . I didn't want in the least to be a hack writer or a part-time one, but a real one, like—who?

We know who.

Camacho is not only an exemplar of the committed writer; his seriousness also elevates the lives of those around him, most notably the radio actors who, before Camacho gave them self-respect, were merely articulate scum. "Thanks to him," one actor says, "we discovered that ours was an artistic profession." And an actress wonders plaintively as Camacho is fading away: ". . . what would people do without us? Who else gives them the illusions and emotions that help them to go on living?"

A Peruvian critic some years ago asked Vargas Llosa the meaning of this novel and he said he hadn't posed that question to himself, but one of his intentions was to prove his own early world and the world of soap opera were not so very different from each other. He illustrates that by tracking a family tragedy that impends as a consequence of the romance with Aunt Julia—the threat to murder Mario, by his father: "I shall put five bullets through you and kill you like a dog, right in the middle of the street," which suggests that everybody's apocalypse is just around the corner, Mario's reality just a short walk from Camacho's fantasy.

Both Julia's and Camacho's tales are parodistic of myriad life-styles and classes, and both are awash in satire and sentimental soapsuds. And yet both come to moments of poignant revelation because they are so very solidly real. They are not ready-to-wear metaphors but curious forms of flesh that endured in the memory of the artist and were finally given shape by an organizing principle he could not define when asked about it. But why should he try to be simplistic after creating such a complex piece of work? "I don't like novels with a moral," he has said, and he offers none overtly. His soufflé of tales might be taken as an argument on behalf of story as pure pleasure, however devoid of sanity or moral tone; or story as a form of salvation and pacification through emotional massage; or story as the vehicle for exploring the rat killers, the compulsive ear lickers, and the wacko script writers who may or may not walk abroad, as a way of proving they're just folks after all: products of the same imagination that invented thee, and me.

1982

PART FIVE

Exotic Life Forms Beyond Fiction

Frank Sinatra:

Pluperfect Music

So Frank is seventy-five this year, and what does that mean? I remember what it meant when he was sixty-eight in June 1984. He was at Carnegie Hall singing "Pennies from Heaven" and "Fly Me to the Moon" and he was in great voice. When he did "Come Rain or Come Shine," a woman in a box called out to him, "Frankie, baby, you're the best."

Frank asked her name and she said it was Angie and he said to her, "You ain't so bad yourself, Angie, you know what I mean?"

"I just wanted to warn you that I love you," Angie said.

"Is that a threat or a request?" Frank inquired.

"I'm leaving my husband for you," she said.

"I think we gotta talk that over a little bit," Frank said.

Angie turned to the audience below to tell us: "I'm gonna wash his underwear, too. I don't care."

"I'm gettin' scared now," Frank said, raising his glass of whiskey. "I'll drink to you."

"You're still twenty-five to me," Angie said.

I'd bumped into Jilly Rizzo, a friend of Frank's, in a New York saloon a few weeks earlier and we talked about the upcoming Carnegie Hall concert, for which tickets were scarce. Jilly said he could get me two, and what's more he'd introduce me to Frank backstage, and would I like that? I said that'd be a little bit of all right, and so there we were (Jilly; my wife, Dana; and me) in Frank's backstage parlor, where half a dozen others were bending his ear.

It was intermission between acts. Buddy Rich and his band, the opening act, had just concluded a hot session and Frank was on next.

A roving waiter brought us a drink and I tried to imagine what you could possibly say to Frank. You couldn't gush. You couldn't say you'd been a fan for forty-eight years. Also, you had no friends in common you knew of. Yes, it's true you were in love with Ava thirty-five years ago and once watched her dance barefoot in Puerto Rico, but you couldn't bring that up, and you didn't know his wife or kids.

Jilly broke the ice by telling Frank that I traveled with tapes, meaning, of course, Frank's tapes. So I talked then about my Pluperfect Sinatra tapes, which a friend of mine and I had concocted to take the best of Sinatra from forever forward to right now and tape them, leaving out all songs that do not make you climb the wall.

Frank listened to my Pluperfect story without much surprise, for his record producers had been doing this for him all his life: *Frank Sinatra's Greatest Hits* and *Sinatra's Sinatra*, for example. But I have to say that nobody ever put together seven tapes such as the Pluperfects, in which you climb the wall every time out.

In one sense, the conversation was good practice for writing this memoir on behalf of Frank's seventy-fifth birthday disks, for I climb the wall more often with these Reprise tunes than I ever did before, given this many choices. There are certain exceptions we will not go into, and even if I am tortured I will not mention their titles, for this is not the critic's corner. This is a story of listening to Frank for forty-eight years, maybe forty-nine, and finding out what it means that he is now turning seventy-five.

So I told Frank how I'd planned to be a drummer in 1942, and when I saw Buddy Rich in a movie playing a tom-tom solo called "Not So Quiet Please" I went out and bought the record before I had a phonograph. I would set it on top of my dresser and let my eyes be the needle and I listened to that solo for six months before I came up with enough cash to buy a friend's used phonograph. Frank remembered the solo. It was in a movie called *Ship Ahoy*, with Eleanor Powell and Red Skelton and Tommy Dorsey and guess who else: Frank. You knew that.

I then enhanced the conversation by asking him a historical question: how he decided to record "There's a Flaw in My Flue," one of my favorites among his romantic ballads, whose lyrics, in part, go like this:

Your lovely face in my fireplace, was all that I saw
But now it won't draw, 'cause my flue has a flaw.
From every beautiful ember a memory arose,
Now I try to remember and smoke gets in my nose. . . .

Frank liked the question and said he'd heard the song on Bing Crosby's
Kraft Music Hall radio show, a segment called "The Flop Parade," and
he thought it was funny; what's more Bing had never recorded it. So
Frank—who felt that the executives at his record company never really
listened to his songs—wanted to make that point; and he asked Nelson
Riddle to orchestrate "Flue" for an opening slot in an upcoming record.

"When they played it," Frank said, "one of the record company guys
says to me, 'What is this?' and I said, 'It's a love song.' I said, 'There's
a flaw in my flue, beautiful.' " And so it flawlessly became, and Frank
made his point doubly, with a leg pull that stands as a comic gem.

The other significant thing that happened at Carnegie Hall was my
wife. She had been a tepid Sinatra fan, growing, if not fond of, then at
least used to him as I played his tapes. She knew him as an actor before
I came along but not really as a singer and here I was clogging her brain
with him on every trip we took. She would sometimes look at me and
say, quietly, "Overdose," and I'd then have to put on the Kiri Te Kanawa
tape.

But unbeknownst, Frank had been growing on her ever since she'd
heard him do "Lonely Town" better than anybody else had ever done
it, and then here he was singing "Mack the Knife" and "Luck Be a
Lady" and swinging everybody's brain from the highest trapeze and even
dancing (which also got to her, for she'd been both a ballerina, and a
gypsy on Broadway), and suddenly there she was on her feet like everybody else when he wound up with "New York, New York": Dana, a convert, no longer susceptible to overdose.

That is the remarkable thing about Sinatra recordings: that you can
listen to them not only forever, but also at great length without over-
dosing, once you have been infected. I say this not only on my own
behalf but on behalf of the entire set in which I move, and which I have
helped infect to the point that Frank is now a common denominator
among this group of seriously disparate ages and types. I am the Me-
thuselah of the set and can remember not only Frank's hits with Tommy

Dorsey's orchestra when they were new—"I'll Never Smile Again" and "There Are Such Things"—but also tunes that never quite made it— "Everything Happens to Me," for instance, which I knew by heart in 1943 and still remember from that era when listening to records was what you did with your friends when the baseball diamond was a major mud puddle.

In the 1950s, there came *In the Wee Small Hours*, which conditioned your life, especially with a young woman with lush blond hair who used to put the record on and pray to Frank for a lover. All that perfumed hair, and it came undone. That certainly was a good year, but it remained for another album, *Swing Easy*, to teach you how to play a record twelve times in one night, which was merely a warm-up for 1983 when you listened to "New York, New York" for the first time seriously and then played it sixty times until 5:00 A.M., also calling your friends in New York and San Juan and Aspen and permitting them to stop sleeping and get out of bed and listen along.

The true thing about this phenomenon is that you do not have to have Frank on video, or in a movie or TV show, or even invent conversation in person with this fellow who is a stranger. You really don't need those presences. All you need is the music the man has made and that has been with you all your life, and which is even better now because you have all the songs of his maturity (which is why these four disks are so valuable, for they collect tunes he did early on and here does so much better). He was new in the forties and still growing in the fifties into such masterpieces as "Drinking Again" (1967), by Johnny Mercer, the greatest of all torch songs Frank ever sang, and also such breakouts as we have here—"I've Got You Under My Skin" (1966) and "The Lady Is a Tramp" (1974) that put earlier white-bread versions out in the back yard. Of course, these views are open to argument but, even so, I will brook none of it here. This is my memoir.

There is another superb thing Sinatra does, which is Irving Berlin's schmaltziest work—"All Alone" and "What'll I Do?" among others— shameless, cornball, wonderful throwbacks to the Tin Pan Alley time when schmaltz was A–Number One, King of the Hill.

It was the schmaltz and also too many trumpets that turned off my son, Brendan, when I played Frank in the car. (He once listened to a Bing Crosby and the Rhythm Boys tape from 1929, and decided the music was prehistoric.) We would fight over tape time in the car, he opting for the Police, me for guess who? This was 1983 and Bren was thirteen. Now he's in college and last month he told me, "We were at a party and this horrible music was on and this girl and I put on a tape of Frank and danced until somebody shut him off."

Two weeks ago he asked my advice on dance tunes and I recommended *Swing Easy* and the albums with Ellington and Jobim, and so now Brendan also travels with Frank tapes, in case of emergency dancing.

The finale of all this is that Frank turned up in our hometown, Albany, as the opening act for the brand-new Knickerbocker Arena, with seventeen thousand seats. Would Albany turn out for him in any numbers? Word had gone out, as it always does with these mythmaking events, that Frank wasn't well, might not show up, that Liza Minnelli was standing by to go on if he crumpled. What's more, Ava had just died and so maybe this was not one of those very good years.

And yet here he came on January 30, six years older than when I'd last seen him, looking smaller and—how not?—older, his seventy-fifth year just barely under way. He's wearing his single-breasted tux with an orange pocket handkerchief, his hair totally silver, adding to his years. Then he opens his mouth. "Come fly with me," he sings and a cheer goes up from the yes, seventeen thousand who have packed the place to hear and see this legendary character who only *seems* to grow old.

A lifetime of staying young at center stage: how can anybody be so good for so long? You listen and know that this is not Frank in his best voice ever but it doesn't matter. It's *his* sound, *his* cadence, *his* tunes, *him*, and it's as good as it can be and that's still very, very good. He moseys to the improvised bar on stage with the Jack Daniel's and the ice bucket and he sits on the bar stool and says: "I think it's about time to have a drink. I don't drink a lot, but I don't drink a little either." And then he opens his mouth again: "It's quarter to three . . ." and the crowd roars and he calms them with his old torch.

And then, finally, he segues into "New York, New York" and the spotlights circle the crowd, which is stomping, and Frank is making love to all here. He opens his arms, points to everybody. . . . "It's up to you, New York, New York. . . ."

Then it's over and the spots cross on him, and the aging bobby-soxers, having come full circle from forty-eight years gone, reach up to shake his hand, and he fades down the stairs and out, and you follow him with your eyes because he is carrying the sound of your youth, the songs of your middle age. And then you think, the song is you, pal, the song is you.

1990

Pablo Casals:

Master Class
at Marlboro

It was the last day at Marlboro for Pablo Casals. He would conduct the final master class of his two-week visit, then leave with his wife, Martita, for Prades, France, a small town in the Pyrenees. Casals spent many years there in exile after the Spanish Civil War, where now an annual Casals Festival of chamber music is held to honor the town's most famous ex-resident.

The eighty-six-year-old master musician, composer, conductor sat on the stage of the converted barn, a pine-walled cube with rough-hewn beams overhead, red and yellow crepe-paper strips two feet wide hanging on the walls to improve the acoustics, and the several windows offering a cool view of the gnarled trees growing out of the green Vermont hillside.

Casals sat facing his pupil, David Soyer, forty, of New York City, a man who has studied the cello for thirty years. The maestro has been at it longer; almost eighty years. Between the two men stood a music stand, and on it the music for Bach's D Major Suite.

The music faced the pupil, not the teacher. At no time in the next three hours, for any of the students who sat across from him, would Casals refer to the music. The Bach suite, Beethoven's Sonata in A Major, Mendelssohn's Song Without Words: they were all as much a part of Casals's mind as the vision of his mother's face.

When his master class in Berkeley, California, was televised, the world heard Casals advise a student on the tempo of a given phrase. "It goes like this," the maestro said. "I remember discussing it with Brahms himself."

Casals has lived a long time. He was born December 29, 1876. Yet he stays young. He is unusually active for a man of such advanced years. He is without the liver-spotted skin of most octogenarians. On the stage at Marlboro last week he moved his arm vigorously with each stroke of the bow. He leaped up frequently to instruct the pupils on the use of their fingers. ("Make your left hand give a little percussion on the strings—like playing the piano. It's neat.") He instructed them in the aesthetic use of the arm in pulling away from the instrument after plucking a note.

And he talked and hummed:

Yes, leave the bow . . . yi, yum, pi . . . yi, yum, pi . . . it's difficult but I think the easiest way is this . . . ahn, ahn, ahn . . . dee, dee, ah, ah . . . very good, very good . . . dot's it . . . yesssss . . . noooooo . . . wait, wait . . . don't do it . . . better, better . . . not so pianissimo . . . that's very interesting . . . everything has to be heard and I didn't hear this part . . . No! What a thing! This way! . . . Don't do that with that song, this is a very rare occasion, the very end of a pianissimo . . . I don't hear it . . . a little more crescendo . . . I don't like that . . . more, more! . . . You are the principal part . . . yes, yes . . . very beautiful.

The audience was mostly musicians, members of the Marlboro Music School's "republic of equals." This is the catchphrase which Marlboro's artistic director, the famed pianist Rudolf Serkin, took from Schuman to characterize the way of life at Marlboro's summer festival. It is a July-to-September season of music, some contemporary, mostly classical.

A brochure describes the Marlboro experience as something "more than a school or a festival—a place where professional musicians, the young as well as the more experienced, can exchange ideas, experiment, and cultivate the highest arts of chamber music."

The school is supported by donations from well-to-do patrons. Also, many musicians pay a "tuition" which runs about $625 for the nine-week season, and which covers room and board. In the winter the school reverts to a liberal arts college with no connection with the music festival other than mutual use of the school's facilities.

The audience of 140 persons who came to see Casals was casual, dressed mostly in knockaround clothing. One man came late, asked for a ticket ("Make whatever donation you feel you can afford," the ticketman said), paid thirty dollars. "I'd like to make a more substantial donation later," he said. "That can be arranged," said the ticketman.

In the audience was a white-haired woman, an ancient, with cotton in her ears. Also listening to Casals like an eager pupil was pianist Serkin, a master himself.

Then came the music, the deep, scratching sweetness of the cellos as the Bach suite was played. The heat of the late morning's high-rising sun drilled in through the roof of the auditorium.

Casals bounced up out of his chair, tapped his feet, stared with downturned mouth at the pupils: "No, no, no . . . ah yes, dot's right. Very good technique."

Said cellist David Soyer, Casals's first pupil of the morning: "We are constantly amazed at the fantastic beauty of Casals's playing. And unbelievable as it might seem, he plays better now than he ever did. And this is a great inspiration to all of us."

At the end of each session the audience applauded. Then at the end of the final session when Casals played the Mendelssohn Song Without Words with Madeline Foley of the Brandeis University faculty, the swan song for Casals at Marlboro this year, the audience broke into rhythmic applause—1-2-3-4, 1-2-3-4. Casals bowed to them, put down his cello, then returned to center stage.

"I don't like speeches, I like facts," he said. "I want to say I'm very sad to leave you."

Then he backed away to greater applause.

This was his third year at Marlboro, the end of a two-week visit, a peaceful interim in a half-year of hectic concertizing. Casals, in June, completed two weeks of conducting Casals Festival Concerts in San Juan; went then to New York where he conducted Bach's St. Matthew Passion, received the key to the city of New York, and received an honorary doctorate at Temple University in Philadelphia.

He then flew to Ravina, Illinois, where before ten thousand persons in a rainstorm he conducted "El Pesebre" ("The Manger"), his oratorio celebrating the birth of Christ, and symbolizing his personal crusade for peace in the world.

Then he came to Marlboro, next to Prades until early August, then once again will go on the road for his peace crusade with "El Pesebre" concerts in Berlin, London, the United Nations (on UN Day, October 24), and finally New Orleans. And then home to Puerto Rico.

Casals said once that a man should "do things with intelligence and conscience." He has lived his own life that way and because of it, and because of his great talent and his care for his talent, he has heaped greatness upon himself. Yet after all, one might ask, isn't it a bit foolish for one mortal man to think that he can bring about peace in today's world?

Casals is enough of a realist to know that it is neither vainglory nor foolishness to try.

As he exited from the auditorium, walking into the bright summer sunlight toward the waiting automobile, his wife trailing him, Serkin embracing him, dozens of admirers having shaken his hand and whispered words of awe and praise to him, he was asked about his crusade. How does it go? Is it achieving what he wants it to achieve?

He grasped the arm of the inquirer and with a knowing smile he retorted:

"I play my oratorio, you know. We can only do what we can."

He smiled with wise eyes.

"But everybody," he added, "has to do what he can."

Then Casals was gone and life at Marlboro swiftly resumed. It was time for lunch and the auditorium where the maestro just gave his hallowed lessons was suddenly a mess hall. Instead of sweet strings there was the click of silverware on dishes. Rudolf Serkin jumped off the stage and was buttonholed.

"I'm sorry, but I cannot talk for long," he said. "I must rehearse for a benefit concert I'm giving tomorrow night with Mr. Benny Goodman."

"Mr. Benny Goodman the jazz clarinetist?"

"No. Mr. Benny Goodman the classical clarinetist."

Mr. Goodman showed up in due time, dressed in off-green gabardine threads, wearing horn-rims, and looking cool and ready to attack Schubert and Brahms. He said he was "an old friend of Rudy's," and that this was his first visit to Marlboro. The concert would be in Stanford, Connecticut.

"All classical?"

"Oh sure."

"No jazz."

"Uh-uh."

Then Rudy and Benny went off to rehearse, as did the rest of the equals at the Marlboro Republic. From one old house came the sound of brass. From another the finger exercise of a violinist. The auditorium—mess hall was now a rehearsal stage where a cantata was in progress. Outside a workman hammered at a piece of lumber for a new building and a persistent bee buzzed around a man who walked up a pathway on the campus. The Goodman-Serkin duo sent Schubert strains out over the maple-tree tops, which rustled with their own soft percussion. Down the road in the new concert hall a Hindemith quartet was in progress.

It was a typical afternoon in Marlboro, and for once, without exaggeration, you could say that music filled the air.

1963

Satchmo:

"All My Days Are the Same"

I've been trying for thirty-six years to write the story of my interview with Louis Armstrong. I did write a small piece for the *Albany Times-Union* the day I talked with him, and when the news editor read it he threw it in the wastebasket with the comment, "Just another bandleader." I retrieved the story and complained to the managing editor, who personally put it in the Sunday edition. It was a reasonably bright, comic story that revealed Satchmo to a small degree and amused a fair number of readers. This whole episode tipped the balance of my discontent and a month later I quit the paper and took a job in San Juan.

I held on to my notes from the interview, for I'd only used a fragment of what Louis and I had talked about, some of which was unprintable in a family newspaper. My awe and reverence for Louis continued to grow through the ensuing years, and somewhere in the late 1970s I conducted an after-dinner poll of who was the most valuable person who ever lived, and Satchmo won with five votes. William Faulkner got four, Michaelangelo three, Beethoven, Muhammad Ali, and Tolstoy two each, and Dostoyevsky and Busby Berkeley one each.

This whole episode tipped the balance of my long silence on Louis, and I began writing the story of our conversation. But I lacked what editors call a "peg" on which to hang the story. My 1956 notes—made on folded, irregularly cut newsprint, which was what reporters took notes on in Albany in those days—had turned yellow and brittle, the sea air of Puerto Rico had rusted the paper clip that held the notes together; also, books by the dozens were being published about Satchmo, and so my interest dwindled, and the unfinished story moldered in my file.

Even so, I did not despair. I kept the Satch notes in the current-projects file, peering in at them now and again, certain that one day a peg would emerge from the lumberyard of my imagination. Alas, one did not. And this whole episode tipped the balance of my inertia and led me, at last, to write the story anyway.

I've been leafing through assorted Satchmo books, by Gary Giddins, by Gunther Schuller, by Martin Williams, by Louis himself, and it is quite wonderful to see all the things that people have said of him, and how much more they know about him and his work than I do; and it is also wonderful to read what he said to other people; for he had great verbal talent in addition to being a musical genius.

But whatever my shortcomings in relation to Louis, and because I do not think my postprandial companions were alone in rating his value in the cosmos, I have decided that writing my footnotes to the life of this Parnassian figure is in order.

It was the second week in March, 1956, and Louis, just four months shy of his fifty-sixth unofficial public birthday—he said he was born on the Fourth of July, 1900, but he was really born on the fourth of August, 1901—was in town with his band, the All-Stars (Trummy Young, trombone; Billy Kyle, piano; Barrett Deems, drums; Arvell Shaw, bass; Edmond Hall, clarinet) to play the Palace. Louis was staying at the Kenmore Hotel, which was odd, for the old hotel, once the place where Albany's gentry and the state's loftiest politicians sipped, supped, and rested their bones in nineteenth-century luxury, was on the slide into fleabagation.

But Satch had played the Kenmore's Rain-Bo Room periodically since it began broadcasting music all over the country via the General Electric Company's radio station WGY, Schenectady. These broadcasts drove romantic couples, even husbands and wives, into spasms of fox-trotting, waltzing, and bunny-hugging in living rooms all across America, and so the Kenmore was, in these years, a mecca for musicians and performers seeking coast-to-coast exposure—Rudy Vallee and Hal Kemp, Duke Ellington and Bix Beiderbecke, Billie Holiday and Mildred Bailey, the Dorsey brothers and Bunny Berigan, all this splendid music originating in beautiful downtown Albany.

These dynamic radio days were long gone in 1956, television having

entered the national life with its usurping ways, and the postwar entertainment tax still driving people to social pursuits other than expensive
nightclubbing. But for all the aforementioned music-oriented reasons,
Louis would still feel good about the Kenmore, and would be loyal to
the place also because, as the story went, he once tried to stay at the
Ten Eyck, the premier hotel of Albany's modern era, and was denied a
room because of his color; and the Kenmore, which had been established
and run for some years by the son of a slave, a man named Adam Blake,
did not bar blacks in the modern age.

When I told Bob Murphy, the proprietor of the Kenmore, that I had
an appointment to see Louis, he told me his Bunny Berigan story. He
came to own Berigan's trumpet, he said, and he gave it to Dan Prior,
the criminal lawyer who had so successfully defended Jack (Legs) Diamond, perhaps the most noted and certainly the most infamous denizen
of the Kenmore, against assault and kidnapping charges in 1931. Murphy
said he acquired the trumpet after Berigan died, but there were those
who said it belonged to a musician in Doc Peyton's orchestra—one of
the Kenmore's several house bands—who didn't pay his bar bill. Some
said Murphy had a great imagination on matters like this. Others said
the truth wasn't in him.

Murphy gave me Louis's room number and I went up in the elevator
to the fifth floor. When I emerged into the hallway I heard the lone wail
of a horn. I didn't know the tune, but Louis would tell me later it was
"Nevada," a tune he played often to warm up his chops. It was a magical
sound, plaintive, out of place in this deserted hallway, a prelude to a
meeting with the maestro.

I'd been listening to jazz all my life, and I knew Satchmo and Kid
Ory and the Hot Five and Satch's big-band tunes before and during the
war, and I dug it all from a distance. Good stuff. Indeed. But then I
saw the man in concert in the early 1950s, when he was presumably
over the hill, no longer the great innovator, and never before had I been
roused to such feverish excitement by a jazz musician. Also, in recent
months, I had been obsessed by his new album, *Ambassador Satch*,
especially a tune called "The Faithful Hussar," or "Huzzah Kuzzah" as
Louis rendered it. For reasons that would be explicable only after prolonged musical psychoanalysis, this song gave me spasms of pleasure,
frenzy, jubilation, ascendancy, solidarity with the human race, and

revelation of internal percussions not previously manifested by my tympanic consciousness.

A pal of mine from the army, Frank Trippett, a Satchmo freak long before I was, had sat next to the man for hours when Satch and his big band played for a dance in a black honky-tonk in the Mississippi Delta in maybe 1943. Trippett was playing trumpet himself in a youthful white jazz band in those years, and he raved about Satchmo often when he and I were beer-drinking regulars at an enlisted men's club in Frankfurt, Germany, listening to Satch sing "Blueberry Hill," and trying to figure out why such a dumb song could sound so great; and the answer, of course, was, that Satchmo was not only the greatest horn player who ever lived, he was also the greatest jazz singer, a genius who could turn sludge into sunshine. "There are no bad songs," he once said.

I knocked at Louis's door and announced myself and he said, "Wait a minute till I get some clothes on," and in a while he opened the door, wearing a handkerchief on his head, a plaid shirt, a pair of boxer shorts, and white socks. His horn was on a chair and he picked it up and finished his warm-up, and then lubricated his chops with vaseline. I sat down and we talked for an hour and a half, the room becoming a thoroughfare at times when his wife, Lucille, came in ("Put your slippers on, Pops," she told him) with friends, and when his valet arrived to unpack his grips and arrange assorted bottles, jars, and tubes on a dresser top—his artifacts of endurance: vitamins, gargles, eye drops, chest rubs.

"They keep me alive," he said. "I paint my chest and it keeps the cold out."

Louis (pronounced "Louis," not "Louie"; his preference) in these days, was a roving ambassador for Rexall drugstores, hustling, in particular, two items that had brought him down from 268 pounds a year ago, to his 173 of the moment. One item was Swiss Kriss, a herbal laxative, and the other was Bisma Rex, liquid or tablets. Bisma Rex, "it cuts gas," Satch advised in the three-page document, "Lose Weight the 'Satchmo' Way," that he handed out to people like me.

"Gas can take you like *that*," he told me. "One time the doctor's thinking I had ulcers and it wasn't nothin' but gas." A druggist put him on to Bisma Rex and soon he was fine. "So I nix out this doctor and go to Bisma Rex," said Louis. "I sent some [tablets] to Eisenhower when he had that stroke. I said to him, 'Man, you wouldn't of had that stroke you had one of these.' "

Even after a night of drinking booze, Bisma Rex and Swiss Kriss were the answer. Satchmo told me he'd given up on beer ("You drink a whole lot of that and nothin' happens") but when he drank the other stuff and something *did* happen, his view was, "If you can crawl to that cab and get to your Swiss Kriss, you gonna be all right in the mornin'."

Satchmo's diet also called for orange juice in abundance—"so delicious . . . you should never get tired of drinking it." He told me that orange juice, "when it's got vitamins in it, is just the same as two pork chops." In sum, said the Satch diet, "orange juice softens it, Bisma Rex cuts it, Swiss Kriss swishes it . . . tee hee."

Louis was coming under attack in these years as a throwback, a man whose music was passé, who was playing an Uncle Tom role for the white folks, who was finding his thrill on Blueberry Hill, but not with anything that was modern or progressive in jazz anymore. There's no doubt his popularity with whites, and with people who loved music but knew nothing about jazz, was on the rise. In another nine years he'd record "Hello, Dolly!" and knock the Beatles off the top of the charts.

How did the man himself react to such musical criticism?

"What is modern stuff?" he said. "If it's good, I listen. To me there ain't no such thing as modern stuff. Just a style the agents picked up and spread around. Dizzy [Gillespie] and Charlie Parker were foolin' around, playin' it themselves, and the agents see there's a pretty good style there and they pick it up. . . . You take [Stan] Kenton, standin' there with a baton. He doesn't instill anything in youngsters but bustin' their lips. In the old days musicians were taught to preserve lips or nothin'. Anybody can blow a horn and pray to God they'll hit a note. In the old days we trained. Half these cats don't warm up. They're followin' the wrong people. . . . One of my solos would fracture them. The oldest record I played, they can't play it. . . .

"Jam sessions these days they just blow. I was in a joint in Pittsburgh for forty-five minutes before I realized these cats were playin' 'Lover Come Back to Me.' . . . You got to explain to the people what you're doin', whether it's 'Tiger Rag' or 'La Vie en Rose.' . . . Take 'Mack the Knife' [Satch's recording of it was, at this moment, a hit, and would spur a revival of Kurt Weill's music], a good old song that's goin' great."

Louis then analyzed Mack for me: "He was a little part of everybody livin'. . . . He was a ladies' man . . . he did everything wrong. He steals, a man draws money out of the bank and disappears and *he's* spendin' money. Who did it but him? Sunday mornin' [dead] on the sidewalk. I seen them there like that. I was a boy seventeen years old and I see it . . . fightin' and shootin'. . . . I never got hurt. I'm still playin' and blowin' the blues."

Any thought of retiring?

"Whatya gonna do? You goin' in a room and bite your nails? You gonna quit just because you're straight with money? Money is just somethin' you need. What good is a roomful when you got nothin' to do with it? Lotsa cats have quit and put that horn down, but they don't come back. You can live that horn. . . . I go to Chicago and New York and there's nothin' but fans in the house. . . . I didn't know there was a time you're supposed to stop. What for, as long as you can still hit them on the nose? . . . Music don't know no age. I feel the same as when I was twenty-eight . . . All my days are the same."

The interview was winding down, and it was getting on to show time at the Palace, where Satch and the All-Stars would play, among other tunes, "The Faithful Hussar," renewing my ascendancy glands. Satch would go on from Albany to keep playing for another fifteen years, growing ill from clogged arteries, kidney trouble, and ulcers; he would undergo a tracheotomy after a heart attack and die of a subsequent attack on July 6, 1971, in his home in the New York City borough of Queens, 34–56 107th Street, Corona (now an official city landmark), his age either seventy or seventy-one, depending on which of his birthdates you accept.

He was a giant in his youth, the first major soloist in jazz, the man to whom every jazz, swing, modern jazz, and rock musician after him has been and is indebted, some via the grand larceny route. Music has changed radically since the seminal days of jazz, but Satchmo's achievement has not been diminished. No one has superseded him in jazz eminence the way Crosby superseded Jolson, and Sinatra superseded Crosby, and the Beatles superseded Elvis, and I will never know who or what really superseded the Beatles.

Everything I loved about Louis's music was present in the Kenmore Hotel room that day in 1956: the fundamental humanity of the man, his wit, his certainty about his talent—as evident in his words as in his solos; and the memories of it all endured in me to this day in February 1992 when I write this. Even the Swiss Kriss endured. Trippett ran into Trummy Young in Hawaii in 1970 and told him the story of how Satch signed his diet for me, and Trummy gave Trippett a photo that Trippett sent on to me—of Satch seen through a keyhole, sitting on the toilet, smiling at the camera. An overcaption reads: "Swiss Krissly," and the undercaption is a Satchmo slogan: "Leave it all behind ya."

As the interview ended, Louis asked Lucille to find a photo of himself and he signed it to me. He looks a few years younger than fifty-six in the photo, and he's blowing the horn. He also signed my copy of his "Lose Weight" diet and he added a line of his wisdom. With my ebony pencil he dedicated the diet on page 1, "For Bill Kennedy," and then on the bottom of page 3 wrote: "P.S. My slogan. The more you shit the thiner you'll *Git*. No shit." And he signed it, Louis Armstrong.

There is one other memory, which happened at the beginning of our meeting when I interrupted his warm-up. Louis got dressed after I knocked, I went in and sat down, and he picked up his horn, feeling unfinished, and he said, "Wait till I hit the high note," and he then played a little while I listened—the end of "Nevada." He blew some low notes, then a few higher ones, and finally he hit the high one and held it for about a week and turned it like a corkscrew and flattened it out two or three ways and sharpened it up and blew it out the window.

Then he put down the horn and smiled.

"Solid," he said.

Oh yeaaaahhhh.

1992

Paul McCartney:

The Major
Possum Game

By now most of the literate Western world knows that Paul McCartney is, or isn't, dead. Illiterates eventually will get the news via television specials.

But what perhaps isn't so generally known is the density of public commitment to discover how, when, where Paul died and was buried and will be resurrected when the revolution comes to sit at the right hand of John Lennon. Equally dense is the public pursuit of the location of Pepperland, and how to get the Beatles to take you there.

It has become a time-consuming pastime of American youth to probe the lyrics, the photographs and the jacket covers of Beatle albums to unearth clues that will solve the riddle of Paul and Pepperland—that mythical paradise from *The Yellow Submarine* film—and the pastime now seems en route to a complexity comparable to the deciphering, by Joycean scholars, of the multiple meanings of the portmanteau words in *Finnegans Wake*; or the quest to prove through clues in Shakespeare's plays that Sir Francis Bacon wrote them; or the pursuit of clues in Sir Arthur Conan Doyle's Sherlock Holmes stories to prove that Holmes lived.

This is so because of a certain willfulness that has made verbal ambiguity and picture puzzles essential ingredients of Beatlism. A Beatle song (or album cover) about which you've never asked the question "What do they mean by that?" is probably a Beatle product you don't rate very high. Their work is full of what Christopher Morley described, in speaking of the Sherlock Holmes stories, as "endless delicious minutiae to consider."

Probably the Beatles didn't intend for their games to take such a bizarre turn, but nevertheless the McCartney death theory is a by-product. Various origins of the notion are being claimed. Tim Harper, a Drake University sophomore from Peoria, wrote about it in his student paper on September 17. John Summer, an Ohio Wesleyan student, developed a complex thesis on the topic. The Michigan University paper printed a story on it, and voice prints of McCartney were made by an associate professor of audiology at Michigan State, proving that McCartney is alive. Disc jockeys at WKNR–FM, Detroit, have been credited with unifying the clues.

Over at Rensselaer Polytechnic Institute's campus radio station, WRPI–FM, in Troy, three student disk jockeys got together last month and talked from 10:00 P.M. to 1:00 A.M. on the subject, with a small studio audience of friends to feed the conversation. Their two phones stayed constantly busy for the three hours with callers who had either propounded theories of their own, or wanted to add to or correct theories given on the show.

The host for the show was Marek Lewanda, nineteen, of Albany, a chemistry major. Also on were Ralph Pascucci, twenty-two, of Manhasset, who uses the radio name of Pat Pending (and, sometimes Regus Pat Off), a mechanical-engineering student; and Jim Nagy, nineteen, whose air name is Freddy Garbo, nineteen, a Fairfield, Connecticut, engineering student who claims to have started the Beatle mystery wagon rolling here last march by citing many clues on his record show. This is the earliest claim we've encountered to date.

What have all these people discovered? News reports have given some but by no means all of the current clues. Herewith old and new:

Starting with the album *Sergeant Pepper's Lonely Hearts Club Band*, the Beatleologists found:

1. Paul sitting down with knees showing, George, Ringo and John with knees concealed;
2. Paul wearing a uniform bearing an arm label with "O.P.D." on it, translated by clue sniffers as "Officially Pronounced Dead";
3. A hand, presumably a traditional death symbol, raised above Paul's head on the cover. The hand over Paul's head is a recurrent item in pictures and cartoons throughout the *Magical Mystery Tour* album's

picture book also. On the *Sergeant Pepper* cover the hand belongs to Stephen Crane, one of many of the noted figures whose likenesses are on the cover.

4. Beside the grave (shown on the cover), which all are watching, is a bass guitar made of flowers. Paul plays bass guitar.
5. On the front of the bass drum on the cover, the words "Lonely Hearts" are printed horizontally. Hold up a mirror to the word "Hearts," bisecting letters lengthwise with the mirror, and it reads: He Die.
6. On the back cover, three Beatles face the camera; Paul's back is to the camera.
7. George Harrison, on the back cover, has his right hand at belt level, probably holding on to a button. But his first finger points upward.

Now: all the lyrics of the album's songs are printed on the back of this album. Should you follow a line emanating from George's finger you will pass through various lyrics with times and numbers, beginning with Wednesday morning at five o'clock (the presumed time of Paul's death); passing upward through the words "ten to six" which is translated as October 6, the date of the car crash in which he was fatally injured— the crash being arrived at through the crashlike sound in the song "Revolution Nine," from the white Beatle album. The upward pointing continues on to "sixty-four" and "quarter to three" which the Troy puzzle solvers feel are meaningful, but haven't yet translated.

Paul was presumably buried on Saturday, October 8, and on October 9, a new Beatle organization was formed with a McCartney impersonator. No reason is given for this date, but the impersonator may have been the winner of a Paul McCartney look-alike contest held in New Jersey —on a date unspecified—and who, after being chosen winner, never showed up to take the prize and was never heard of again. (Ah ha!)

Saturday was chosen as the burial date because of two items: first, the words of the song "Being for the Benefit of Mr. Kite" (from *Sergeant Pepper*), in which "the celebrated Mr. K performs his feat on Saturday at Bishopsgate." This is considered to be a reference to John Lennon, whose middle initial is thought to be K. The second item is that the Mr. H of the same song is said to be George Harrison, and the lyric says "ten summersets he'll undertake on solid ground."

Now "undertake" is the key to understanding both that reference and also the related cover of the new Beatle album, *Abbey Road*. The cover picture shows, left to right, George, Paul, Ringo and John walking across Abbey Road (where they have offices in London). To the left is a cemetery (maybe), to the right is a police hearse (maybe), or at least a police van.

Paul is wearing a business suit and no shoes, reportedly the burial costume for certain people in Italy. (Why Italy? Because.) Paul also has a cigarette (a coffin nail?) in his hand. Harrison wears jeans, like a gravedigger, they say; Ringo wears black like a clergyman, and Lennon wears white, like an undertaker (?). The clincher in the photo is a Volkswagen parked to the left of the street, part of the license reading "28 IF." The translation: Paul would be twenty-eight if he lived. Some argumentative people say only twenty-seven.

There are other clues: Paul wearing a black flower in his lapel and the other three Beatles wearing red roses (*Magical Mystery* album); also, on "I Am the Walrus," as the music fades, faint words are spoken which—reportedly—come from *King Lear* and are said to be: "Bury my body . . . O untimely death . . . Is he dead?"

Now. Take the cover of *Magical Mystery Tour*. "The Beatles" is printed by using star clusters to form each letter. Put this up to a mirror and it reads: 23 JYA 38. Apparently "23" doesn't mean much. Yet. But "JYA" in Chinese Mandarin dialect reportedly means "final resting place," and as to "38"—3 is a mystical ascending number and 8 is infinity turned sideways.

And don't forget the sound of the banshee—an Irish death wailing figure—on "Goodnight" (white Beatle album); and the bus in the sky (*Magical Mystery* picture book) which isn't much different from the symbolic Irish death coach that traditionally rides in the black sky (so they say). McCartney is an Irish name, isn't it?

So now, at last, we come to Freddy Garbo's masterwork: the discovery of the location of the island which may be Pepperland (where the Beatles will take you if you call the right number in London and say: "Turn me on, dead man," and can prove you know all the clues).

First, get a copy of the Rolling Stones album *Their Satanic Majesties*, which has all of the Beatles' faces hidden in the flowers on the 3D cover photo. (This is obviously a come-on clue to another Beatle clue, right?) Turn to page 2 of this four-page album and find the center of the printed maze where it says "It's Here." Put a pin through the center of that maze. Close the cover, reverse the pin so that it now enters the pinhole from the cover side instead of from page 2, and let it stick into page 3. It will touch, precisely, a fragment of a map which Freddy found to be part of Brazil.

The map shows the Salado River at coordinates (he says, but my atlas seems to disagree) 64 west longitude (When I'm Sixty-four—*Sergeant Pepper*), and 26 south latitude (the four Beatles have 26 fingers extended in one photo in the *Magical Mystery* picture book). Follow the Salado River ("Lucy in the Sky with Diamonds" says "Picture yourself in a boat on a river . . . everyone smiles as you drift past the flowers . . .") and you will come to an island at the river's mouth, called "Florianopolis" which, says Freddy, means Place of Flowers, and, natch, the Beatles' faces are found amid flowers on the cover.

Is Florianopolis Pepperland? Or is Pepperland the island John Lennon bought in the Mediterranean but doesn't want any publicity about?

Freddy believes that all this is a hoax played chiefly by Lennon. He also feels that Americans who are playing the game, and who really believe they can get to Pepperland by discovering the clues, are people who are trying to shorten the odds against their ever getting to paradise. "They say," says Freddy, "that if I guess the clues, I'm going to win a lifetime for free with the Beatles."

But Marek Lewanda wonders, not unreasonably: "Why should the Beatles want random people in America to live with them?"

All three disk jockeys believe that some clues are valid—such as Paul without shoes, the hand over his head—but they don't know what it all means. "I'm thoroughly convinced," said Lewanda, "that he's alive." None of them believe in Pepperland.

McCartney was interviewed last week in Scotland and claimed to be alive, though earlier he said if he were dead he'd be the last to know. And if people want to believe he's dead, said a Beatle spokesman, they aren't going to let anything as flimsy as the truth interfere.

Well, we want to make it clear here that we haven't been taken in by all this. We did some research of our own and translated "Ob-La-Di, Ob-La-Da," the title of a Beatle song (White Album), and came up with some viable goods. Unscrambled, "ob-la-di" comes out "*libado*," the past participle of the Spanish verb "libar," meaning suck, and therefore sucked, or colloquially, "sucked in." As to "ob-la-da," that is the scrambled past participle—*bolada*—of the Spanish verb "*bolar*," which means, to bowl, or throw a ball, but in colloquial Spanish means "hoaxed." Get it?

To clinch our case we ran through the proper names of the women who appear in the songs on the white Beatle album—Martha, Julia, Sadie, Honey Pie, Mother Superior, Molly, Prudence and Georgia. Taking the first two letters from each name we arrived at MA-JU-SA-HO-PI-MO-SU-MO-PR-GE.

This, of course, when unscrambled, translates as MAJOR POSSUM GAME. And we all know how a possum loves to play dead.

There are some letters left over after this maneuver which obviously express the Beatles' sentiments about all this, just as they express our own, namely P-H-O-U-I, which, linguists will note, when rendered phonetically, emerge as FOOEY, from the raspberry fields of the same name.

1969

Jiggs:

"What's the Matter with Father? I Saw Him Drink Water."

Jiggs. When I was growing up, reading him every day and especially in color on Sunday, he didn't seem any more Irish than half a dozen of our neighbors who looked like him. He seemed to me just another American victim of success, trapped by his money and his wife Maggie's social climbing in a world he loathed. He preferred old friends at the saloon, or at the construction job (Jiggs carried a hod before he got rich). Maggie chastised such recidivism by throwing rolling pins at his head.

I eventually came to realize that both Jiggs and my neighbors were indeed Irish-Americans, and that Jiggs spoke for his look-alikes in their ascendancy out of poverty into the sweet-smelling region of money. It was the specifics of these contrasting worlds that made the story of Maggie and Jiggs valuable originally and keeps it valuable today as peerless social history. Reencountering Jiggs in this book (*Jiggs Is Back*, by George McManus) is like shedding four decades, or six. It returns us to the time when the quartet sang at Rooney's saloon until the boiler factory next door complained about the noise.

In his prime Jiggs had eighty million readers in forty-six countries and sixteen languages. His creator, George McManus, bragged he was as rich as Jiggs: he made $12 million in the forty years he drew the strip. Oliver St. John Gogarty, the Irish writer, told McManus he was a genius, and Gogarty was right. Nobody invents like McManus anymore. He once spent two weeks drawing one picture for the strip—a single panel of Times Square, drawn for the Sunday pages on New Year's Eve, 1939. Compared to what today passes for cartooning, Jiggs qualifies as a kind of *War and Peace* of the Golden Age of the funny papers. Charlie

Chaplin said he studied Jiggs with profit, and what comic couldn't? It was heroically funny work; Jiggs, for instance, reminiscing to Maggie about her family: "Your grandpap . . . lived to be eighty and never used glasses. He drank out of the bottle. . . . Your uncle Bimmy lived in the kitchen so he wouldn't have to go so far to eat."

"I was just thinking," says Maggie, "how marvelous it is that all my relations are talented in the world of music."

"Yes," says Jiggs, "it is marvelous that you think so."

McManus probably heard such lines in the same way I did—uttered by Irishmen about Irishmen, self-criticism being a cherished Irish heritage second only to criticism of others.

There is grand hyperbole in the world of Jiggs, but it also cuts close to the real bone: realism in the funhouse, which is the foundation for so many of the major comic strips that were. To be sure, some were born in cuckooland: *Popeye* and *Li'l Abner* and the *Katzenjammer Kids*, and there were the improbable worlds of *Mandrake the Magician* and *Buck Rogers*.

But think of that realism: a world hostile to children in *Little Orphan Annie* and *Little Annie Rooney*; trendy adolescence at the soda fountain in *Harold Teen*; the boxing world in *Joe Palooka*; adventure in exotic Asia and Africa in *Terry and the Pirates* and *Tim Tyler's Luck*; and then the mainstay—the family—in *Mickey Finn* and *Moon Mullins* and *Gasoline Alley* and *Blondie* . . . and *Jiggs*.

The funnies taught us about all those sweet truths that would become the essence of Hollywood's happy-ending movies. There was no divorce in the funny sheets, and no death. Life was wacko and it went on forever. Jiggs went on until 1954, when George McManus died. McManus had kept up with life, evolving the strip to conform to changing times. When the rolling pin went out of style Maggie threw vases instead. I don't remember the demise of Jiggs as a strip. Maybe my attention wandered, or more likely it was because the funnies went minimal, editors double-shrinking them to save space, treating them like poor relations which, predictably with such treatment, most of them became. *Pogo*, a latter-day wonder, is gone. *Beetle Bailey* endures, and so does *B.C.* and the remarkable *Peanuts*; and now Gary Trudeau with *Doonesbury* and Berke Breathed with *Bloom County* and Bill Watterson with *Calvin and Hobbes* are keeping the art form respectably savage and original and funny.

But it's just not like it was and it probably won't be, either. We've climbed out of the saloon era, the soda-fountain era, and today Little Annie Rooney would have to be a hooker. The great comics of yore exist only as artifacts of an ebullient past. When you enter into that past in the book that follows you will, among other excursions, go on vacation across the country with Maggie and Jiggs. And when it's over you'll return to the old train station in the neighborhood where Jiggs began and you'll see the neighbors turning out to welcome the old gent.

"My he looks grand," says one neighbor. "He's not staggerin' a bit either."

Not a bit. He stands up to time.

Welcome back, Jiggs. And stick around. We got some on ice.

1986

The Photography of Stillness:
Muckraking the Spirit

"**O**ne reason I so deeply care for the camera is just this. . . . Handled cleanly and literally in its own terms, as an ice-cold, some ways limited, some ways more capable, eye, it is, like the phonograph record and like scientific instruments and unlike any other leverage of art, incapable of recording anything but absolute, dry truth."

This is James Agee, writing in *Let Us Now Praise Famous Men*, that extraordinary, inexhaustible book about Alabama tenant farmers. I came to the photographic work of Walker Evans for the first time when I discovered the book eleven years ago, and, together with Agee's moving words, it helped fire me up and turn me into a muckraker in the slums. I had seen Evans's work before in photo anthologies, which I used to devour, but only in bits and pieces. My brother-in-law was a photographer with a dozen such collections, and I would sit there thinking Wow! Fantastic! at confronting all that absolute, dry truth of life.

Recently, a friend who had abandoned photography in favor of writing had me almost convinced that its power to evoke the response it did when the camera was still young had seriously declined. I think he was a little bit right. I look at David Douglas Duncan's *Self-Portrait: U.S.A.* (Abrams), on the Miami Beach and Chicago conventions of 1968, and I know I'm supposed to react because I always reacted to such hand-somely mounted authenticity by an old master. But I don't. I've seen too many political delegates in funny hats. I know the shallowness of their knee-jerk loyalties. I understand convention rituals, for I've been there for years through television. The disappointed faces of youthful McCarthy supporters are sad antiques from the sixties. And so it's not entirely Duncan's fault that his book just lies there. Yet he's got to take some blame, for he didn't prevail over my saturation the way another recent book, Bruce Davidson's *East 100th Street* (Harvard), prevailed over my very personal saturation with the slum.

Davidson's book has been out a while and has expanded his reputation as a photographer of the first rank. In going through it, I was struck by the similarity of some of his photos to those of Jacob Riis, the daddy of all muckrakers, in the classic Riis work, *How the Other Half Lives*. That was published first in 1890 and has been republished periodically ever since. The newest version has also been published by Harvard and contains forty-six Riis photos. Unfortunately, Harvard printed them on inferior paper, kept them much too small and arranged them in a pinched and cluttered layout that has all the feeling of a Sears, Roebuck catalogue. Davidson's book is a triumph of simple design. It gives the photos their due, although overly dark printing of my copy obscured details I saw clearly in the same photos printed elsewhere. Harvard should shape up.

Recognizing Riis as an ancestor of Davidson, realizing Walker Evans was also part of the family, I went through Peter Pollack's monumental (708 pages, 742 photos) work, *The Picture History of Photography* (Abrams), published first in 1958, and vastly expanded for a 1969 edition that takes the state of the art up through Davidson. I found in it work by the Mathew Brady group, Eugene Atget, Lewis Hine, Harry Callahan and others, which also belonged to this special category that has moved me so much; and I began to see why it did. On top of this came two more new books: *Walker Evans* (Museum of Modern Art), a superb collection of Evans's work, much of it done in the 1930s but never before published, and here accompanied by John Szarkowski's fine introduction, which illuminates Evans's eccentric and aristocratic personality as well as his art; and *Face of an Island* (Grossman), a pictorial record of Negro slaves and their descendants in the early 1900s and 1920s on Saint Helena Island off South Carolina. The photos were taken by Leigh Richmond Miner, an unknown but highly accomplished photographer who worked contemporaneously with Atget and Hine. A botanist, art teacher and dabbler in many arts, Miner packed away his glass-plate negatives and ignored them. He died in 1935. A few years ago, the plates were rediscovered and now have been edited into a beautifully printed book that recreates a time in America most of us have never seen pictured anywhere.

The thing that brings all this work together for me is the absolute stillness of the best photos; not only the absence of action but the absence of overt or easy emotion within the picture itself. Evans could easily have indulged in pathos, but absolutely purged his work of anything resembling it. Riis never bothered with manipulating emotion because he was too busy tracking down yet another scene of horror and degradation. Miner is also free of it. Davidson isn't quite.

In relating to the rural poor, or slum people, we often conclude that they deserve our pity. What they deserve is our comprehension, which Evans unfailingly gives us: a man in his Sunday best, an ill-fitting, wrinkled coat, but in no way apologetic; looking, in fact, like an eccentric personnel manager who can't quite decide whether to hire you or not. And in a Miner picture, old Jesse Dorkins, about 1905, sits in the doorway of his rotting shack, dressed in tatters, hands on knees, woolly hair and beard in snarls, mouth slightly open, lower lip jutted. He is in the throes of no particular emotion we can recognize, but his condition cannot help but move a viewer to an emotional comprehension of the cancerous residue that slavery has left in his life.

It's difficult to convey this meaning without pictures to illustrate the point; but it may come clearer by comparing this stillness I'm talking about to the short stories of Isaac Babel or Hemingway, or to Jerzy Kosinski's *Steps*, works that evoke emotion because the artist has not tried to capture emotion itself but conveys successfully the facts from which emotion is made and leaves our imagination free. It is the difference between the photo of a man caught at the precise instant he is being made aware of a tragedy in his life, and the same man weeping after hearing the news. The first photo would help us understand a particular man. The second is everybody's soap opera.

There is another stillness, especially in Evans, a stillness of things: doorways, rooms without people, storefronts, suggesting not emotion but a phase or way of life. Davidson also has this, but he is less concerned with life purified than he is with irony: a GOD BLESS OUR HOME sign on the wall of a demolished house, Pope Paul's photo blessing filthy rubble. This is jazzy propaganda, but too easy for an artist. He also manipulates subjects unnecessarily, posing a lovely girl in a paper-strewn vacant lot: beauty amid barrenness, a forced comment.

These are only occasional complaints about Davidson. He has done something rare to see the slums in a new way at this late date. Also, his personality must convey total trustworthiness for people to reveal themselves to his camera as they do—naked, shooting up, dealing, buying, pimping, hustling, dying in squalor. Pollack says Davidson has a powerful influence on young people considering photography as a vocation, and I understand why. Like the great ancestors of his art, he has seen and understood, then caught those moments of stillness when people define themselves not by doing but by being. This moves us, for we recognize a vital part of ourselves in the center of that stillness; which means art has done something important.

1971

Marshall McLuhan's
Message Is . . . ?

(PHASE I—Let there be light.
Turn on the electronic age)

If the medium is the message, is Marshall McLuhan the medium?

If the medium is the massage, is Marshall McLuhan the masseur?

Question, question.

Communication:

Marshall McLuhan doesn't like pictures. He shouted at a cameraman in Albany a week ago. He communicated to (them) (those with power over cameramen), saying: "That man is here again with his infernal machine."

This followed a dictum: "That will be the last picture." (The message.)

But then the infernal machine returned, was banished.

Clash of media.

"The spoken word can't compete with these instruments for commanding attention," said McLuhan. "To try to talk to a snapshooting process is impossible."

Communication (Joke type) (McLuhan speaking in Italian dialect):

The captain of an Italian ocean liner turned on the public-address system to address passengers and crew.

"I got-a two pieces of-a news. One bad-a news, one good-a news. Ah'm a give you the bad-a news first. We are lost. Second. We're a half an hour early."

(Conclusion from the message: Marshall McLuhan doesn't trust his

364

facts to speak for themselves. He is as insecure as any after-dinner speaker.)

McLUHAN APHORISM (Hereinafter known as MLA). "A funny man is a man with a grievance. Politicians might pay attention to this as an index of public feeling."

MLA (2) "Real news is bad news. Good news is advertising. It takes a lot of bad news to sell the good news. Advertisers will eventually catch on and turn the good news into bad news."

MLA (3) "The only people who read ads are the people who already have the product. Advertisers tell us this through their research. They read the ad to find out if the product is doing what it is supposed to do."

(Transitional McLuhanism: prefatory to the message) (Hereinafter known as TMP): "We don't know who discovered water, but it wasn't a fish."

(Conclusion): "Nobody knows the business he's in. He knows the other fellow's."

(Listener's conclusion: this is the message to us all: if you're a fish, look at the water you're in.)

(PHASE II—The End of Nature)

"Nature ended with Sputnik and Telstar. Nature became art. The whole planet became a programmable entity."

(Message: don't look back.)

"New environments are lost on those looking in the rear-view mirror. . . . It is much safer to look back. You've been there and know what it's made of. . . . It's Bonanzaland. . . . It has nothing to do with the present world."

(PHASE III—Fact, Scientific)

"Touch doesn't create connections but intervals. Touch creates a gap which is filled in which creates rhythm."

(Observation on scientific fact:)

"Bucky Fuller [i.e., Buckminster Fuller, creator of the geodesic dome] is an ear man, not an eye man. He's tribal. . . . We're retribalizing."

TRANSLATION
(From *Saturday Review*)
(By Robert Lewis Shayon)

One of McLuhan's basic propositions is that we are crossing a technological frontier dividing the age of the collectivist from that of the
individualist: We are being retribalized. The all-at-onceness of the
"field approach" to problems is rapidly replacing the fixed, visual
approach of applied or "resolute" knowledge.

The Title of this piece: Clarity Is a Four-Letter Word (plus
three)- - - - -)

WE PAUSE HERE FOR TELEVISION IDENTIFICATION:

MLA (4) "Television is not pictures. It's X-ray. It's involvement in
depth. . . . It can encompass millions of years of human development
in a few seconds."

Addenda (The addenda will take the form of words): The effect of the
television age, McLuhan more or less said, is not a biological thing;
rather it belongs to our nervous system.

(PHASE IV—Self-Revelation)

"I never have a point of view in anything I say. Keep moving. A point
of view means staying in one place. That sort of thing came in with the
printed word and the telegraph. Newspapers have no point of view. They
have to add one on the editorial page."

(Equal time is herewith offered to the American Society of Newspaper
Editors and the Objectivity Clubs of North America. Rebuttal must be
relayed, voice-over, through your local television channel.)

Question: WHAT IS CULTURAL CONFUSION?

(Joke) (The message): "The teacher asked the students what they
thought the world would be like without Thomas Edison. One student
answered: 'If it weren't for Edison we'd all be watching television by
candlelight.' "

STATEMENT FROM THE AUDIENCE (1): Marshall McLuhan is not
confused.

COMMENT FROM THE GALLERY: "What a crowd, eh?" "It proves
that all you got to do is make yourself unintelligible."

SELF-REVELATION (concluded)

"I never have a point of view. I never make a value judgment. I never try to win arguments. If you say to me 'I couldn't disagree with you more,' I bypass you. I could waste a lot of time trying to convert you and people are never converted by arguments. People who live by argument are fragmented."

(A CRY FROM BELOW): "But if we have no sense of direction, then we are living in a world of anarchy."

McLUHAN: "Yes. Exactly."

VOICE: "Huh?"

McLUHAN: "Most people would rather muck along with anarchy than confront the need for order. I don't say I know how this can be done."

(PHASE V—Art)

TMP (2) "Expo '67 was a success because it had no story line."

Message: "Artists of the twentieth century are trying to explain why they have pulled the story line out of action. We can no longer use connected space [i.e. connected narrative, i.e. the well-made novel, i.e. the neat movie, i.e. the neat newspaper story] in printing, or in point of view. We can only use a mosaic. The New York World's Fair was a flop because it had a story line."

Conclusion: What he means is that we must have gaps in things.

Question: "Who fills in the gaps? The viewers."

Elaboration on the role of the artist: "The future of the future is the present. It always was and it is now. The only person with enough sense to look at the present is the artist, and when he presents his findings he's branded as a kook or a nut. What is ahead is already here."

(PHASE VI—Medicine)

TMP (3) "When Pasteur said he discovered bacilli which were invisible, he was thrown out of the medical profession as a charlatan."

Message: In the electronic age, forces are invisible. "And yet we try to arrange these things visually. Astronauts when they leave the earth take their environment with them. (WHICH PROVES): Environments are more potent than anything they contain. The medical profession pays no attention [to environment] as a cause of disease or disorder. They regard the body as a container. This is enough to create sickness on a very large scale."

(PHASE VII—Sex)

"The miniskirt is abstract art, like Giacometti. It is not as erotic as old visual garments were. They were very involving. But the old idea of eroticism was not involving, but specialist. Hot. Twiggy is not hot, but real cool."

(ARBITRARY CUT-OFF POINT):

"I am not here to propose models for solution, but means of awareness."

Click.

Fadeout.

Go to black.

1967

Postscript: This oddity, homage to McLuhan's hit-and-run inscrutability, grew out of his visit to Albany on October 3, 1967. I covered his speech, in which he revealed to the audience for the first time what I decided to title (since he hadn't) the "Theory of the Tactility of the Russian Peasant," which was his sudden but prophetic perception on the train to Albany that masses of people the world over, and especially in America, would soon become ungovernable in ways comparable to the Russian peasant masses that spent six months of the year in bed ("because they liked it," said McLuhan). His conclusion for America: "We are headed for tactile living that we are not prepared for."

Diane Sawyer:
The Subject Is Beauty*

My friend McGarr says Diane Sawyer is the most beautiful woman in the world. McGarr is rarely wrong on these issues. I would say she is, without doubt, the most beautiful blond woman of my era. This remark is retroactive and considers the temporary supremacies of Grace Kelly, who was exquisite, and Catherine Deneuve, who remains so today. Diane matches them but generates more heat, more light: ancillaries to empyrean beauty.

Being beautiful is useful, but by itself it will not make you the queen of all journalism and other psychic realms. Tick off all the beautiful women in your life who settled for being ornamental. Think of those burdened with stupidity. I knew a beautiful child who evolved into a gorgeous adolescent and at thirty was a hag.

We are all responsible for our faces, which makes Diane an exceedingly responsible citizen. At forty-one she embodies the truth that beauty of the first order is nuclear: that it arrives with the embryo, but also that it must be nurtured, or else it decomposes. We mustn't overvalue beauty. We know that. However, we usually do. Great beauties are so rare that we make goddesses of them and then behave like foolish mortals.

Beauty of Diane's kind creates the illusion of perfection. Even in

* This story was written for *Esquire* magazine's ongoing series, "Women We Love." I admired Diane's early sojourn on the CBS morning show, but admired her even more when, as her first reporting assignment for *60 Minutes*, she came to Albany in 1984 to do a profile on me. My billiard room had not yet been built, so I am still in the dark about her pool game.

interviews with her she emerges as flawless. She argues charmingly against this, citing her contact lenses, denigrating her hair as thin and mousy. But the contacts are neutral objects, and she is wrong about her hair, which is also perfect.

I have yet to find any women who fault her or begrudge her anything. They like her style and intelligence, and they say she is what a woman should be. Men also say this. I am one of those fond of saying this.

Naturally she cannot be perfect. Let's face it: there are many things we do not yet know about her. How is her pool game? Her soufflé? Can she carry a tune? Our knowledge of these things will come in time. Meanwhile, we accept her perfection and admit our love.

1987

"Tropicality" Defined

We were talking about being in the tropics, the essence of the tropics, tropicality and so on. We dispensed with the jungle and got down to the sun, the sea, skin, a tumbler of rum and ice, and the beach.

Peter Reed of St. Croix happened along and heard us utter the word "beach." "I hate the beach," he said. "I spend a lot of money buying up beaches and selling them for the sand in concrete."

This did not seem to reflect the tropicality we were searching for, but it made a point: that the beach has more than one function in the tropics. (When we say "tropics" we mean subtropics. Nobody in our set ever goes to the beach in the real tropics unless they are an alligator.)

The beach, for instance, looms large in the memory of Bill Katz, the Albany, New York, curmudgeon you might have seen buzzing around Mexico in the mid-1960s. Bill doesn't remember which town he buzzed, except that "it was small, off the beaten track, had a Catholic church, one hotel, a lot of flowers and a café. Men were walking around with guns, and Indians with bows and arrows came out of the jungle to play bingo. The church, of course, ran the bingo game."

Bill checked out the beach, which looked beautiful. But as he looked at it he knew he would worry about sharks if he swam; and furthermore the hotel clerk had warned that the water this day was thick with jellyfish. So Bill went back to the hotel bar and drank rum and had a wonderful afternoon just thinking about the beach.

Our own time with jellyfish came off the island of Icacos, not far from Fajardo, Puerto Rico. When we dove from the boat the water was brimming with baby jellyfish: abundant, benign, almost invisible. It was like swimming along with cellophane noodles. Yet we are here to report that inhaling baby jellies is not harmful to your health if you do it in moderation.

We recall trying to be tropical on a beach at Acapulco, testing out the Dos Equis on somebody's veranda, trying to stay out of the sun (for when we had hair we were red-haired) but being steadily foiled by passing vendors who wanted to sell us sunglasses, or coconut meat, or a watch; and finally we took our quest elsewhere.

We are often deceived in this quest by what seems like genuine tropicality but which turns out to have originated in 1942 in Warner Brothers' wardrobe department: that white suit, for instance, that Sidney Greenstreet used to wear whenever he sat beneath his three-bladed fan. We bought a white suit to wear last July in Puerto Rico, but San Juan was so hot that very few people were wearing any clothing at all. And Panama straw hats. Do you really think people in Panama wear hats? Do you know what a sweat band can do to your forehead when the temperature hits 103?

Tropicality turns out to be a concatenation of values revealed to us only by prolonged synthesis. After considerable deliberation, for instance, we have eliminated sand as an essential element of tropicality. Sand is not necessary. Sun is usually thought to be essential, but dusk is just as good. Dusk is so good that we wrote a poem about it years ago in Puerto Rico. Here is our poem.

> Dusk is a musk
> For intellectuals like usk.
> Most people don't give
> A particular fusk.

Poetry is not necessary for tropicality, but water seems to be. We have been debating whether watching the moon over Crooked Lake in upstate New York has any usable elements of tropicality and decided no. Too far north. Tropicality needs the tropics if it has any aspirations to authenticity.

It truly needs the sea. Sheila Smith of New York City grew up by the sea and concludes that the sea air, the smell of salt on your body when you come out of the water, is all very sensual; and sensuality is certainly an ingredient of tropicality. We sometimes envision ourselves being sensual by sitting under a palm, appreciating the water a few feet away that may or may not lick at our toes. But for Laurie Bank Berry, who was raised in Mexico, such contemplation isn't enough. "I don't just look at it," she said, "I swim in it."

Supremely correct, of course. For some people. Without offering contradiction, let me suggest that wetting oneself (and we are extremely fond of wetness) is not an indispensable ingredient of basic tropicality. We have hundreds of images relevant to our time in the tropics: sweat, for instance (another form of wetness), and sunburn, and rust, and mildew, and sand fleas, and the expensive watch our wife, Dana, left on the dashboard, and which melted. None are necessary.

Skin may be necessary but it can be elusive. We discussed this with Larry Ries of Saratoga Springs, New York, who, with his wife, Madeleine, had just returned from Sarasota, Florida. Larry, a noted skin observer, almost had the opportunity for expansive observation during a visit to Sarasota's Lido Beach, which is a nude beach, or was until the week before Larry got there. Four women covered only with skin had been arrested by police and a sign posted: "Appropriate Dress Required." And so, by the time Larry arrived, women on the beach were merely topless. So there you are.

Corlies (Cork) Smith, a New York book editor, came closest to defining the essence of tropicality when we raised the question with him. "Everything slows down," he said.

Bingo. Here come the Indians.

This is the secret formula. This is why people get sand in their shoes, though we haven't heard of it happening lately in just those terms; and it is also why, and how, beach bums are born.

What occurs when the essential mix is present is a calming of the spirit, an absence of distraction, an opening into the freedom merely to be. If we were to draw a picture of the elements of our own tropicality there would be a chair, an umbrella for shade, rum, limes, ice and nothing to do, no place to go in order to be. We can be right here. This is the place to be.

We would be staring out at the rolling and breaking surf, looking up at that coconut palm out of the corner of our eye, careful that our ankles aren't getting sunburned, sipping the rum, talking to the listener across the table, and considering how the past has yet again come full cycle and moved with incredible speed into this unsuspectedly vital present. The sea would break on, the sun would secede, the rum: well, it would be important to deal in moderation with the rum or else miss dinner entirely.

Tropicality is the condition that pervades the place you didn't know existed until five minutes ago. Once perceived it must not be abandoned, for it has brought you very close to certain ultimate truths. But then, alas, you begin to understand that you can't catch it by the throat and take it home; that you must let it go. And so you immediately start scheming how to come back next month, or next year, and reconstitute it.

Return is possible, of course, but not easy. Conditions must be right. Above all: on the return trip do not forget the limes.

1985

Rudolph Valentino:
He's No Bogart

Clarence Brown, a noted director of silent films, wrote to film historian Kevin Brownlow in 1966: "I have had the opportunity and the pleasure and the good luck to direct the two people I consider were the greatest personalities of the screen—Rudolph Valentino and Greta Garbo. You'll be hearing about Valentino, who's been dead for forty years, and you'll be hearing about Garbo from now on as you have in the past. See how many of the other stars are remembered in ten years. Garbo and Valentino are the two who are going down through posterity."

His full name, says one biographer, was Rudolpho Alfonzo Raffaele Pierre Filibert Guglielmi de Valentina d'Antonguolla. He was Italian, a 1913 immigrant. He became famous in 1921 in *The Four Horsemen of the Apocalpyse* and he died in August 1926, after surgery, at the age of thirty-one, having made a series of immensely successful costume pictures—*Monsieur Beaucaire*, *Camille*, *A Sainted Devil*, *Eugenie Grandet*, *The Conquering Power*, and three that were shown a week ago at the Saratoga Performing Arts Center film festival: *The Eagle*, directed by Clarence Brown, and costarring Vilma Banky and Louise Dresser; *Son of the Sheik*, his last film, also with Miss Banky; and *Blood and Sand*, with Lila Lee and Nita Naldi.

In one scene in *Blood and Sand* (remade in later years with Tyrone Power and Rita Hayworth), a woman spectator at the bullfight is so overcome by the sensual appeal of Valentino the torero that she rips off the top of her dress and throws it to him.

"Many life-hungry women," wrote Jim Tully in *Vanity Fair* in 1926,

375

"have literally been turned out of theaters in which Valentino appeared on the screen."

No women behaved life-hungrily enough to be turned out of the Saratoga theater last week, but when Valentino stroked Vilma Banky's neck in *The Eagle*, there was a slight but audible chorus of sighs. And in *Blood and Sand*, in which he romances his true love, Lila Lee, and his profane love, that campy vamp Nita Naldi, he exuded, according to at least one female patron who was willing to be interviewed, the aura of James Dean, also Vittorio Gassman, also Tyrone Power ("but better").

"The one person he doesn't look like," said the woman, "is Rudolph Valentino."

Since this had been her first Valentino film, her comment was a tribute to the old boy's ability to transcend his own myth and image. She, like most people who came to age after the silent film era had passed, knew only the Valentino legend, the man whose death caused unbounded female grief in the land, the man whose movies usually carried an undressing scene (in *Blood and Sand* he bares a shoulder, an arm, and two sockless ankles and shins) for the female audience. The legend was based on those few often-seen photos of Valentino that show his slick, glossy black hair, his sideburns, his unsmiling full mouth, his dark eyes. The era of Latin Lovers was perennially referred to in the press, and Sunday supplements often trudged the old photos out of their files. But of them all—John Gilbert, Ramon Novarro, Antonio Moreno, and others—the greatest, it was always said, was Valentino.

A statue in Beverly Hills commemorates eight major figures of silent films: Mary Pickford, Harold Lloyd, Conrad Nagel, director Fred Niblo (who did *Blood and Sand*, but, more important, *Ben Hur*, the lead role of which Valentino declined, saying "Where can I go after *Ben Hur*? I have no place to go but down"), Tom Mix, Will Rogers, Douglas Fairbanks, Sr., and Valentino.

Valentino was an acknowledged hero to Hollywood, legendary while still alive, an economic glory to the industry. When he died, an era died. When sound tracks killed the silents, they also killed most of those lovely lovers with unmanly voices.

The era of Clark Gable arrived, and in December 1931 Gable was cocky enough to comment (as quoted by Walter Winchell): "I modestly anticipate a Valentino future." O. O. McIntyre also noted that year:

"Those horrible Valentino sideburns are in again," attesting to an effort, at least in certain quarters, to revive some portion of that romantic image. (It remained for the hippie culture to really revive sideburns.)

But revival was impossible. The era of the Valentino style was as dead as its central figure. The closest thing to Valentino in the subsequent years was Robert Taylor (who starred with Garbo in a remake of *Camille*). He was equally handsome, but the women had already seen Gable in his undershirt, saw him spank unruly women, and a new romantic style was born. Tyrone Power (who did *The Mark of Zorro*, a remake of a silent Fairbanks film of the same name, and similar in plot to *The Eagle* with its masked hero posing as a foppish dandy) was another Valentino offshoot—the intense and pretty swashbuckler.

We passed from Gable's supremacy (over Taylor, Power, and other challengers) and into the time of Bogart, who brought the potentiality for meaningful fantasy to the average man. Bogie wasn't a pretty boy. He wasn't even handsome like Gable. He wasn't a stripper, not even an undershirt man. He was just tough. Also, he was hip. And hipness was suddenly a romantic quality.

The male audience could also get carried away by Bogie in a way that wasn't possible with Valentino, who was a bit too dainty. Valentino played a tough sheik, a fearless torero, a masked outlaw. But he didn't seem authentic. When Bogart punched a gossip columnist in a nightclub, off-screen, it wasn't a publicity stunt. It was an extension of the personality we'd seen him manifest on the screen. Valentino got his publicity by press agentry, by having a canary and black bedroom, by naming his hilltop hacienda Falcon's Lair, and so on.

What Valentino did have, and this is what impressed that first-time woman viewer, was a real talent for silent film acting. The women doted, to be sure, on that brooding look that said he was an obviously exciting lover. But he was also capable of facial expressions that reflected what the film's moment called for—innocence, stupidity, guilt, semi-debauchery, stunned incredulousness, a mind full of high jinks, foppish fear, willful vengeance, and much more.

Very likely it was this talent that gave his handsome face its notorious fame; for dozens of other handsome faces flashed once, then disappeared. Gable also had this talent-plus-looks, probably in equivalent degree. Bogart didn't have much in the way of traditional good looks, but his face went with his toughness, and he had more talent than Gable and Valentino put together.

However they differed, the element they all had in common was the star "personality." Albert Camus wrote that "to have a personality of your own is an idea which is peculiar to a certain form of civilization. Other people may find it the worst of misfortunes."

In the bygone era of the stars, having such a personality was essential. You reasserted it, as Valentino did in each film, and you packed the movie houses forever. People knew you, loved you.

It may seem unfair to give the last word of a Valentino essay over to Bogart, but Bogie, because of his intelligence, would seem a far better candidate for "going down through posterity" (as Clarence Brown predicted) than Valentino or Gable. The point is not whether we're talking of silent films, or even good films. The point is what you do with your personality.

We can be curious about Valentino if we've never seen him, and maybe we'll go back for more. But it will very probably be mere curiosity, soon sated. Fun. With Bogart, it's not just the fun of films, or absorbing the work of a film star. It's not even the study of such a sociological phenomenon as Valentino was. The issue is, much more interestingly, an awareness of life, and our enduring attraction to people who have that awareness to an extraordinary degree. It pervades Bogart's personality, but not Valentino's. Valentino knew what made women sigh, but Bogart knew what made them tick.

1969

Cassius Clay
Arrives

At five minutes to ten there was plenty of 5–1 and 6–1 in the lobby of the Palace Theater. There were a few takers, such as the man who liked the odds, and the fact that Joe Louis hasn't picked a winner in eight fights.

The sentiments were overwhelmingly the same: this Clay can't fight. Liston catches him and it's all over.

The Theater Network Television image of ringside at Miami Beach flashed onto the Palace screen, showing the jammed ringside.

"Imagine paying $250 to see this thing?" a man said.

Cassius was doing a cha-cha-cha in his corner, and on the screen announcer Steve Ellis was chatting with Joe Louis, dapper with his mustache, bow tie and gray hair. The great champs were introduced at ringside: Rocky Marciano, Sugar Ray and contender Eddie Machen. Then came the challenger: Cassius. The first sound was a boo and then mild applause in the Palace.

The camera closed in on the champion, the glowering mask, the sullen jowls of Sonny Liston, looking unblinkingly at the challenger.

"He won't have to hit Cassius. He'll scare him to death."

But then the fight began and the crowd that expected a quick knockout watched Clay pedal back away from the champion, who pushed forward, shuffling like an old Joe Louis, but awkward, full of power but missing with a wild left and a dozen jabs. The marvel was Cassius's head. Sonny couldn't hit it.

"Come on Cassius," was the cry. "Stay away from him. Don't get him, mister. Keep running, Clay." Clay pushed his glove in Sonny's face, danced and bobbed.

"How do you like this Clay?"

Applause went up at the challenger's performance and it was clear even then that fight fans had a new favorite. "Twenty-two and he's still got a long way to go, if he don't get killed."

The second was a quiet round. Mike Ferrandino and Tim Sullivan in the Palace balcony were enthused, vocalized their enthusiasm.

"Keep moving . . . coast . . . keep coasting . . . don't close your eyes."

It was a slow round but: "Well, he goes two full ones anyway."

Came another voice: "I got my five dollars' worth. I seen two rounds."

In the third round Sonny was on the ropes and the sentiment you could hear was "Come on Clay . . . look, Clay's got Liston so mad he don't know what he's doing . . . uh oh, Clay's slowing down . . . yeah, this is it . . . Clay's groggy . . . he's got him now . . . he's hurt somewheres . . . he ain't even trying to get away."

Post-round analysis was that Clay had been hit in the gut, the solar plexus, under the heart, someplace where it counted.

Steve Ellis announced in the fourth that Sonny had a puff below his right eye. Cassius's newfound friends warned him: "Keep that glove in his kisser . . . you might make five rounds if you stay away from them corners."

In the rest period before the fifth, Clay proved again his talent for making faces and Joe Louis commented: "I think Clay surprised the whole world." Then came the news from Steve Ellis that Clay was blinking, had something in his right eye. Everybody knew what that meant: "This is the buildup for the next fight . . . he's got his alibi all ready . . . this is it . . . this is the round . . . he ain't tryin' to throw a punch . . . what is it? . . . neither one is doing anything . . . now what the hell is going on? . . . the fix is in."

Joe Louis explained in the rest period it could have been Vaseline in Cassius's eye. The fans believed it was a rematch.

In the sixth: "It's gravy from here. I got six to five it wouldn't go this far." But then Cassius came out dancing and he was a hero again: "He's got some heart . . . you gotta have heart . . . he's a cocky kid, that's what he is."

The round was slow to start, with Clay jabbing and Liston especially slow-moving. It ended slow, with jabs and feints, and then with a closeup of Liston in his corner: "The ugly bear is cut." The camera focused on the left side of his face, where a welt had risen. And then suddenly Cassius was in the middle of the ring, dancing, his arms in the air. And then the referee raised his arm in victory.

And then: "Oh my God."

Cassius was rarely off camera then, speaking, screaming, throwing kisses, and when the microphone wasn't near, just mugging crazily to fortify his image as the sprout who makes faces at the world.

Cassius explained his victory: "I'm the greatest. . . . I don't have a mark on me. . . . I'm only twenty-two years old. . . . I must be the greatest. . . . You must listen to me. . . . I'm the greatest. . . . I whupped him. . . . He couldn't touch me. . . . I'm one of the prettiest things that ever lived."

And then, of course, he recited his poetry:

> "I was gonna take him in eight,
> As you can see.
> But he wanted to go to heaven,
> So I took him in seven."

Joe Louis on camera called the fight the "biggest upset in boxing history." It was all of that. It reversed the field of opinion of the world in twenty minutes.

"Boy," said Bucky Greenwood. "He's the greatest."

"Cassius is faster than Liston," said Arnold Harris. "I like him as a champ. He fought. He fought."

Said Danny Andrews, five-time Golden Gloves featherweight champion locally: "Liston was a great champ, but he never talked to interest people and pull people on his side."

Said fourteen-year old Hubert Ballou:

> "Liston, the bum,
> Is done."

1964

Ballet:

Everybody Loves
a Fat Girl,
Right?

"Want to dance with the ballet?" the headline read.

Does a kid ballplayer want to play with the Yankees? Do actress hopefuls want a screen test? Does anybody want to hit the lottery?

News stories heralding the tryouts for the children's parts in the New York City Ballet's upstate premiere performances of *The Nutcracker* on July 4 to 7, indicated forty-one children would be used in the performances. But when Una Kai, the blonde ballet mistress of the company, looked out at the 173 very young ladies in anxious waiting, she shortened their odds considerably: "There are only twenty-five parts, so a lot of you are going to . . . I'm sorry . . . But . . ."

The tall, erstwhile ballerina, wearing street clothing, a blue dress of miniskirt length, semi-high heels and gold jewelry stood in the middle of the rehearsal hall at the Saratoga Performing Arts Center. The 173 children lined three walls, two deep, looking generally professional in leotards, tights, ballet slippers (a few in toe shoes) and in varying color combinations of black, white, pink, blue, and one young lady in purple.

The call was for 3:00 P.M. but at 3:25 it was bedlam in the hall with a long line of girls still not registered. But the line dwindled at last and the ballet mistress shushed the noise and put the gawking parents and dance teachers out of the room. Then she broke the children into age groups, eight to nine, nine to ten, ten to eleven, twelve and older.

She confronted the oldest group and asked for those with only a year or so training, or less, to raise their hand. The children eyed her like army recruits looking with suspicious eyes on a corporal asking for volunteers. Nobody raised a hand.

"I really only need advanced dancers out of this group," she added, and a few finally confessed to being beginners and were weeded out. The older group was sent outside to wait. Young ballerinas bite their nails when they are apprehensive, just like ordinary little girls.

"Now," said Miss Kai, "all you eight-to-nine people . . . make a straight line . . . shhhhh . . . Now we're going to salute. . . . Feet together . . . 1-2-3-4-5-6-7-8 . . . Salute on 7-8. . . . Stand at attention. . . . That doesn't look like attention. . . . Be a soldier. . . . 1-2-3-4-5-6-7-8 . . . Put your hand down when I come back to the count of one. . . ."

The eight-to-nine people saluted with something less than precision. No Rockettes they. Miss Kai eyed them and went to the far end, where the smallest of the small people stood. She drew out four. Those not picked looked straight ahead, wondering what it meant. After all, this couldn't be the end. Nobody even danced yet.

Miss Kai lined up the nine-to-ten people, and repeated the process, picked eight, then the ten-to-eleven people. She had two dozen lined up, and sized them by height. And it was obvious now who were the chosen few. It was obvious (Wasn't it?) (No, probably not) that the choice was being made on the size of the girls, not on their balletic talent.

Then she had the group sized completely, eighteen girls only out of perhaps 125. The eyes of all followed her every motion. She moved back to the front of the hall and talked to them all again.

"There's no dancing involved in these parts," she said. "It's really by size and shape that I've chosen. Don't feel too badly."

Lips quivered, small faces registered large shock. The filing out en masse was the evacuation of a disaster area. Miss Kai explained privately her method of selection: "I just chose by size and shape. I couldn't take any fat ones. I chose all the skinnies."

Her purpose was to tailor the children to the elaborate and fanciful costumes already made—the toy soldiers, the angels. The advance publicity was explicit: nobody more than four feet ten inches would be chosen. But it didn't say anything about poundage.

The older group was called back from the hallway and broken into several groups of ten. From about fifty, seven would be chosen for dancing roles that called for the use of hoops. Miss Kai started the eliminations by having each group twice do grands jetés across the floor. Quickly she eliminated the fat girls, pointed them to the corner. Then she narrowed the field to about twenty and told the rest: "We can't use you. Thank you for coming." A child who tried mightily to influence the ballet mistress by always being in the foreground, always looking into the mistress's eyes when she danced, doing not what came naturally but very likely what Mama told her would work, was eliminated.

"You can't use me?" she asked.

"No, we can't use you," Miss Kai said.

That child's problem was that she was just not very good, not in the same league with the seven accomplished young people finally chosen, one of them a boy who travels to New York City each week for his dance classes. These seven, said Miss Kai, were also chosen for their slenderness, but technique, ability were important.

When the selections were complete and all but the twenty-five chosen ones were dismissed, it was time for insistent mothers. "They told my daughter to wait, but she never danced." . . . Mistake, sorry. "My daughter is a little confused. She said she was picked and then not picked." . . . No, not.

And the losers: "I don't think it was fair. I didn't get a chance to dance. . . . See that girl over there in the blue dress? She's crying. . . . My sister made it. . . . See the girl in pink? She made it. . . . The ballet lady told the bigger girls that she rejected them because they were too fat. I don't think that was very nice."

Everybody loves a fat girl, right?

Wrong.

1968

Roberta Sue Ficker
Is Going to Become
Suzanne Farrell

"A lot of it is taste," said Suzanne Farrell.

A lot of what is taste? Well, liking Suzanne Farrell, for instance. That doesn't put you in a minority, but there is an element that thinks she is still young, not mature enough to lead a ballet company yet, said one eminence of the critical world. That could be. Also it couldn't. Take George Balanchine, for instance, who creates ballets for her, who gives her the plums such as the lead in his revised version of "Slaughter on Tenth Avenue." Take him.

"Mr. B. does like me," said Suzanne, "and not some other ballerinas. And he's been criticized for that."

Being ill-equipped indeed to decide whether or not Suzanne Farrell should, or should not, lead a ballet company such as the New York City Ballet, of which she has been a part since 1961, let us begin by affirming the future: that if she isn't ready now, she will be. The affirmation stems more from faith than from reason, faith in a particular kind of talent that shows itself, even to an outsider's eye, to be a singular thing.

Watching her perform was like rereading *Young Man with a Horn*, the Dorothy Baker novel in which the young Bix Beiderbecke–like hero plays cornet like no one else on the scene, a boy coming from nowhere into the full-blown world of jazz and establishing his authority with a flourish. The same theme was repeated with less subtlety in *The Hustler*, pool-playing wunderkind fresh in from the street whipping Minnesota Fats, the great one.

It is the quality of being recognizably extraordinary.

It was recognizable throughout July when the New York City ballet performed at Saratoga Performing Arts Center, and it was indeed recognized by this noncritic of the dance on the night that Suzanne Farrell, twenty-two, born Roberta Sue Ficker of Cincinnati, a roller-skating, tree-climbing tomboy until Kismet and other talent scouts directed her toward a career in ballet, was performing on stage at Saratoga, first in "Barocco" and then in "Slaughter."

She finished the classically elegant "Barocco," with music by Bach and movement by Balanchine, and then she was, all of a sudden, that doomed stripper in the skit within the play, the "Slaughter" sequence from "On Your Toes," with music by Rodgers and Hart and movement by Balanchine. But this movement was also by Farrell. There was Roberta Sue showing Gypsy Rose and Sally, and all the rest of them who were alive and kicking on the runways of 1936, what they should have looked like but no doubt didn't when they did their stuff. Bump bump. Kiss and toss a flower. Grind grind. Twirl a pretty garter.

Could this be the same girl whose performance of a Stravinsky-Balanchine ballet was described as "a living piece of kinetic sculpture"? Was this the girl with "every physical gift, from the pure, beautiful Botticelli face to the long, strong and pliant body whose turnout already has an air of authority"? Was this "the seraphic Farrell"?

One and the same.

" 'Slaughter'? It's fun," she said. "It's easy because it's just a pleasure. It's fun because I get to be a nasty girl, which believe it or not is a diversion for me."

But that stripper routine. The authority she brought to it.

"I've never been," she said, smiling demurely, meaning not, of course, that she had never been a stripper, but meaning that she had never even seen a stripper in the native habitat of strippers. And so the logical assumption is that Roberta Sue had been choreographed to a fare-thee-well by Mr. Balanchine. But no.

"He didn't tell me precisely how to do it," she said. "Most of that is my own personality."

She relishes this label of versatility.

"People say Suzanne Farrell is a lyrical dancer. That's nice but I don't want to do only 'Swan Lake.' I don't want to be typed. I love doing 'Barocco' first and then 'Slaughter' because I'm saying: 'See, audience, you thought I could only do that. I can do this too.' "

Has success spoiled Roberta Sue then?

"Maybe I am spoiled, like my mother says. She says I was spoiled as a child, but I don't think I'm spoiled. I had a certain amount of luck, but I worked hard."

Her mother took her off the street, down from that tree when she was eight and sent her to ballet class in the hometown. The teacher recognized the talent, the gifted talent, and wrote Balanchine's School of American Ballet suggesting an audition for Roberta Sue. Diana Adams, the ballerina, came to Cincinnati and agreed that this girl, then fourteen, should go to New York for an audition. She auditioned—"For Mr. B."—on her fifteenth birthday, won a scholarship from the Ford Foundation to study at the Balanchine school, and in November 1961 joined the company of the New York City Ballet.

The talent—how did it emerge, and why?

"I was rather normal," Miss Farrell said, sitting in a backstage room at the Saratoga theater and exuding longitude of hair, face, finger and limb, but not much latitude—five foot seven, she weighs only 108 pounds. "I wasn't sold on ballet in the beginning. I wasn't crazy about it, didn't want to be a ballerina. When we would start working on the recitals I was always the boy. Always the prince, never the princess, because I was always the tallest. I wondered, 'This is what ballet is all about? A career of lifting other girls?'"

But ah, wait. Then Roberta Sue got her first tutu, and performed for the first time on a legitimate stage.

"I looked out, and the music and the auditorium and the audience hit me, and I said 'This is what I want to be.'"

She worked, read books on ballet, formed the New York City Ballet Junior with her friends, which consisted of slumber parties at which girls talked about ballet and saw "who could jump higher, whose leg could go higher, who could do more pirouettes."

"I never saw the New York City Ballet," she said, "until 1959 when I played hooky and went to Bloomington to see it."

She was thirteen then and remembers no particular dancer, only that all the people on stage, "even in the corps," danced. "If I were to stay in the corps all my life," she said, "I knew I'd get to dance, not be just a tree."

So when she did get into the New York City Ballet as a member of

the corps she stayed in it only ten months, a short-timer, and then got
her first solo.

"Mr. B. cast me in the part but left town and didn't see me. It was
in 'Serenade' and everybody said I was very good. Even the other ballerina said I was very good, but I couldn't go up and say 'George,
everybody says I was very good.' "

But no doubt someone did, for Balanchine cast her next in "Barocco."
And after that the ballet mistress of the company came and said, "Mr.
Balanchine wants you to learn Titania in 'Midsummer Night's Dream.' "
And Miss Suzanne Farrell (a name out of the phone book) said: "T-t-t-
who?" and thought the ballet mistress was kidding. But she wasn't. And
after Titania came two ballets, "Meditation," and "Movement for Piano
and Orchestra."

"Mr. B. choreographed them for me," said Miss Farrell, "and I
thought: 'I guess he likes me.' " That was in 1963 and since then it has
been as much stardom as a ballerina can get in a company full of such
illustrious performers as Melissa Hayden and Jacques d'Amboise and
Edward Villella and Patricia McBride and Marnee Morris.

The preference Balanchine shows for Miss Farrell is not solely professional. "The last two weeks in June," she said, "Mr. B. and I went to
Europe for a gastronomic tour—strictly for the food in Paris. He needed
the rest and we love French food." The trip dropped her out of her daily
routine and so when she opened in the first few performances of the
Saratoga season she felt inept.

"My first couple of 'Nutcrackers' and my first 'Barocco' were pretty
bad," she said. "It may not have looked so bad to some but it did to
me. 'Farrell,' I said, 'how did you ever get where you are?' "

The question was such a good one that we asked for an answer. And
her explanation of what is really inexplicable is this: that it is a combination of luck, work, God-given talent. "And you also have to have a
brain. Not an IQ brain, but brain in the common sense."

And it involved perseverance: "If I was going to do something I was
going to do it well. If I'm not good at a thing I won't do it."

It involved single-mindedness of purpose: "I was going to school in
New York and, when it became obvious to me that ballet was going to
be my career, I said, 'Forget the diploma and go to ballet. You can go
to school later.' "

Also it involved George Balanchine.

"All I could think of," said Miss Farrell, "was how desperately I wanted to please Mr. Balanchine. Sometimes he wouldn't even look at me, and I'd think, 'He doesn't like me anymore.' But I understand what he wants, and what he means when he says something. Other kids in class hear what he says and don't understand, or can't do what he says, or don't want to. I can. And I want to."

And the future? That is as mystical as the past, centering evermore on Mr. B.

"I want to stay as long as I can in this company with Mr. B.," she said. "He's the greatest. If I can't be with him I don't think I want to be a dancer. I don't think. But if I did, I would continue to do Balanchine ballets, promote Balanchinism. If he isn't around there wouldn't be a certain amount of magic in the air."

1968

The Cotton Club Stomp

The Cotton Club, the movie: could it (could any movie) really be worth $47 million? Could it have escalated to that from a mere $25 million during the year I worked on it? Will it be the comeback film for Francis Coppola? (Yes.) What's a novelist like me doing in this movie, or in the movies at all? Doesn't Hollywood poach novelists for lunch at the Polo Lounge? Shouldn't I have stayed home in Albany, unpoached, unpoachable? Think of Scott Fitzgerald, who didn't stay home. Think of Nathanael West, who squandered his too brief days writing clunkers. Think of James Agee, who *died* of movies (and gin and cigarettes). Think of it.

David Thomson, a critic and fiction writer in San Francisco, thought about it and asked me why I was bothering to write movies. I said I was having a fine time, didn't expect much, wasn't naive. He smiled, said that when characters in my novels say they aren't naive you know something fearful is about to happen to them. It may be that I'll one day want to strangle the entire population of Beverly Hills. Intimations of this are already afloat on the easterly breezes. But so far the game is well worth all the candles I burned collaborating with Coppola.

The beginning, in mid-July 1983, was an offer to come to New York and write dialogue for him. I qualify as a lifelong movie freak and erstwhile movie critic; I admired Coppola's work in *The Conversation* and *Apocalypse Now*, and I thought *The Godfather I* and *II*, which he and Mario Puzo wrote from Puzo's whiz-bang novel, were peerless modern films. So I checked into a hotel on Central Park South and went to work with this mythic character who earns his myth the hard way.

We talked for two days about the story, and we began the survival pattern that would continue for weeks: noshing on imports from Zabar's, DDL's deli, and the Yellowbird saloon in Astoria, sipping Vinoforte from Coppola's winery, Irish whiskey from you-know-where, and orange juice by the gallon. We planned to talk longer, but when the choreographer came in to discuss the script there was nothing new for him to see. So while Coppola coped with things musical, I stepped into the next room, wrote Scene One, and off we went. Out of an IBM Selectric, a pile of books on Harlem, gangland, and jazz, out of a phonograph playing Duke Ellington from morning till dawn, there came, in ten days, a raunchy, eighty-two-page, unfinished monster called the Rehearsal Draft, the script the actors worked with for three weeks.

Coppola had set up shop in a sizable but ramshackle second-story suite in the Kaufman Astoria Studios, a block-square concrete bastion of movie history where the Cotton Club's 1929 interior was being sumptuously reconstituted by production designer Richard Sylbert. The suite, which was being somewhat renovated (the roof was leaking seriously onto our noshables), had been in use since the 1920s—by legend, as dressing space for Gloria Swanson when she made *Queen Kelly* with Erich von Stroheim, for the Marx Brothers when they made *The Cocoanuts*, and so on.

But not until the *Cotton Club* crowd moved in had it been the arena of such rarefied expectations, such a stratospheric budget, such palpable rancor, scandalous rumor, public babble, contagious frenzy, and mass gastrocolonic anxiety. A few weeks into the project, Richard Gere passed through my office, nonplussed. "I've never seen anything like it," he said. "Everybody's afraid they're going to be fired."

I wasn't afraid. I was too new to the world of movies to be anything but an amused and earnest observer. Gere was not afraid either. He was the star. But he wasn't a happy star. He had script approval in his contract, and so far he hadn't approved of much of the script. I can't blame him. The script then was a peculiar document. Only Coppola and I knew what was really going on with it, and sometimes I wasn't too sure about Coppola. Or me either.

Coppola had been hired by producer Robert Evans, who started the film from Jim Haskins's documentary picture book *The Cotton Club*. Evans, who originally planned to direct the film himself, asked Coppola to rewrite the early scripts created by Mario Puzo and rewritten somewhat by Evans. Coppola chose to start anew, and the Puzo-Evans scripts were set aside for reasons that preceded my arrival. Coppola signed on as director after writing two scripts, and then I came in.

The subject we were dealing with was this preeminent Jazz Age and Depression-era nightclub which existed from 1923 to 1935 at 142nd Street and Lenox Avenue in Harlem, the black neighborhood that was a parallel carnival to the Great White Way of Broadway. But the club had a most ironically exclusionary racial structure. It was patronized only by whites, employed only black help and black entertainers, was owned by white gangsters (principal figures: Owney Madden, a Liverpool Irishman, and George "Big Frenchy" DeMange), who allowed in no black customers, with some exceptions—prestigious blacks, performers' relatives, black racketeers, a limit of twelve—who were relegated to the worst booths.

The white customers who after the crash of '29 could still afford a $2.50 cover charge per person came in evening clothes, from abroad, from royal circles, from high political perches, from Hollywood, Broadway, and gangland. Solvent tourists from Cleveland were also admitted. Some thought of their excursion into Harlem as "slumming," but that was rich man's contumely. This so-called slum was producing a major shelf in the pantheon of black entertainment: Duke Ellington, Cab Calloway, Ethel Waters, Lena Horne, Jimmie Lunceford, Lucky Millinder, Bill (Bojangles) Robinson. Harlem was wide open, very wide, all night long. Satchmo, Billie Holiday, Fats Waller were playing in clubs— Connie's Inn, Pod's and Jerry's, the Savoy, Small's Paradise. But the Cotton Club was supreme.

The Cotton Club Girls were a major draw, categorized as "high yellow." Near-white miscegenational beauties—mulattoes, quadroons, octoroons, tall (five-foot-eight minimum), elegantly but scantily clad sex objects (stride bikinis beneath transparent chiffon, fishnet hose)—they were exotic temptations to the racial voyeurs, in a phrase, "tall, tan, and terrific." The club was a "window on the jungle . . . a cabin in the cotton" which those with passports might safely and pleasurably enter.

A Cotton Club Girl, Estrellita Brooks Morse, came to the set one day during rehearsal. Tall, light-skinned, her solid-gray hair coiffed in waves, dressed to the teeth, she was, in her late sixties, still a knockout.

"My God," she said of Dick Sylbert's set, "this is just like the Cotton Club!"

She spoke of her performing days, the girls wearing Wheatcroft body makeup to cover veins or blemishes: "Everybody was looking right up you. You couldn't have no marks." She remembered the gangster owners pampering the girls: Big Frenchy always soft-spoken, Owney Madden sending champagne backstage. She remembered celebrity customers, and George Raft treated like family when he turned up.

The Cotton Club Girls, along with the "ponies" (shorter dancers of darker hue), the Cotton Club Boys, and the musicians, were Harlem royalty. Howard (Stretch) Johnson, a Cotton Club Boy who became a professor of sociology and was the film's technical adviser, spoke of his excitement at being catapulted from a small-town environment into the heart of the black entertainment world. But he added: "The Cotton Club radicalized my perspective. I saw the close connection among high society, the mob, and the politicians, and that there was not much chance to make it without their consent."

Our script sought to reflect such things, matching a pair of black dancers, the Williams brothers (Maurice and Gregory Hines), who perform at the club, with a pair of Irish brothers, Dixie and Vincent Dwyer (Richard Gere and Nicolas Cage), who work for Dutch Schultz (James Remar), a beer baron waging war on Harlem numbers bankers. Gregory Hines falls in love with a Cotton Club Girl (Lonette McKee) who can pass for white. Gere falls for Dutch Schultz's mistress (Diane Lane).

What we created was a gangster story about race and subjugation, about rising in the world through show business, all this pervaded by music and dancing. What we also had was six hundred people building sets, creating costumes, arranging music, rehearsing dancers, or just waiting for the script—at a cost of $250,000 a day, a throbbing condition that can put a certain stress on a writer.

The stress was like deadline pressure in journalism, the copy moving so rapidly from typewriter into word processor that Coppola stood up, pounded the table, and declared: "This is the city desk!" Fourteen-, sixteen-hour workdays were not unusual, and once we worked thirty-four hours without sleep. Coppola called this sort of stint "the death trip." From July 15 to August 22, when shooting began, we produced twelve scripts, including five during one forty-eight-hour, nonstop weekend. We lost track of the number of scripts we turned out, but it was somewhere between thirty and forty.

A new script, by my definition, is one with major new dynamics, and we had more of those than any writer needs. One of Coppola's methods of rewriting was to lift the climax of reel six, say, and put it in reel two. This does things to reel three that you probably hadn't counted on, and also leaves you with a problematical hole between reels five and seven. At times he would ravage the entire script, insert long-dead sections of old scripts, and offer up an unrecognizable new document. Work would then begin anew to make it make sense.

This created such confusion that I wrote in my notes: "If this has any coherence it will be a miracle of ingenuity." But one can also argue that the ingenuity lurked in the major transpositions he made that led to intensification of the dramatic line.

The continuously unfinished, unfathomable script vexed the production department and created an army of critics and second-guessers who read each new version as if it were the last word. Coppola viewed each version as raw material. Like the actors, he and I were in rehearsal for the final product.

"When does this scene take place?" I asked him after one major reshuffling.

"I don't know the whens," he said.

In retrospect it seems akin to writing a novel that turns out to be a short story. Any number of scenes and characters were created only to be later demolished. Coppola decided after one conversation with an Irish twist to it that we should include James Joyce in the story. He handed his aide, Tony Dingman, his copy of *Ulysses* and said, "Find us something." Tony riffled the pages, stopped at page 67, where Leopold Bloom thinks about his daughter, Milly, and recalls Boylan's song:

> Those girls, those girls,
> Those lovely seaside girls.

We had no seaside in *The Cotton Club*, so I invented an Irish wedding at which the best man toasts the bride, from Atlantic City, and quotes the song. Gere was playing cornet with a rickytick band at the wedding, which was the excuse for the scene. Coppola decided I should play the best man because I look rather Irish from the side and front. I revved up for this, but then in a revised script not only was I missing but so was Joyce. Gere remained, however.

Concision is the operative word with Coppola, who will intercut even a short scene with another one to accelerate the pace. I thought I was already a concise writer, but after Astoria I created a screenwriting axiom: what you wrote yesterday, cut in half today.

I brought to this new form the logic of a storyteller, if I may presume myself to be logical, a strongly visual imagination conditioned from early childhood by the movies, a penchant for dialogue, and this matter of concision, which I think of as journalistic knowledge. "Get the story in the first paragraph" is the same advice I got from a screenwriter: "Jump into the bottom of the scene." The recurring need is to home in on the significant action, find the kernel of continuity, dramatize it, pare it to the bone, move along, and do it again.

In film the poetry lurks in the ensemble effect—the script's architecture, the cameraman's eye, the designer's sense of color and form, the actor's narrowed glance, the bare bones of a single line, an insistence on action, an absence of serenity, complexity banished to avoid confusing the mass audience. When it works well it is a lovely gift to the world, but it has its limitations. Since we were fiddling with *Ulysses*, I remarked that no movie will ever approach Joyce's complexity. Coppola retorted that we are only at the beginning of cinema, that future technology will reduce moviemaking costs to penny-ante figures compared with today's blockbuster costs, and that *this* was the avenue to poetry and complexity. He said a filmmaker might one day inexpensively make a hundred movies to put *Ulysses* on film. "Cinema could be something unbridled," he said. "Cinema is more than the little movies we make, more than what we do with it."

Coppola's faith in technology is a way of bypassing the Hollywood moguls, who, he feels, have been isolating him. If *The Cotton Club* is a hit he will again be Storm King of the Mountain. But the box-office failure of his last three films has forced him into a corner, feinting at shadow and substance alike. He aspires to make the moguls irrelevant, an appealing prospect for any American innovator, and if he succeeds, film will move in a new direction.

Still, I don't think any number of movies (pick a number) will convey the complexity of life-through-language Joyce achieved.

About the second week in August, Coppola dropped on my desk a copy of our Estimating Draft of August 8 with a cover message from Robert Evans. "Dear Francis" came the Evans voice in large scrawl.

> You asked for my comments, my first one is the Cotton Club script of August 8th is on the way to being not good—but great. Spent much, much time—on both the structure & text of the enclosed further comments—Hope they are of some help. At least you know I'm not "just another pretty face" but rather just trying to do the best I can. Love ya, Evans. Please accept both dialogue & structure as my only *interpretation* for your eyes only—and only to be used as a possible springboard for the "Coppola" pen. E.

Reading this, a question arose in my mind about the Kennedy pen. It wasn't mentioned, although every version of the script carried the joint byline of William Kennedy and Francis Coppola. Soon after, the movie trade publications reported on the start of shooting, listing Coppola and Mario Puzo as the writers.

Elaborate feature stories, arranged by Evans's minions, appeared in the *Los Angeles Times*, *Newsday*, *The Wall Street Journal*, none mentioning my pen. I knew I was really in trouble when the film production's phone directory was printed. The apprentice editor and the trainee director were listed, but I was not. Michael Daly told me that when he started reporting on the film for his lively *New York* magazine article last spring he was told by Evans's publicity man that I was just a "script consultant," and his impression was that I was not important to the film.

Evans resented the radical script changes that followed my arrival. Coppola told me Evans was saying I had Coppola in my power. I had met Evans when he passed through our office. "Loved your book," he said, not specifying which one. Daly said he later spoke to Evans about me and he recalled Evans remarking: "Who *is* he? He wrote some book. . . ."

My presence also fouled Evans's fund-raising efforts. His pitch to the press, and therefore to prospective investors, was that *The Cotton Club* was being made by the same trio that had created *The Godfather*—Evans, Coppola, and Puzo. Coppola's view of Evans's contribution to *The Godfather* is somewhat different. "What Evans did on *The Godfather*," said Coppola, "was like what five other executives did."

Anyway, I was the Invisible Writer. Arguments on behalf of my visibility were raised with Evans by my agent, my lawyer, by Coppola's people, without effect. Evans was quoted in December by *The Wall Street Journal* as saying, after I'd been on the project six months, that Puzo's script had gone through fourteen versions. But Puzo was never on the set, had nothing to do with this deception. Evans wasn't on the set either. He stayed home, enraging Coppola with his long-distance second-guessing of the production. In anger Coppola refused to let him view the rushes.

When Evans sent in another set of notes on our script, Coppola threw them in the wastebasket and told the man who'd delivered them: "I don't want his notes. He's double-crossed me thirty-three times, and anybody who double-crosses me thirty-three times I don't want anything to do with."

I asked Coppola what he perceived as a double cross, and he replied: "He never gave up on the fact that he wasn't directing, and that he wouldn't hover and second-guess me. I said, 'If I'm the captain of the ship I don't want you behind me telling me what to do.'"

The film had the hovering disease from the moment Coppola signed on to direct a production crew he hadn't hired. The nay-saying to everything he did or said was endemic. It first came to a head the day he told me he might quit the film that night and go to Paris. A meeting followed with money men, Evans, production honchos, and Coppola. I was in the next room working. After an appropriate amount of screaming back and forth, Coppola said he'd be on his way to Paris at five o'clock unless it was put in writing that he was in absolute control.

"Settled," said Evans.

"I want a deal *today*," said Coppola.

"I apologize," said Evans. "I didn't know . . ."

"By five o'clock," said Coppola. "Call the lawyers."

"Settled," said Evans.

"Yes or no today or I'm gone," said Coppola.

"You're a stand-up guy," said Evans.

"I've got a ticket," said Coppola.

"You're a stand-up guy," said Evans.

Though Coppola won the day, the nay-saying continued. Also, the working out of Coppola's financial deal dragged on until he actually did walk off the set and go to London for two days. Contention ended the day he fired eighteen people, most of the production department.

The feud with Evans went to court eventually, and Coppola won the right to keep artistic control. Evans won the right to see the film at long last. He didn't like it, and wrote Coppola more notes. Coppola said the only changes would be in response to preview audiences' comments.

"Evans won't even be told where the preview is," Coppola said. "And if he finds out, he'll have to pay admission to get in."

Evans's word was, at this point, that the film was an expensive flop.

"He saw the second-to-last cut of *The Godfather*," said Coppola, "and he said the same thing."

By mid-August 1984, Evans and another investor had sold their shares of the film. Evans's buy-out figure was $6 million. Total control went to the principal investors, Edward and Fred Doumani, Las Vegas casino owners who have $30 million invested; to Barrie Osborne and Joey Cusumano, who had been the line producers from October 1983 forward; and to Coppola, who at last became director-without-kibitzer.

The cost of the film was said in court in Los Angeles to have reached $58 million, but that was anti-Coppola hyperbole that included the interest cost on the Doumanis' investment, which is not borne by the production. The money angle is invariably overstressed in any Coppola venture. He's been bad-mouthed as a director whose excesses cause the production great expense, and the uncertainty in his working method does feed into that. But on *The Cotton Club* Cusumano sees it differently.

"They pissed away ten million dollars," he said, recounting astronomical featherbedding, overcharging, and luxurious excesses outside Coppola's control. "Francis was instrumental in saving money in this film," said Cusumano, and he cited cutting of the work force by sixty people at Coppola's urging (not including the eighteen Coppola fired himself), a saving of almost $2,000 a week for each worker.

As to the script, ours was a relentless effort to cut costs. Our early, uninhibited draft would have cost $50 million, to the shock of us all. Within days we had another draft costing a mere $27 million. I like to think that, if only for a little while, I helped save somebody $23 million.

The length of the script was also a problem. The magic number was 120 pages, a minute a page. Our draft was 130 pages and worrisome. So late one night I pruned dialogue and description, excised widows, adjectives. No scenes were lost, and in the morning even Coppola didn't know what was gone, but the script was 120 pages. The cutting meant nothing to the length of the movie, but people stopped worrying about the length of the script.

I'm probably exaggerating only slightly in saying that at the outset many people viewed the script as an execrable document, and the film as an unredeemable disaster. That I never felt that way is the result of my enduring faith in the rewritability of anything. It also reflects my escalating belief that Francis Coppola was really going to do what he said he was going to do.

As people viewed the rushes—the lush photography, assorted beautiful people, talented singers and dancers, those curiously funny and virulent gangsters—a tonal change became evident: hey, this still needs a miracle, but maybe it's gonna work.

Then came the first cut of the film: stunning, but draggy. At the second, much tighter cut, cheers went up. Coppola went west to visit and showed the film to George Lucas (who liked it). In New York he showed it to the Doumanis and the executives of Orion Pictures, the studio distributing the film.

Coppola had cut it to two hours flat for the Orion screening, and when it ended, the Orion moguls and the Doumanis smiled, nodded, and walked away. Coppola, confused, furious, took this as high ungraciousness. A meeting followed immediately in the Orion boardroom, and the moguls by then had had the chance to construct a response to this nonpareil artifact: Too much tap dancing. It goes too fast. Needs some air. Love Gere, love Diane Lane. Let's have more love scenes. Where's those scenes I loved in the rushes? What the hell are you gonna do about that crazy ending?

I thought this the weakest version I'd yet seen, and by then I'd seen four. Coppola was worried that if the film ran too long, exhibitors would be limited to one showing a night, halving the revenue. But by the end of the Orion meeting he knew he'd cut too much.

The next day in the editing rooms Coppola and Barry Malkin, his editor and former schoolmate, to whom he listens faithfully, plus Malkin's assistant, Bob Lovett, and myself, went through the film and voiced a communal response to each scene, suggesting elisions, transpositions, restorations. By day's end there was a new cut with eleven minutes added, which made all the difference, for when I spoke to Coppola a week later by phone and asked him how the second showing for Orion had gone, he said it was "a big hit, definitely an up reaction. Everybody's happy. They're sending me telegrams and baskets of food."

The cut was soon locked, and the early mixing of sound and image began, the aim being to ready the film for Christmas 1984. The word of mouth was invariably positive; even those who had hedged their views were falling through their hedges onto Coppola's increasingly greening pastures. Some were saying it might even be a great movie.

Coppola cooked dinner at his New York apartment one night, and I put him through an after-dinner quiz on his willingness to direct by consensus, for he had, indeed, heeded many people's reactions.

"It's like a violinist who responds to the pressure of the string," he said. "Is he or the string making the note? The answer is, both. . . . If I were more satisfied with my vision of the piece in the first place I wouldn't be as susceptible to the other creative people. But I'm the one holding the yes and no functions."

He spoke of three elements—the script, his own research, and the actors. "All give you a direction as to how to go, and these are fused in the alchemy of the production. . . . You think as you go, following the instincts of the individual artists. . . . You base it on the original script, but you don't deny what you fall into. . . . It looks like chaos, but it's actually a logical process . . . in which you observe very carefully what happens when you add a new given.

"I specialize," he said, "in being the ringmaster of a circus that's inventing itself."

During the trial in Los Angeles over control of the film, the judge opined that the arguments in the case reminded him of *Rashōmon*—multiple private, conflicting perspectives on reality. Dick Sylbert told me a story—an old one, I think, but no less funny for that—about a production of Tennessee Williams's *A Streetcar Named Desire*. The bit actor playing the doctor who escorts Blanche DuBois to the asylum was asked about the plot. "It's about this guy who carts a lady off to the nuthouse," he explained.

Any single view of the bizarre phenomenon called *The Cotton Club* is subject to similar limitations. Coppola may have the widest perspective, since he was the epicenter. "My life is like this every day," he said one night as he was homogenizing assorted flavors of frenzy. But then, who in such a position as his can take a long perspective on anything?

And so I offer the following conclusions as a particular angle on events by a newcomer to the game. I came on as a short-timer but saw more than I expected. Coppola gave me the option to follow the film to the end, and I took him up on it. Not since I helped establish a daily newspaper from scratch has immersion in the raw experience of communal creation had such appeal to me. The pay wasn't bad either, and I've got a novel in my head in which moviemaking is part of the story. So I stayed on, writing scenes in dark saloons and in automobiles and in frantic production offices. I stayed on even to rewrite the Looping Script, because about 90 percent of the dialogue had to be lipsynched and rerecorded. Flat ad libs (lots of those) were upgraded, dead lines excised, and Richard Gere's role was enhanced.

What seems unusual about the final product is the combining of two nontraditional versions of two genres: the musical comedy and the gangster film. In the musical comedy ("an idiom," said Coppola, "I had been imbued with by my father since I was a kid"), the song-and-dance numbers are not story stoppers but weave through the fabric of the film. Realism segues into Expressionism, the gangsters emerging as genuine brutes as well as comedians. The narrative musical ending turns the film on its ear, giving it an unexpected dimension, yet confirming what we've suspected all along: that this is not a historical tale, it's a fable. And that ending was Coppola's vision from the outset. The film celebrates black beauty, black talent, black private life (i.e., just people: no pimps, no whores, no junkies, no race riots), and black love, the likes of which hasn't been seen on-screen in recent memory, if ever.

It will further popularize Ellington, Calloway, tap dancing, and black performers in general. My guess is it will make stars of Gregory Hines, Lonette McKee, Diane Lane, James Remar, Bob Hoskins, and maybe others. Richard Gere's price will go up.

I haven't seen the ultimate version of the film. Coppola went west again, this time with the Lock Cut, presumably untouchable. But he found a way to pick the lock, and changes continued, with old scenes restored, John Barry's underscoring largely purged of violins in favor of saxes, Bob Wilber recreating the original sounds of Ellington and Calloway. And so some surprises are in store for me. The greater surprise will be the critical and public response. If it's a hit, that will be quite nice. If it flops, some of us will take the rap.

My critical apparatus says it will be well received, but what do I know? I'm only the writer. However, I am no longer the Invisible Writer. I am pleased to report that Coppola and I will share "story by" credit with Mario Puzo, and Coppola and I, alone, will share screenplay credit. My open letter to Bob Evans on this point is this: "Dear Bob, You didn't ask for my comment on this topic, but here you have it anyway: Go poach yourself. Love ya, Kennedy."

Having said this, I now begin the reimmersion in fiction, which is to say language, the thing I missed most in my year at the movies. Coppola said more than once that he thought I'd be directing my own films in four or five years, but I think not. He's suited to the ringmaster role, but I believe I would gnash my teeth to cinders in a matter of weeks. Autonomy is more my style, and solitude. And so now I'll get back to that. The limo is waiting downstairs to take me to work.

1984

The Making of
Ironweed

It is raining on Finny's car, a shell of a boxy old Hudson sedan that rests wheellessly on blocks in a vacant lot on Colonie Street in Albany, just west of the railroad viaduct over Broadway. Two men, fat and filthy Finny, and tall and filthy Michigan Mac, are asleep in the car. Finny is alone in the back seat as Helen and Francis arrive, their breath visible at this witching hour of Halloween, 1938. Francis opens the curtain that serves as the car's window.

"Hey, bum, you got a visitor," he says.

"Who the hell are you?" Finny asks as he wakes up.

"It's Francis. Move over and let Helen in. I'll get you a jug for this, old buddy."

Finny smiles through his rotten teeth.

"Yeah, sure," he says, and Helen reluctantly climbs in and sits beside him.

"Don't be scared," Francis tells her.

"It's not that," says Helen.

"She knows," Finny says with a leer that gives new meaning to the word "pervert." "She's been here before."

Francis and Helen say their farewells as Helen settles in for the night, her last refuge from the soul-chilling weather, and Francis walks up Colonie Street, heading vaguely toward the home he hasn't seen in four years, hasn't lived in for three decades.

It's peculiar, this reality. Synchronous. Colonie Street, one block west of the set, is where my maternal grandfather's large family flourished for two generations; and it was in their house that as a child I began to study their lives. Forty years later, pieces of their reality, much transformed, emerged onto the pages of two of my novels. There never was such a figure as Francis Phelan in our family, which is perhaps one of the reasons I could invent him so freely.

Whatever his origin as a creation, Francis entered the imagination of film director Hector Babenco, and so now, on this simulated Halloween in the spring of 1987, Francis Phelan is fully fleshed in the person of Jack Nicholson; and his paramour, Helen Archer, is incarnate in Meryl Streep. These two illustrious actors, with supporting actors of fine verve and talent, James Dukas and Jeff Morris, plus Babenco, in yellow slicker and railroad conductor's cap on backward, are all reconstituting imaginary history on a street where it truly might have come to be.

How this began, Babenco recently recalled in conversation. He had heard about my writing, and when he saw a copy of *Ironweed* he bought it. Raised in Argentina, later resident in Brazil, Babenco is multilingual, but *Ironweed* was the first book he had ever read from beginning to end in English.

My story made him feel good, and Babenco at first thought that was because it had been his pioneer reading achievement in the English language. "But three, five months later," he said, "the book wasn't leaving my system—the anguish and pain of the characters, the compassion for them. And I decided to move forward."

The novel had been optioned by two producers, Gene Kirkwood and Joe Kanter. Babenco went to see Kirkwood, found that another director was also interested in the book but a year away from actually making a film from it. Kirkwood tried to interest Babenco in another project.

"But I wanted not to be denied," Babenco said. "It was unbearable when I felt so deeply about the material of *Ironweed*." He went back five or six times to Kirkwood. "It was an emotional decision, not rational. I fought like a desperado."

Then one day Babenco called me, we arranged to meet in New York, and we talked for three hours about *Ironweed* and about literature, on which he had been raised. I knew nothing about his work so he arranged a screening of his fourth and latest film, *Kiss of the Spider Woman*, which was opening in New York two days hence.

I thought it a wonderfully intelligent film, and successfully structured on levels of reality and fantasy, both of which were also elemental to any film that might be made from *Ironweed*. We then went to lunch and in the midst of it I called Kirkwood and said we could make a potentially fine film with Babenco *now*, not a year hence. He agreed, I went back to the table, we shook hands, and that was that. That night the rave reviews for *Kiss of the Spider Woman* came out in the New York papers, and Babenco began to get calls to make other movies.

But he was already booked.

A recurring question asked of me is how does it feel to translate your novel into a film, and how do you do it? Let me begin with an authoritative negative vision of any such effort, this from Ingmar Bergman: ". . . we should avoid making films out of books. The irrational dimension of a literary work, the germ of its existence, is often untranslatable into visual terms—and it, in turn, destroys the special, irrational dimension of the film."

This has been historically true so often that all we can do is hunt and peck for the exceptions. Consider a handful: Vladimir Nabokov's *Lolita*, made by Stanley Kubrick; Steinbeck's *Grapes of Wrath* and Liam O'Flaherty's *The Informer*, both made by John Ford; James Jones's *From Here to Eternity*, made by Fred Zinnemann; Robert Penn Warren's *All the King's Men*, made by Robert Rossen. I believe these are all major achievements in American film art, yet none come anywhere near expressing the fullness or complexity of the novels on which they were based. How could they? An elephant cannot become a horse. But, then again, what does that have to do with breeding horses?

The novel, as receptacle of the entire spectrum of the imagination—visual, linguistic, poetic, spiritual, mystical, historical, etc., etc., etc., until the receptacle is full—can be duplicated only in its own mirror image, not in any other medium. Allow me to use this fragment of a paragraph from *Ironweed:*

Francis watched this primal pool of his own soulish body squirm into burgeoning matter, saw it change and grow with the speed of light until it was the size of an infant, saw it then yanked roughly out of the maternal cavern by his father, who straightened him, slapped him into being and swiftly molded him into a bestial weed. The body sprouted to wildly matured growth and stood fully clad at last in the very clothes Francis was now wearing. He recognized the toothless mouth, the absent finger joints, the bump on the nose, the mortal slouch of this newborn shade, and he knew then that he would be this decayed self he had been so long in becoming, through all the endless years of his death.

I would like to have that paragraph budgeted for filming.

I'm with Bergman that it *is* rather literarily irrational and doesn't translate into visual irrationality. I don't doubt that some elements of it *could* be translated ("soulish body" would be difficult), but it would be through special effects, probably cartoonish in their final form and, as such, reductive, with no place in this film.

There *are* irrational elements in our film: ghosts, fantasies, and hallucinatory sights, sounds, and behavior. But these things *do* translate. Babenco and I decided on what would work, what wouldn't. If folks say they don't work, he'll take the rap (so will I, somewhat, and that's all right). If they say they *do* work we will both bust our buttons.

Film is a director's medium. Yes, yes. East is east. A rose is a rose. Who would doubt it? Well, producers sometimes, writers sometimes, actors sometimes, also critics, charwomen, and rachitic, one-eyed shut-ins, who all know how to do it better. But if Babenco isn't in charge then it's the committee system at work, the bureaucratic underworld: Casey, North, and Poindexter, doing a soft-shoe imitation of Ronald Reagan shuffling off to Managua.

Film is Babenco's medium and I sit in the front row of the loge and cheer. I did not *expect* a full translation of the novel. The novel is the novel, and that's still that, no matter what else happens. The fact is, however, that when a writer undertakes the writing of a script from a novel of his own, it is tantamount to self-amputative surgery. You eventually pose in front of the mirror without a left ear, a right thumb, with a thigh partly sliced away, the left leg dangling at the ankle, and then you decide that you're ready for the premiere. Just comb the hair a little to the left, wear gloves, bulky trousers, and a high shoe, and who'll notice? You may even set a new style.

This is not serious. Cutting a novel to pieces is not serious. But shaping a story for another medium *can be* a totally different sort of artistic exercise of the imagination. Consider Bergman's imagination prior to his writing the screenplay for *Fanny and Alexander*. There lay his whole life to be culled for a final, celebratory, five-hour movie. (Three hours and a half in the United States.) A *fifty*-hour movie would not have been able to tell his story, but he singled out episodes, shaved history here, amputated his psyche there, and he produced a masterpiece for the finale (we still hope he changes his mind) of his career as a filmmaker.

He found harmonies, in the editing of his life and imagined times, that conformed to film size, just as I hope Babenco and I found the same when we structured our movie. That is how it was for me at the start, at any rate: the writer believing he is significant in shaping the film. And he is. But, of course, the process has only just begun. There follows the shoot, and then the editing, and then the screenings.

Listen to Raymond Chandler, noted literary hard-boil, speaking on behalf of beleaguered screenwriters:

> If you oppose the routine minds, they are angered by your opposition. If you do not oppose them, they say you are a hack without integrity. What Hollywood seems to want is a writer who is ready to commit suicide in every story conference. What it actually gets is the fellow who screams like a stallion in heat and then cuts his throat with a banana. The scream demonstrates the artistic purity of his soul, and he can eat the banana while somebody is answering a telephone call about some other picture.

Chandler bade a qualified farewell to lovely Hollywood with that essay, and spoke volumes for the eloquent but powerless underdog. But here I arrive in a later year, working not within the studio system but with an independent producer, Keith Barish, of Taft Entertainment Pictures/ Keith Barish Productions (and we will get to him), and with a contract that gave as much control to a writer as my lawyer has ever negotiated, or seen.

Would that control have been there if push ever came to shove? I can't say. The issue was never tested. At dinner after a screening I made a remark that included the phrase "commitment to the writer," and another writer-director who was present laughed himself into a colonic spasm.

"Commitment to the writer? In Hollywood? There's no such thing," and he resumed his spasm.

Well, let's put it this way then: this film is the exception that proves the rule. The key has been in Keith Barish's desire to make a serious movie (he also co-produced *Sophie's Choice* from William Styron's novel) from a literary work that the major studios in Hollywood were afraid to touch. Barish, who personally monitored the shooting of the film in Albany, also showed great (and justified) faith in Babenco, letting him run his own shop with a minimum of interference, and letting him cut his own movie.

During the early months Babenco was approached by several major actors who were interested in playing Francis, but we always had one eye on Jack Nicholson, whose Irishness, toughness, and wit were perfect for the part. No one could remember Nicholson ever evincing the sensitivity or vulnerability essential to Francis's character, but then again had any role ever tested those traits in him?

Babenco visited Nicholson, found he'd read the book and wanted to play Francis. Nicholson then read the script and liked it, and so began the quest to raise the money to pay him his price. I met Nicholson at a saloon in New York one night when negotiations were under way but breaking down. "I don't want a nickel more than the Bank of England will give me on my name," he said with a smile.

But no Hollywood studio was willing to meet that demand for a film like *Ironweed*. And then Marcia Nasatir, who would become a producer of the film, introduced Babenco to Keith Barish. Barish, in partnership with Taft, met Nicholson's price, agreed to finance the film, and became the principal producer.

At some point in these negotiations I was walking with Babenco toward a Chinese restaurant in New York City when the reality of what was taking place reached him.

"We are going to make this *movie!*" he said. Then he clenched his fists, and with both feet leaving the ground, he leaped into the cinematic stratosphere.

.   .   .

He came down to earth in Albany, and why not? Production designer Jeannine Oppewall was sent to check out the terrain in North Carolina as an alternative, but discovered that Albany looks more like Albany than North Carolina does.

And so the movie people moved in and took over Albany's imagination. Celebrity watches were inaugurated to get Jack's and Meryl's autographs. A Hooverville was constructed in the old freight yards behind Watervliet. River Street in Troy was magically reconstituted as Pearl Street in Albany. The trolley came back to Lark Street in Albany, on a block where it had never run. The local newspapers wrote two stories a day about it all, growing angrier by the hour at the absence of openness by the movie people, who were more or less sworn to silence (or else), the press only grudgingly coming to understand that you don't talk about the movie until you are sure there is a movie to talk about.

Some 1,500 locals signed up as extras, and in time some of them would form into a social group and call themselves Weedies. The scriptwriter and his wife, Dana, would spend three days as extras, playing a pair of swells in the Gilded Cage scene, where Meryl so vividly personifies the lost Helen and her vanished dreams of musical glory. Eighty people—crew, extras, stars—would crowd into the long-abandoned Boulevard Cafeteria, which had been reconstituted as a Gay Nineties saloon.

We were all audience for Meryl's film debut there as a singer. "He's Me Pal" is her tune, which she sang for sixteen rehearsals and takes, the final take being, without doubt, the best, and the one that is used. But from the first rehearsal, she owned all of us—crew, extras, all— who wept, laughed, cheered her performance.

Please excuse this total breakdown of objectivity, which is a response to what seems a widely shared perception that Meryl Streep is the best actress alive. Sixty-four people from the production showed up the next day to see the dailies of her performance. Veteran film people, for whom dailies were usually a closed ritual for a select few hierarchs, found the recurring crowds at these daily showings an unusual phenomenon. A picnic atmosphere prevailed, with beer, soda, and popcorn for all, and heavy applause followed the screening of Meryl's song, just as it had on the set.

"She rocked 'em," said Jack.

I remember hearing Robert Duvall say once that people *always* think dailies are great, nobody knocks them; and this was certainly the general rule on this film. The excitement was cumulative as the film ripened, as the austere lushness of Lauro Escrorel's cinematography unfolded, as the principals came to understand the characters they had been inhabiting over the weeks. Tom Waits is wonderfully comic as the mournful Rudy, and Carroll Baker, an age away from her *Baby Doll* persona, not only personifies the virginal Irish wife, she even looks like one of my aunts.

And then there is Jack.

He's on screen maybe 85 percent of the time, in a role he was born to play. By his own measure, the only character from any of his films who is remotely kin to Francis Phelan is Randle McMurphy in *One Flew over the Cuckoo's Nest*; but Jack is more complex, more diverse as Francis. Jack has been a screenwriter, and a director, and he seems always to be looking at himself as a set of specimens under glass: varietal strains of a single species. In four takes maybe he'll repeat himself once, but the odds are against it. He willfully shifts nuances to give the director a choice.

Jack isn't exactly what you'd call a family man. A nonfamily man is perhaps closer to how he represents himself, and there is certainly an overriding element of that in the psyche of Francis Phelan also. My objectivity falls by the wayside again as I remember Jack's performance in the kitchen with his wife, twenty-two years after he'd abandoned her; and then on top of this his confrontation in the back yard with the ghosts of his entire life. Here is the range of a great actor made visible, the leap from contrition and self-abasement into a fierce and life-preserving anger at the haunting anxieties that are trying to drive him mad.

Francis hears the music of the ghosts in the yard and he moves toward, not away from, them. "You goddamn spooks," he yells. "You ain't real. You're all dead, and if you ain't you oughta be. I'm the one is livin'. I'm the one puts you on the map. So get your ass gone!"

I couldn't have imagined a better performance. (And I did imagine it.)

I say bravo.

The film began shooting on February 23, and wrapped June 6, and during the entire time I was at work on the last quarter of a new novel, *Quinn's Book*, which I'd been writing for five years. Ninety-five percent of the *Ironweed* script had been completed before the shooting began, we modified a few scenes as we went, and I spent at least part of almost every day on the set, involved in the production in myriad ways.

But I also worked every day on *Quinn*.

Somewhere in March I made a bet with Babenco that I would finish my novel before he wrapped the movie. If he won, he'd get the box of Cuban cigars I'd been given as a gift. (I no longer smoke.) If I won, he'd owe me a case of elegant Beaujolais. (I do drink a glass of wine now and again.)

I lost the bet by six days, Babenco is smoking the cigars, and I am buying my own wine. I do think, however, that this answers another recurring question of me: whether I will stop writing fiction, as have some novelists who worked in Hollywood. My answer is that I am a practicing novelist who once in a while writes a screenplay and tries to keep some semblance of control over what is done to it.

Late in September I went to Los Angeles and watched an early version of the movie on videotape, studying it for three days in my hotel room and offering cuts, elisions, restorations, and assorted gratuitous suggestions. I observed, with new incursions of pain, that certain favored scenes were no longer in the film. Alas, alas, Mr. Writer. Once the film is in the editing room your time of influence has passed. Now there remains only that inexorable problem of time, and it will not yield its hegemony over your space.

The full film came to three hours, was quickly slashed to two hours and forty-five minutes, then to two hours and twenty-four, then Babenco said he and editor Anne Goursaud (and with suggestions from Jack) had cut it to two hours fourteen. The editing was ongoing, the shaving proceeding apace. Soon it would be shorter.

I remember a conversation I had with a professor at Yale who said he thought all movies should be reduced to twenty minutes. Was this happening to my story? The worst scenario was Raymond Chandler's vision of the Hollywood producer fifty years ago consoling the writer about cuts: ". . . the scenes that regretfully had to be thrown away were graven on the producer's heart, and in the lonely watches of the night he tells them over to himself and weeps. . . . How sadly will he drain the life blood from your story and hand you back the embalmed remains as if it was just what you wanted—or at least what you ought to want, if you are a reasonable fellow and willing to face the facts of life."

Was this happening to me? Well, you knew all this going in, sap. Why are you having illusions about the process now? Welcome to L. A. Welcome to the movie business.

I went back to the beginning of the tape and watched the two hours and twenty-four yet again. Keith Barish said the distributors at Tri-Star were crazy about this version. Soon I would see the two-fourteen on the big screen. Babenco called to ask whether he should have an ambulance standing by for me.

And then I saw it, and as I watched I realized that all that was left for me to do was root for the home team. What I was seeing was concision in process, a winnowing of (if it succeeded) a work of art.

Film, it seems to me, yearns for coherence. The novel does also, but the novel can tolerate sideshows and excrescences that wouldn't be allowed by most modern filmmakers. Because the novel requires an exercise of the intellect, an intimacy with the reader's mind and reasoning powers, it can meander and ruminate, it can luxuriate in language alone, and gain in depth from these excursions. But because film is an exercise in immediacy, of raw life perceived in the instant that it happens, those meanderings are judged to be irrelevancies that dilute or divert the principal focus of the story. Stay in the center ring and never mind the sideshows, is the revered wisdom.

I watched the big two-fourteen.

And then it was over.

It was better than the two-twenty-four.

One of the scenes I'd missed most had been restored. Other things were gone and I missed them somewhat, but not much. The film did cohere. It was faster, better, sharper with ten minutes cut away. Jack thought it was still too long. I didn't. There was talk of showing it to presumably dispassionate people with movie savvy to gain perspective. Babenco was against this. He felt he already had perspective and I agreed with him. To hell with the committee system. He had produced a work of art of a high order.

It wasn't the final cut, it was only the two-fourteen.
But it was a work of art of a high order.
That's what I thought.
But don't trust me. I'm only the writer.

1987

The Homeless:

Do They Have Souls?*

Lead up to the topic question gradually. First ask, Do people who own their own homes have souls?

Yes.

How about people who pay rent?

Not too many of these have souls.

What about people who live in cars?

Very few of them have one.

And those who live in cardboard boxes?

Only if they live entirely inside the box do they stand a chance of having a soul. People who live with their legs outside the box are lost, for the soul dissolves when it rains. One man who slept in his box for two years woke in a torrential storm to find himself floating and his soul gliding into the sewer at flood level.

What do you remember about being homeless?

Nothing. I have always had a home. I have always had a suit and a proper necktie.

What of your father?

He always owned a suit.

Your grandfather?

* This was my response to a request from a *Newsday Magazine* editor that I peruse some photos of the homeless and then write something. The excellent photos, some of them excruciating to look at, were by a veteran photojournalist named Andrew Holbrooke.

He had a home but lived in a room with ashes.

Your great-grandfather?

He lived in a ditch.

Your great-great etc. grandfathers?

They lived in the muck: "fingers sink the toes sink in the slime these are my holds . . . the tongue gets clogged with mud that can happen too only one remedy then pull it in and suck it swallow the mud or spit it out it's one or the other and question is it nourishing," said Beckett.

How many kinds of homeless are there?

Twelve.

Name them.

Men, women, children, animals, and eight others.

Do burglars get Christmas presents?

Yes.

How about prostitutes?

Yes, if they are good.

Do you remember Hell's Kitchen?

Like it was yesterday. Nothing was more wicked, with its three-cent whiskey. They arrested 82,000 in New York in 1889, and ten thousand were under twenty.

Well yes, but it's not that bad today.

Maybe not, but over in Hell's Kitchen Park right now you could pick up maybe seventy-five people smoking crack, or dealing it, or selling their bodies to buy it. Nowhere to go, said the park's twenty-one-year-old crack whore who needs $300 a day to stay tuned. And the same theme pervades Joyce Kilmer Park over in the Bronx: crack was made for fools like me, but only God can smoke a tree.

Now that you've gotten around to God, let me ask another question: is Ronald Reagan homeless?

Yes.

Does he have a soul?

No.

Will he be remembered for the war on drugs, or the budget deficit, or fraternizing with Gorbachev?

No, he will be remembered for his remark that people who sleep on heating grates in the street are there by choice.

Why do people hate the homeless?

People hate the homeless because they are there. If they were elsewhere people would love them.

Are you your brother's keeper?

I would like to be, but the last time I saw him I didn't get to see him, because he was wrapped in plastic.

Why didn't you unwrap him?

Because the plastic was keeping him warm.

Would you lend your grocery cart to a homeless woman?

Certainly not. She would fill it with cans and bottles.

But that's how the homeless make their living, by turning in empty cans and bottles to redemption centers.

There is no redemption.

Why is that?

Because God is on vacation.

If they do not get caught in the rain, at what point do homeless people lose their souls?

"Deterioration of the sense of humour fewer tears too that too they are failing too and there another image yet another a boy sitting on a bed in the dark or a small old man I can't see with his head be it young or be it old his head in his hands I appropriate that heart," said Beckett.

In what way may someone cease to be homeless?

Sleep under snow. Stay away from heating grates. Eat garbage and die. Step to one side when you see a body falling out the window and check immediately with the landlord for vacancies.

Is there any way to make the homeless into human beings?

No.

This is terrible. Isn't there anything we can do to change this situation?

Not unless you want to deteriorate into a leper licker. However, prosperity is just around the corner, and job applications are being taken by all Pentagon contractors.

Will we ever stamp out crack?

No.

Will there always be homeless people on the street?

Yes, thank God, as long as there are heating grates.

Have you ever met a homeless person with a soul?

Once. A woman with two grocery carts and two dogs. She was weak and could not push and pull all her belongings at the same time. She pushed a little, stopped, came back and pulled the second cart, to which the dogs were attached.

How can you be sure she had a soul?

She was taking care of the dogs, which were not herself.

What did you do for that woman?

I gave her twenty dollars, all I had in my pocket.

What did she say?

Nothing. She tried to smile.

Did the gift assuage your guilt over the homeless?

Yes. I felt like a saint.

Was this a lesson to you?

Indeed, for if we all give money to the homeless we will cease to feel guilty and the homeless will then disappear from the corner of our eye.

Are there any images you would like to leave with us?

Yes, I recall two alcoholics with only three legs between them, and a very drunken Rumanian going blotto under a piece of carpet next to a steam pipe, and a homeless couple smiling and sharing a cigarette, or maybe it was a joint, and a homeless man celebrating his condition with wine, beer and coffee, and a homeless woman wearing three coats, at least, and a homeless man with a white Jesus beard eating a crust of bread, and in these faces there is desolation, anticipation of the void, and sometimes a grimace of defiance, or, to conclude from that as Beckett did, "to conclude from that that no one will ever come again and shine his light on me and nothing ever again of other days other nights no . . ."

Amen.

1988

PART SIX

Albany Resurgent: More Reports from the Native

O Albany!:

Remarks to the Publication Party

There is a great deal of goodwill in the air these days, especially, it seems, toward me and my books, notably the book at hand, *O Albany!* So many good things have happened to me this year that my life has become improbable, something that even I wouldn't write in a novel. Readers say my life is far-fetched; but they never say that about what I write, do they? Maybe the chapter on the South Mall in *O Albany!* (where the state paid for everything three times) is far-fetched. Maybe the whole billion-dollar South Mall is as far-fetched as the chapter on Dan O'Connell, Albany's political boss, controlling the city for fifty-six years. But is that any farther-fetched than the Erastus Corning chapter—one man elected mayor eleven consecutive times, forty-two consecutive years, a national record? Maybe it's Albany that's far-fetched—an improbable city.

It is probably legitimate to call me a chauvinist, though I'll deny it. Lavishing this much attention on a place is bound to draw this accusation; but I submit that *O Albany!* is not an uncritical document. Some said the tone of it was not condemnatory, and this is probably true. I'm more enlightened and amused by our political history and our scarlet record as a city of sin than I am outraged by it. I think one line in the book gives retrospective shape to the creed that has guided our political trajectory for the better part of a century—Charlie Torche's brilliant perception that "honesty is no substitute for experience."

The point of being a bemused cheerleader of Albany life stems in part from my long-smoldering resentment of the denigration of the city by transients. The negative image is often reinforced by journalists who come to town to cover the legislature and never see much more of the city than the inside of the two or three saloons that serve Capitol Hill. I recall one such transient wrote a supremely hasty commentary on the city and *The New York Times* published it in its travel pages. I was angered to the point of structuring a rebuttal, but when my agent spoke to a *Times* editor, the piece was cut off before it was written. "We always get that kind of response when we print a critical piece," said the editor. And so that particular criticism was never rebutted, but it is rebutted now through this book. Now we have our innings.

We all here know what a special place this city is. I don't have to convince you. It has its flaws, but whatever they are they are more than compensated for by the city's piquancy, its pizazz. Maybe this isn't the chateaubriand, or the filet mignon, of American cities, but it certainly is one hell of a corned-beef sandwich.

The mention of food reminds me of drink, and suggests another of my favorite lines from the book. This is from one of my drinking uncles who was asked one day would he like a drink. He answered, "The last time I refused a drink I didn't understand the question." And so with that, let's have a drink and get on with the conversation.

1983

Jack and
the Oyster

You could say that the world is Jack's oyster because the oyster is Jack's world. You could say that Jack is the pearl in Albany's oyster, as one headline writer already did. You could say that the oyster created Jack's world, or that the oyster creates a world of jack. Somebody once called the oyster a succulent bivalve. An Albany columnist wrote frequently about the oyster and never forgot to mention that it was a succulent bivalve. Every once in a while he might have said that the oyster was the quintessence of bivalent succulency, but no. Somebody else once said that the oyster was sexually ambivalent, that God told it to go fertilize itself and it did. The Albany columnist never wrote about that part of God's handiwork. Ambivalent bivalvency he might have called it, but no.

Jack, and this is true, has been shucking oysters for eighty-one years. No, you say. Well, that's the way things happen in Albany. People go along doing things for eighty-one years and then the word gets around that they've been doing it and people say, No. What I say is, Go take your no and fertilize it. Jack *has* been shucking oysters for eighty-one years. When I saw Jack, he was recovering from pneumonia and was in a moment of hiatus (*huître* is French for "oyster"; *hiatus* is Latin for "gap" or "opening." For example: "The hiatus in Phutatorius's breeches was sufficiently wide to receive the chestnut"—*Tristram Shandy. Hiatus*, in a rare meaning, is also "a gaping chasm," as in an oyster after Jack has finished shucking it).

Jack also shucks clams. In 1984 it was estimated that he had shucked three million clams during his lifetime. Was that true?

"Who could predict that for sure?" said Jack.

Which did he open more of, clams or oysters?

"Clams. They seemed to go for the clams. But I'd say it was close to even."

What of the method?

"When you open the oyster you take it off the top shell and put it on the bottom shell and they come out a whole lot cleaner."

Do you always know the top from the bottom?

"Oh, sure. The bottom is round, the top is flat."

And clams?

"Only one way to open a clam. From the top."

Jack opened a clam for me one night in late 1984 in the kitchen of his restaurant at 42 State Street in Albany. His hair was pure white, he wore his horn-rimmed glasses and had his apron over his collar and tie as he picked up the clam knife, palmed the clam (Jack shucks righty), flicked the knife into the clam's hiatus-to-be, beveled the doomed mollusk in palm, swung the knife this way with the first deft stroke, then entered the blade deeper into the violated chasm, rebeveled the now twained shell, raised the top half on its hinge, and revealed a clam— from the Old English *clam* or *clamm*, corresponding to the Middle High German *klam*, and to the German *klamm*, meaning "to cramp, fetter, constrict, or pinch," which is certainly what life was doing to that clam before Jack freed it into eternity for me with his clam knife—and revealed, as I was about to say, the most magnificent clam I have ever seen. Jack could have searched through a sugar barrel full of clams and wouldn't have found another with such a sunburst of pure clamency, untouched by the knife, a paragon of hemisected, unviolated abundancy, its liquor intact on the half shell, redolent, as one might expect, of the divine odor of clam juice.

How had Jack opened, protected, framed the perfect clam?

"Like everything else. Practice."

I did not eat the clam that Jack opened. I regret that. If I had, I could now say that I ate the most beautiful clam in North America, admittedly a clam claim difficult to prove. But let us here set that clam aside, as did Jack, and get back to Jack and the oyster.

Jack is Jack Rosenstein, now ninety-one, born at 21 Broad Street in the South End of Albany on June 5, 1893, to Isaac and Rebecca Rosenstein, late of Russia. Isaac was a cigar maker ("Very good cigars, no brand. Them days you didn't need a brand"). Jack went to work as a newsboy at age seven in 1900, working the corner of Maiden Lane and Broadway in front of Keeler's European Hotel, "225 rooms, 35 with bath, Gentlemen Only, Known From Coast to Coast." Jack remembered Sunday mornings he'd be there calling out "New York or Albany paper" (the proper newsboy pronunciation is PAY-pee), and the drummers who had been up all night (Keeler's never closed) carousing, after a week of selling their wares, would yell out at Jack: "Get away from there. We wanna sleep." And Jack would nod and call out, "New York or Albany paypee."

When Jack was nine, somewhere in 1903, the owner of Keeler's took meaningful notice of him and gave him a job running errands. Jack got to know the hotel, especially the kitchen, from which he would run orders of oyster fries and oyster stews to private homes. He sometimes, after eleven at night, delivered to the Tenderloin, when that Albany attraction was partially situated on Dallius Street, an old South End thoroughfare named for a seventeenth-century Dutch cleric.

"There was two five-dollar houses in them days," said Jack.

"Davenport's?"

"Right. Davenport's."

"Read's?"

"Lil Read's was a two-dollar house. Stanley's was a five-dollar house."

"Wasn't there a Creole place on Dallius Street too?"

"That was farther down."

The proprietresses would say, "Give fifteen, twenty cents to the boy," and Jack saved that change, the beginning of his $400 fortune, about which more later. Then one night one of the oystermen at the hotel didn't come to work, and Jack was put at the oyster and clam counter with the two other oyster openers.

"I can see all the oysters piled up, and all you kept doing was opening them and opening them. The boss took a likin' to me, and so they put me on the night shift, working oysters [clams also]. That's where I got the practice. Oysters I was a little slow on, but I opened them very good."

Is it harder to open an oyster than a clam?

"To some people it is." But not to Jack. "My training there made the big difference."

There were three oystermen working during the meal hours, with chutes where they threw the empty shells. Some of the oystermen broke oysters, then clandestinely threw them out. The boss would go below after dinner, however, and inspect the baskets at the bottom of the chutes. "He never found a broken one in my basket. But he did in theirs."

Jack had learned about oysters and clams from the very same boss, the hotel owner, William (Sheriff Bill) Keeler. "He used to put me in front of him. He'd say, 'These are your hands, and I'll teach you how to open them clams and open them good.' He told others I was the cleanest clam opener he ever saw, but he didn't mention it to me."

One day Bill Keeler called Jack in and asked him where he'd go on a week's vacation. "Them days you didn't know what a vacation was." Coney Island, said Jack. "Okay," said Bill, as Jack remembers it. "Your pay will go on. But say nothin' to nobody." Jack was getting five dollars a week. On Christmas Day, Bill gave him a five-dollar gold piece. "This is your Christmas," said Bill. "Say nothin' to nobody." After a while Bill called Jack into the cashier's office. Bill was big and stocky, had a large mustache, and wore a black skullcap, a unique garment in Albany. It had a hook above the center of the forehead to which Bill could raise and affix his spectacles when he so chose. In the office Bill asked Jack: "How much they payin' you?" Jack mentioned the five dollars, and Bill said, "I'm raisin' it two dollars, but I won't put it in your envelope. I'll pay you out of my own pocket." Because grown men, the oystermen Bill had brought up from Crisfield, Maryland, where people really know how to shuck oysters, were only getting twelve dollars a week.

Bill Keeler knew about oysters because at age thirteen in 1854 he went to work in the oyster and fish business. Then in 1864 he and his brother John opened an oyster house at 85 Green Street in Albany. Bankers, farmers, editors, bootblacks frequented Keeler's, two hundred at a time, for the famous oysters—raw, stewed, fried. This was the advent of the oyster age in Albany, and it wrought significant change in the city's way of life. Success on Green Street with fries and stews led the Keeler brothers to open, in 1884, at 56 State Street, the restaurant that would exist until 1969 and prevail as one of the great four-star restaurants of this country: Keeler's State Street. It was an American-style restaurant, but it continued in the tradition established in 1838 by Delmonico's, the pioneer French restaurant in America. That is to say, it offered a highly diverse and often exotic menu, well organized by subject, superbly cooked to gourmet taste, splendidly served in elegant surroundings, and with all gustatorial whims and perversions catered to in the extreme.

Bill went off in 1871 to become an Albany alderman, street commissioner, and sheriff, but retained the partnership with his brother until 1886, when they split. Bill went over a block to Maiden Lane and Broadway and opened his own restaurant, which soon became Keeler's European Hotel (for men only), and it was such a success that Sheriff Bill eventually bought half the square block and built a place that became a cynosure of the good life, the sporting life.

In time the hotel included a bowling alley, pool and billiard rooms, a barbershop with four baths, private dining rooms upstairs where families might dine or where hanky-pankers might pank privately. A restaurant for ladies was added, but the ladies were not allowed to stay overnight. Bill built a lake to furnish ice for his guests, bought a poultry farm to keep his kitchen stocked, and bought an oyster bed in Lynnhaven, Virginia.

The earliest menus I've turned up, one dated from March 12, 1897, and another from January 5, 1902, consist of four pages of dense, small-print listings (eighty-seven entries in 1902 on ways to eat clams and oysters: rockaways and rocky points, lynnhavens, bluepoints, littleneck clams). In 1838 on its pioneer menu, Delmonico's offered only five oyster dishes plus oyster soup. The oysters were menu headline items at Keeler's: LYNNHAVEN HALF SHELL 40–30 [cents], it read in 1897. OYSTERS NOW ON HAND was the 1902 banner, in type larger than the name of the hotel's.

The pattern continued at Keeler's State Street after Bill Keeler's hotel burned down. In 1932 and 1944 oysters were the main attraction: BLUE-POINTS, 45 CENTS, it read, the same price both years.

Politicians and celebrities came in great flow to Keeler's Hotel. (Jack couldn't remember any of them. ("I was never interested in that. I was in the kitchen.") They consumed oysters by the barrel—five thousand oysters, three thousand clams signed for by Sheriff Bill in a three-day period in October 1914; that is, eight thousand mollusks in thirteen barrels, at a total cost of eighty dollars, or about one cent apiece wholesale.

"Nobody else handled them like Keeler's," said Jack. Other places had insufficient turnover on oysters, and sophisticated Albany oyster eaters demanded they be served fresh, as they always were at Keeler's—three oystermen working as fast as they could to answer the demand. A few years ago Jack estimated he could open fifteen clams in a minute, twelve oysters in two minutes. He works with a stabber, a long knife that was brought to Albany by the Crisfield oystermen. For anybody who has tried to open an oyster for the first time, six a minute seems like Olympic speed.

Alas, it's nothing of the sort. The oyster-opening record, according to Guinness, is held by Douglas Brown, who on April 29, 1975, at Christchurch, New Zealand, opened one hundred oysters in three minutes and one second. Guinness lists and knows no clam-opening record, which is almost shameful. But my guess is that it would be at least double the oyster figure. Clam eating, on the other hand, is laggardly. The record is 424 littlenecks, out of shell, in eight minutes, or fifty-three per minute, by Dave Barnes at Port Townsend Bay, Washington, on May 3, 1975. This compares with the oyster-eating record—held by Ron Hansen of Sydney, Australia—of 250 oysters, out of shell, in 2:52.33, or 87.0413 oysters per minute. My theory is that clams need a bit of a chew, but that the silky oyster slides swiftly and sleekly down the gullet.

I have not a whit of doubt that Jack could have established the speed record in his youth had that been his goal. There are unplumbed depths to Albany people: the road not taken. But Jack had another ambition: he wanted to become a waiter. "*Ah*," said Sheriff Bill, "so you want to rob the customers, too." And so Jack went to work nights, a dollar a day plus the nickel and dime tips. By 1913 his fortune had climbed to $400, and with a fellow oysterman, Bill Evans, who knew oysters but had no money, he opened an oyster bar and wholesale delivery business to other restaurants, up the hill from Keeler's Hotel, on Lodge Street. Jack and Evans didn't get along; so Jack left and opened a hole-in-the-wall restaurant—four tables, a kitchen, and a marble oyster bar—back down the hill at Beaver and Grand streets.

Jack married Jane Millerstein from Troy in 1916 and began to prosper. Jane was cashier, Jack counterman. When a customer came in, Jack would take the order, call it through a partition—"One oyster fry"— then run into the kitchen and cook it. He took over a piano store next door and broke through the walls to expand. He took over a coal company that closed, put in private dining rooms, expanded his menu, and by 1937 employed seven waiters, five cooks, two checkers in the kitchen, an oysterman, and was selling eight hundred to one thousand oysters every other day. That year, '37, an Albany bank offered Jack the mortgage on a failed restaurant at 42 State Street, a block over from where Keeler's Hotel used to be and a few doors down from John Keeler's restaurant at 56 State. Jack moved in and has been there ever since, now seating 140 in the dining room, a bar adjacent where you wait for a table, banquet rooms upstairs; and during August, when transiency is at its peak, Jack's Oyster House serves five hundred meals a day, not including banquets. Jack's sons, Arnold and Marvin, run the place, and Jack's grandson, Brad, is apprenticing.

Photographic blowups of the town when Sheriff Bill was a presence adorn the walls. Jack was always a physical presence, working eight, ten hours a day until pneumonia and other ills hit him, and when we met he was sitting out front in his black suit and red tie, longing for last year's pep and yearning to get back to the kitchen with his apron and stabber. "I'd love to get in there. It runs good, but it'd run a whole lot better if I was there."

Jack used to go on vacation to Miami Beach, stay a month. "But it got monotonous sitting around doing nothing." So he quit vacations. "All I did was take care of my business. I always wanted to be here, never wanted to be away."

Jack's life embodies the golden platitude that America is a republic of equals, the land of opportunity. But even during America's incipient time Jefferson spoke of our "aristocracy of merit," and that seems closer to the truth of what Jack reveals to us. Bill Keeler and Jack Rosenstein, like the Walrus and the Carpenter—Bill with his big mustache, Jack with his tools—led a parade of oysters out of the nineteenth century through most of our own century, and Jack's sons are keeping the parade going toward the twenty-first.

We know that some things changed along the parade route. Bill Keeler's sons turned the hotel's Broadway dining room into a cabaret, the first in Albany, and an orchestra and entertainers played to turn-away crowds. "The crowds, you'd have to see it to believe it," said Jack. "But the old man didn't like it. Didn't care for that kind of business."

So Bill Keeler retired, and in 1918 he died in Virginia, nearer, my oyster, to thee. His hotel burned on the morning of June 17, 1919, and a fireman lost his life, but more than a hundred guests got out safely. The hotel had had a small fire in an earlier year, and an employee called Bill Keeler at home to tell him. "Why call me?" said Bill. "Why don't you call the fire department?"

I told Jack I was trying to personify the value he represented, and I asked him what he thought was the key element of his life's work. "That it's been done right," he snapped back.

I ate a dozen oysters while we talked, bluepoints, which Jack always loved best, except maybe for rocky points, which are larger, and there is therefore more of them to love. Did Jack love oysters the way I did?

"No, I never ate them. I can eat a clam, but I don't care for them much either. But I can't eat an oyster. I tried to cultivate a taste for them, but I couldn't."

"Yet you and the oyster," I said to Jack. "You were partners all your life."

Jack laughed at that. "That's right," he said.

"Did you ever think about what the oyster means? What it is?"

"*Nah.* Never did."

Nevertheless, there goes Jack, there goes Bill, walking up from Maiden Lane and Broadway—up to Lodge Street, and then down to Beaver and Grand, and then over to State. A hundred million oysters are following their trail, or is it two hundred million? Well, it's a lot.

> "It seems a shame," the Walrus said,
> "To play them such a trick.
> After we've brought them out so far,

And made them trot so quick!"
The Carpenter said nothing but,
"The butter's spread too thick!"

"O Oysters," said the Carpenter,
"You've had a pleasant run!
Shall we be trotting home again?"
But answer came there none—
And this was scarcely odd, because
They'd eaten every one.

"The question now with oysters is," said Jack, "will you be able to get them? It's hard to get oysters, but that's the business. Will you get them?"

1985

The Capitol:

A Quest for Grace and Glory*

We were sitting on the steps that lead down into Capitol Park west, making notes on the hundreds of people who had been here during the lunch hour on this perfect summer day of 1985. The great office buildings on Capitol Hill, Albany's acropolis, had disgorged their hungry, sun-seeking denizens, who quickly opened their lunch bags or lined up at the score of sidewalk pushcarts to buy fruit, and egg rolls, and hot dogs, and they lolled on these steps and on the park's sweet greensward until time and the egg rolls ran out. Then they went away.

Now the day was making long shadows, and all that remained of the lunchers was a bit of their spoor: grease spots on the steps. Three young boys rode up on bikes, and two of them rolled their trousers and waded into the park's small pool, where minigeysers rise and fall in season. The boys were questing for coins that profligate dreamers sometimes toss into the water along with their secret wishes. The third boy approached the steps and asked if the man taking notes was a reporter.

"Sort of," he was told.

"You look like one. What you writin' about, the buildings?"

"About this big one, the Capitol. It's very famous and very old."

"Is it?"

"Yep. They started to build it 122 years ago."

"Wow!" said the boy. "That's almost a century."

Excess beyond comprehension: precisely.

* This essay was written as a companion piece to a book of photographs of the Capitol by Dan Weeks, Stephen Shore, Judith Turner, and William Clift.

The Capitol is, in all respects, a presence beyond human scale. Inside it or outside it, the eye is gluttonous, the brain festive, the imagination overtaxed. It is the architectural snowball that became an avalanche, exceeding all expectations except those of the men who first conceived it, who wanted the symbols of America to inhere in it; and so they do. What also inheres is the monumentalism of one of the last load-bearing masonry buildings in America and a sprawl of superlatives that have become its historical baggage.

There is, for instance, the cost of building it. Governor Lucius Robinson (1877–1879), a frugal man, called it "a public calamity . . . without parallel for extravagance and folly." By 1899, after it had been a-building for thirty-six years, the legislature refused to spend any more money finishing it and declared it complete. Cost to that point: $25 million, the most ever expended on a building in North America. But it was hardly complete, and the new governor in 1899, Theodore Roosevelt, immediately undertook alterations that by 1902 proved to be not only unsatisfactory but dangerous. Alterations are still going on today, as is the effort to finish it.

It will never be finished; is, indeed, unfinishable. But it demands eternal attention, deserves completion or restoration of certain splendid parts, and calls out indignantly for elimination of the abuses that have been perpetrated through the years on its glorious corpus. If all the words written in, about, and because of the existence of this corpus were suddenly turned into raindrops, the entire population of the world would be awash in a deluge of vowels and consonants. This book adds a few drops to that deluge, with reverence and beauty: the reverence in these words, the beauty in the photographs that follow them.

The American Architect and Building News in 1881 called the Capitol "one of the greatest buildings of the century." An early critic said of the Senate Chamber (the work of the eminent architect H. H. Richardson and one of his upcoming associates, Stanford White) that it was "the most beautiful room in the United States." Another critic wrote that the Chamber "surpasses in magnificence any legislative hall on this continent."

The Assembly Chamber, the madly bold design of Leopold Eidlitz, a major architect and theorist to his contemporaries, was described by a critic in *Scribner's Monthly* in 1879 as "the most monumental and most honorable work of public architecture this country has to show for itself."

But it proved to be structurally unsound, stones fell onto the desks of fearful legislators, and after only nine years the great ceilings with their groined arches were reconstructed and lowered, their grandeur diminished.

Richardson's Great Western Staircase in the Capitol, also called the Million-Dollar Staircase (it cost more than a million), has been described by a present-day architectural historian as "possibly the most intricate one in the western world." Also, the feud over styles of design among the Capitol's architects (Thomas Fuller was the first, replaced by the triadic team of Richardson, Eidlitz, and Frederick Law Olmsted, they in turn replaced by Isaac Perry) was viewed, in its day, as "a controversy in architectural politics unprecedented in our history."

This sort of maximizing can go on, has gone on, and is well documented. But let us consider certain new and current elements of the Capitol's history and turn our attention to a series of views of the building's four exterior sides, the likes of which only birds have heretofore seen.

These photos were made by Dan Weaks, who works with a truck that is outfitted to raise his camera to a height well above normal eye level. We seem to be looking at the Capitol's eastern façade, for instance, from the perspective of a helicopter hovering over State and Eagle streets, our eye at the building's dead center in the imaginary cross hairs of a telescope. Weaks takes multiple photos of his subject, then pieces them together like a jigsaw puzzle to create his pictures-that-never-were. The human scale is always there, those tiny, ambulating blurs in all his foregrounds; and while they are most aptly in scale against the great façades, they are also the presences without which there would be no such epic scope to photograph.

Stephen Shore's color photographs of the Capitol's exterior give us a perspective of another sort: a sidewalk realism, but with natural light that is constantly recoloring the great building. Now it is a wan beige in the summer sun, now a bone gray, or a rich, shadowed tan, or a bright, sunlit white with greenish shadow, or a stark bluish-gray on a day when the matching gray trees have shed all their leaves, and yet the grass is still as green as when summer was here.

Shore finds his blue skies reflected equally blue in the Capitol windows, and also in the windbreaker of a woman on a park bench. He finds the lion guarding the porte-cochere entrance beneath the eastern steps to be not one lion but three: twice reflected in the glass and the polish of a parked Le Baron. He will discover an upward angle that proves the Capitol's façade is predominantly the work of stone carvers, from another angle that it is all Romanesque arches, and from yet another a nonesuch grid of parallel and perpendicular lines. A long look at the Shore photos is repaid by revelation. In one foliated corbel he finds a handsome hound with his tongue out. He has, perhaps, discovered a stone carver's pet, but he has also discovered that the hound's cranial fracture and bisected left ear are part of a line of mortar that has repaired, with great finesse, serious damage to the corbel caused by weather, or vandals.

The abundance of such carvings, the extraordinary stonecutting, all done with tools passed on from medieval time, both crafts all but vanished from the world in this age of steel and poured concrete, give anyone randomly touring the Capitol's interior a passport to a lost age, an age of belief in which a symbol carried ancestral weight: a log cabin in the wilderness, a broken chain beneath an emancipated slave.

On the first floor by the Senate staircase a tour guide was instructing visitors about the carvings that adorn the balustrade. Darwin's theory of evolution was new when the staircase was being built, said the guide, and the designers decided to begin at the bottom with the symbolic carving of a single cell, and then rise, with the ever-increasing complexity of living things, to the fourth floor, when the final carving would depict man at the summit of living ascendancy.

But many of the carvers were Catholics who would have none of such heathen jabber, and they refused to carve man at the top. So evolution, said the guide, now ends with the elephant.

We followed the carvings upward and near the fourth floor found the rhino, the hippo, the mammoth, and a penultimate elephant; but we interpret the last carved panel not as an ultimate elephant but as a recumbent camel. I think the carvers were having their way with life, just as they did with death in a carving on the Million-Dollar Staircase showing an antlered stag with a huge arrow in its back. The carving is captioned "Non Effugit."

The photos of Judith Turner provide another vision of Capitol abstractions: the geometry of pillars and pedestals, stairs and shadows. She turns her cubist eye on a precubist world and finds poetry in polished marble, combed sandstone. She is the minimalist any visitor to the Capitol must become or else lose sight of the delicacy of the basket woven into a corbel by a carver, or the backlighting that silhouettes an archway, or a tumultuous rush of lines and angles that overpower a corner until one sees the sinuous bobcat in the background, climbing the foliage of an adjacent arch: and vision is arrested, and delighted.

William Clift wants space to be encompassed. In his photos he seeks out a stairwell, a portico, a corner of the Assembly Chamber, the fireplace wall in the Executive Chamber before it was redecorated, the Capitol by night from a distance, the press room on the third floor, a view to the north over three Capitol dormers. He finds beauty not in isolated elements but in the ensemble effect, in the way a given place accumulates furniture, and flags, and a vista, and a perimeter.

His photographs suggest another truth: that the Capitol is a museum not only of stone carving and architecture, but of portrait painting, of political photography, of military artifacts. The Capitol is a rich repository of flags, guns, uniforms, letters, and photos from the Civil War, other wars. In a small cavelike room under the Million-Dollar Staircase, you must handle the photos with white gloves: tintypes of women taken off dead soldiers on Southern battlefields, or photos of Union soldiers taken by Mathew Brady's studio, or a letter from a wounded soldier to his lieutenant, asking that his buddies write him and yearning from his hospital bed to rejoin the company.

These things are not entirely accessible to the public but await display in a Civil War room or a military museum yet to be created. Some items are on view in corridors of the Capitol: a Confederate doctor's surgical case alongside his foot artillery sword, blades with two moral edges; and the uniform worn by Colonel Elmer Ephraim Ellsworth, born in Saratoga County, sometime resident of Troy, and the first Union officer to die in the Civil War: shot through the chest by the proprietor of an Alexandria, Virginia, hotel, from whose roof Ellsworth had pulled down the Confederate flag. When President Lincoln heard the news of Ellsworth's death, he wept.

Now move along. There's the courtyard, once planned by architect Fuller as a sculpture garden to educate the public about art, but never completed. Now it is half full of a latter-day copper roof that covers the Capitol's one-story cafeteria, added in 1923. Ventilators, a ladder, the green corrosion of the copper roof, and not much else dominate the dismal, unsightly central core of the great building. There are plans to create an open garden in that courtyard, with fountains and statuary and with access from all sides, and maybe that will happen one day.

We can go upstairs now to the Legislative Correspondents' room and see how it's changed in the twenty years since we last used its facilities, and the answer is: not much. What is new is that it's quiet. You don't hear typewriters, you don't even see them, because they've been replaced by video display terminals. Photos of certain favored governors line the upper walls of the downstairs part of the room: Teddy Roosevelt, Tom Dewey, Al Smith, Big Bill Sulzer, the only governor to be impeached, and Martin H. Glynn, the *Albany Times-Union* editor who was Sulzer's lieutenant governor, and who replaced him.

A young Nelson Rockefeller looks out from the east wall and Dan Barr, who used to report on politics for the *Times-Union* and who later became a Rockefeller press aide, is having coffee with a visitor on The Shelf, the upstairs portion of the press room that juts out over half the lower room. This is the truly historical section, where the pool and card tables and the beer are kept. And it is where Harry Truman one day played "The Missouri Waltz" on the piano. The boys had a sign made up and sent it to Harry for his signature, and it is there on the piano now. It first read: "Harry Truman Played Here, Oct. 8, 1955." Harry signed it but inserted the words "the piano" after the word "played," and added in a footnote: "Just to make plain what was played," for like everybody else in politics, Harry knew that a twenty-four-hour poker game was a significant element on The Shelf.

Dan Barr was a young reporter in the mid-1950s when he encountered the poker game. Some of the regulars were Jimmy Desmond and Dick Lee of the New York *Daily News* and Warren Weaver and Doug Dales of *The New York Times*, Emmett O'Brien of Gannett News Service, and Arvis Chalmers of the *Albany Knickerbocker News*. Dan knew you couldn't just sit down and play poker, that you had to be invited. So he watched the game patiently for six months, and then one day Jimmy Desmond looked up and said to him, "Well, kid, you wanna play?"

Dan brought Rockefeller up to the press room one day, his first visit, and the governor was depressed by the dinginess of it. Said Dan: "Nelson told Emmett O'Brien and other old-timers here that he'd renovate the

place, extend The Shelf, clean it up, and modernize it." The cadre of
the press corps took this offer under advisement, then told the governor,
"No thanks. We want it just the way it is."

That's the way it still is, and it's not bad at all as press rooms go. It
looks like a press room, and it feels like a press room, and while there
is only a card game maybe once a month nowadays, the stakes are the
same as they were in the fifties: a quarter, half a dollar, and a dollar.
"Inflation has never hit this place," Dan Barr said.

In William Clift's photo of a downstairs corner of the press room, the
face of Mario Cuomo stares out at the viewer. Governor Cuomo,
the incumbent at this writing, personally oversaw the refurbishing of the
Executive Chamber, the most recent of the Capitol's modern restorations.

Governor Cuomo took us on a tour of the room that, before his tenure,
had been called the Red Room, after its red rug and draperies, and was
used mainly for press conferences. The sumptuous appointments of the
room's designer, architect Richardson, had been long since replaced
with mock-colonial furniture and chandeliers; radiators had blocked the
full-length windows; the handsome Philippine mahogany walls had been
gouged in numerous places to hang paintings; and a mighty clutter of
chairs and lights and wiring for cameras and microphones had overthrown
the room's original purpose: to give dignity and elegance to the office
of the chief executive.

Now press conferences are held elsewhere, a replica of the original
multicolored floral rug is on the floor, the colonial revival, the red decor
and the radiators are all gone, and the walls have been patched, polished,
and stripped of paintings. Will the paintings go back up?

"Only if I lose the election," said the governor, who prefers mahogany
to bad portraiture.

The room looks today very like it did when Governor Alonzo B. Cornell
entered it for the first time on September 30, 1881: luxurious, tasteful,
aesthetically pleasing. It is now used for ceremonial occasions, visitors
come through on tours, and the governor paces in it. He does not use
the eight-and-a-half-by-five-foot desk that Grover Cleveland and Theodore and Franklin Roosevelt used when they governed the state. "If I
sat at it," the governor said, "the newspapers would say I've got a Benito
Mussolini complex." He works in a smaller office, adjacent to the chamber, using a smaller desk that once belonged to F.D.R.

What does the governor think about such rooms, about the Capitol itself, and what it stands for?

"I love it," he said, and he pointed to the splendid fireplace that, as he explains to visiting schoolchildren, used to be the only source of heat in the chamber.

"Then I take the kids to the window and have them look out at the modern South Mall, so different from all this old way of life here, and I tell them that there were human beings here a hundred years ago, and there'll be human beings here a hundred years from now, and that we're only part of a continuum.

"I feel like a visitor here myself," the governor went on, "and the more time you spend on history, the more you feel that way. I'm very leery about changing anything or spoiling anything. We have to preserve things for generations that haven't been born yet, and being in this room makes you think that kind of thought."

The great structures of American political history were designed to dominate the communities that gave them power, their domes and towers thrusting upward to the heavens with the message that the law must be exalted. Albany's Capitol was to have a tower, but all designs proved either unwieldy or excessive, and it was never built. Even without it the building has dominated the city, and the state, for a century.

The sleek towers of its new neighbor, the South Mall, more formally known as the Nelson A. Rockefeller Empire State Plaza, now rise higher, but the Capitol is not diminished. It remains a giant among buildings, radiating the complex and multiple meanings of lawmaking, political debate, and the historical record of it all. It looms before us at the top of State Street hill like Franz Kafka's castle, and like that remarkable literary creation, it suggests a quest for grace, not by the individual in this case, but by the community.

Those long years of building the Capitol, the myriad restorations, the eternal tinkering with it, and the indefatigable will to finish the unfinishable, all bespeak a communal need to perfect a work of art: to embody meaning that may be venerated now and forever. The Capitol is, no doubt about it, an imperfect work of art, but it is nevertheless a very great one.

1986

Talking to
the High Court

When Chief Judge Sol Wachtler asked me to speak here he suggested I might create a bridge between this city and this court.* "Those of us who have been coming to Albany for the last century to serve on our state's highest tribunal," he wrote, "have come to love the city as our own."

Albany has actually been home to the high court for more than three and a half centuries, beginning in the era of the Patroon, Kiliaen van Rensselaer, whose feudal manor of Rensselaerswyck encompassed a million acres of the land that surrounds us here. In 1635 the Patroon appointed a Schout, who was sheriff, district attorney and high judge all in one, and empowered him to choose three Schepens, or aldermen of a sort, to administer government and justice. None were trained in law, so the Patroon sent them a book, *Freedoms of the Patroons and Colonies*, and cleverly noted to his judges that "those who cannot read shall immediately have the same read to them by others." The Patroon later sent two more volumes—Damhouwer on criminal procedure, and the Ars Notariatus, thus establishing the first law library in this old, old place of law and justice.

The seat of this new legal power was a shingled wooden building inside the walls of Fort Orange, at what's now the foot of Madison Avenue. The courtroom was seventeen feet long and ten feet wide, with judges' chambers on the second floor, to which the Schout and the Schepens

* The New York State Court of Appeals.

440

adjourned by climbing up a ladder through a trapdoor. This is when people first began to refer to this as the high court.

The court of Rensselaerswyck was so powerful that for years it resisted the efforts of the director general of the whole New Netherland colony, Peter Stuyvesant, to impose his authority here. The Schout of Rensselaerswyck, an arrogant fellow named Brandt van Schlictenhorst, went so far as to tear up all the law ordinances Stuyvesant ordered him to publish. One ordinance regulated a tax on tap beer, and some among us may recognize that this resistance to authority in matters of beer has been handed down to us in Albany, most notably during Prohibition, when the Albany political machine, in defiance of federal law, ran its own breweries.

Stuyvesant finally arrested van Schlictenhorst, evicted his court and created a new one, the Court of Fort Orange and Beverwyck, the oldest court in the state—a year older than the first New York City court. This court sat in a building called the Stadt Huys at the foot of Hudson Avenue, and it was here in the 1680s that Albany County, known as the Mother of Counties because of its enormous size, was created and subdivided—in 1683; and where in 1686 the city of Albany received its charter from Governor Thomas Dongan. That golden decade of the 1680s will also be remembered for other reasons—as the time when the first game of pool, and also the first peanut, were introduced to Albany.

The court outgrew the old Stadt Huys and a new one was built about 1743. And only Faneuil Hall in Boston, and Independence Hall in Philadelphia, could ever match it for historical significance; for here in 1754 was held the first Colonial Congress, with Benjamin Franklin presiding; and from its steps on July 19, 1776, the Declaration of Independence was read to the Continental army troops and the citizens of Albany.

Here also justice was served in a most expeditious and handy way. Convicted felons were taken out in front of the Stadt Huys and whipped; and convicted murderers were taken to the basement and hanged. In time the place was called the Common Gaol & City & County Hall, and justice was carried on here until 1808 when the county and city, and the state, all moved their offices to the new Capitol—we now call it the old Capitol—which stood just a bit southeast of where the present Capitol stands.

That year of the big move was also the year of the first accurate survey of a canal route between the Hudson River at Albany and Lake Erie. It was when Robert Fulton's steamboat, the *Clermont*, renamed the *North River*, docked here for her second season on the river; and when Albany theatergoers saw their first tigers—a male and female from Asia, down at the Thespian Hotel hall on North Pearl Street.

The court continued its work in the old Capitol until 1821, when a constitutional convention created the predecessor of this court—the Court for the Trial of Impeachments, and the Correction of Errors. But the Court of Errors was unwieldy with thirty-seven members, most of them politicians who knew or cared little about the law, and who voted on appeals without consulting either lawbooks or the few genuine judges who served on the court.

Judge Francis Bergan, in his book on this court, quotes the great *New York Tribune* editor Horace Greeley as writing of the "confessedly deplorable state of our higher courts of justice, choked with litigation which lingers from year to year and ruins clients by its enormous expensiveness without bringing their suits to a conclusion."

The population growth in the country at this time was fantastic, the Germans and the Irish coming in by the hundreds of thousands annually, and Albany felt it keenly, eventually becoming a city dominated by the Irish.

Yet the courts were constricting life at a time when the world was changing and expanding radically. In 1847, for instance, down at the Delavan House, the fancy hotel that stood where Fleet Plaza is today, a man named W. C. Bull read aloud the first telegraphic message sent by sound, an achievement noted all over the world. Albany was so impressed that it immediately opened direct communication with distant lands, the first being St. Louis, Missouri.

Such major changes in the society often seemed prophetic of divine anger to some who gave allegiance to the highest court of all. William Miller of Pittsfield founded a sect called the Millerites, and they predicted that 1843 would see the Second Coming of Christ. The Millerites grieved when Christ didn't turn up, but they recalculated and said he was really due in 1844. When he didn't show up then either they decided the world would end November 9, 1847.

Wrong again. The world kept going, including the New York State Legislature, which passed the Judiciary Act of 1847, creating this—the highest court of this state. The court has gone through many wrenchings, expansions and transformations in the years since then. In 1883 it moved into an elegant new courtroom in the present-day Capitol, and stayed there until 1916, when it began its move to this extraordinary building.

There are more connections to be made between the court and the city, more bridges to be built, but there is no time today to build them. And so I'd like to close with the remarks of two men, both sometime visitors to Albany, both close observers of our system of justice in this country. The first is Finley Peter Dunne, the Irish writer, who was well aware that justice eluded many of the Irish a hundred years ago, and who had this to say: "I tell ya, Hogan's right when he says 'Justice is blind.' Blind she is, and deaf—and dumb—and has a wooden leg."

And then Daniel Webster, the great American statesman whose whole life was government and law. "Justice," he said "is the greatest interest of man on earth."

I'm sure I speak for multitudes past and present when I say that we are proud this exalted court exists in our midst, but more than that: we are privileged beyond measure that it exists at all.

1986

Jody Bolden or
Bobby Henderson:

Either Way the
Music Was Great

"I made up my mind," Jody Bolden was saying, "that when I got down there I'd be relaxed and I wouldn't even think commercial. I thought of all the people who liked my music and I had them in mind, and not that it was gonna sell a million copies. And I had a beautiful piano to make it on and so I was more relaxed than any record session I was ever in. And for people I knew, I just wanted to play good songs, and we picked out the relaxin' tunes."

Jody Bolden, one of the very highly regarded pianists of the jazz age, but one whose fame was always way behind his talent, was sitting up in his bed at Albany Medical Center, talking about a major event in his life—the new record due for release before the year is out.

The record is called *Home in the Clouds*, the title of a tune Jody wrote in collaboration with Kaye Parker somewhere between 1927 and 1929 at Benny Carter's club in New York. Anybody who has ever heard Jody play piano for more than a few hours has probably heard the tune at least once, heard him play it and sing

> When the man in the moon
> scatters silver over the sky,
> We will hum any tune, make each
> song a sweet lullaby. . . .

The record is a rare development, for as anyone connected with music will tell you, the market today is all rock music, and jazz is just not very commercial anymore. But the record will be issued anyway, on the

Halcyon Label, apt name, a record firm owned by Marian McPartland, herself a highly regarded jazz pianist.

But the taping was a product of the devotion of two longtime jazz fans—John Hammond, now director of talent acquisition for CBS, and Hank O'Neal, a federal employee who first heard of Jody in 1957 when he was given a copy of *A Night at Count Basie's.*

The story, as Hank O'Neal tells it, dates to that record, when he first listened attentively to Jody Bolden's highly original style; and it leaps then to 1969 when John Hammond played a tape for O'Neal at Hammond's CBS office and asked if he recognized the musician.

"That's Bobby Henderson," O'Neal retorted, and claims he only needed four notes to make the identification. The tape had been made by Hammond at Mike Flanagan's Petit Paris Restaurant in Albany, where Jody played regularly before his illness sidelined him. The name "Bobby Henderson" is unfamiliar to many Albanians who know Jody only as Jody; but it is his straight name, and the one he uses on all his records.

O'Neal, who was visiting in Albany last week, said he told Hammond: "You're a big CBS executive, why don't you record this?" O'Neal, in his notes for the record jacket, continues the story:

"John said it was a pity that no one would record Bobby. The major companies just don't care very much about jazz and their interest in sixtyish, largely-unknown Negro jazz pianists is totally non-existent.

"And so," O'Neal adds, "it became a personal project to find someone to sponsor a record of Bobby." The sponsor turned out to be Sherman M. Fairchild, head of Fairchild Aviation, and Fairchild Camera and Instrument Co., a man O'Neal describes as "a longtime friend of jazz behind the scenes (and striding piano players in particular)." Striding piano, or stride piano, is the jazz genre into which Jody Bolden's work fits, along with the work of James P. Johnson, Fats Waller and Art Tatum.

Says O'Neal of Jody: "He's a more tasteful player than either Tatum or Fats. Tatum would put forty-eight notes in a measure when you could've gotten away with twelve. And he [Jody] doesn't get so boisterously out of hand as the music sometimes did with Fats—on songs like 'Your Feet's Too Big' or 'Fat and Greasy.' "

Most of Jody's late years were lived in Albany, away from the mainstream where most musicians practice their art. And so, as O'Neal pointed out in the liner notes to *Home in the Clouds*, Jody/Bobby has "not been a major part of the new trends in jazz that have developed since he left New York City in 1937. He really never needed to be. He simply plays jazz that is eternally fresh, always tasteful, and ever appealing. It may have been a few years, but Bobby does not have any catching up to do."

Jody, born in 1910, began taking piano lessons when he was eight, when Mamie Smith, the blues singer, used to come to his house in Harlem to visit. By the time he was fifteen he was serious about the piano—"practicing, practicing," he said. "At that age I never felt I could play. You'd listen to guys like Ellington and Fats and they'd really grown up in music. But after a while they were very inspiring."

He made a record when he was seventeen, backing up a young singer named Martha Raye. Jody credited John Hammond with getting him that record date.

"Martha was sixteen," Jody recalled. "She had long pigtails and she was well developed for a young girl, and her mother used to travel with her. All those musicians, man, had big eyes for Martha."

The record was cut but never released. Jody got work with a band, then met Fats, who took him on as a protégé. He credited Fats with giving him the self-confidence to play solo piano, and then introducing him to crowds with the words, "Now you've got to hear my boy play."

An underground kind of fame developed for Jody, and then came a record date in 1933 and fate stepped in. The subway Jody was on had a breakdown and when he got to the studio his recording time was gone. And he waited twenty-three years for another chance—the night in 1956 that John Hammond walked into a nightclub on Albany's Eagle Street called the Kerry Blue, run by Jean Garrison, and with Jody as the star attraction.

It would be Hammond's rediscovery of Bobby Henderson, and in the next two years Jody would make four records, most notably *A Handful of Keys*, on which he gives a good but disappointing rendition of one of his greatest numbers, "Twelfth Street Rag," but which also has his best recording, "Blues for Fats"—fourteen choruses of it. One jazz critic, Johnny Simmen, thought this to be "one of the outstanding piano performances in music. Any kind of music, I mean . . . Bobby's inspiration never falters."

Jody had settled in Albany in 1946 and ten years later was telling people, "I just want to be known as an Albany man who played music." Such musicians as Rex Stewart and Roy Eldridge and Trummy Young and Omer Simeon and Hot Lips Page would drop by the Kerry Blue to play alongside Jody, or just listen to him make that two-handed sound that filled the room.

What kind of music was it?

"I just play with ten fingers," Jody said.

"Some piano players only play with one hand," someone said.

"You got to have at least eight fingers," Jody said. "You can't make it with less than that."

Jody seemed to have two dozen fingers and, at his peak, incredible accuracy and unbelievable speed. A tune like "Twelfth Street Rag" would send listeners into ecstasies of excitement, bring them to their feet to cheer the maestro.

It had been like that from the early days, when he was playing in such Harlem nightclubs as the Famous Door and Pod's and Jerry's, and then at the club where he met Billie Holiday.

"She sang great, man, from the first time I ever heard her. She was working in a joint in Prohibition, maybe it was the Clam House, in New York, and a lot of musicians I knew wanted me to hear her. So we go by the Clam House and Billie was accompanied by this girl named Vi and Vi played a lot of piano, and Billie sang. She was a natural from the start and it only took the right people to hear her. So then I got up to play a tune and Billie was amazed because I was so perfect accompanying her. And then I played 'Sweet Sue' for an encore and I knocked her out."

In her book, *Lady Sings the Blues*, Billie wrote in passing that "By then Bobby Henderson was playing for me. I still think he was the greatest."

He played for Billie at a place called Jerry's Log Cabin in Harlem, on 133rd Street—his first nightclub job. Willie (the Lion) Smith was on the bill, and Jody replaced him. Jody remembered Willie fondly: "Among piano players Willie was one of the senior citizens, man."

Willie was on his last night at the club when Jody arrived, and he recalled: "I froze when I got in the place, cause I never had seen so many famous musicians—Goodman, Bunny Berigan, the Dorsey brothers, the whole crowd. The boss of the place got me up to play and I played Gershwin's 'I Got Rhythm.' I was nervous, but the boss says 'You play piano,' and I says 'Little bit.' Surprisingly I got a terrific hand. Somebody was liking it."

1969

Postscript: We were all was still liking it when *Home in the Clouds* was released in 1969. It was Jody, all right, but past his peak. The lung cancer that was destroying him slowly had affected the use of his arms. He died December 9, 1969, about the time the record came out.

When he and I talked in his last days of how he looked at his career he said, "I don't want people to forget me." Now when I listen to his records, I feel great joy at being in his company again, but also an enduring sadness; for though the music on all his records (even one with him playing a tinny, honky-tonk piano) was always of a high order, it was never high enough to capture the complete Jody, the great Jody. And so people who come to him only through his records can never know how truly good he was. Only those who heard him play live have that now. I have that and it's a great thing to have.

The Charcoal Man:

Warming Up to the Press

George Dobert didn't know why anybody would be interested in hearing about the making of charcoal nowadays.

Because it's kind of odd, he was told; kind of unusual; the kind of thing you never think about anybody doing. Charcoal is just there at the supermarket when you want it, ready-made, like a jar of artichokes. Maybe you could show me the equipment, how it's done.

"It's just burned out in the yard in a pile."

"The wood?"

"Yep, the wood."

"Any particular kind of wood?"

"Nope. Any wood will burn."

"Well, could you show me the equipment you use?"

"You want to come out I'll show you the shovel and the rake."

So the jaunt was made up the winding road to Taborton and eventually to George H. Dobert's farm on The Kipple, a road that was just a meandering wagon path when George Dobert was born seventy years ago, and wasn't much more than that when he bought his farm forty-eight years ago. A big farm. A hundred acres. Maybe two hundred, George said, worrying not at all about being specific with a stranger. But when he got there forty-eight years ago he could look across his land and up to the higher part of the mountain and see the house that was there even then, that is now a bigger house. But that isn't all that's changed. A whole forest has grown up in between George's house and that other one. And it is out of that forest that the logs came that he—and his father before him—turned into fire wood, or charcoal.

"How long I been burnin' coal? If you want to know the truth, since I started to walk."

George also has raised some beef cattle and dairy cattle and planted his own potatoes and lettuce and lived off the land, and the charcoal was something else that brought money in. Did he live off the charcoal?

"It takes everything," he said. "If I just wanted to farm I'd starve to death."

He never did farm a whole lot, and then lightning hit his barn and it burned down and he lost some of the animals, but anyway it was inevitable that he'd go out of the dairy business, what little there was.

"Today if I had to sell a quart of milk I'd have to have everything inspected. Fellow down here below the church used to sell milk in the summertime, and the doctor had to come up and inspect it. If I was to sell a quart of milk today I'd give it away before I sell it. Give it away. When I came up here you didn't have that stuff. Make butter and take it in town and sell it. Now there ain't no cows from here to Sand Lake."

What about the charcoal, what do you do with it?

"You sell it."

"For starting coal furnaces, for instance?"

"Where do you know they got houses like that nowadays? Nobody got them kind of furnaces anymore."

"The most they buy it for is to have a cookout, and barbecuin'," said Mrs. Dobert, who, having said that, got up and left the front porch.

"How much do you sell in a year?"

"I have no idea. Some years I didn't burn anything. Now pretty near everything is oil furnaces. See oil trucks goin' up and down the road every day. And everybody works in the city today. That's where I oughta went. Them that went didn't care for anything else but making the big money, gettin' five dollars an hour. Didn't get that burnin' coal. Sometimes you don't sell ten dollars' worth a week. Just now it's a little better. All winter didn't sell hardly any."

"What about the profit, say from about fifty bushels?"

"I ain't sold fifty bushels can't say when, must be four, five years ago. Maybe longer. Used to have a roofer and he'd take forty bushels at a time. I didn't measure. He furnished the bags. I don't know what happened to him. Guess the bigshot died and they got someone else in

there. Everything's changing and changing fast. Coal ain't like it used
to be. Sometimes you'd go to the city and sell forty, fifty bags. That ain't
much. That ain't a day's pay. I ain't peddled now to the city in seven
years maybe. I ain't got no trucks or anything. Just a team of horses. If
I went to the city with them they'd have me arrested. I'd be holding up
traffic all over."

Now one of his sons (he had eleven children) delivers charcoal to
some stores, but not very much by George's reckoning.

"Gettin' old anyway. All through as far as I'm concerned. All through
crawlin' around all night."

"Crawling around?"

"You got to watch it, maybe every two hours."

"How big is the pile?"

"Sometimes you burn a little, sometimes big ones."

"We'll say a pile half as big as this porch. How deep would it be?"

"Ten feet and that there burned, and it settles down and sometimes
the inside ain't burnt."

"Now this may seem like a dumb question, but how do you keep it
from just turning into ashes?"

"Cover it with dirt. Put a heap of wood, and cover it."

"The dirt doesn't smother it?"

"Nope." George Dobert snorted at the ignorance of the stranger. "You
just start a little fire and get it going. I don't know how you explain it.
Just start a fire. And then you got to watch it every time or it'd burn
right up."

"So it just smolders then. For how long?"

"Couple of weeks, and maybe it wouldn't be all charcoal then. Maybe
some of it wouldn't be burnt."

"What about when it rains?"

"That's good. Sometimes it gets so red hot it won't smoke even."

George took the visitor out of the barn and showed him a bin of
finished charcoal, about a quarter full. Cords of hemlock and maple and
birch were stacked along the driveway to the barn, and an old plow was
gone to rust. In another barn were the horses. What kind of horses? Just
horses. And then a truck and a large sleigh that the horses draw in the
winter, which is a bad time for burning coal because it's too cold to

keep watching it all through the night. The truck belongs to George's son who works with the logs and the charcoal now that his father is pretty much out of the business.

"I ain't gonna stay here forever," George said. "Some don't live as long as I did."

He looked down at the tree full of wild apple blossoms and that reminded him of another change in life.

"They wonder why people die," he said, "eatin' all that arsenic. They spray it on everything. I eat apples I peel 'em. They even spray the potatoes. Fella bought a whole load of potatoes and planted 'em and they never sprouted. Another fella up there bought a pig and gave it a cabbage leaf and the pig got sick. Vet said the only thing he could see was that he got poisoned. But I lived here forty-eight years and I guess I'll live forty-eight more. Live, like the fella says, as long as I see somebody else livin'."

It was dusk now and the mosquitoes were out and biting. The stranger swatted them as George's eyes smiled through his steel-rimmed spectacles. He had started out reticent, untrusting. Now he was relaxed and garrulous, talking again without prodding about the city, where he envied the big money. "Even when they get makin' five dollars an hour it ain't enough for them and they go on strikes. Times are changin'. Times are changin' so fast you can't keep up with 'em."

The visitor made a note and George wondered: "You gonna put that in the paper too?"

"Probably."

And George shook his head in amazement at what people find important to write about in the newspapers these days. George couldn't get over it.

"Say," he said, "you're gonna have to send me one of them papers."

"Positively," said the visitor, who then drove back down the mountain into the middle of 1970.

1970

Postscript: Some months after this story appeared in print a lawyer from Troy came up to me at a party and said, "George Dobert got a kick out of that story you wrote about him." I said I enjoyed it too because it had gotten at an odd and antique truth about rural life. Then the fellow said, "No, he got a kick out of it because he thought you were an Internal Revenue man when you called him. He thought you were checking him out." And so whatever George had told me about making charcoal had to be read in an entirely new light. It also may help explain why, in the story, Mrs. Dobert leaves the porch so suddenly after bringing up the subject of barbecuing. I taught this story regularly in my journalism class for years after, explaining that reporters should understand clearly that there is a decided difference between the truth and the whole truth.

Barney Fowler:

The Quest for Curmudgeonous Joy

Barney Fowler.

In some quarters, the name slides through the teeth like sandpaper. Elsewhere, teams of police and patriots stand and recite the pledge of allegiance to Fowler and all his works. His mail, he says, totals twelve thousand letters a year, and people call him in the middle of the night to shout obscenities. For a time he received a flood of pornographic mail, catalogues and photos in plain brown wrappers, the consequence of a practical joke played on him by Albany students who had been targets of his verbal abuse. He took two pies in the face on campus here to raise money for the Telethon. People remember him Red-baiting professors who were giving anti-draft counseling to students in the 1960s, and he is the coiner of an alternative name for State University at Albany that some people find alliteratively appalling: "Dirty Doodleland."

I remember Barney Fowler when he didn't wear any socks. He was then the Saturday city editor of the *Albany Times-Union*, a relative newcomer from Schenectady, where he had been a columnist for fifteen years on the *Union-Star*. Sockless he came from Schenectady, bearing harpoon, bow and arrow, and writing nature stories about wild Adirondack animals and fish, which he would skewer with arrow, spear with harpoon. Sockless he would go into the woods (also matchless and without benefit of gunpowder), and survive alone for a week or two, then come back to the city room and turn out one sockless story after another about skewered and sockless Adirondack animals. Hal Kallenburg, the late *Times-Union* columnist, took note of the phenomenon and made the pronouncement that enlightened us all: "Barney had a great disappointment in life. He expected to be born a bear."

Barney Fowler is now sixty-seven and has been in the news business for fifty-three years, most of that time as a columnist. He recalled some of his high points recently, during an interview at his desk in the *Times-Union* city room. Chain-smoking and deep-inhaling Camels as he turned out one of the six columns he writes every week, he summed up the essence of his role as a curmudgeon: "I'm totally opinionated and will remain that way."

He applies the word "curmudgeon" to himself with lavish affection. As he practices it, curmudgeonism has its basis in a circumlocutory quest for love. Self-love is part of the syndrome, as is his professed love of opinion: right opinion, wrong opinion, it doesn't matter.

He is for the death penalty. And although he says he has stayed away from the abortion issue, he admits he is somewhat against it, somewhat for it. "I believe in abortion for rape, incest and mother's safety cases." He is against the abuse of booze and drugs by Albany students. He is against letting television cameras into the courtroom. He is for tolls on the Barge Canal, ever since he became aware of million-dollar yachts with white-jacketed waiters on them cruising the canal toll-free. He is against politicians using state autos in private matters and has spies everywhere noting state license plates on cars out for Sunday drives. He has long been against snowmobiles, "the most emotional thing I ever touched on."

"I had members of the Snowmobile Association come to the paper and threaten a boycott because of my attitude," he recalled. "Everyplace I'd go, they'd attack me."

He egged them on by recalling that a psychiatrist once told him the snowmobile was a compensatory sex symbol used by people with a lack of sexual ability. "All you got to do is say that in print . . ." Fowler said with a Freudian wink.

He is also responsible for what has been alternately called the "Million-Dollar Outhouse" and the "Fowler Sanitation Spa" on the Northway. He campaigned relentlessly for a comfort station on his route between the newspaper and the North Country animal territory.

He also campaigned against boats discharging sewage into state waters, viewing the boat owners of the state as captains of "floating toilets."

"It's the kind of thing that irritates people," he said. "A man pays thirty thousand for a boat and opens up the paper to see it called a floating toilet."

Fowler has also campaigned to have the SUNY campus police armed to keep down muggings of students, has plugged diligently on behalf of the beleaguered Adirondack Park Agency (which, peripherally, is concerned about bears), and remembers fondly the time he campaigned against feminism in a debate with Betty Friedan in Albany.

"I think that was the funniest goddamn thing that ever happened to me," he recalled. Members of a women's press club in Albany had been reading his antifeminist views and invited him to debate somebody. The somebody they chose turned out to be Ms. Friedan, and a full house turned out to see them tangle.

"I was certainly not against women as such," Fowler said, "but I didn't like some of the things they were asking for."

His views, more than once during the debate, caused Ms. Friedan to yank the microphone out of his hand. "I told her I was trying to act like a gentleman and I wished she'd try to act like a lady," he recalled. Ms. Friedan called him a male chauvinist pig.

"I picked that up," Fowler said, meaning he used it in his column. "I rather liked it."

How does it feel, he was asked, to be a provocateur?

"If you're geared for things, you can smell controversy a mile off," he said. "I've been in this business long enough to know that you've got to provoke something; so in turn you provoke thought, and you get two sides to it."

His attack on the university began when some of his informants ("A lot of my stuff came from the cleaning and maintenance people," he explained) found, back in the 1960s, some disheveled sections of the campus during sit-ins and other protests. That's when Dirty Doodleland was born in the imagination of Barney Fowler. He carried the campaign on for years and vented his wrath against administrators who refused to impose discipline on students who wrecked furniture, burned holes in carpets and left garbage in their wake. To get a first-hand look at campus damage, he disguised himself as a painter, stuck a paintbrush in his overalls, and walked through the campus carrying a bucket of water. What he saw, he didn't like.

"Seriously, I began wondering why they didn't start weeding out some of these characters. If this had happened when I was younger, I would have been expelled forthwith. This whole damn thing just keeps going and they accept it."

Does this mean Barney Fowler condemns the entire student body, administration and faculty of the university? Not entirely. Last year he praised the administration for seeing fit to cancel a Drink and Drown Party that students were planning.

Also, he appeared on campus once and debated students ("They've got active minds, let me tell you") on the issue of student flogging. He said he believed in it only in certain cases, and not in cases of damaged furniture.

He has campaigned against exposing the students to speakers like Abbie Hoffman, and once, when he called the Albany Student Press to ask for a subscription, an editor hung up on him. From then on he referred to the paper as the Campus Rag.

He also entered into an exchange with an Albany professor who "analyzed my writing and found it 'clumsy and archaic.' I never forgot the word archaic because I didn't know what it really meant."

For all those on campus who united against him, if indeed they did, a much larger number off-campus united behind him, not just on the university issues but on all the controversies he provokes. His mail, he said, runs about 80 percent positive, 20 percent negative, a nice balance, in his opinion. He once mentioned the availability of a set of plans to make a bluebird house and received six hundred requests in the mail. "One of the most popular things I ever did," he said.

His attacks on the university have diminished of late, but does that mean the skirmishing is over? "I reawaken the thing once in a while," he said, "just to keep it going."

Fowler understands his audience the way Louis Armstrong understood his trumpet. He strokes them six times a week with his ursine and his bullish invective, giving them the news they want to hear. He will take the pornographic mockery and pie in the face from Albany students, but he also knows that when he translates the pie story into a column item, the students will get the raspberry and he will get the mail.

And when it pours in, lavishing love on the columnist, Barney Fowler will scratch his bald head in glee, light up another Camel and start shaping yet another set of plans designed to entrap that curmudgeonous creature of thin air, the Bluebird of Fowlerian Happiness.

1981

Radicalism and Dwight MacDonald:

Not What They Used to Be

Radicalism isn't what it used to be.

It's as different as Dwight MacDonald is from Kenneth Pitchford—in the clothes they wear, in the cut of their beards, in how far they will go to change America. The difference is also between youth and age, for even though Pitchford is not a youth—he's thirty-seven—he considers himself "an honorary youth," and he looks, acts, talks, poeticizes and loves the world like a hippie.

MacDonald, on the other hand, dresses like a rumpled fugitive from Weber and Heilbroner, and while he exudes intelligence, sardonic wit, political perspicacity and excess acidity over Lyndon B. Johnson, it is clear that he is a victim of tradition. He believes America is worth saving.

Poet Pitchford feels it is only worth abdicating.

Their ideologies clashed Thursday night at Albany State University during a lively teach-in on the Vietnam War. The teach-in was a prelude to Friday's "strike" by students and some faculty to protest America's involvement in the war. About two hundred people, mostly dressed anti-flamboyantly (which made Pitchford's oversize rings, love beads and rainbow shirt all the more exceptional), hooted and whistled and applauded the speakers as they expressed the various ideologies on the left—from socialism to pacifism, from nonviolent liberalism to what MacDonald called "infantile ultra-leftism and mechanical Marxism."

The students were the listeners at the outset as MacDonald—longtime radical journalist, former editor of the magazine *Politics*, erstwhile writer for *Fortune*, now a columnist for *Esquire* and occasional writer for *The New Yorker*, and certainly one of the most omnipresent critics of America's war stance to be found between oceans—expounded on the condition of politics at the moment in the United States.

He abhorred Johnson—"the most catastrophic president we've ever had. . . . He'll go down in history beside Herbert Hoover, a little lower"—and he was for Senator Eugene McCarthy for President. He urged the students to be cautious about accepting the Johnson announcement that he will not seek reelection. "Don't let down your guard," he warned. "I really don't know what he's up to."

He saw the McCarthy victory in the New Hampshire primary as "a turning point in the history of this country—it led to the exit of Johnson." He talked of how young college students shaved their beards and lengthened their skirts to campaign door-to-door for McCarthy and he found this to be probably flattering to the people who were canvassed by these kids. "They probably were flattered to be paid so much attention by young, intelligent upper-class youths," MacDonald said. He also lamented for Senator Robert Kennedy: "Poor old Bobby has got all the money. But he hasn't got these kids."

MacDonald wore his badges proudly. He had been a 1930s radical. He cited his Trotskyist affiliation way back then and even told a joke at his own expense: "Trotsky said of me that everybody has the privilege of being stupid, but MacDonald abuses the privilege."

MacDonald concluded his talk by saying that among Johnson's many mistakes was the arrest of Dr. Benamin Spock and four others for antidraft counseling. "It's given a great shot in the arm to the whole peace movement," he said. Then he wished the students luck with their "strike" and concluded: "Up the resistance!"

It was altogether an affable, witty and fairly tough speech. He drew sustained applause and in no way prepared for what was about to happen.

The first sign was when George Hein, a chemist from Newton, Massachusetts, who is a worker for Resist, an antidraft organization, began the antipolitical line that would explode into verbal hippie bombs subsequently. Briefly the line is that traditional politics is useless as a way of making change in American society. "So," he said, "I would suggest alternatives outside the system. . . . Get people to ask: can you have alternatives to the system?

"A year ago," he said, "burning draft cards was for kooks. Today it's not. Very respectable people do it."

When he said that the edge of civilization was not—as Dwight MacDonald joked, where you can no longer get the morning *New York Times*—but that it was "where people act out of conscience," the applause was loud and long.

Somehow MacDonald was made to seem in the wrong. Vaguely. But somehow.

Then David Mermelstein, an economist who teaches at Brooklyn Polytechnic Institute, opened the soft salvo at MacDonald. He said he didn't like MacDonald's reference to "Red China," and said: "I think it's time all of us get over the cold-war talk and make it just plain China." Then he attacked MacDonald with his big guns: talking about Herbert Hoover the way MacDonald did made it seem that there was something better about Roosevelt, something good about Democratic liberalism and bad about Republicanism.

For a split second Mermelstein sounded like a disconsolate Republican, but then quickly he made it clear that he thought, like Hein, that politics was irrelevant, and never touches the true seats of power in America—the Pentagon, the federal bureaucracy, the State Department. "We better not rely on liberal politicians to save us," he said. "I have no confidence that Robert Kennedy and McCarthy will not use napalm against guerrillas should other wars break out in Latin America."

MacDonald took the microphone with a funny smile and commented: "I really must have a word."

The audience had somehow—vaguely, but somehow—turned on him, applauding Mermelstein so enthusiastically after applauding MacDonald so enthusiastically. (Actually the audience applauded everybody enthusiastically, just as long as they were emotional and left of center, which everybody was.)

MacDonald termed Mermelstein's view "ultra-leftism that says don't worry about politics, because it won't solve our problem." He said there was no chance for a real revolution in America under present circumstances, and therefore: "I think we should do what we can do."

Mermelstein answered back, MacDonald added a quip or two. Then Hugo Bedau, professor of philosophy at Tufts University, took the microphone and told the audience that "You may think there's a bunch of drunks up here tonight. But what you're watching is the left in disarray."

The discussion moved back and forth over the organization Resist, over the role of blacks and whites on the Left, and when Mermelstein said: "It doesn't make any difference who is President—Nixon or McCarthy, the N.L.F. will push us out of Vietnam," then MacDonald told him: "I think you've added mechanical Marxism to infantile leftism."

But MacDonald's push for activism within the framework of the existing social and political structure was beginning to grate upon the students. A young blonde predicted a successful socialist revolution in the United States, and then Kenneth Pitchford made his presence heard for the first time. He angrily told MacDonald: "We're against your old-fashioned, leftist, brainwashed ideology. Just today Long Island University and Columbia have gone up and there's another group that's going to liberate N.Y.U. What we're for is un-hung-up sexual freedom, we're for love, we're for sharing, we don't want any of this (obscenity). We want freedom and we want it now!"

The applause was enthusiastic.

Said MacDonald: "This figure is irresponsible. He's doing the job for J. Edgar Hoover and L.B.J."

MacDonald kept his cool. He pooh-poohed the campus takeovers during the past week as irresponsible also. The talk went on, but that was the peak moment. A Negro student defended hippies. A white student defended hippies. A white student trembled as he deplored violence and praised Gandhi. Then came the intermission, time for punch, time to gather into little knots and talk about all the talk. Somebody asked MacDonald if he supported Fred Halstead, the Socialist candidate for President.

MacDonald laughed unkindly. "You think I learned nothing in the thirties?" he asked the student.

"Do you get this kind of flack all the time when you speak?" MacDonald was asked. And he laughed again, generously.

"The younger generation. Yeah, sure," he said.

The crowd dwindled to about seventy and milled around the punch pitchers and the leftist literature from North Vietnam, from the Socialist party, from American writers on Vietnam, and after a half-hour the teach-in reconvened for poetry readings.

Muriel Rukeyser, the noted poet, was one of four who read. Both she and Harriet Zinnes read their own poems plus the works of others that impinged on the war. Robin Morgan, who is the wife of Kenneth Pitchford, read her own work, plus works by Vietnamese poets who have written eloquent antiwar poetry.

But poet Pitchford was far and away the high point of the poetry hour, not from his poeticizing, which in itself is notable and has been well-received in the past by critics of repute, but rather because of his posture on America.

"I'm tired of words," he said. "I think poetry is dysfunctional."

He spoke of too much emphasis on literary conventions when black and white men are dying. And then he spoke of the essence of his revolt of the moment: ". . . the fight against white elderism."

"I'm talking to white middle-class kids," he said, and he urged that "we declare ourselves a separate nation. We'll have our own press, the underground press. We've got our own music, Country Joe and The Fish. We've got people who'll do plumbing for us. We won't recognize America. We might recognize Cuba. We won't have any land so people who want to visit us won't need passports. . . . This is a revolution of music, of sex, of drugs, of joy. . . . We're now thinking about a Constitutional Convention and a Declaration of Independence. When in the course of human events one people can't bear another . . ."

The applause was enthusiastic.

Dwight MacDonald was gone. In more ways than one.

1968

Requiem for a Lady at the Bottom of the World

That fact that people die alike does not mean that they lived alike. A truism. Why say it? Because when you think of Jenny's death you think of all the things that they will say about her. They'll say she was a wino. And once they've said that they don't have to say anything else. Because the people who are ready to believe that winos are all of a stripe, that they live alike and die alike, will toss Jenny into that wino bin of theirs.

A mistake. Jenny wasn't like the others. (The others weren't like the others either.) But for the purpose of simplifying Jenny's case we can admit that she was different in all the important ways from the wino folk around her. What they had in common was a façade, which is strangely vital at the bottom shelf of the world. Jenny had no façade.

"I'm shy," she said. "People scare me."

One of the underachievers; one of the psychological have-nots. The secrets of power in America, Saul Bellow the novelist once said, will never be revealed to innocents and underdogs. Jenny was the underdog. Also the innocent. What power could ever accrue to the likes of her?

She had worked as a short-order cook. She had a talent for sewing. One woman who knew her had the sense she might have been a master seamstress if she'd been able to put her mind to it. She was proud of the athletic ability she had in her youth (she was 41 in September); captain of her basketball team in Virginia, she kept telling her friends. Status, of course; rather a sad status when at age 41 you must go back to your high school years to find a moment when you were somebody.

She was a mother, indirectly but absolutely. Her husband, Connie, short for Constantine (such a royal name that mocked the decline he fell into), had found a child in a vacant lot. The child's mother was still there when Connie found the baby, naked. "He didn't even have no diaper," Connie said.

"You want that little ol', thing, you can have him," the natural mother told Connie. And Connie took him, and raised him. Brought him home to Jenny. They called the boy Jubjub; nicknames were a way with them: Jenny called Connie Moosie, and Connie called Jenny Little Girl.

Connie was also a wino, and people who saw the child without understanding anything of the family unit, thought the boy was a kind of mascot, a pet for winos. But he was the child of two alcoholic people who loved him. In the years when Jubjub passed the age of reason, when he got his prize possession, a bicycle, he became a wild boy. He slept in doorways. He became a truant. Jenny the surrogate mother, who came from a family of ten herself but raised no family except another woman's castoff, loved the child. Like her own, some said. But Jenny could not know whether that was true or not, having had none of her own to compare.

The boy loved Jenny. When the wine corroded her, gave her constant diarrhea, Jubjub got money. Don't ask how he got it. He got it and bought Kaopectate, that his mother drank to bind her body. It was one of many sicknesses that Jenny and Connie fell heir to. Two of Jenny's sisters died of lung ailments, and Jenny had lung trouble for as long as anybody could remember. Connie had hepatitis, leg trouble, hemorrhages through the nose. Two years ago he became as victimized as Job, not with boils but with peripheral neuritis so that nobody could touch him, not his arm, not his leg, not his shoulder, not anyplace, because he hurt everywhere. He lay down on the top of a stoop on Dongan Avenue and he listened to a radio somebody put beside his ear and he stopped drinking and stopped eating and prepared to die. When anybody hurts as much as Connie hurts they assume that death is the only consequence.

But friends took him to the hospital and after a few weeks he was out and well; thin as glass and just as fragile, but off the wine and with the neuritis gone, a kind of new man.

Jenny was in the hospital at the same time. Her vital capacity was minimal, her lungs all but collapsed. She occupied a bed on a floor below Connie in the Albany Medical Center and some said they were

going to die together. But then she too recovered and they came regularly
to meetings of the Better Homes and Community Organization in the
South End, the neighborhood organization that functions in the midst of
bordellos and wino caves and the squalid life of the poorest of Albany's
poor.

Connie cracked jokes and dressed in the way that he still clung to in
his most sober times: dapperness out of a long-gone time when dapperness was status too. Jenny listened, but with her bright mind she was
the first to detect irony. Full of self-awareness, she saw through others
who became grotesque when they articulated their cockeyed little
egos. Jenny was a smart one. Would have made a wonderful seamstress.
Would have made a wonderful mother. Would have made a wonderful
cook. Wonderful wife. Wonderful homemaker. Had a husband. Had a
child. Had a talent, could sew. Too bad, Jenny, too bad you never
flowered.

Jenny was dying. Sick since 1948. Very sick for the last seven years.
So thin she wasn't there at all inside those baggy clothes. Yours sincerely,
wasting away. And everybody knew she was dying. Connie's father came
to see them when they were both deep in the sickness, deep in the wine.
You wouldn't want to read about how bad the room was that they were
both living in that day. Connie was sick and bleeding. Jenny was on
the couch with her stick legs out at the end of a blanket.

"You're in the bed," Connie's father said.

"I know," Connie said.

"Woman," the father said to Jenny, "what are you gonna do?"

"Papa," she said, "I'm not gonna do nothin'."

"You know what that means?"

"I know."

The father did not argue with despair. Possibly a task force of hu-
manists and sociologists and social therapists and miracle workers could
have reclaimed Jenny. But the father was not a task force.

"You don't have to settle for this despair," an optimist said to the
gray-haired old man.

"You do have to settle for it," the old man said.

And so Jenny moved through her last days. She still narrowed her
eyes with knowingness, she still called people Doll, if they were men,
and Dolly if they were women, she was still able to respond when Connie

was comatose and hemorrhaging, no matter how sick she was herself; and though all these human responses were perpetuated in her twig-like frame, she was dying. And everybody knew.

Jenny couldn't get her breath last week. And every breath hurt, every breath drew a moan from her. Connie collected himself and took her to the hospital and knew when he left her that she was really dying this time. Really. He went home and slept and dreamed he was fishing. Dreamed he caught onto a great fish that tugged him almost into the water himself; then he'd pull it in; then it'd swim away and when he finally pulled the line in he found a little horseshoe kind of hook at the end of the line, empty. The waters he was fishing in were muddy, a sign of death. The empty hook: a good try, but too bad.

"Somethin' bad gonna happen, Jubjub," he told the boy. "Somebody gonna leave us."

She died Monday at 2:15, the death certificate said. It didn't specify whether it was A.M. or P.M. The police tried to find Connie but it was Wednesday before he knew the police had called at his house. A neighbor told him. He wondered: why the hell the police lookin' for me? I ain't done nothin'. And he went to the station where the desk sergeant said they weren't looking for him at all. Bureaucratic confusion. And then a friend from Better Homes called him and told him: Your wife passed away.

He sat in the big armchair at his father's house, having unsuccessfully tried to get some extra money so Jenny wouldn't have to be buried strictly with a welfare funeral. He wanted to add a few hundred, get something more than a pine box. But he couldn't get it.

At the edge of life himself, Connie remembered how Jenny's sister said she shouldn't marry Connie. "I was a rough young guy in those days," he said. "I didn't care about nothin'. But I changed." And Jenny and Connie stayed married for 16 years.

Connie was in that state of random grief. Now he would weep, now laugh. Now he would grow nostalgic, now he would think of the future.

"I'm through with women," he said. "No joke. I had my time. I don't care if she was born with gold. I had my woman."

Nuns from Saint Rose College gave Jenny a dress to be buried in. It was a black wool dress. The nuns knew her from their attendance at the Better Homes meetings. Of course they didn't have to know her to give something to a woman with nothing at all. The Saint Rose nuns who attend the Better Homes meetings are some of the very few people who know or care about people like Jenny.

At his father's house Connie talked about death with the old man.

"There's no rent to pay up there," the old man said.

"I wanna look good when I go up there," Connie said. "I look good now, don't I?"

"No," his papa said. "You look too bad even to die."

Connie took that as a joke. But he spruced up and went to the undertakers and arranged for Jenny's $250 funeral, paid by the County Welfare Department. Later he went home to bed, and at 3 A.M. he got up and walked to the bus station to meet one of Jenny's relatives who was arriving. But the relative never came, and Connie walked back home in the cold.

1967

Baseball at Hawkins Stadium:
"Here's Your Son, Mister."

I owned a rubber baseball, a glove, a bat, and a uniform at such an early age I can't know how young I was. I know from photographs that I was using them well before my precocity with spheres, diamonds, numbers and letters allowed me to enter first grade at age five in 1933. My uncle Peter pitched to me on the front lawn, and my great-aunt Lella caught the pitches I didn't hit. The glove was a pair of leather slabs without padding, and for catching a ball it was as practical as a tin plate.

By perhaps 1935 or 1936 the New Deal had come to North Albany, and the Rooseveltian minions in the Works Progress Administration were building tennis courts and leveling the huge open field behind Public School 20 (and next door to our house), where everybody played baseball and football and golf and where, Lou Pitnell tells me, he and I caught fly balls and grounders hit by the tall, thin, fiftyish foreman of the WPA gang, a man named Mac, while Mac's underlings cleared rocks, moved and raked dirt, planted grass, and beautified the sandlot where cows had grazed when this was a pasture on the Brady farm.

I've tried to dredge Mac up from memory but he's not even a phantasm. But I remember Lou Pitnell's glove from those days: very stiff leather but with a good pocket, and my own: a yellow first baseman's mitt that I still have, although the yellow is now mostly black, and the rawhide webbing has rotted. That glove was why I usually played first, even though I was a right-hander. Lou threw righty but batted lefty, something I never understood in people until I began to write about politics. Bob Burns, another sandlotter, remembers very few left-handed players—

The author strikes the stance of an incipient home-run hitter. When he grew up and lofted one over the fence, they moved the fence.

Billy Corbett, Billy Riedy—but no lefty pitchers whatever. Neither of us can explain this phenomenon.

If I don't remember Mac I do remember the other "older guys" who hit and caught fly balls and grounders ("hittin' 'em out" was the official name of this game)—a rollicking band of aging players who came out for exercise, and a communal reveling in the sport of their youth, many nights after supper when it wasn't raining.

There was my uncle Peter; and Andy Lawlor: tall, thin, saturnine, with a long-fingered glove that had no padding, and a heart ailment that allowed him to pitch but not hit or field ("Never run for a bus; let it go and catch the next one," his doctor told him); and his brothers Jim and John (Knockout) and Tommy (Red), Tommy a pepperpot shortstop who remembered his own sandlot days in Carroll's Field near the railroad tracks, owned by my great-grandfather, Big Jim Carroll. Tommy played in the Twilight League, the organized semipros, and Joe Murphy played in the Class D Eastern Shore League (where Jimmy Foxx came from), and John (Bandy) Edmunds, the man we all remember as North Albany's best player, went up to play professionally but wouldn't wear a uniform because of his bandy legs, and came back home to work as a fireman.

But Bandy had no qualms about showing his legs when he played behind School 20. He hit and fielded in his cap, socks, spikes, and jockstrap, caught long fly balls behind his back, and then, with a whirl and a bullet throw back to the hitter, he would announce: "There's only a few of us left." Certain North Albany women conveyed to the parish priest their outrage at Bandy's jock show, or so I've been told—I can't remember this protest either—and from then on Bandy had to play wearing trousers, what's the free world coming to?

The School 20 field was where baseball began in my head, my heart, my right arm—with the kids and with the men. As kids alone we played pickup of any sort: "Roll-y at the bat," which required you to field a fly and then throw a grounder toward the bat lying on the ground, and if you hit it you took over as fungo man; or maybe, when it was one of those golden days, you could round up two outfielders and three infielders for two teams and have a game of sorts; or maybe even two full squads for a *real* game, if it was a sunlit Saturday.

I was about eight when I started taking banjo lessons from a local jazz guitarist and banjoist, Mike Pantone, who was sometimes on time for the lesson, sometimes so early that I was still playing ball; and so the very portly Mike would dig in behind the plate and umpire for us till the game ended and the music began.

The organization of Little League teams, with managers, uniforms, a stadium, all the necessary equipment, was not even a likely dream for us. We often played with cracked bats and coverless balls whose interior string was held together by black tape. The diamond was in three different places—the first where Mac and his men had put it, then another that we built ourselves to fulfill our most fervent need: to hit toward the chicken-wire outfield fence. I remember vividly the day I lofted my first home run over its distant uprightness, after which the field was moved again—it was too close to the parked cars, and we lost too many balls in the high weeds beyond the fence—moved to a site utterly remote from fences, and my days as a home-run hitter vanished abruptly and forever.

I learned to hit through the hole to right, coached by my father, who

had played second base for a much achieved Van Woert Street team
("The Little Potatoes, they're hard to peel"), at the turn of the century.
He was a Yankee fan, as was Lou. I liked the Giants and the Red Sox.
I gave my father a book on the Yankees, the only book I ever knew him
to read all through. I later gave him one on the Red Sox but I don't
think he even cracked it. He took me to Yankee Stadium and we saw
Lou Gehrig hit what seemed to be a mile-high infield fly that turned out
to be a home run over the right-field fence.

My father read newspapers, as we all did in the family, and his good
pal was Charley Young, the sports editor of the *Knickerbocker Press*. We
subscribed to the *Knick* and the *Times-Union* and the *Albany Evening
News*, and frequently the *Daily News* and the *New York Mirror* turned
up, all these papers bringing the writings of Dan Parker and Paul Gallico
and Jimmy Powers and Damon Runyon into the living room; and so
baseball became almost as pervasive and significant in my life as church
and school.

School was inimical to life on opening day when the Albany Senators
of the Class A Eastern League took to the field at Hawkins Stadium in
Menands, just north of North Albany, our back yard, really. The stadium
seated about 8,500, but eleven thousand would crowd in for special
games. All season long we'd find a way to get in, either by shagging a
foul ball that came over the wall, and which got you in free when you
returned it, or waiting for the friendly Menands village cop (Lou remembers he was overweight and his name was Thorpe) to hook us up
with a ticket buyer ("Here's your son, mister"), for if you arrived with
a parent, then the boy scrambled under the turnstile, free. Bob Burns
also recalls crawling under the fence near the bleachers. I don't remember doing this, and Joe Keefe says he lacked the bravery such crime
required. Sometimes we actually paid to get in.

Joe remembered Tony (I think we called him Como) Catelle, a dramatic
center fielder for the Senators who caught fly balls with dives, falls,
tumbles, and other acrobatics, and Joe thought this was how it was done
until he saw Joe DiMaggio let the fly balls drop quietly into his peach
basket with that easeful DiMaggian ubiquity.

It is perhaps banal to remember Babe Ruth, but it is inevitable.
Nobody went to school when he came to Hawkins Stadium, first on

August 9, 1929 (I missed that one), and maybe five more times in the thirties, one of those nights memorable to us all because the Babe poked one into right center that landed on the roof of the Norwalk burial vault company where spectators sat to watch the games free; and that was the longest ball anybody—Lou, Bob, me—ever saw hit in Hawkins, although the same was said of the Babe's center-field blast in '29. Hyperbole is always generational. The Babe himself said in Albany that the longest ball he ever hit was in Tampa, and it went about five hundred feet.

Richard J. Conners, the New York State assemblyman from Albany, who was both the Senators' official scorer and local correspondent for the *Sporting News* from the early thirties to the postwar years, and a neighbor of mine for much of my life, tells me the Babe hit his last home run at Hawkins Stadium in an exhibition game with Brooklyn, against the Senators, on July 25, 1938.

The attendance record that night, with all passes suspended, reached an all-time high: 11,724 fans cheered the Babe and saw him swack a curve ball ("It broke like it was rolling off a table. I don't know how he ever hit it," said the catcher) over the right-field wall.

The Babe was expansive that night and said Albany was a "real good baseball city, one of the best minor-league cities in the country." He also reported that he was offered the job of managing Albany when it was in the International League, but friends warned him against taking it; and yet he might have accepted had the salary been right. But it wasn't.

When the Senators weren't at Hawkins, we followed them with great passion even so—hearing the away games announced on radio by, first, Doc Rand, then his son, Gren, who weren't away themselves, but reading the teletype in an Albany radio studio. They would vivify the wire news with sound effects, a snap of their fingers signifying a crack of the bat, their imagination supplying the "curve ball that cut the outside corner," when all the wire offered was "strike two." We believed in the snap and the curve and were grateful for the fantasy.

We remember Pete Gray, who played with Elmira against Albany during the war, when most able-bodied players were in service, and in 1945 played a big-league season with the St. Louis Browns: an odd figure, a showpiece, really, but a triumph of willfulness over the adversity that had been his since his right arm's amputation in childhood.

We particularly remember Ralph Kiner because, of all Albany Senators, he rose highest, becoming a major slugger for the Pirates (Albany was then a Pirate farm team, and so my National League allegiance was torn between New York and Pittsburgh) and a Hall of Famer (fifty-four home runs in '49, forty-seven in '50, and, in the '49 season, the first player in history to hit four home runs in four consecutive times at bat—twice.) He played left field for Albany in 1941 and 1942 and was a home-run hero even then. Bob Burns remembered the fans calling him "Wiggles" because when he gave three shakes of his tail it meant the next pitch stood a very good chance of going over the wall.

Baseball players were not only local heroes, they also, on occasions, turned into real people. They ate in the Morris Diner, where we all hung out. Kiner roomed across from Bob Burns's house on Lawn Avenue. And Lou remembered seeing Jake Powell, an outfielder with the Yankees, at one of the late-thirties World Series games. When Jake saw Lou Pitnell, Sr., the North Albany barber who had cut his hair when he played with the Albany Senators, Jake gave him and his son a very big pregame hello, another reason for young Lou to be a Yankee fan forever.

Maybe the funkiest Albany saga is the story of Edwin C. (Alabama) Pitts, who was doing time in Sing Sing in 1935 for being the getaway driver in an armed robbery, when the Giants played a prison team as part of spring training, and somebody noticed Pitts had talent at the plate as well as at the wheel.

Dick Conners, who still lives in North Albany and was a friend of Pitts, told me the Pitts story.

The owner of the Senators in 1935 was Joseph Cambria, who put Albany into the International League, where it played from 1932 to 1936. Cambria, a noted figure in Baltimore laundry circles before entering baseball, heard about Pitts's talent, met him at the Sing Sing gate when he was paroled, and brought him to Albany. Albany's greatest local hero at that time was Johnny Evers, a Troy native but an Albanian by adoption, who had played big league baseball for eighteen years, twelve of them with the Cubs; was the National League's most valuable player in 1914, and part of the great double-play combination that Franklin P. Adams had so deftly defined in the *New York World*:

Trio of bearcubs and fleeter than birds,
Tinker to Evers to Chance.
Ruthlessly pricking our gonfalon bubble,
Making a Giant hit into a double,
Words that are weighty with nothing but trouble:
"Tinker to Evers to Chance."

After he left big-league baseball, Evers signed on with Cambria as general manager of Albany, and in June of 1935 he inherited Alabama Pitts. Cries rose up against a felon playing for the Senators, and William G. Bramham, head of the minor leagues, ruled against Pitts.

Evers took the case to baseball's commissioner, Judge Kennesaw M. Landis. Evers had already put himself squarely behind Pitts. "I have been in baseball all my life," he said. "If this boy is not allowed to play, I will sever all connections with the game for good. That's a broad statement, but I mean every word of it."

Landis ruled for Pitts, who came to Hawkins Stadium to play outfield, and, as Ring Lardner once put it, although he was a mediocre fielder he was also a very poor hitter. However, he was deft at cards, and Dick Conners took him to play (across the street from my house) with Dr. Jay McDonald and Jake Becker, among others; and on the way home Pitts told Dick: "Don't stay in the game when I raise a second time. I can read those cards."

Of course Dick imparted this news to the others and that was that for Alabama's poker-playing in North Albany. He concluded his days four years later with another kind of gambling—knifed to death in Gastonia, North Carolina, while dancing with another man's wife.

Pitts only lasted in Albany for six weeks, but the Senators went on for twenty-three more years, peaking in 1948 when attendance reached 210,804, or about 3,100 per game—and standing room only for Sunday doubleheaders. They went on to win the pennant in 1949. But a decade later professional baseball died in Albany, with attendance down to forty thousand, and in 1960 the splendid Hawkins Stadium was razed, and sold to developers who put up a large cut-rate store called Topps. A friend of mine spoke for all baseball fans when she said, "Topps is the bottoms."

Baseball came back to Albany in 1983 when the Albany-Colonie Athletics, farm team of Oakland, was established in Heritage Park, near

Albany Airport. In 1985 the team became the Yankees—a New York Yankee farm—and that year 324,003 people came to watch, an all-time seasonal attendance record for Eastern League baseball. I live on the other side of the river and since the games are no longer in my backyard, I follow them with great goodwill, but chiefly in the morning paper; and soon that too will pass, for the local Yankees are moving to Long Island. At this writing the local baseball scene looks very bleak.

When I left North Albany for the first time I took a job at the *Glens Falls* (N.Y.) *Post-Star* as a sportswriter. I covered all sports, wrote a column, and became a dogged fan of Red Smith, Joe Palmer, and Jimmy Cannon, who were heroic sportswriters of that age; and when I was drafted during the Korean War my time with sports served me well. The army made me a sports editor of a weekly newspaper, and so for the next two years I was so immersed in games that the rest of the world was minimalized.

This, of course, was temporary insanity, and at the end of my stint with the army I abandoned sports for the police beat, politics, and fiction, more expansive ways of indulging dementia. But sports, and especially baseball, lurked insidiously in my imagination and, when I began to write long fiction, the figures from childhood and sportswriting days demanded attention. Their stories seemed then, and now, elemental to my own life and the life of my family.

One of my great-uncles was Eddie (Coop) McDonald, a third baseman who was a maestro of the hidden-ball trick. He had three years (1911–1913) with Boston and Chicago in the National League that were respectable but less than stellar, and another ten or more great years with minor-league teams in Birmingham, Chattanooga, and Little Rock as a player and manager. He was a beloved figure in the family, in my own memory, in Albany, and in the baseball world, and I drew on his baseball experience, but not on his personal life, when I created Francis Phelan, the derelict hero of *Ironweed*. Francis was a drunk, Coop a teetotaler.

There is a quasi-mystical postscript to the *Ironweed*–Albany Senators connection. When the film was shot in Albany the old all-night Boulevard Cafeteria, one of my youthful haunts, empty in 1987, but its stained-glass windows and murals still handsomely intact, was refurbished by the movie crew and used as the Gilded Cage, the saloon where Francis

(Jack Nicholson) and his friend Helen go, and where Helen (Meryl Streep) sings so memorably. The Boulevard building was, and is, owned by Matt (Babe) Daskalakis, a first baseman for the Senators in the team's latter days in the mid-1950s. Since the movie, Matt has opened the place as a saloon, restaurant, and the only place in town where you can dance to the music of the 1930s and 1940s. Some things, clearly, were meant to be.

If I have come full circle from those games of catch and fungo in the mid-1930s to a latter-day faith in the annual ritual of baseball, it is not with any speculative or mythifying baggage, or any abstract rationale for what has come to pass, but rather it is with the still-visible specifics of memory: my uncle Peter swinging a bat and revealing to me what he looked like when he was fourteen; umpire Mike Pantone wearing a catcher's mask too small for his head, but protecting his nose; that rainmaker of a flyball that Gehrig hit; that jazz of language that came out of a Jimmy Cannon column.

These things accumulated and did what they did to me, and now here I am again, about to enter into my annual six months of daily anxiety over the fate of the New York Mets. I have good reasons for this, of course, as you now know.

1992

Family:

My Life in the Fast Lane
Dana's Ironic Hiccups
Snapshots: Two Grandfathers

My Life in the Fast Lane

The Knights of Columbus existed for one boy, who became one young man, as a never-quite-accessible playland where what could not be was always superior to what was. Things could not be for the boy because at the outset he was too small to lift the bowling balls or catch the medicine ball, too short to reach the functional level of the pool table, too young to smoke the cigars that the card players (playing pinochle, incomprehensible game) were smoking. Sometimes he spat in the shallow but wide brass spittoons and felt accomplished, and he learned to call the players by name: Tom Riley and Pete Burns and Freddy Whitmore and Hooks Keenan and Bill Fealey and John Corscadden, John who preferred kibitzing to playing and was a champion at his preference.

The club, a Catholic men's fraternal organization, was built in 1872 at 131 North Pearl Street in downtown Albany, a three-story brownstone with a large hall suitable for basketball, bingo, and holiday bacchanals of a restrained order. One became a full member after taking three symbolic degrees—events of prayer and ritual, the third of which was so mysterious, exciting, and astonishing that George M. Cohan wanted to produce its equivalent as Broadway theater. But, the degree being secret, that was not allowed.

The boy's father, uncles, cousins and assorted neighbors were full members of the Knights, as the club and its building were both called. One favored great-uncle, Pat McDonald, erstwhile sportsman, gambler and politician (a common Albany hybrid), was club superintendent, and when the boy visited Pat's and his wife Lizzie's third-floor apartment, the whole club seemed like family real estate.

One entered up several stone steps and, with difficulty, pushed open the huge right door that gave onto the main hallway, which had about it the odor of stillness. To the left were the front and back parlors, empty of people but full of handsome furniture that discouraged comfort. To the right a semicircular staircase led up to the second-floor cardroom, always busy after four in the afternoon, and to the library, always empty at any hour. It also led downstairs to the basement, wherein were manifested the club's magical elements: two pool tables and six bowling alleys.

Dike Dollard and Patsy Mulderry, both elderly millionaire paving contractors, might be playing pool for pennies, then quarreling over the

---

The author at twenty, circa 1948, squatting front left, next to Jimmy Finnegan, who threw the widest hook the author ever saw. The bowlers all worked for Simmons Machine Tool Corporation.

Members of the Knights of Columbus National League, in uniform. The author's father, William Sr., is at far right of front row; the author's uncle, Pete McDonald, is at far right of back row. A portly cousin, John (Case) McDonald, is second from left, front row.

outcome, while the aging former police court judge from the North End, John J. Brady, waited to play the winner.

The boy learned from his father and his most proficient uncle how to use a cue, how also to palm and roll the small duckpin balls; and so at an early age a pool table, boy-size, appeared at home, and bowling became a sport to grow into. It was pursued with intense pleasure, then with fanaticism: bowling four nights a week by the time college came along.

Its appeal increased, for as practiced nighttimes at the Knights, bowling reconstituted, indoors, the allure of the baseball diamond (a depopulated and fading area of concern by late adolescence); which is to say it offered team competition among peers, with individual skills highly prized, and the sense of play and the quest for camaraderie fulfilled.

In his association with women, the young man grew equivalently fanatical; but women came to the Knights only for parties, dances and bingo; club life excluded them otherwise. John Corscadden remembered some members sending their women friends to the movies across the street while the men nightly, every night, hung around the club. One of Johnny's pals, Eddie Fisher, remembered the pattern of taking his date home and *then* going to the club, where life went on until perhaps midnight, adjourning finally to the Grand Lunch across the street for "coffee and."

Corscadden and Fisher were pals of Pete McDonald, a wild man who was the boy's principal uncle, a man who did many basic things well: bowling, talking, shooting pool or darts. Eddie Fisher remembered the night Pete put a newspaper over the dart board and said, "Name a number," then hit it, said "Name another," and hit it, and like that.

Corscadden was fast and good at basketball and brought a team into the gym in the early thirties and made money for the club. He was offered a basketball scholarship at a prep school with the understanding that it could lead him to Colgate; but he declined. "I was too smart," he said. "I wanted to be around with the gamblers. I was a dope, really. That's the answer to it."

Fisher had a 202 bowling average, very high, and didn't even own his own ball. He used one left in a locker by Sullivan the undertaker. Then one day Sullivan took the ball home and Fisher's average dropped twenty points.

Bowling was central to club life, the alleys busy all week (no mixed leagues until the forties). Joe Falcaro, the world champion, bowled at the Knights once. Johnny Corscadden remembered Falcaro putting ointment on his thumb to keep it from cracking, which reminded Fisher of the trip the K of C team took to a tournament in Detroit, where Fisher met a man with a cracked thumb. Fisher showed the man how to keep coating the crack with New Skin and cotton until a cloth scab developed; and the man went on to be the tournament's high scorer.

Some of the men bowled five-dollar jackpots after the league action at the club, which was when the boy's father made the double-pinochle split (4-6-7-10 pins)—"In my whole life I never saw it made," Fisher said—and earned a twenty-dollar tip from a gambler who made money on the match.

Pete McDonald rolled a 299 game in one of the jackpot matches (his team lost the match) and told the boy (and the young man for years after): "When you roll 300, come around and talk to me." Pete was there ten years later when the young man rolled a 299 himself and therewith shut Pete up about the 300.

The young man joined the Knights at seventeen but found life had changed. He played pool okay, yes; bowled 256 on alleys five and six and led the league with high single for a while; and he sang in the glee club as best he could ("I can't sing but I will," was his motto), but the uncles weren't bowling anymore, and neither was his father. His uncle Pat, still superintendent but very old now, was tending to his dying wife.

Life in the club was dying also, for several reasons. The Catholic bishop wouldn't let the club open a bar, not even a beer bar, and members defected, the boy's father among them, though he never drank. Men joined the Elks Club over on State Street, for that had become the principal sociopolitical bowling alley in town: the place where the significant Albany pols hung out. At the bar.

In the sixties the K of C would be bulldozed to make room for a highway, and the remaining members would begin a new life in a new building uptown. But even in the early fifties the club, for the young man, was little more than a group of empty rooms with nostalgia racing through them, just as he had when he was a boy. Bowling had degenerated into respectability, and pool seemed a sin no one committed seriously anymore. Sadly, it was no longer important to belong to the club: not this club, not any club.

And anyway, by then the young man had developed bowler's finger: an ignominious traumatic arthritis that prevented him from throwing a hook; and his average dropped from the 180s to the 130s. Oh, the shame just to think of it. In a much later year, trying out a ball with a fingertip grip, he regained his hook; and soon thereafter, with little preparation, bowled a 600 triple. The restoration had begun.

But alas, he then developed bowler's groin, and chose at once to retire the sport and build a swimming pool. Today he no longer has need of nighttime games, much preferring the game of solitude. But he talks from time to time of adding a room to the upstairs of the house, with space enough for a pool table, regulation-size, such as might have been found in the basement of the K of C circa 1938. This, however, is largely talk. One doesn't really need a pool table in one's life. Everyone knows this.

Postscript: Times do change. Now, in 1992, there is a pool table, regulation size, in the upstairs of the house. The past has been recaptured and it is almost as good as it used to be.

1986

Dana's Ironic Hiccups

What you are about to read is a scientifically researched, literary-related, medical article which also contains advice to newspapermen on a foolproof courtship technique. Consider yourself warned.

The medical portion, which is the weighty part of this piece, begins early in 1964 when I was writing a story on Robert Frost's grave in Old Bennington, Vermont. His gravestone was still absent, and unfinished, a year after his death, and on the existing stones in the Frost plot there were errors in the birth and death dates of his wife and three of his children, and the name of his son was misspelled. A poet devotes his life to precision and finds in death that his numbers are scrambled.

I was in the throes of this irony when Dana, my wife, developed the hiccups. This was not unusual, but as we drove through the Vermont countryside, the hiccups kept on, and on, and on. I maintained a prolonged silence and then, remembering that sudden terror cured hiccups, I erupted with a fiendish yell into her left ear. The hiccups continued.

She held her breath, slid down in the seat to change the gravitational pull on her esophagus, and the hiccups grew raucous, out of control, gave her a pounding headache. I stopped at a store and bought aspirin and got her a glass of water. The aspirin palliated the headache, but had no effect on the hiccups.

As we rode along I saw her tear a piece off the small brown paper bag that the aspirin came in. She folded it to the size of a finger joint and put it behind her ear. Then there was silence, and no more hiccups. I waited a few minutes before I said to her: "I saw what you did and I don't believe it." She told me it was a Puerto Rican hiccup remedy her

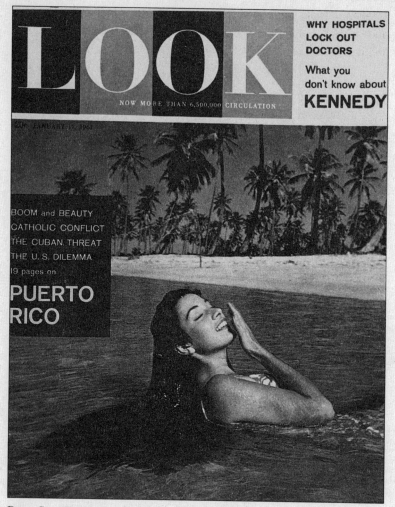

LOOK

NOW MORE THAN 6,500,000 CIRCULATION

20¢ JANUARY 17, 1961

WHY HOSPITALS
LOCK OUT
DOCTORS

What you
don't know about
KENNEDY

BOOM and BEAUTY
CATHOLIC CONFLICT
THE CUBAN THREAT
THE U. S. DILEMMA
19 pages on
PUERTO
RICO

Dana Sosa Kennedy, wife of the author, as she appeared on the cover of
Look magazine in 1961 when the magazine profiled Puerto Rico. This
cover sold more copies for *Look* than any other issue of the magazine up
to that point, except for the portrait of John F. Kennedy's first family.

grandmother had told her about, and that she had just now remembered it.

The months moved along, Dana got the hiccups now and then, dutifully put a piece of brown paper behind her ear, and away went the hiccups. I then began my twenty-eight-year-long bout of medical research to understand hiccups better, and I came to know that they are sudden, spasmodic contractions of the diaphragm, which produce sharp intakes of breath, this intake cut off when the windpipe constricts, thus creating the *hic* in hiccup. Anybody might hiccup, including a fetus.

The diaphragm's contractions can be brought on by such things as stress, hepatitis, alcohol, overeating, strokes, orange soda, sudden excitement, cold showers, and, in one case reported in the *New England Journal of Medicine*, by an ant crawling around on the patient's eardrum.

To cure the hiccups you hold your breath until you turn purple, or you breathe into a paper bag, or eat a teaspoon of sugar, or drink a glass of water upside down, or suck a lemon wedge soaked in Angostura bitters, or tickle your throat with a cotton swab, or sneeze, or have your doctor insert a soft rubber tube four inches into your nose and then pull the hose back and forth to stimulate the area behind your soft palate. Also you can take drugs: nifedipine, chlorpromazine, quinidine, phenytoin, valproic acid, carbamazepine, or, if drugs don't work, you can ask your physician about having your phrenic nerves surgically cut. Because this latter cure could stop you from breathing, most physicians will probably tell you to go back to lemon sucking.

Dana had no need to resort to any of these cures. She possessed the foolproof piece of brown paper. She did, that is, until the night we were parking at the Troy Country Club and she was stricken by a violent hiccup attack. We had no brown paper, for I was tiring of carrying paper bags wherever we went, so I said to her, "Why don't you put a paper behind your ear?"

You'll notice I didn't say "piece of brown paper" but merely "paper," which was a product of my journalistic training to get at what is essential in the world.

The hiccups stopped immediately.

During her next hiccup attack I told Dana again, "Why don't you put a paper behind your ear?" Hic, hic, hic.

"You didn't say it right," she told me. "You have to say '*Why* don't you put a paper behind your ear.' " So I said it that way and the hiccups went away.

On our way to New York another attack erupted. I looked at her and said, "Why don't you put a paper behind your elbow?" Very funny. Hic, hic. "Why don't you put a paper behind your paper? . . . Why don't you put an ear behind your elbow? . . ." Hic, hic.

"*Say it right!*" she screamed, and so I did, and the hiccups went away.

She got them later and grew furious when I failed to say "Why don't you . . ." etc.; but I didn't even know she had them. When I said it they vanished. Again, at a party, she had them and couldn't get my attention casually, so she came over and said, "I have the hiccups." And I said, "No you don't," and she didn't. She got them again when I was reading, and I heard them and looked at her, and before I said anything they stopped, so we then moved into the postliterate control stage, where language no longer mattered.

Of course the news of this miracle cure traveled widely in our set and was widely disbelieved. The power of suggestion . . . drawing on the right side of the brain . . . belief in an authority figure . . . self-hypnosis, etc., were offered as facile explanations.

Then our friend Tom Smith developed an unbelievably loud and intractable case of hiccups at a party, underwent the sugar, water, fright, and other cures without effect, decided to ignore them and told a story, at which point they erupted so frequently he could not finish the story, a tragic event for Tom. And so Dana came over to him and told him to lie down on the couch. She put a piece of brown paper behind his ear and his hiccups went away.

Dana cured our daughter Katherine's hiccups over the phone, and when our daughter Dana's five-year-old son, Casey, was about to drink some sugar water to cure his, I said, "You don't need that, Case. Just put a paper behind your ear." And my wife said, "Yes, Case, *why* don't you put a paper behind your ear?" And Casey looked at us in terror, on the verge of flight: my grandparents have gone bananas. But we only smiled and noted that he had stopped hiccupping.

Dana cured a supermarket clerk at the checkout counter, our friends took up the cause and cured themselves and their friends, and Vera Gagen declared, "It's a movement!"

We were walking in Rome when Dana got the hiccups and when I looked at her she said to me, "Don't say anything. I like my hiccups and I want to have them for a while." And I said to myself, This is the completed circle. But I was wrong. Dana walked on ahead and I stopped to take a note on her behavior. She turned and saw me writing and said, "Oh no," and lost her hiccups.

Last week Dana was all by herself when the hiccups arrived. She smiled and received them with great pleasure. Old friends, seldom encountered these days. She thought of paper but cleared her brain of it immediately in order to erupt for a while with diaphragmatic joy. Hic, hic.

"But then," she said, "it all flooded back to me. Brown paper, ear, *why* don't you . . . ." And all by herself, without prompters, without casual hypnosis, without resort to the right side of the brain, or serious paper, she divested herself of windpipe occlusions.

Nevermore, alas, nevermore.

As for myself, I recall having hiccups only once during all this time and Dana cured them by saying you know what. But then I had an uncharacteristic sneezing attack—four is usually my limit and I had already counted sixteen sneezes—when Dana said to me, "Why don't you put a paper behind your ear?" and the sneezes stopped immediately. I decided this had happened to me because I was on a self-imposed deadline to write this piece and needed closure that was still scientific but different.

Then late one evening I was telling Dana all the messages I'd received for us during the day and she yawned. I mentioned another message, she yawned again.

"I'm boring you with these messages," I said.

"Not at all," she said, and she stopped yawning. I then remembered another message and here came another yawn. I laughed.

"I'm not bored," she said, "and stop saying I am."

Yet another message, yet another yawn. Hilarious. But now she was furious at my laughter, and insisted vehemently she was yawning because she was tired and not out of boredom. I stopped talking and wrote notes on all this and she yawned throughout my note taking. I could not stop laughing, she could not stop yawning.

"Do you have any Tums?" she asked.

I gave her two and said no more and we both ended the evening with our mouths closed.

That ends the clinical part of this story.

My advice to newspapermen on the subject of courtship takes the form of a story that begins in 1956 in San Juan in the kitchen of a couple who were good friends of mine, and were also relatives of the very young and very beautiful dancer, Dana Sosa, who had just closed in a show on Broadway and had come to Puerto Rico to see her family. A party was arranged, a number of courtly males were invited, and, if I must say so, and I must, I was then in my courtly stage.

I was stunned by Dana's beauty and, as soon as I could, I maneuvered her out of the large living room and into the small kitchen, where three was a crowd, four a mob. Soon I had the scene narrowed to two, Dana and me, and I was extolling her hair, her face, etc., told her I longed to know all about her life, on and off Broadway, and that since I was writing three columns a week for a newspaper in San Juan, why didn't I write a column about her?

Dana, being a showperson not averse to publicity, agreed. And so I began my interview, which culminated in an extremely serious question four days later: How would you like to get married? To me. She took the question back to New York with her a few days after that, and in two weeks she was back in San Juan with the answer, which was: I'd like that. Twelve days later, thirty-six days after we met, we were married.

That was 1957 and ever since then she has been nagging me about that interview I never wrote. I insisted I'd write it one of these days, and so here it is, though it probably isn't what she expected. But it is now May 1992, and we recently celebrated our thirty-fifth wedding anniversary, and her Broadway story (*New Faces of 1956*, *Pajama Game*, *Me and Juliet*), and her modeling and her magazine-cover-girl days, and her time with the Joffrey Ballet, and the fact of her enduring beauty, have been told scores of times. But has anyone ever written about her hiccups? Not until now.

This story is full of ironies, just like Robert Frost's graveyard plot. Dana will now have to stop nagging me about the interview, and, through my three decades of private, dispassionate research, medical science has a vast new supply of data to analyze for the benefit of the human race. People always say that God works in strange ways, but so do newspapermen in love.

1992

Snapshots: Two Grandfathers

My grandfathers, George Kennedy and Peter McDonald, died before I was born. I came to know something of them through talks with my parents and other relatives, a few artifacts, death certificates and obituaries, and two photographs that defined them for me forever.

Both photos are working class portraits.

The portrait of George Kennedy is with three other men who are, I believe, from the Albany Water Department, these four pausing in their work on the granite blocks and water lines of an Albany street to pose with their tools: shovel, pickax, two-handed valve wrench, wheelbarrow, and George, second from left, holding a prybar. George has a stubble of white whiskers in the photo, looks hunched and grizzled, and was probably near the end of his life. He is wearing a vest and a gold-plated chain for his pocket watch. I inherited the chain, perhaps also the watch, but I can't be sure the watch was his. The chain is functional, the watch (whoever owned it) doesn't work.

George had come to Albany at age twenty in 1880 from County Tipperary, worked as a laborer, and risen to become yardmaster at the George H. Thacher & Co. foundry, which made railroad carwheels for the New York Central Railroad. He eventually brought over two of his brothers and two sisters, who all settled in Albany. He died in March, 1923, of lobar pneumonia at age sixty-three. His wife, Hannora Ryan (remembered as the sweetest of women, and who came from the next town over from George in Tipperary), had died in February, 1896, also of lobar pneumonia, at age twenty-nine. My father, William, said she never recovered from the birth of his sister, Mary, some months earlier.

The Kennedys lived on Van Woert Street, a long, almost solidly Irish

George Kennedy, the
author's paternal grand-
father, late in life, second
from left holding prybar.

block at the edge of Albany's Arbor Hill, but considered part of North
Albany, when my father was born in 1887. They later moved to a house
next door to an ice house and, in 1890, when my father was three,
somebody torched the ice house, the Kennedy house burned with it, and
they lost everything. George moved from yet another home on Lawrence
Street so my father wouldn't have to cope with the horse and carriage
traffic when he went to school, and, finally, he moved back to Van Woert
Street and stayed there.

In George Kennedy's photo with the work gang, his days of authority
as yardmaster are behind him, as is his time as foreman at the Rathbone,
Sard foundry (five hundred men employed, among them my father, who
did piecework as a stove mounter but quit when the wages per piece
dropped from $1.35 to $.55). The iron and steel business went west
toward the coalfields, and the coal stoves my father was mounting were

made obsolete by the advent of gas. The times turned against George Kennedy and in his late days he was again a simple laboring man.

I have a younger photo of George with his daughter, Mary, taken in 1917 when she was twenty-two. George is at his social best: clean-shaven, hair tidily combed, wearing a dark suit, striped shirt with white collar, dark tie, and the watch chain. He looks strong, is square-jawed and handsome in this photo, but there is a grimness to his mouth and his eyes are sad. He lived the last twenty-seven years of his life without his sweet wife, without a woman in the house, except when one of his sisters came by to clean the place. He could not raise the baby Mary and also work, so he raised only my father, a wild, electric boy who was nine when his mother died. Hannora's maiden sister raised Mary until she married.

The street photo of George came to me from Mary in the 1960s, and I was so moved by it that I thought of having it blown up to poster size as a way of advertising my origin; but that seemed as pretentious as trying to deny an origin, and so I let it go unsung until now, when the chance to write about it thrust me into a search of the family archives, and led to my first conversation with Mary Craig Hurley, eighty-nine, who is almost my in-law, and who lived on Van Woert Street, directly across from George.

Mary remembers George from eighty years gone. She sees him about 1912, when she is nine and he is fifty-two, at a Van Woert Street house party—"all of Van Woert Street would be there"—and again at the annual clambake in Donovan's backyard; and George is always dancing and singing "The Stack of Barley," an Irish reel.

"He did a marvelous dance," Mary said, "and he had a good singing voice. I remember the words that he sang: *'Oh my little stack of barley was the cause of all my misery . . .'* He was a wonderful man, a good-livin' man."

I am sure George Kennedy knew my mother's father, Peter McDonald, who was born in Albany and lived on Colonie Street, a block away from Van Woert.

Peter's photo, which hung in reverential space in our kitchen all my early life, is with a train and track crew, all standing with Engine 151

Engineer Peter McDonald, the author's maternal grandfather, fifth from right, in front engine 151 of the New York Central, with train and track crew. Peter's brother, James, is far left, front.

of the Central. (Everybody in the family played 151 when Clearing House, the numbers game, was vogue.) Peter is fifth from right, handsome, wearing a stylish scarf under his jacket and overalls, the only man in the photo so garbed. Swift Mead, an old-time boxer and saloon keeper, said of Peter: "He was a dressed-up guy, always with a clean uniform. A hard-workin' man."

Peter began as a laborer and rose to become passenger locomotive engineer on Engine 151. He was given a medal for making a record-breaking run with the Twentieth Century, the Central's greatest train, from Albany to Buffalo. The medal has been lost and the record of the run I haven't yet found. But I believe it was a true record, for his children, my mother, Mary, my uncle Peter, and my aunt Katherine, would not have invented such braggadocio.

Peter fathered five children, two of whom did not survive infancy. He took sick in April, 1916, the sickness lingered, and he died in January, 1918, of pleural pneumonia and myocarditis at age forty-three. His widow, Annie Carroll, the only grandparent I knew, lived with us, and helped raise me. She died of complications after a stroke in 1951. I can't remember her mentioning Peter, but I believe they had a very good marriage.

I inherited Peter's scuffed black leather wallet in which he kept a record, during his illness, of his 107 visits to and by an Arbor Hill doctor, Marcus D. Cronin. In the last seven days of Peter's life Dr. Cronin came to the house twice a day. The doctor bills came to $96, which my grandmother eventually paid in two installments, in May and December, 1918. At the time of Peter's death, both of his daughters were working in an office, and supporting their mother and rambunctious young brother, Pete. I have very few memories from any of the three about their father. They were effusive in their love for him, but his death was four decades gone when I began to ask questions. I did inherit that wallet and his railroad pass for 1913, and military enrollment papers for World War I; also a postcard he sent to my mother in 1913 when she was at Camp Tekakwitha on Lake Luzerne in the Adirondacks. "Howdy toots," he wrote her. "Don't get drowned." He said he was taking an engineer's exam Monday and he signed it *P.A.P.*

A clipping with his obituary was also in the wallet. "Mr. McDonald was stricken with an attack of pleural pneumonia about six months ago and it greatly weakened his heart. He had made a wonderful fight against great odds for the past four months, but his condition had been gradually growing worse up to yesterday when his heart finally gave out."

They don't write obits like they used to.

The photographs of Peter and George are close to being terminal images: George, old in his sixties; Peter in his prime, at his career summit, a few years from a wasting early death. If you block off the chin stubble George looks like my father. As is, Peter looks like his son, Peter. My father inherited from George the love of song and dance (he was a prize waltzer), and Peter and his sisters inherited the wit that kept me laughing all my life. Neither inheritance shows up in the photos, but what is there are starting points for a continuity of family and meaning. These men —widower and widow maker—are emblematic of what their children became, and of what they passed onto *us*, the next generation: a veneration of ancestors, an appreciation of the working class, a bemusement with genetic gifts.

We really can't know how guardedly, how limitedly they lived, any more than they could have imagined life in the Space Age. Even my father didn't believe it when men walked on the moon. "You damn fool," he told me, "you can't *get* to the moon."

The streets and houses and people my grandfathers knew, the jobs they held—most are gone now, or obsolete. But George and Peter aren't. There they are, standing for their portrait photos, offering up the gift and the challenge of creative memory. They look into the camera and say to us, "We were, now you are." Anything after that is found gold.

1992

Some of the selections in this book first appeared in the following periodicals: *The Atlantic, The Carillon, Esquire, GQ, Life, Look, The Miami Herald, Michigan Quarterly Review, Mirabella, National Observer, The New Republic, Newsday, Quest, The Recorder, San Francisco Examiner, The San Juan Star,* and *Vanity Fair.*

"Jiggs: 'What's the Matter with Father? I Saw Him Drink Water' " was originally published as the introduction to *Jiggs Is Back* by George McManus, Turtle Island Foundation. "The Making of *Ironweed*" appeared as "(Re)creating Ironweed" in *American Film* and later as the introduction to the book *The Making of Ironweed,* Viking Penguin. "The Capitol: A Quest for Grace and Glory" was published in *The Capitol in Albany,* photographs by William Clift and Stephen Shore, Aperture. "Baseball at Hawkins Stadium: 'Here's Your Son, Mister' " first appeared in *The Birth of a Fan* edited by Ron Fimrite, Macmillan.

Grateful acknowledgment is made to the following for permission to reprint previously published material, some of which first appeared under different titles:

The Miami Herald: "Early Assignments: Tracking the Missing Leopard."

The New York Times: "A Speech: Be Reasonable, Unless You're a Writer"; "Ernest Hemingway: His Dangerous Summer"; "*The Grapes of Wrath* at Fifty: Steinbeck's Journals"; "*Nothing Happens in Carmincross*: Benedict Kiely's Deathly Variety Show"; "Gabriel García Márquez: The Autumn of the Patriarch"; "Mario Vargas Llosa: *Aunt Julia and the Scriptwriter*"; and "Frank Sinatra: Pluperfect Music." Copyright © 1976, 1982, 1985, 1987, 1989, 1990 by The New York Times Company. Reprinted by permission.

The Paris Review: "Fragments of a Talk with *The Paris Review: Ironweed* and Style."

Review: "Carlos Fuentes: *Distant Relations*" and "Ernesto Sábato: *On Heroes and Tombs*." By permission of *Review* and the Center for Inter-American Relations, Inc.

The Times Union (Albany): "Early Assignments: Langford, Prominent Cat, Dies"; "Albert the Swimmer"; "Bernard Malamud: On *The Fixer*"; "J. P. Donleavy: Captivated by Ginger: A Non-Interview"; "The Beat Generation: Ginsberg's Albany Pain"; "E. L. Doctorow: Shimmering *Loon Lake*"; "Frank Sullivan: Serious Only About Humor"; "Pablo Casals: Master Class at Marlboro"; "Paul McCartney: The Major Possum Game"; "Marshall McLuhan's Message Is . . . ?"; "Rudolph Valentino: He's No Bogart"; "Cassius Clay Arrives"; "Ballet: Everybody Loves a Fat Girl, Right?"; "Roberta Sue Ficker Is Going to Become Suzanne Farrell"; "Jody Bolden or Bobby Henderson: Either Way the Music Was Great"; "The Charcoal Man: Warming Up to the Press"; "Radicalism and Dwight MacDonald: Not What They Used to Be"; and "Requiem for a Lady at the Bottom of the World."

Viking Penguin: "Damon Runyon: Six-to-Five: A Nice Price," an introduction to *Guys and Dolls: The Stories of Damon Runyon.* Copyright © WJK, Inc., 1992. By permission of Viking Penguin, a division of Penguin Books USA Inc.

The Washington Post: "The Beginning of the Writer: Eggs"; "Samuel Beckett: The Artful Dodger Revealed"; "*Players*: DeLillo's Poisoned Flowers"; "O'Hara's Letters: A Quest for Celebrity"; "Lygia Fagundes Telles: *The Girl in the Photograph*"; and "Julio Cortázar: *A Manual for Manuel*." © 1977, 1978, 1982, 1989 *The Washington Post*. Reprinted with permission.